PMI-ACP® Exam Prep

Questions, Answers & Explanations

PMI-ACP® Exam Prep

Questions, Answers & Explanations

Tim Bagnall, PMI-ACP
Christopher Scordo, PMP, ITIL

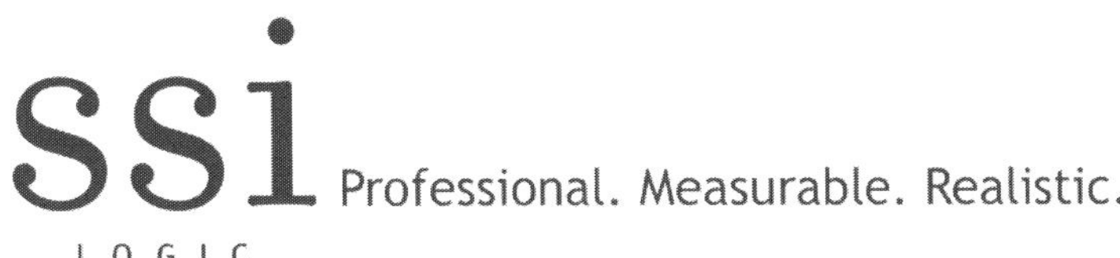

Copyrighted Material

Edition 2013.

Published by SSI Logic

ISBN-10: 098947030X
ISBN-13: 978-0-9894703-0-8

All inquiries should be addressed via email to:
support@ssilogic.com

or by mail post to:
SSI Solutions, INC
340 S Lemon Ave #9038
Walnut, CA 91789

Table of Contents

Introduction

Practice Exams and Quizzes

INTRODUCTION

Welcome

Thank you for selecting SSI Logic's *PMI-ACP® Exam Prep – Questions, Answers, and Explanations* for your PMI-ACP® study needs. The goal of this book is to provide condensed mock exams and practice tests which allow you to become comfortable with the pace, subject matter, and difficulty of the PMI Agile Certified Practitioner (PMI-ACP) exam.

The content in this book is designed to optimize the time you spend studying in multiple ways.

1. Practice exams in this book are condensed to be completed in one hour; allowing you to balance your time between practice tests and other methods of study.

2. Passing score requirements in this book are slightly higher than the real exam; allowing you to naturally adjust to a higher test score requirement.

3. Practice exams included in this book cover the entire scope of the PMI-ACP exam, while shorter quizzes focus only on specific Knowledge Areas outlined in the *PMI-ACP® Examination Content Outline.*

The practice exam content in this book is structured into two general types of exam preparation:

- "Lite" Mock Exams, which allow you to test your knowledge across condensed versions of the PMI-ACP exam; designed to be completed within one hour.

- Knowledge Area Quizzes, which reflect brief practice tests focused on specific exam topic areas, outlined in the *PMI-ACP® Examination Content Outline,* designed to be completed in 25 minutes.

We wish you the best of luck in your pursuit to become a PMI Agile Certified Practitioner (PMI-ACP).

PMI-ACP® Exam Overview

About the PMI Agile Certified Practitioner (PMI-ACP®) Certification

The PMI-ACP certification is managed by the Project Management Institute (PMI®) and is designed for project management practitioners who are using Agile practices in their projects. Since 2011, the PMI-ACP certification has become one of the most widely recognized credentials available, for professionals who implement Agile methodologies.

The PMI-ACP certification is a globally recognized credential, and individuals are encouraged to remain active via PMI's Continuing Certification Requirements (CCRs). Only individuals who maintain active PMI-ACP credentials may refer to themselves as PMI Agile Certified Practitioner. Individuals do not need to be a member of PMI to earn the PMI-ACP credential.

The minimum requirements in attaining the PMI-ACP certification:

- Education: At a minimum, A high school diploma is required
- General project experience
  - 2000 Hours (a minimum of 12 Months) working on project teams earned within the past 5 years
- Agile project experience
  - 1500 hours (a minimum of 8 months) working on agile project teams or in agile methodologies within the last 3 years.
- Project Management Education: 21 PMI contact hours of accredited education
- Ethics: Agree to PMI's Code of Ethics and Professional Conduct
- **Pass the PMI-ACP Exam**

PMI-ACP Exam Details

The PMI-ACP exam is designed to objectively assess and measure project management knowledge. Concepts covered in the PMI-ACP exam are derived from the *PMI-ACP Reference List,* comprising 11 different reference texts that articulate Agile practices. This list of reference books can be found on the PMI website.

The actual exam is offered in a computer based testing (CBT) environment. A summary of the exam structure and passing requirements are as follows:

- There are 120 total multiple choice questions which make up the PMI-ACP exam
- 20 randomly placed "pretest questions" are included, and do not count towards the pass/fail determination
- Individuals have 3 hours to complete the exam
- While PMI does not publish a precise passing score, individuals should

assume a score of 65% is required (65 of 100 questions)

The PMI-ACP Exam Content Areas

The two content areas, along with specific topic "Knowledge Areas", are listed below.

Agile Tools & Techniques (50% of exam)

- Communications
- Planning, monitoring, and adapting
- Agile estimation
- Agile analysis and design
- Product quality
- Soft skills negotiation
- Value based prioritization
- Risk management
- Metrics
- Value stream analysis

Agile Knowledge & Skills (50% of exam)

- Level 1 (18 knowledge/skills) (33% of exam)
- Level 2 (12 knowledge/skills) (12% of exam)
- Level 3 (13 knowledge/skills) (5% of exam)

As depicted above, the two primary content areas of the PMI-ACP exam contain a total of 13 topic areas.

Practice Exams and Quizzes

PMI-ACP Lite Mock Exam 1
Practice Questions

Test Name: PMI-ACP Lite Mock Exam 1
Total Questions: 40
Correct Answers Needed to Pass:
30 (75.00%)
Time Allowed: 60 Minutes

Test Description

This is a cumulative PMI-ACP Mock Exam which can be used as a benchmark for your PMI-ACP aptitude. This practice test includes questions from all exam topic areas, including sections from Agile Tools and Techniques, and all three Agile Knowledge and Skills areas.

Test Questions

1. Calculate the Net Present Value of the following investment candidate. The initial investment cost is $10,000. The discount rate is 0%. At the end of year 1, $500 is expected. At the end of year 2, $8,000 is expected. At the end of year 3, $1,500 is expected.

   A. $10.00

   B. $1.00

   C. ($1.00)

   D. $0

2. 2.) Xavier has just written test code as part of the four step process of TDD. What step is Xavier performing?

   A. 4th

   B. 2nd

   C. 1st

   D. 3rd

3. Of the following, which is the best definition of an agile leader?

   A. Someone who empowers the team to procrastinate and evade key decisions for the sake of performance.

   B. Someone who empowers the team to be dependent and reliant upon on the team leader for all decisions.

   C. Someone who empowers the team to be undisciplined and chaordic.

   D. Someone who empowers the team to be self-organized and self-disciplined.

4. Identify the lean manufacturing process used for inventory control adopted by agile to help control workflow?

   A. 5Y

   B. Kaizen

   C. Yokoten

   D. Kanban

5. To help explain the definition of local safety in his agile practitioner class, Cody uses a chart showing a cumulative distribution function of estimated task times. On the chart, the 90% confidence

level has a value of 120 minutes, the 50% confidence level has a value of 70 minutes, and the 10% confidence level has a value of 10 minutes. What is the local safety of this task?

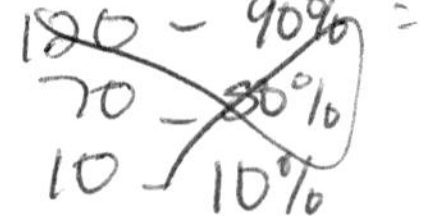

A. 50 minutes

B. 70 minutes

C. 60 minutes

D. 110 minutes

6. Rachel is going over the agile knowledge and skill area of communications management. Which of the following is the best definition of communications management?

A. Managing communication between the team to reduce team conflict and inefficiencies.

B. Reducing communication between the development team and stakeholders to prevent the inefficiency that communication causes in the software environment.

C. Managing communication between a few key team members so that they may in turn convey information to their subordinates.

D. Managing communication between team members and stakeholders to promote effective collaboration.

7. Which of the following example user stories is NOT closed?

A. A trainer can administer site content.

B. A trainer can delete old training programs from student plans.

C. A trainer can sign up students for detailed nutrition programs

D. A trainer can review student weight lifting progress.

8. What earned value management (EVM) variable captures cost variance?

A. CV = EV - AC

B. CV = AC - EV

C. CV = PV - EV

D. CV = EV - PV

9. What does the XP phrase 'caves and common' mean?

A. A caves area where programmers may have peace and quiet for developing user stories and a common room for eating lunch and other social activities.

B. A single room where on one side is an open space with information radiators and a whiteboard for meetings, and on the other side are programming cubicles.

C. A common area that is public to team members and where osmotic communication and collaboration are at play, and a caves area that is a reserved space for private business.

D. A common area reserved for iteration reviews, daily stand-ups, and retrospectives and a caves area reserved for the development team.

10. What does a wireframe help portray to a customer?

A. A finished product design.

B. A design concept showing content, layout, and intended functionality.

C. A competitor's design.

D. A chart of remaining story points to be developed in the iteration.

11. Select the definition of osmotic communication

A. A concept of communication where people sharing the same workspace take in information unconsciously

B. A concept of communication where only verbal information is exchanged

C. A concept of communication that excludes body language and other non-verbal information

D. A concept of communication for software developers to exchange best coding practices

12. As a product owner, Hanna believes in the value of 'incremental delivery.' Why might Hanna see value in incremental delivery?

A. As product owner, she can delay valuable feedback until the end of the project.

B. As product owner, she can review old product code.

C. As product owner, she can start to create the product roadmap.

D. As product owner, she can review a tangible product and update or refine requirements.

13. With respect to agile project management, what term is used to describe "making decisions in an uncertain environment?"

A. Rumination

B. Control

C. Ascendancy

D. Governance

14. Of the following, which is the best definition of prioritization?

A. The vector ordering of product features with respect value.

B. The scalar ordering of product features with respect to value.

C. The fixed ordering of product features with respect to value.

D. The relative ordering of product features with respect to value.

15. Which of the following lists the four Agile Manifesto values?

A. 1) Individuals and collaboration over processes and tools, 2) Working software over comprehensive documentation, 3) Customer collaboration over contract negotiation, and 4) Responding to change over following a plan.

B. 1) Individuals and interactions over processes and tools, 2) Comprehensive documentation over working software, 3) Customer collaboration over contract negotiation, and 4) Responding to change over following a plan.

C. 1) Teams and interactions over processes and tools, 2) Working software over comprehensive documentation, 3) Customer collaboration over contract negotiation, and 4) Responding to change over following a plan.

D. 1) Individuals and interactions over processes and tools, 2) Working software over comprehensive documentation, 3) Customer collaboration over contract negotiation, and 4) Responding to change over following a plan.

16. During Vanessa's daily stand-up meeting update, the agile team helped her make a quick decision on what type of memory she should use for object access. When a team makes decisions together, it is known as:

A. A participatory decision model

B. A ad hominem decision model

C. A user-first decision model

D. A done-done decision model

17. How long does creating a charter typically take in the Crystal development process?

A. A few hours.

B. From four to eight hours.

C. A few months.

D. From a few days to a few weeks.

18. Select the parameter that does NOT belong in the agile iron triangle:

A. Schedule

B. Scope

C. Cost

D. Constraints

19. Trey and his agile team are using story points to estimate development effort of user stories. What is a story point?

A. A fixed and interval value of development effort.

B. A fixed and relative value of development effort.

C. A dynamic and nominal value of development effort.

D. A fixed and ordinal value of development effort.

20. Thomas is explaining the purpose of a product roadmap to Christy, a new agile developer. Select the response that best defines a product roadmap.

A. A high level overview of the product requirements.

B. A high level overview of the sprint backlog.

C. A high level overview of the iteration backlog.

D. A highly detailed document describing the product requirements.

21. What is a WIP limit?

A. A limit of how many sprints can be performed at one time.

B. A limit of how many user stories can be authored at one time.

C. A limit of how many WIPs can be in process at one time.

D. A limit of how many object classes can be performed during a sprint.

22. What is a sprint backlog?

A. A list of the product features to be developed in a sprint.

B. A list of all product features to be developed in a release.

C. A list of possible product features to be developed in a sprint.

D. A list of product features.

23. What does the agile estimation technique of ideal days ignore, discount, or simplify?

A. Non-working days, single developer implementation only, and ideal uninterrupted work

B. Delays, obstacles, non-working days, and the possibility that multiple developers may work on the user story

C. Weekends, holidays, and ideal working conditions

D. Delays, obstacles, and ideal working days

24. Of the following, select the rationale for why an empowered team considered an important team attribute in agile?

A. Empowered teams need extensive management involvement in order to understand customer need

B. Empowered teams need minimal management involvement and thus can focus on leading and delivering value instead of being lead

C. Empowered teams adapt slowly to changing requirements and therefore can reduce scope-creep risk.

D. Empowered teams remain inflexible to changing customer requirements and focus on delivering to specification.

25. An agile team often uses velocity when estimating. What is velocity?

A. A measure of the number of user story points or stories completed per iteration

B. A measure of the number of user story points completed per day

C. A measure of the number of iteration plans completed per iteration

D. A measure of the number of user story points completed per release

26. Define velocity as used in agile estimation.

A. A measure of the number of user story points planned per release.

B. A measure of the number of user story points planned for an iteration.

C. A measure of the number of user story points or stories completed per iteration.

D. A measure of the number of user story points completed per day.

27. Select from the following types of contracts, the one most suited for the agile framework.

A. Fixed-price with incentive

B. Fixed-requirement

C. Fixed-scope

D. Fixed-price

28. As agile team leader, Stacey intends to schedule a brainstorming session to generate ideas that may help solve some of the team's current issues. Which of the following is NOT a good brainstorming technique that Stacey should use?

A. Delaying any criticism that may hamper idea generation.

B. Hosting the meeting in a neutral and comfortable environment.

C. Having an engaging and experienced facilitator lead the brainstorming session.

D. Never follow up with the results, conclusions, or action items of the brainstorming session.

29. Select a technique that promotes agile 'knowledge sharing.'

A. A non-skilled team

B. A monolithic team

C. A cross-functional team

D. A mono-functional team

30. Select the correct ending to the sentence. When estimating relative work effort in the agile methodology, ideal days are estimated for

A. the entire development team.

B. a pair of programmers.

C. the entire iteration team.

D. a single developer.

31. When drafting a persona for agile modeling, which detail is the most important to include?

A. A picture

B. All are important details

C. An Age

D. An Address

32. Patty is reviewing an agile artifact that serves as a high level overview of the product requirements and when certain features are expected to be completed. What artifact is Patty most likely looking reviewing?

A. A project roadmap

B. A process roadmap

C. A product roadmap

D. A planning roadmap

33. Select the response that is a typical information radiator for an agile project.

A. A task board

B. A 10-day weather look ahead for all team members' local weather

C. An archive of team e-mails

D. A project plan document

34. Of the following, which response defines an information radiator?

A. An online guide for how to review project information.

B. A visual representation or chart that shows project status regarding a tracked project-related metric.

C. A raw file of project data.

D. A visual depiction of a Pascal coding technique.

35. What does collocation and osmotic communication enhance among team members?

A. The natural flow of questions, ideas, and information sharing

B. The natural flow of top-down decision making

C. Inter-team rivalry and competition for improved productivity

D. A reduction in the use of body language and other visual cues

36. What is the activity called when a team constructively criticizes its performance for the purpose of improving performance going forward?

A. A refactoring

B. A retrospective

C. A re-imaging

D. A resolution

37. Planning poker, where team members make collective decisions, is an example of:

A. A relative decision model

B. An exclusionary decision model

C. An ordinal decision model

D. A participatory decision model

38. If a user story is said to be able to be scheduled and developed in any order, it satisfies which characteristic?

A. It is estimable

B. It is independent

C. It is Negotiable

D. It is small

39. What is one method that can be used to improve communication for a team that cannot be collocated?

A. Using video conferencing whenever possible

B. Making all workers work the same hours, even if it means the graveyard shift for some team members

C. Making workers fly in on Monday and fly out on Friday

D. Using e-mail exclusively

40. When value stream mapping it is important to identify areas of waste that exist in the process. The pneumonic device WIDETOM may be used to remember the different forms of muda (or waste). What does the E in WIDETOM stand for with respect to waste?

A. Extra processing

B. Earned Interest

C. Entity Flow Reversal

D. Emission

PMI-ACP Lite Mock Exam 1 Answer Key and Explanations

1. D - Net Present Value: A metric used to analyze the profitability of an investment or project. NPV is the difference between the present value of cash inflows and the present value of cash outflows. NPV considers the likelihood of future cash inflows that an investment or project will yield. NPV is the sum of each cash inflow/outflow for the expected duration of the investment. Each cash inflow/outflow is discounted back to its present value (PV) (i.e.,, what the money is worth in terms of today's value). NPV is the sum of all terms: NPV = Sum of [Rt/(1 + i)^t] where t = the time of the cash flow, i = the discount rate (the rate of return that could be earned on in the financial markets) , and Rt = the net cash inflow or outflow. For example, consider the following two year period. The discount rate is 5% and the initial investment cost is $500. At the end of the first year, a $200 inflow is expected. At the end of the second year, a $1,000 is expected. NPV = -500 + 200/(1.05)^1 + 1000/(1.05)^2 = ~$597. If NPV is positive, it indicates that the investment will add value to the buyer's portfolio. If NPV is negative, it will subtract value. If NPV is zero, it will neither add or subtract value. [Agile Estimating and Planning. Mike Cohn.] [Value based prioritization]

2. C - The TDD process has four basic steps: 1) Write a test, 2) Verify and validate the test, 3) Write product code and apply the test, 4) Refactor the product code. An example may be that a user has to enter an age value. A good test is to make sure the user data entry is a positive number and not a different type of input, like a letter (i.e., write the test). The programmer would verify that entering a letter instead of a number would cause the program to cause an exception (i.e., v&v the test). The programmer would then write product code that takes user entry for the age value (i.e., write the product code). The programmer would then run the product code and enter correct age values and incorrect age values (i.e., apply the test). If the product code is successful, the programmer would refactor the product code to improve its design. Using these four steps iteratively ensures that programmers think about how a software program might fail first and to build product code that is holistically being tested. This helps produce high quality code. [The Art of Agile Development. James Shore.] [Product quality]

3. D - A common misconception in agile is that an agile team does not need a leader. In fact, all agile teams need a leader, but the way in which the leader leads is fundamentally different than the typical traditional project manager/project leader method. Some have theorized that this misconception stems from the desired 'self-organizing' quality of the agile team. And although the 'self-organizing' agile team is empowered to take ownership and responsibility of the product and make some decisions itself, it nevertheless requires a leader to help provide guidance, mentoring, coaching, problem solving, and decision making. Some key aspects required of an agile leader include: empowering team members to decide what standard agile practices and methods it will use; allowing the team to be self-organized and self-disciplined; empowering the team members to make decisions collaboratively with the customer; inspire the team to be innovative and explore new ideas and technology capabilities; be a champion of and articulate the product vision to team members so it will be motivated to accomplish the overall objective; remove any obstacles and solve any problems the team may face in its effort; communicate and endorse the values and principles of agile project management to stakeholders that may be unfamiliar with agile; ensure that all stakeholders, including business managers and developers, are collaborating effectively; and, be able to adapt the leadership style to the working environment to ensure that the agile values and principles are effectively upheld. [The Art of Agile Development. James Shore.] [Knowledge and Skills: Level 1]

4. D - Kanban, Japanese for billboard or signboard, is a scheduling system for just-in-time (JIT) production developed by Toyota in the 1940s and 1950s. It is a way of controlling and reducing inventory by using cards or signs to order (demand signal) requisite parts for a manufacturing process from other dependent systems (supply). Kanban has been adopted by agile to help control workflow. [Lean-Agile Software Development: Achieving Enterprise Agility. Alan Shalloway, Guy Beaver, James R. Trott.] [Planning, monitoring, and adapting]

5. A - The local safety is the difference between the 90% confidence estimate of task time and the 50% confidence estimate of task time. Remember that estimates for task time are typically a range of estimates and not a single value; think of estimates existing as a cumulative distribution function. A 50% confidence estimate is essentially an aggressive estimate where the estimator only has a 50% confidence that the task will be completed within the associated time value. A 90% confidence estimate is essentially a conservative estimate where the estimator has a 90% confidence that the task will be completed within the associated time value. [Agile Estimating and Planning. Mike Cohn.] [Agile estimation]

6. D - Effective communication is a cornerstone of agile. Communication is the act of transferring information among various parties. Communications management is a knowledge and skill area of agile that highlights this importance. PMI has several definitions regarding communications management and agile builds on top of these to add its own perspective: 1) Communications Planning: Determining the information and communication needs of the projects stakeholders 2) Information Distribution: Making needed information available to project stakeholders in a timely manner, 3) Performance Reporting: Collecting and distributing performance information. This includes status reporting, progress measurement, and forecasting, and 4) Managing Stakeholders: Managing communications to satisfy the requirements and resolve issues with project stakeholders. From an agile perspective: communication among the team is built into the process and facilitated through collocation, information radiators, daily stand-up meetings, retrospectives etc.; Although it is hoped that the product owner, customer, and user can be heavily involved with the project and also use these communication techniques, a plan for conveying information to stakeholders may be needed if this is not the case. [Agile Software Development: The Cooperative Game –

2nd Edition. Alistair Cockburn.] [Knowledge and Skills: Level 1]

7. A - The best answer is "A trainer can administer site content" because it is an activity that has no clear end point or exit criteria. The other selections include activities that have a clear end point. [User Stories Applied: For Agile Software Development. Mike Cohn.] [Agile analysis and design]

8. A - Unlike traditional project management methods that evaluate risk and variance and trends in formal meetings, agile incorporates risk analysis and variance and trend analysis into iteration review meetings. Risk and variance and trend analysis may be performed in agile using information radiators, like a risk burndown chart, and the use of traditional earned value management (EVM) to measure cost and schedule variance (CV and SV, respectively). [Agile Estimating and Planning. Mike Cohn.] [Knowledge and Skills: Level 3]

9. C - The XP phrase 'caves and common' refers to the creation of two zones for team members. The common area is a public space where osmotic communication and collaboration are largely at play. The caves is a private space is reserved for private tasks that require an isolated and quiet environment. For the common area to work well, each team member should be working on one and the same project. [Agile Software Development: The Cooperative Game – 2nd Edition. Alistair Cockburn.] [Knowledge and Skills: Level 2]

10. B - In the agile design process, prototypes help the customer understand current design state. Three common types of prototypes are HTML, paper (i.e., sketches), and wireframes. A wireframe is a sketch of a user interface, identifying its content, layout, functionality, is usually black and white, and excludes detailed pictures or graphics. A wireframe can be created on paper, whiteboards, or using software. [Agile Estimating and Planning. Mike Cohn.] [Agile analysis and design]

11. A - Osmotic communication is a concept of communication where information is shared between collocated team members unconsciously. By sharing the same work environment, team members are exposed to the same environmental sounds and other environmental input and unconsciously share a common framework that improves communication. [Agile Software Development: The Cooperative Game – 2nd Edition. Alistair Cockburn.] [Communications]

12. D - A cornerstone of Agile development is 'incremental delivery.' Incremental delivery is the frequent delivery of working products, which are successively improved, to a customer for immediate feedback and acceptance. Typically, a product is delivered at the end of each sprint or iteration for demonstration and feedback. In this feedback technique, a customer can review the product and provide updated requirements. Changed/updated/refined requirements are welcomed in the agile process to ensure the customer receives a valuable and quality product. A sprint or iteration typically lasts from two to four weeks and at the end a new and improved product is delivered, incrementally. [The Art of Agile Development. James Shore.] [Knowledge and Skills: Level 1]

13. D - Highsmith defines agile project governance as "making decisions in an

uncertain environment." [Agile Project Management: Creating Innovative Products – 2nd Edition. Jim Highsmith.] [Knowledge and Skills: Level 2]

14. D - An agile team must always face the prioritization of product features in its product backlog. From release planning to iteration planning, an agile team must prioritize the user stories/ features of its product to ensure that high-quality and high-value features are developed first to help facilitate an optimized and early return on investment (ROI). An agile team typically prioritizes requirements or user stories/features in terms of relative value and risk; value is defined by the customer (i.e., customer-value prioritization). Two common methods to prioritize product features are: MoSCoW and Kano. The MoSCoW method categorizes features into 'Must have,' 'Should have,' 'Could have,' and 'Would have' features. The Kano method categorizes features into 'Must haves (threshold),' 'Dissatisfiers,' 'Satisfiers,' and 'Delighters.' Must haves are features that are requisite. Dissatisfiers are features that adversely impact perceived value and should be eliminated. 'Satisfiers' are features that increase perceived value linearly, where the more you add the more the customer is pleased, but are not required, and 'Delighters' are features that increase perceived value exponentially to please the customer. To prioritize features based on risk, a risk-to-value matrix can be used. A risk-to-value matrix has four quadrants, with the horizontal axis having low and high value, and the vertical axis having low and high risk. User stories are assigned to one of the four categories/quadrants: low-value, low-risk; low-value, high-risk; high-value, low-risk; high-value, high-risk. A cost-to-value matrix can also be made in this manner. All prioritization in agile is 'relative,' meaning that the priority of one user story is relative to other user stories and not prioritized on a fixed scale. [Lean-Agile Software Development: Achieving Enterprise Agility. Alan Shalloway, Guy Beaver, James R. Trott.] [Knowledge and Skills: Level 1]

15. D - The Agile Manifesto defines four values. The four values list primary values and secondary values, with primary values superseding secondary values. The values are 1) individuals and interactions over processes and tools, 2) working software over comprehensive documentation, 3) customer collaboration over contract negotiation, and 4) responding to change over following a plan. [Manifesto for Agile Software Development. Agile Alliance.] [Knowledge and Skills: Level 1]

16. A - To build trust among the team, agile believes heavily in participatory decision models where team members collaborate to make decisions. Although a team leader or scrum master will need to make some decisions individually, many decisions can be made by the team collectively. These agile principles are also known as collective ownership, self-organization, and self-discipline. In collective ownership, the team members are equally responsible for project results and are empowered to participate in decision making and problem solving processes. [Agile Retrospectives: Making Good Teams Great. Esther Derby, Diana Larsen, Ken Schwaber.] [Knowledge and Skills: Level 2]

17. D - The Crystal development process is cyclical/iterative. Its primary components are chartering, delivery cycles, and project wrap-up. Chartering involves creating a project charter, which can last from a few days to a few weeks. Chartering consists of four activities: 1) Building the core project team, 2) performing an Exploratory 360° assessment, 3) fine tuning the methodology, and 3) building the initial project plan. [Agile Software Development: The Cooperative Game – 2nd Edition. Alistair Cockburn.] [Agile analysis and design]

18. D - The agile iron triangle includes cost, scope, and schedule as its parameters. Constraints is a parameter included in the agile triangle, not the agile iron triangle. [Agile Project Management: Creating Innovative Products – 2nd Edition. Jim Highsmith.] [Knowledge and Skills: Level 1]

19. B - Story points represent the relative work effort it takes to develop a user story. Each point represents a fixed value of development effort. When estimating the agile team must consider complexity, effort, risk, and inter-dependencies. [Agile Estimating and Planning. Mike Cohn.] [Agile estimation]

20. A - The product roadmap - owned by the product owner - serves as a high level overview of the product requirements. It is used as a tool for prioritizing features , organizing features into categories, and assigning rough time frames. Creating a product roadmap has four basic steps: 1) Identify requirements (these will become part of the product backlog), 2) Organize requirements into categories or themes, 3) Estimate relative work effort (e.g., planning poker or affinity estimation) and prioritize (value), and 4) Estimate rough time frames (estimate velocity, sprint duration, and rough release dates). [The Art of Agile Development. James Shore.] [Agile analysis and design]

21. C - A lean manufacturing philosophy is to eliminate waste. One defined waste type in the lean philosophy is inventory, which is also referred to as work in process (WIP). WIP is material or parts that have started production but are not yet a finished or "done" product. Inventory is considered wasteful because it costs money to purchase, store, and maintain. One way of reducing inventory is to reduce the WIP at individual machines or servers by only moving as fast as your slowest machine or processor (the system bottleneck). Agile also strives to control its WIP through WIP limits by completing all features to a "done" state before beginning development of new features. One can think of an iteration or sprint as a process that can develop a certain amount of features. In this analogy, the WIP limit is equivalent to the sprint backlog. By maintaining a WIP limit equal to the sprint backlog, no features should be incomplete at the sprint review. [Lean-Agile Software Development: Achieving Enterprise Agility. Alan Shalloway, Guy Beaver, James R. Trott.] [Planning, monitoring, and adapting]

22. A - The sprint backlog is a list of product features or work items to be completed in a sprint. It is typically fixed for the sprint unless it is overcome by important customer requirements. [Lean-Agile Software Development: Achieving Enterprise Agility. Alan Shalloway, Guy Beaver, James R. Trott.] [Agile analysis and design]

23. B - Instead of using story points, agile teams may estimate the relative sizes of user stories using ideal days. Ideal days represents the amount of days - uninterrupted by meetings, personal life, non-working days, or any other delays, obstacles or distractions - that it would take a single person to build, test, and release the user story, relative to other user stories in the backlog. [Agile Estimating and Planning. Mike Cohn.] [Agile estimation]

24. B - Empowered teams - ones that are self-organizing and know how to solve problems with minimal management involvement - are a cornerstone of the agile methodology. This is the antithesis to the classic viewpoint of the traditional project manager who is seen as someone that controls all decisions and delegates tasks to a team with little feedback. An agile team must include all members and stakeholders to make decisions, and make decisions expediently. Because it is essential that the user/customer be involved with development, it is encouraged that the user/customer is closely integrated with the agile team with collocation/on-site support being ideal. An agile team feels empowered when it collectively assumes responsibility for the delivery of the product (i.e., taking ownership). [Coaching Agile Teams. Lyssa Adkins.] [Knowledge and Skills: Level 1]

25. A - Velocity is a measure of the number of user story points or stories completed by a team per iteration. An agile team can use its previous velocity recordings as a method of estimating how many user story points it may complete in the next iteration. [Agile Estimating and Planning. Mike Cohn.] [Agile estimation]

26. C - Velocity is a measure of the number of user story points or stories completed by a team per iteration. An agile team can use its previous velocity recordings as a method of estimating how many user story points it may complete in the next iteration. [Agile Estimating and Planning. Mike Cohn.] [Agile estimation]

27. A - Time, budget, and cost estimation is an important knowledge and skill area of agile. According to Highsmith, the nature of the agile method, whereby it welcomes changing scope, means that it lends itself well to fixed budgets and a fixed schedule because changing scope makes it difficult to estimate a total cost. Generally speaking, the budget and schedule constraints are known but before a project will commence there needs to be an agreed upon set of base product functionality defined in an initiation phase; fixing scope reduces an agile team's innovative tendency to provide improved value. For companies that are familiar with fixed-price contracts, where requirements are agreed upon before contract closing, adopting agile can be a weary initial venture. Instead, other contract vehicle types are recommended for agile efforts. These include: a general service contract for the initiation phase and separate fixed-price contracts for iterations or user stories; time-and-material contracts; not-to-exceed with fixed-fee contracts; and, incentive contracts (e.g., fixed price with incentive; cost-reimbursable with award fee). [Agile Project Management: Creating Innovative Products – 2nd Edition. Jim Highsmith.] [Knowledge and Skills: Level 1]

28. D - A successful brainstorming event should strive to consider the following points - Host the meeting in a neutral and comfortable environment - Have an engaging and experienced facilitator lead the event - Send participants an overview, with goals, schedule, and what ground rules, beforehand - Have a multi-disciplinary/diverse team to get a broader perspective - Delay any criticism that may stifle idea generation. [Agile Retrospectives: Making Good Teams Great. Esther Derby, Diana Larsen, Ken Schwaber.] [Knowledge and Skills: Level 1]

29. C - In agile, effective 'knowledge sharing' is a critical factor for success. It involves the near real time communication of key information among all team members and stakeholders. To promote knowledge sharing, agile uses standard practices built into its process, such as using generalized specialists/cross functional teams, self-organizing and self-disciplined teams, collocation, daily stand-up meetings, iteration/sprint planning, release planning, pair programming and pair rotation, project retrospectives/reflection, and on-site customer support. And, of course, the sixth principle of Agile is " The most efficient and effective method of conveying information to and within a development team is face-to-face conversation." In this sense, Agile prefers and encourages collocation for all stakeholders and team members for the simple fact that face-to-face conversation is the best method of communication and, in turn, effective knowledge sharing. [Becoming Agile: ...in an imperfect world. Greg Smith, Ahmed Sidky.] [Knowledge and Skills: Level 1]

30. D - Instead of using story points, agile teams may estimate the relative sizes of user stories using ideal days. Ideal days represents the amount of days - uninterrupted by meetings, personal life, non-working days, or any other delays, obstacles or distractions - that it would take a single person to build, test, and release the user story, relative to other user stories in the backlog. [Agile Estimating and Planning. Mike Cohn.] [Agile estimation]

31. B - A persona is a notional user of the system under development. Being much more detailed than actors in use case modeling where generic user names are assigned (e.g., end user), personas try to elaborate on users with detailed descriptions to provide context to the developers. Some personas have such notional details as name, address, age, income, likes and dislikes, and other specific details. [User Stories Applied: For Agile Software Development. Mike Cohn.] [Agile analysis and design]

32. C - The product roadmap - owned by the product owner - serves as a high level overview of the product requirements. It is used as a tool for prioritizing features , organizing features into categories, and assigning rough time frames. Creating a product roadmap has four basic steps: 1) Identify requirements (these will become part of the product backlog), 2) Organize requirements into categories or themes, 3) Estimate relative work effort (e.g., planning poker or affinity estimation) and prioritize (value), and 4) Estimate rough time frames (estimate velocity, sprint duration, and rough release dates). [The Art of Agile Development. James Shore.] [Agile analysis and design]

33. A - Typical information radiators on an agile project include: project burndown charts, task boards, burnup charts, and defect charts. [Agile Software Development: The Cooperative Game – 2nd Edition. Alistair Cockburn.] [Communications]

34. B - An information radiator is a visual representation of project status data. [Agile

Software Development: The Cooperative Game – 2nd Edition. Alistair Cockburn.] [Communications]

35. A - Osmotic communication helps ensure the natural flow of questions, ideas, and information sharing among the agile project team. [Agile Software Development: The Cooperative Game – 2nd Edition. Alistair Cockburn.] [Communications]

36. B - During reflection or retrospectives, an agile team reserves time to reflect on the work it has completed with the objective of continuous improvement. In these self-assessment/team-assessment events, topics can include: lessons learned from successes and failures; team standards that worked, failed, or were not properly followed; and other areas of improvement. [Agile Retrospectives: Making Good Teams Great. Esther Derby, Diana Larsen, Ken Schwaber.] [Knowledge and Skills: Level 2]

37. D - To build trust among the team, agile believes heavily in participatory decision models where team members collaborate to make decisions. Although a team leader or scrum master will need to make some decisions individually, many decisions can be made by the team collectively. These agile principles are also known as collective ownership, self-organization, and self-discipline. In collective ownership, the team members are equally responsible for project results and are empowered to participate in decision making and problem solving processes. [Agile Retrospectives: Making Good Teams Great. Esther Derby, Diana Larsen, Ken Schwaber.] [Knowledge and Skills: Level 2]

38. B - The acronym INVEST (independent, negotiable, valuable, estimable, small, and testable) helps the agile practitioner remember the characteristics of a good user story. I – Independent stories can be developed in any order and avoid dependencies which can make development more complex. N – Negotiable user stories mean that both the customer and developer should feel free to analyze and adapt a user story to meet customer needs. V – A valuable user story describes how the product feature will provide value to the customer. E – Estimable user stories are ones that developers can readily estimate the effort or duration required for developing them. S- Small user stories are ones that take about two to five days of work to implement. T - Testable user stories are ones that can be verified according to acceptance criteria to ensure value. [Agile Retrospectives: Making Good Teams Great. Esther Derby, Diana Larsen, Ken Schwaber.] [Planning, monitoring, and adapting]

39. A - A high-performance agile team is one that is ideally collocated for osmotic communication and face-to-face interaction. However, collocation isn't always feasible in today's multinational environment. For distributed teams, several practices are available to provide the best form of effective communication in the absence of being collocated: team intranet sites, virtual team rooms, and video conferencing over e-mail when possible. Geographic separation, especially on a world-wide scale, causes the team to consider language and cultural differences, and time zone differences. [The Art of Agile Development. James Shore.] [Knowledge and Skills: Level 2]

40. A - Value stream mapping is a lean manufacturing analysis technique adopted by agile. A value stream map may be used to analyze the flow of information or materials from origin to destination to identify areas of waste. The identified areas of waste are opportunities for process improvement. Waste can take many forms and can be remembered using the pneumonic device WIDETOM. W - waiting; I - inventory; D - defects; E - extra processing; T - transportation; O - over-production ; M - Motion. A value stream map is typically mapped or charted collaboratively with a team so it may define and view the entire process together, pinpointing areas of waste within the process. Processes that add value (processing of a part or feature) are generally referred to as "value-added" and processes that do not (e.g., waiting for a part to arrive) are generally referred to as "non value-added." Generally speaking, one wants to reduce, to the largest extent possible, the non value-added time (i.e., areas of waste). [Lean-Agile Software Development: Achieving Enterprise Agility. Alan Shalloway, Guy Beaver, James R. Trott.] [Value stream analysis]

PMI-ACP Lite Mock Exam 2 Practice Questions

Test Name: PMI-ACP Lite Mock Exam 2
Total Questions: 40
Correct Answers Needed to Pass:
30 (75.00%)
Time Allowed: 60 Minutes

Test Description

This is a cumulative PMI-ACP Mock Exam which can be used as a benchmark for your PMI-ACP aptitude. This practice test includes questions from all exam topic areas, including sections from Agile Tools and Techniques, and all three Agile Knowledge and Skills areas.

Test Questions

1. Roger as an experienced agile team leader is keen on having an empowered team. What does an empowered team mean?

A. A team that is risk-averse and focused solely on minimizing risk.

B. A team that solves problems through the use of customer feedback mechanisms.

C. A team that is capable of "powering" up to different iteration velocities to reach customer expectations.

D. A team that is self-organizing and takes ownership of the product it is developing.

2. Barry and Jill have just overturned the lowest and highest values, respectively, during a planning poker meeting when estimating a user story that Barry is to develop. What typically happens next in planning poker?

A. Because Barry is the developer, the team should use Barry's estimate.

B. An average of the two values should be used as the estimated work effort to complete the user story.

C. Both Barry and Jill should be allowed to defend their decisions and the team should repeat the voting process until consensus is reached by the entire team.

D. Randomly pick one of the cards as the user story work effort estimate.

3. Why is knowing about CASs important for an agile practitioner?

A. Because understanding that software projects are themselves similar to CASs reminds practitioners about the importance of adapting to a changing environment.

B. Because understanding that software projects are themselves similar to CASs reminds practitioners about the importance of avoiding scope creep.

C. Because understanding that software projects are themselves similar to CASs reminds practitioners about the importance of fixing a changing environment.

D. Because understanding that software projects are themselves similar to CASs reminds practitioners about the importance of avoiding too many interacting, adaptive agents that can disrupt progress.

4. John, as project leader, mentors and coaches his team. He always makes sure to highlight important team achievements. What is John doing when he provides mentoring and coaching?

A. Refactoring the team

B. Guiding the team

C. Reforming the team

D. Motivating the team

5. Which of the following is the best definition of an agile leader?

A. Someone who delegates all tasks to the development team without any collaboration

B. Someone who empowers the development team to take ownership of the product and make important decisions in a collaborative environment.

C. Someone who retains control of key decisions and delegates all functions and tasks to team members.

D. Someone who empowers the development team to make inconsequential decisions to give it the feeling of self-organization.

6. Pick the response which is NOT a characteristic of the agile validation process.

A. Confirms the product meets specifications and requirements.

B. Confirms the product meets user needs.

C. Helps ensure quality.

D. Performed frequently.

7. Jessica is using the lean technique of 5Y for root cause analysis. What agile knowledge and skill area does 5Y fall under?

A. Problem-saturation strategies, tools, and techniques

B. Problem-reversing strategies, tools, and techniques

C. Problem-mitigation strategies, tools, and techniques

D. Problem-solving strategies, tools, and techniques

8. From the following, select a common agile framework/methodology.

A. Static systems development method (SSDM)

B. Dynamic product development method (DPDM)

C. Dynamic systems development method (DSDM)

D. Extreme systems development method (XSDM)

9. Which of the following helps an agile team promote simple and effective communication?

A. Through the use of lengthy memorandums.

B. Through collaborative release planning

C. Through the use of formal boardroom meetings.

D. Through the use of e-mail.

10. What term often used in agile estimation refers to the amount of user stories or story points completed in an iteration?

A. Frequency

B. Acceleration

C. Speed

D. Velocity

11. Hanson and his team are using a framework in their agile effort where the team follows a prescriptive five step process that is managed and tracked from the perspective of the product features. Which framework is Hanson's team incorporating into its agile effort?

A. Defect driven development (3D)

B. Test driven development (TDD)

C. Acceptance test driven development (ATDD)

D. Feature driven development (FDD)

12. Of the following, which is NOT a phase of Highsmith's agile project management?

A. Monitoring & Controlling

B. Adapting

C. Speculating

D. Closing

13. Not all agile efforts succeed the first time, what is a common cause of failure?

A. Accrued budget debt from failing to adhere to waterfall scheduling.

B. Accrued schedule debt from using a sustainable, 40 hour work week.

C. Accrued technical debt from putting off quality standards.

D. Accrued social debt from putting off team building events.

14. Which of the following best defines collaboration?

A. Achieving personal goals.

B. Achieving objectives independently.

C. Achieving objectives through cooperative team work.

D. Achieving growth targets.

15. Of the following, which is the best definition of prioritization?

A. The relative ordering of user stories with respect to value and risk.

B. The scalar ordering of user stories with respect to value and risk.

C. The fixed ordering of user stories with respect to value and risk

D. The vector ordering of user stories with respect value and risk.

16. Having a high emotional intelligence is important to promote effective communication in an agile team. What is one of the seven components of emotional intelligence as defined by Higgs & Dulewicz?

A. Chaordicness

B. Controlled recklessness

C. Interpersonal sensitivity

D. Sympathy

17. Calculate the return on investment of the following: Gain: $1,000; Cost: $10,000.

A. -70%

B. -90%

C. 90%

D. -80%

18. Xavier has just refactored his production code after testing it as part of the four step process of TDD. What step is Xavier performing?

A. 1st

B. 4th

C. 2nd

D. 3rd

19. Jane and her team are discussing with the business stakeholder what the expected behavior is of a particular user story. What step is Jane on in the ATDD four step process?

A. 2nd

B. 3rd

C. 4th

D. 1st

20. Jane and her team are distilling information from a discussion with the business stakeholder into specific tests for a user story. What step is Jane on in the ATDD four step process?

A. 1st

B. 2nd

C. 4th

D. 3rd

21. Of the following, select the best adjective that describes an agile team's, project and quality standards.

A. Refined over time

B. Defined in the agile manifesto

C. CMMI-defined

D. Fixed from the get go

22. Sarah, as an agile leader, knows that she should practice with an adaptive leadership style. What are the two dimensions Highsmith uses to define adaptive leadership?

A. Adaptive agility and anticipatory agility

B. Being agile and doing agile

C. Being agile and practicing agile

D. Adaptive agility and prescriptive agility

23. Select from the following a key soft skill negotiation quality.

A. Adaptive compromise

B. Adaptive leadership

C. Adaptive reflection

D. Adaptive following

24. In agile estimating and planning, what is 'retained' revenue?

A. Revenue retained through the development of new product features or services that prevent existing customers from stopping use of the existing product.

B. Additional revenue realized through the sales of new product features or services to existing customers.

C. New revenue realized through the sales of products or services to new customers.

D. New revenue found in a hidden value stream.

25. What process, performed frequently, helps ensure high product quality?

A. Planning poker

B. Affinity planning

C. Milestone reviews

D. Verification and validation

26. Which scrum meeting is often timeboxed to four hours?

A. Release plan meeting

B. Daily stand-up meeting

C. Affinity planning meeting

D. Sprint planning meeting

27. Of the following, select the rationale for why an empowered team considered an important team attribute in agile?

A. Empowered teams adapt slowly to changing requirements and therefore can reduce scope-creep risk.

B. Empowered teams remain inflexible to changing customer requirements and focus on delivering to specification.

C. Empowered teams adapt to changing requirements and thus can focus on delivering value in a volatile marketplace

D. Empowered teams remove themselves from being responsible of product quality in order to reduce association with project failure.

28. Kathy, the head of a multi-national corporation, is considering hiring an agile team to develop a new database system. However, the agile team Kathy is working with tells her that estimating final cost can be difficult. Why is it more difficult to estimate cost on an agile project?

A. Because agile welcomes the changing scope that customers may request to stay relevant in the marketplace.

B. Because customers have little experience with the agile quality to cost and value triangle.

C. Because the cost of product development is not fixed.

D. Because agile works outside the purview of a fixed schedule.

29. Rebecca and her agile team are discussing the project and quality standards it will hold itself accountable against for a new effort. When it typically the best time to have this discussion?

A. After the first iteration

B. At the beginning of an effort

C. After refactoring

D. After the first accepted user story

30. In agile and other project management styles, team motivation is a critical factor for success. What is one method to improve team motivation?

A. Focusing only on business objectives.

B. Fostering a competitive environment.

C. Spending quality time together.

D. Highlighting a developer's deficiencies public for the sake of team feedback.

31. Prototyping is a common project management technique to reduce risk. Select the response which is NOT a common form of prototyping in agile projects.

A. XAML

B. Paper

C. HTML

D. Wireframe

32. Becky, as project leader, intends on building a high-performance team. What is a practice or technique she can use to build a high performance team?

A. Isolating team members for focus

B. Criticizing team members openly

C. Promoting competition

D. Building trust

33. Select a common agile framework/methodology.

A. Agile codified process (ACP)

B. Agile framework process (AFP)

C. Agile lean process (ALP)

D. Agile unified process (AUP)

34. Jill and her team are scheduled to hold a reflective improvement workshop the next business day. Which agile project management methodology uses reflective improvement workshops as a key tool to apply its principles?

A. Extreme Programming

B. Agile Unified Process

C. Crystal

D. Feature Driven Development

35. In which framework are core roles categorized as the following three: product owner, scrum master, development team?

A. Extreme programming (XP)

B. Scrum

C. Lean software development

D. Agile unified process (AUP)

36. What type of team takes ownership of a product and requires minimal management supervision?

A. Power team

B. Empowered team

C. Magnitude team

D. Impact team

37. Peter is at a planning event where the relative development effort of user stories of a large product backlog is to be estimated. The team is to assign user stories to various soft drink sizes (small, medium, large, extra-large). What type of planning event is Peter most likely attending?

A. Planning game estimating

B. Agility estimating

C. Planning poker

D. Affinity estimating

38. Which of the following best defines negotiation?

A. Agreement found through customer choice.

B. Agreement found through discussion.

C. Agreement found through inspection.

D. Agreement found through reflection.

39. Jules is describing the SMART acronym used for task analysis in an agile seminar. What does the A stand for?

A. Aggregate

B. Altruistic

C. Achievable

D. Accurate

40. Help Julian select a key principle of lean software development.

A. Increasing inventory

B. Amplifying defect detection

C. Quality stream mapping

D. Eliminating waste

PMI-ACP Lite Mock Exam 2 Answer Key and Explanations

1. D - Empowered teams - ones that are self-organizing and know how to solve problems with minimal management involvement - are a cornerstone of the agile methodology. An agile team feels empowered when it collectively assumes responsibility for the delivery of the product (i.e., taking ownership). [Coaching Agile Teams. Lyssa Adkins.] [Knowledge and Skills: Level 1]

2. C - Planning poker is based upon the wideband Delphi estimation technique. It is a consensus-based technique for estimating effort. Sometimes called scrum poker, it is a technique for a relative estimation of effort, typically in story points, to develop a user story. At a planning poker meeting, each estimator is given an identical deck of planning poker cards with a wide range of values. The Fibonacci sequence is often used for values for planning poker (i.e., 0, 1, 1, 2, 3, 5,8,etc.); another common sequence is (question mark, 0, 1/2, 1, 2, 3, 5, 8, 13, 20, 40, and 100). A planning poker meeting works as follows: 1) a moderator, not estimating, facilitates the meeting. 2) the product owner/manager provides a short overview of the user story and answers clarifying questions posed by the developers. Typically the product owner does not vote. 3) Each estimator selects an estimate of work effort by selecting a card, 4) Once everyone has selected a card, everyone overturns their card concurrently, 5) Estimators with high and low estimates are given a chance to defend positions. 6) The process repeats until there is consensus. The developer who owns the user story is typically given higher credence. [Agile Estimating and Planning. Mike Cohn.] [Agile estimation]

3. A - A complex adaptive system, or CAS, is a system composed of interacting, adaptive agents or components. The term is used in agile to remind practitioners that the development of a product is adaptive in that previous interactions, events, decisions influence future behavior. The term chaordic (a made up word blending chaotic and order) is sometimes used when describing CASs. Literature points to three key characteristics of chaordic projects: alignment and cooperation, emergence and self-organization, and learning and adaptation. [Agile Project Management: Creating Innovative Products – 2nd Edition. Jim Highsmith.] [Knowledge and Skills: Level 3]

4. D - Having a motivated team is essential for any project, regardless of whether it is agile or not. Motivated teams work together better, have strong productivity, and exceed expectations. Some simple steps to increase motivation are 1) spending quality time together; where team members get to know one another on a personal level to build a sense of community, 2) providing feedback, mentoring and coaching; where team members are congratulated and thanked on jobs well done and also mentored or coached to improve in skill and capability, and 3) empowerment; where the team is empowered to make many key decisions which, along the way, builds trust and shows that leadership believes in the capabilities of the team. [The Art of Agile Development. James Shore.] [Knowledge and Skills: Level 1]

5. B - A common misconception in agile is that an agile team does not need a leader. In

fact, all agile teams need a leader, but the way in which the leader leads is fundamentally different than the typical traditional project manager/project leader method. Some have theorized that this misconception stems from the desired 'self-organizing' quality of the agile team. And although the 'self-organizing' agile team is empowered to take ownership and responsibility of the product and make some decisions itself, it nevertheless requires a leader to help provide guidance, mentoring, coaching, problem solving, and decision making. Some key aspects required of an agile leader include: empowering team members to decide what standard agile practices and methods it will use; allowing the team to be self-organized and self-disciplined; empowering the team members to make decisions collaboratively with the customer; inspire the team to be innovative and explore new ideas and technology capabilities; be a champion of and articulate the product vision to team members so it will be motivated to accomplish the overall objective; remove any obstacles and solve any problems the team may face in its effort; communicate and endorse the values and principles of agile project management to stakeholders that may be unfamiliar with agile; ensure that all stakeholders, including business managers and developers, are collaborating effectively; and, be able to adapt the leadership style to the working environment to ensure that the agile values and principles are effectively upheld. [The Art of Agile Development. James Shore.] [Knowledge and Skills: Level 1]

6. A - Because each iteration typically produces a working product that is built and integrated and iterations are typically two to four weeks in length, there is frequent verification and validation to ensure product quality. Verification is the confirmation that a product performs as specified by a customer (e.g. as indicated by a user story) and validation is the confirmation that a product behaves as desired (i.e., meets the customer's need). Sometimes a product may be built and integrated to specification - that is, it can be verified - but it does not meet the intent of the customer - that is, it cannot be validated. [Agile Software Development: The Cooperative Game – 2nd Edition. Alistair Cockburn.] [Product quality]

7. D - Literally thousands of decisions are made in the course of a project. Many of these decisions are made in response to problems that inevitably arise and confront the agile team. Therefore it is essential that an agile team is properly versed in problem-solving strategies, tools, and techniques. Some common problem-solving techniques include: ask it loud; revisit the problem; 5Y; sunk cost fallacy; devil's advocate; be kind, rewind; asking probing questions; and reflective/active listening. [Agile Retrospectives: Making Good Teams Great. Esther Derby, Diana Larsen, Ken Schwaber.] [Knowledge and Skills: Level 1]

8. C - Common frameworks or methodologies used within agile include: scrum, extreme programming (XP), lean software development, crystal, feature driven development (FDD), dynamic systems development method (DSDM), agile unified process (AUP). [Agile Software Development: The Cooperative Game – 2nd Edition. Alistair Cockburn.] [Knowledge and Skills: Level 2]

9. B - Effective communication is a cornerstone of agile. Communication is the act of transferring information among various parties. Communications management is a knowledge and skill area of agile that highlights this importance. PMI has several definitions regarding communications management and agile builds on top of these to add its own perspective: 1) Communications Planning: Determining the information and communication needs of the projects stakeholders 2) Information Distribution: Making needed information available to project stakeholders in a timely manner, 3) Performance Reporting: Collecting and distributing performance information. This includes status reporting, progress measurement, and forecasting, and 4) Managing Stakeholders: Managing communications to satisfy the requirements and resolve issues with project stakeholders. From an agile perspective: communication among the team is built into the process and facilitated through collocation, information radiators, daily stand-up meetings, retrospectives etc.; Although it is hoped that the product owner, customer, and user can be heavily involved with the project and also use these communication techniques, a plan for conveying information to stakeholders may be needed if this is not the case. [Agile Software Development: The Cooperative Game – 2nd Edition. Alistair Cockburn.] [Knowledge and Skills: Level 1]

10. D - Velocity is a measure of the number of user story points completed per iteration. An agile team can use its previous velocity recordings as a method of estimating how many user story points it may complete in the next iteration. David's team's velocity is 20. [Agile Estimating and Planning. Mike Cohn.] [Agile estimation]

11. D - Feature driven development (FDD) uses a prescriptive model where the software development process is planned, managed, and tracked from the perspective of individual software features. FDD uses short iterations of two weeks or less to develop a set amount of features. The five step FDD process is: 1. Develop overall model; 2. Create the features list; 3. Plan by feature; 4. Design by feature; 5 Build by feature. [Agile Software Development: The Cooperative Game – 2nd Edition. Alistair Cockburn.] [Knowledge and Skills: Level 2]

12. A - The agile project management phases, in sequence, are: Envisioning, speculating, exploring, adapting, closing. [Manifesto for Agile Software Development. Agile Alliance.] [Knowledge and Skills: Level 1]

13. C - The top 12 causes of agile failure (failure modes) according to Aaron Sanders: 1. A checkbook commitment doesn't automatically cause organizational change or support. 2. Culture doesn't support change. 3. Culture does not have retrospectives or performs them poorly. 4. Standards and quality are lost in a race to project closing. 5.Lack of collaboration in planning. 6.None or too many Product Owners. 7. Poor project leadership or scrum master that doesn't place trust in the team and allow it to be self-organizing and self-disciplined. 8.No on-site agile promoter or coach. 9.Lack of a well built, high-performance team. 10. Accrued technical debt if strict testing standards are not upheld. 11.Culture maintains traditional performance appraisals where individuals are honored and the team aspect is lost. 12. A reversion to the traditional or 'old-way' of doing business occurs because change is hard. [Coaching Agile Teams. Lyssa Adkins.] [Knowledge and Skills: Level 3]

14. C - Collaboration is a key soft skill negotiation skill. It involves working in groups to create ideas, solve problems, and produce solutions. [Coaching Agile Teams. Lyssa Adkins.] [Soft skills negotiation]

15. A - An agile team must always face the prioritization of product features in its product backlog. From release planning to iteration planning, an agile team must prioritize the user stories/ features of its product to ensure that high-quality and high-value features are developed first to help facilitate an optimized and early return on investment (ROI). An agile team typically prioritizes requirements or user stories/features in terms of relative value and risk; value is defined by the customer (i.e., customer-value prioritization). Two common methods to prioritize product features are: MoSCoW and Kano. The MoSCoW method categorizes features into 'Must have,' 'Should have,' 'Could have,' and 'Would have' features. The Kano method categorizes features into 'Must haves (threshold),' 'Dissatisfiers,' 'Satisfiers,' and 'Delighters.' Must haves are features that are requisite. Dissatisfiers are features that adversely impact perceived value and should be eliminated. 'Satisfiers' are features that increase perceived value linearly, where the more you add the more the customer is pleased, but are not required, and 'Delighters' are features that increase perceived value exponentially to please the customer. To prioritize features based on risk, a risk-to-value matrix can be used. A risk-to-value matrix has four quadrants, with the horizontal axis having low and high value, and the vertical axis having low and high risk. User stories are assigned to one of the four categories/quadrants: low-value, low-risk; low-value, high-risk; high-value, low-risk; high-value, high-risk. A cost-to-value matrix can also be made in this manner. All prioritization in agile is 'relative,' meaning that the priority of one user story is relative to other user stories and not prioritized on a fixed scale. [Lean-Agile Software Development: Achieving Enterprise Agility. Alan Shalloway, Guy Beaver, James R. Trott.] [Knowledge and Skills: Level 1]

16. C - Higgs & Dulewicz (1999) defines emotional intelligence using seven components: 1) Self-awareness, 2) Emotional resilience, 3) Motivation, 4) Interpersonal sensitivity, 5) Influence, 6) Intuitiveness, and 7) Conscientiousness. [Coaching Agile Teams. Lyssa Adkins.] [Soft skills negotiation]

17. B - Return on Investment (ROI): A metric used to evaluate the efficiency of an investment or to compare efficiency among a number of investments. To calculate ROI, the return of an investment (i.e., the gain minus the cost) is divided by the cost of the investment. The result is usually expressed as a percentage and sometimes a ratio. The product owner is often said to be responsible for the ROI. [Agile Estimating and Planning. Mike Cohn.] [Value based prioritization]

18. B - The TDD process has four basic steps: 1) Write a test, 2) Verify and validate the test, 3) Write product code and apply the test, 4) Refactor the product code. An example may be that a user has to enter an age value. A good test is to make sure the user data entry is a positive number and not a different type of input, like a letter (i.e., write the test). The programmer would verify that entering a letter instead of a number would cause the program to cause an exception (i.e., v&v the test). The programmer would then write product code that takes user entry for the age value (i.e., write the product code). The programmer would then run the product code and enter correct age values and incorrect age values (i.e., apply the test). If the product code is successful, the programmer would refactor the product code to improve its design. Using these four steps iteratively ensures that programmers think about how a software program might fail first and to build product code that is holistically being tested. This helps produce high quality code. [The Art of Agile Development. James Shore.] [Product quality]

19. D - Acceptance Test Driven Development (ATDD) is similar to Test-driven development (TDD) in that it requires programmers to create tests first before any product code. The tests in ATDD are aimed at confirming features/behaviors that the intended software will have. The iterative cycle of ATDD with its four steps can be remembered as the four Ds: 1) Discuss, 2) Distill, 3) Develop, and 4) Demo. 1) Discuss: The agile team and customer or business stakeholder discuss a user story in detail. Talking about the expected behaviors the user story should have and what it should not. 2) The development team takes those items learned from the discussion and distills them into tests that will verify and validate those behaviors. The distillation process is where the entire team should have a good understanding of what "done" (or completed) means for a user story. That is, what the acceptance criteria are. 3) After distillation, the team develops the test code and product code to implement the product features. 4) Once the product features have been developed, the team demonstrates them to the customer or business stakeholders for feedback. [Lean-Agile Software Development: Achieving Enterprise Agility. Alan Shalloway, Guy Beaver, James R. Trott.] [Product quality]

20. B - Acceptance Test Driven Development (ATDD) is similar to Test-driven development (TDD) in that it requires programmers to create tests first before any product code. The tests in ATDD are aimed at confirming features/behaviors that the intended software will have. The iterative cycle of ATDD with its four steps can be remembered as the four Ds: 1) Discuss, 2) Distill, 3) Develop, and 4) Demo. 1) Discuss: The agile team and customer or business stakeholder discuss a user story in detail. Talking about the expected behaviors the user story should have and what it should not. 2) The development team takes those items learned from the discussion and distills them into tests that will verify and validate those behaviors. The distillation process is where the entire team should have a good understanding of what "done" (or completed) means for a user story. That is, what the acceptance criteria are. 3) After distillation, the team develops the test code and product code to implement the product features. 4) Once the product features have been developed, the team demonstrates them to the customer or business stakeholders for feedback. [Lean-Agile Software Development: Achieving Enterprise Agility. Alan Shalloway, Guy Beaver, James R. Trott.] [Product quality]

21. A - All agile efforts have project and quality standards that the team defines collaboratively at the beginning of an effort and refines collaboratively throughout the effort. Project and quality standards help an agile team with team cohesion and provide a structure, albeit one that can adapt as the project evolves, to promote a self-disciplined environment. There is no 'one size fits all' standards definition in agile; because every project is different, it has been shown that the team should define which project and quality standards it should hold itself against and strive to conform to those standards while also being open to adapting those standards throughout the project to optimize performance and delivered value. Project standards can range from where the daily stand-up meeting is located and how long each participant has to share his or her progress and challenges to highly specific software coding styles, methods for test-driven development, and what the team's definition of 'done-done' means. [Agile Software Development: The Cooperative Game – 2nd Edition. Alistair Cockburn.] [Knowledge and Skills: Level 1]

22. B - Highsmith defines adaptive leadership as two dimensional: Being agile and doing agile. Being agile includes focusing on cornerstones of agile project management, like incremental delivery, continuous integration, and adapting to changing requirements. Doing agile includes several activities that an agile leader must do: do less; speed-to-value, quality, and engage and inspire. [Agile Project Management: Creating Innovative Products – 2nd Edition. Jim Highsmith.] [Soft skills negotiation]

23. B - Key soft skills negotiation qualities for the effective implementation and practice of agile are: emotional intelligence, collaboration, adaptive leadership, negotiation, conflict resolution, servant leadership. [Coaching Agile Teams. Lyssa Adkins.] [Soft skills negotiation]

24. A - Retained revenue is revenue retained through the development of new product features or services that prevent existing customers from stopping use of the existing product. [Agile Estimating and Planning. Mike Cohn.] [Agile estimation]

25. D - Because each iteration typically produces a working product that is built and integrated and iterations are typically two to four weeks in length, there is frequent verification and validation to ensure product quality. Verification is the confirmation that a product performs as specified by a customer (e.g. as indicated by a user story) and validation is the confirmation that a product behaves as desired (i.e., meets the customer's need). Sometimes a product may be built and integrated to specification - that is, it can be verified - but it does not meet the intent of the customer - that is, it cannot be validated. [Agile Software Development: The Cooperative Game – 2nd Edition. Alistair Cockburn.] [Product quality]

26. D - In the agile framework scrum, sprint planning and sprint review meetings are often timeboxed at four hours. [The Art of Agile Development. James Shore.] [Planning, monitoring, and adapting]

27. C - Empowered teams - ones that are self-organizing and know how to solve problems with minimal management involvement - are a cornerstone of the agile methodology. This is the antithesis to the classic viewpoint of the traditional project manager who is seen as someone that controls all decisions and delegates tasks to a team with little feedback. An agile team must include all members and stakeholders to make decisions, and make decisions expediently. Because it is essential that the user/customer be involved with development, it is encouraged that the user/customer is closely integrated with the agile team with collocation/on-site support being ideal. An agile team feels empowered when it collectively assumes responsibility for the delivery of the product (i.e., taking ownership). [Coaching Agile Teams. Lyssa Adkins.] [Knowledge and Skills: Level 1]

28. A - Time, budget, and cost estimation is an important knowledge and skill area of agile. According to Highsmith, the nature of the agile method, whereby it welcomes changing scope, means that it lends itself well to fixed budgets and a fixed schedule because changing scope makes it difficult to estimate a total cost. Generally speaking, the budget and schedule constraints are known but before a project will commence there needs to be an agreed upon set of base product functionality defined in an initiation phase; fixing scope reduces an agile team's innovative tendency to provide improved value. For companies that are familiar with fixed-price contracts, where requirements are agreed upon before contract closing, adopting agile can be a weary initial venture. Instead, other contract vehicle types are recommended for agile efforts. These include: a general service contract for the initiation phase and separate fixed-price contracts for iterations or user stories; time-and-material contracts; not-to-exceed with fixed-fee contracts; and, incentive contracts (e.g., fixed price with incentive; cost-reimbursable with award fee). [Agile Project Management: Creating Innovative Products – 2nd Edition. Jim Highsmith.] [Knowledge and Skills: Level 1]

29. B - All agile efforts have project and quality standards that the team defines collaboratively at the beginning of an effort and refines collaboratively throughout the effort. Project and quality standards help an agile team with team cohesion and provide a structure, albeit one that can adapt as the project evolves, to promote a self-disciplined environment. There is no 'one size fits all' standards definition in agile; because every project is different, it has been shown that the team should define which project and quality standards it should hold itself against and strive to conform to those standards while also being open to adapting those standards throughout the project to optimize performance and delivered value. Project standards can range from where the daily stand-up meeting is located and how long each participant has to share his or her progress and challenges to highly specific software coding styles, methods for test-driven development, and what the team's definition of 'done-done' means. [Agile Software Development: The Cooperative Game – 2nd Edition. Alistair Cockburn.] [Knowledge and Skills: Level 1]

30. C - Having a motivated team is essential for any project, regardless of whether it is agile or not. Motivated teams work together better, have strong productivity, and exceed expectations. Some simple steps to increase motivation are 1) spending quality time together; where team members get to know one another on a personal level to build a sense of community, 2) providing feedback, mentoring and coaching; where team members are congratulated and thanked on jobs well done and also mentored or coached to improve in skill and capability, and 3) empowerment; where the team is empowered to make many key decisions which, along the way, builds trust and shows that leadership believes in the capabilities of the team. [The Art of Agile Development. James Shore.] [Knowledge and Skills: Level 1]

31. A - In the agile design process, prototypes help the customer understand current design state. Three common types of prototypes are HTML, paper (i.e., sketches), and wireframes. A wireframe is a sketch of a user interface, identifying its content, layout, functionality, is usually black and white, and excludes detailed pictures or graphics. A wireframe can be created on paper, whiteboards, or using software. [Agile Estimating and Planning. Mike Cohn.] [Agile analysis and design]

32. D - Building a high-performance team is critical to any project's success. A high performance team has the right team members, is empowered, has built trust, works at a sustainable pace, has consistently high velocity/productivity, takes regular time for reflection to review work, has a team lead that removes any obstacles and provides mentoring and coaching, is self-organized and self-disciplined, and is collocated. Several management techniques can be used to build or foster a high-performance team environment, some techniques include: removing obstacles that slow down a team's performance, having high expectations of team performance, and coaching and mentoring the team to achieve its best performance. [Coaching Agile Teams. Lyssa Adkins.] [Knowledge and Skills: Level 2]

33. D - Common frameworks or methodologies used within agile include: scrum, extreme programming (XP), lean software development, crystal, feature driven development (FDD), dynamic systems development method (DSDM), agile unified process (AUP). [Agile Software Development: The Cooperative Game – 2nd Edition. Alistair Cockburn.] [Knowledge and Skills: Level 2]

34. C - Reflective improvement workshops are a cornerstone of the Crystal methodology. While all agile methodologies incorporate reflection into their standard practices, Crystal terms the practice 'reflective improvement workshops.' [Agile Software Development: The Cooperative Game – 2nd Edition. Alistair Cockburn.] [Planning, monitoring, and adapting]

35. B - The core roles in scrum are the product owner, scrum master and development team. [Ken Schwaber. Agile Project Management with Scrum. Chapter 1.] [Knowledge and Skills: Level 2]

36. B - Empowered teams - ones that are self-organizing and know how to solve problems with minimal management involvement - are a cornerstone of the agile methodology. An agile team feels empowered when it collectively assumes responsibility for the delivery of the product (i.e., taking ownership). [Coaching Agile Teams. Lyssa Adkins.] [Knowledge and Skills: Level 1]

37. D - Affinity estimating is a method to predict the work effort, typically in story points, of developing a user story. It is particularly useful for large product backlogs. Although several methods exist, the basic affinity estimating model involves sizing user stories on a scale from small to large. The scale can be a Fibonacci sequence or t-shirt sizes and is typically taped to a wall in a large conference room.

Participants then attach their user stories to the wall as estimates. It is often done in silence and has several iterations until the user stories have been estimated. [The Art of Agile Development. James Shore.] [Agile estimation]

38. B - Negotiation is a key soft skill negotiation skill. It involves discussion or conversation to work towards a common understanding between two parties. [Coaching Agile Teams. Lyssa Adkins.] [Soft skills negotiation]

39. C - The acronym SMART (specific, measurable, achievable, relevant, and time-boxed) helps the agile practitioner remember the characteristics of a well-defined task. S – Specific tasks are ones that clearly contribute to the development of a user story. It should not be vague. M – Measurable tasks are ones that the team and customer can verify. A - Achievable tasks are ones that developers may realistically implement and understand. R - Relevant tasks are ones that unequivocally add value to the user story. T - Timeboxed tasks are ones that can have an estimate assigned of the amount of effort or time needed for development. [Agile Retrospectives: Making Good Teams Great. Esther Derby, Diana Larsen, Ken Schwaber.] [Planning, monitoring, and adapting]

40. D - The principles of lean software development are: Eliminate waste; Amplify learning; Decide as late as possible; Deliver as fast as possible; Empower the team; Build integrity in; See the whole. [Lean-Agile Software Development: Achieving Enterprise Agility. Alan Shalloway, Guy Beaver, James R. Trott.] [Knowledge and Skills: Level 2]

Knowledge Area Quiz Communications Practice Questions

Test Name: Knowledge Area Test: Communications
Total Questions: 15
Correct Answers Needed to Pass: 11 (73.33%)
Time Allowed: 25 Minutes

Test Description

This practice quiz specifically targets your knowledge of the Communications exam topic area.

Test Questions

1. Which agile methodology has as one of its core principles the concept of osmotic communication?

   A. Scrum

   B. FDD

   C. Crystal

   D. XP

2. What should a scrum master do if he or she notices disruptive behavior during a scrum?

   A. Abruptly cancel the meeting.

   B. Let the team, as self-organizing, resolve the issue.

   C. Ignore the disruptive discussion knowing that it will be handled during the next performance review.

   D. Call attention to the disruption and order that everyone pay attention to the speaker.

3. How often are stand-up meetings typically held on an agile project?

   A. Bi-weekly

   B. Daily

   C. Every other day

   D. After an iteration

4. Sheila as team leader, wants to design a comfortable, collaborative team space for her agile project. What can she do as a basic guideline?

   A. Arrange seating to group by team function

   B. Minimize team member interaction

   C. Have a dedicated whiteboard

   D. Have large swaths of blank wall space devoid of project information

5. Select the response that is NOT an advantage of using an information radiator.

   A. Improves team communication

   B. Makes communication less time consuming

C. Makes it easy for all team members to track progress

D. Removes the need for project planning

6. How does an agile team promote customer engagement?

A. With regular communication between the customer and team.

B. With incentives and kickbacks for approving completed features.

C. With a defect information radiator showing customer meeting absences.

D. With bi-weekly communication between the customer and team.

7. What type of information do information radiators typically portray?

A. A histogram showing the highest velocity of all agile teams worldwide.

B. The weather, local time, and stock exchange quotes.

C. User story development status, system defects, iteration feature development status.

D. The text of user stories with highlighting showing a need for clarification from stakeholders.

8. Not all company cultures are right for the agile methodology. With respect to communication, what type of culture is a good fit for the agile methodology?

A. A culture with a highly focused distribution of power that requires many levels of clearance for communication

B. A culture that values open, face-to-face communication

C. A culture with strict communication channels and clear hierarchical divisions

D. A culture that retains physical separation between the agile team and customer or customer representative

9. As team leader, Walter must interact with the customer frequently. What is one significant requirement of the team leader with respect to communication?

A. Walter must communicate the results of scrum tests with the development team.

B. Walter must facilitate communication between the developers and customer.

C. Walter must communicate the fail tests he wrote before an iteration to the customer.

D. Walter must facilitate communication on the functional requirements specification document.

10. How often are information radiators updated?

A. Every week

B. At the end of each iteration

C. Constantly

D. Never

11. Empathy is a valuable human emotion for generating trust in a team. What types of empathy on an agile project can help build trust?

A. Customer-programmer empathy and programmer-tester empathy

B. Customer-stakeholder empathy and customer-product owner empathy

C. Stakeholder-customer empathy and customer-programmer empathy

D. Customer-product owner empathy and programmer-tester empathy

12. What is an effective method for improving team collaboration?

A. Emphasize the use of top-down decision making.

B. Emphasize the use of comprehensive documentation.

C. Emphasize the isolation of team members.

D. Emphasize the use of face-to-face communication.

13. What do team members discuss in the daily stand-up meeting?

A. Work breakdown structures

B. Stakeholder inconsistencies

C. Software development methods

D. Current progress and any issues or impediments that are impacting progress

14. In the scrum methodology, how long do daily stand-up meetings, or scrums, typically last?

A. 2 to 4 hours

B. 1.5 to 2.0 hours

C. 30 to 60 minutes

D. 15 minutes

15. In the scrum-based agile project management methodology, what are stand-up meetings called?

A. Daily scrum

B. Pit

C. Sprint

D. Dailies

Knowledge Area Quiz Communications Answer Key and Explanations

1. C - A core principle of the Crystal methodology is osmotic communication. [Agile Software Development: The Cooperative Game – 2nd Edition. Alistair Cockburn.] [Communications]

2. B - A high-performance, self-organizing team should realize and correct the disruptive behavior. [Coaching Agile Teams. Lyssa Adkins.] [Communications]

3. B - A stand-up meeting is typically held daily and is often referred to as the daily stand-up meeting. [The Art of Agile Development. James Shore.] [Communications]

4. C - A warm, welcoming environment that promotes effective communication, innovation, and motivated team members is an important aspect to consider when designing team space. Guidelines for a better agile team space include: collocation of team members; reduction of non-essential noise/distractions; dedicated whiteboard and wall space for information radiators; space for the daily stand-up meeting and other meetings; pairing workstations; and other pleasantries like plants and comfortable furniture. [Agile Retrospectives: Making Good Teams Great. Esther Derby, Diana Larsen, Ken Schwaber.] [Communications]

5. D - All successful projects, regardless of management philosophy, require project planning. The use of information radiators on an agile project offer several advantages. They reduce lengthy communication, allow for all team members and stakeholders to review project status throughout a project, and reduce the need of other more time-consuming communication methods, like e-mails or memorandums. [Agile Software Development: The Cooperative Game – 2nd Edition. Alistair Cockburn.] [Communications]

6. A - An agile approach heavily emphasizes the need for direct customer involvement to ensure product quality and value. One way to promote customer engagement is to have regular communication between the customer and team. [Agile Software Development: The Cooperative Game – 2nd Edition. Alistair Cockburn.] [Communications]

7. C - An information radiator displays project status-related information, such as user story development status, burndown charts, and task boards. [Agile Software Development: The Cooperative Game – 2nd Edition. Alistair Cockburn.] [Communications]

8. B - An open, face-to-face communication culture is the best suited culture for an agile team. [Agile Software Development: The Cooperative Game – 2nd Edition. Alistair Cockburn.] [Communications]

9. B - As a team leader or agile project manager, you must facilitate communication between the development team and customer to ensure that requirements are understood and implemented correctly. One of the four Agile Manifesto values underscores customer collaboration. The team leader must facilitate this collaboration to deliver value. [Agile Software Development: The

Cooperative Game – 2nd Edition. Alistair Cockburn.] [Communications]

10. C - Constantly is the best answer. Information radiators should be updated whenever the posted data has changed to keep all team members and stakeholders up to date. [Agile Software Development: The Cooperative Game – 2nd Edition. Alistair Cockburn.] [Communications]

11. A - Customer-programmer empathy and programmer-tester empathy help generate team trust on an agile project. [The Art of Agile Development. James Shore.] [Communications]

12. D - Face-to-face communication enhances team collaboration. [Agile Software Development: The Cooperative Game – 2nd Edition. Alistair Cockburn.] [Communications]

13. D - In a daily stand-up meeting team members discuss current progress and any issues or impediments that are impacting progress. Each team member shares what he or she has achieved since the last meeting, what he or she will achieve before the next meeting, and what obstacles may prevent him or her from achieving progress. [The Art of Agile Development. James Shore.] [Communications]

14. D - In the scrum methodology, daily stand-up meetings, or scrums, should last no longer than 15 minutes. Some scrum instances use stop watches to track time and use a 'talking stick' to help indicate whose sole turn it is to share pertinent information. [The Art of Agile Development. James Shore.] [Communications]

15. A - In the scrum-based agile project management methodology, daily stand-up meetings are referred to as 'scrums' or 'Daily scrum.' [The Art of Agile Development. James Shore.] [Communications]

PMI-ACP Lite Mock Exam 3 Practice Questions

Test Name: PMI-ACP Lite Mock Exam 3
Total Questions: 40
Correct Answers Needed to Pass:
30 (75.00%)
Time Allowed: 60 Minutes

Test Description

This is a cumulative PMI-ACP Mock Exam which can be used as a benchmark for your PMI-ACP aptitude. This practice test includes questions from all exam topic areas, including sections from Agile Tools and Techniques, and all three Agile Knowledge and Skills areas.

Test Questions

1. What is the activity called when a person performs a self-assessment to understand how he or she may improve performance?

A. A retrospective

B. A resolution

C. An INVEST analysis

D. An appropriating

2. Jill is explaining the importance of an agile team being empowered. What does an empowered team mean?

A. A team that is management-driven and focused solely on pleasing the management.

B. A team that relies on external leadership to show it the path forward.

C. A team that is self-organizing and knows how to solve problems with minimal need for oversight

D. A team that solves problems through the use of market research.

3. What does the product backlog serve as initially in an agile project?

A. A rough estimate of product requirements

B. An exact estimate of product requirements

C. A rough estimate of product standards

D. An exact estimate of product standards

4. What is a control limit?

A. An objective range that indicates if a process is considered stable.

B. An objective range that indicates if a process is improving in residual activity.

C. A threshold value that indicates if a process is improving in reaction time.

D. A threshold value that indicates if a process is declining in responsiveness.

5. Rebecca and her agile team have assembled to play a game of planning poker to make decisions about the relative work effort of the product's user stories. When a team collectively makes decisions, what is the decision model known as?

A. Anticipatory

B. Estimation

C. Participatory

D. Planning

6. In agile modeling, what is a good example of a name given to a persona?

A. App buyer

B. App developer

C. App host administrator

D. James Quill

7. Of the following, which is a key soft skill negotiation quality?

A. Creative intelligence

B. Intelligence quotient

C. Artificial intelligence

D. Emotional intelligence

8. On a burndown chart, how does the charted 'ideal/estimated work accomplished' series appear?

A. As a curved, downward sloping line

B. As a straight, upward sloping line

C. As a straight, downward sloping line

D. As a curved, upward sloping line

9. Which agile framework has a project life cycle with the following five stages: feasibility study, business study, functional model iteration, design and build iteration, and implementation?

A. Dynamic systems development method (DSDM)

B. Static systems development method (SSDM)

C. Extreme systems development method (XSDM)

D. Dynamic product development method (DPDM)

10. In terms of communications management, how does an agile team promote simple and effective communication?

A. Through collaborative brainstorming events

B. Through the use of e-mail.

C. Through the use of formal boardroom meetings.

D. Through the use of lengthy memorandums.

11. Which agile framework emphasizes the practice of collective ownership, continuous integration, and pair programming?

A. Scrum

B. Crystal

C. DSDM

D. XP

12. A portion of Tom's agile team is not collocated but rather geographically dispersed throughout the world. What is one factor the team should consider when conducting its business?

A. Whether or not to consider cultural and language differences to promote an effective communication method.

B. Whether or not to reflect after an iteration.

C. Whether or not to use earned value management as an agile accounting method.

D. Whether or not to conduct risk-based spike tasks.

13. As an agile certified practitioner, Patricia emphasizes the virtue of fine-grained communication in the daily stand-up meeting. How is this virtue a sign of a healthy stand-up meeting?

A. Having fine-grained coordination during a stand-up meeting is a false indicator of a healthy stand-up meeting. The team should have a broad focus to remain open to innovative ideas from other sectors of industry.

B. Having fine-grained coordination during a stand-up meeting indicates a lack of defects and well tested and integrated code.

C. Having fine-grained coordination during a stand-up meeting indicates that each team member is solely focused on his or her own obstacles and uninterested in other team members' progress or obstacles.

D. Having fine-grained coordination during a stand-up meeting indicates that the team understands how important it is to have a sharp, inter-dependent focus for the duration of the meeting.

14. Henry and his team are assigning story points to a particularly vague and unclear user story. What should the agile team typically do in such a case?

A. Assign the user story an arbitrarily high number

B. Assign the user story with the mode of all previously scored user stories

C. Assign the user story the mean of all previously scored user stories

D. Remove the user story from the backlog

15. What is a positive indicator that agile may be appropriate to an organization as a new project methodology?

A. That the adopting organization values a competitive, non-collaborative environment for the sake of boosting revenue.

B. That the adopting organization will review the product once at the end of the release when all requirements have been reached.

C. That the adopting organization values strict, inflexible project management techniques.

D. That the adopting organization will assign dedicated customer representatives to the project effort.

16. Which is the best definition of prioritization?

A. The vector ordering of user stories with respect value.

B. The fixed ordering of user stories with respect to value.

C. The relative ordering of user stories with respect to value.

D. The scalar ordering of user stories with respect to value.

17. Ursula has several user stories that she and her agile team need to provide an estimate for regarding their relative size to one another. What scoring system might Ursula and her team use to estimate relative size?

A. Story marks

B. Story pips

C. Story points

D. Story cards

18. What can an agile team do to promote an innovative and collaborative team space?

A. Rotate team member roles

B. Isolate team members by function

C. Separate team members by function

D. Reserve a space for daily stand-up meetings

19. In the XP principle of continuous integration, what happens after new code has been tested and integrated into the production code base?

A. The production code is reviewed in its entirety by pair programmers.

B. The production code is tested.

C. Other code is integrated before testing the production code.

D. The production code is postfactored to add redundancy measures.

20. Jill and her team just performed an Exploratory 360. Which framework is Jill most likely leveraging in her agile effort?

A. XP

B. Crystal

C. AUP

D. DSDM

21. What are some activities that an agile team would NOT be performing in Highsmith's agile project management closing phase?

A. Creating the project vision

B. Completing remaining project work

C. Authoring user documentation

D. Authoring product release instructions

22. When value stream mapping it is important to identify areas of waste that exist in the process. The pneumonic device WIDETOM may be used to remember the different forms of muda (or waste). What does the I in WIDETOM stand for with respect to waste?

A. Inspection

B. Interest

C. Inventory

D. Installation

23. The agile triangle includes what three parameters?

A. Cost, scope, value

B. Scope, schedule, constraints

C. Value, quality, constraints

D. Scope, cost, schedule

24. Bob and Laurie share the same work environment and so are in tune with each other's daily progress as a result of hearing the same environmental sounds. What type of communication are Bob and Laurie participating in when neither must use words to know, in part, about what the other person is thinking or feeling?

A. Background sensory communication

B. Active listening

C. Subliminal communication

D. Osmotic communication

25. Select a common agile problem-solving technique.

A. Be kind, probe

B. Devil's in the detail

C. 1Y

D. Asking probing questions

26. Why is verification and validation performed frequently on an agile project?

A. Because a product release typically lasts several sprints, verification and validation take place frequently to keep sprints on track.

B. Verification and validation are not performed frequently.

C. Because a product release typically lasts several iterations, verification and validation take place frequently to keep iterations on track.

D. Because iterations are typically short in duration and a working product is delivered at the end of each iteration, verification and validation must take place frequently to ensure product quality.

27. Stacey, the head of a multi-national corporation, is considering hiring an agile team to develop a new database system. However, the agile team Stacey is working with tells her that estimating final cost can be difficult. Why is it more difficult to estimate cost on an agile project?

A. Because agile contracts have no scheduling or planning

B. Because customers have little experience with the agile quality to cost and value triangle.

C. Because agile welcomes changing scope.

D. Because the cost of developers is constantly in flux.

28. Which of the following duties is expected of a servant leader?

A. Affinity planning.

B. Team enabling.

C. Kanban tracking.

D. User story authoring.

29. Why should fixed-price contracts be avoided for agile development?

A. Because fixed-price implies that the time and material costs shall not exceed certain thresholds which causes undue stress on agile accounting practices.

B. Because fixed-price implies that the schedule is fixed which no agile development effort should bind itself against.

C. Because fixed-price implies that the revenue structure is fixed to a point that is problematic for development compensation.

D. Because fixed-price implies that scope is fixed and discourages the development team from exploring innovative ideas outside the scope that may add value to the product.

30. Why is a warm, welcoming team space environment important in agile development efforts?

A. Because it promotes an inflexible atmosphere.

B. Because it produces more efficient software code.

C. Because it decreases employee retention.

D. Because it promotes effective communication, collaboration, and innovation.

31. Jessica as a product owner believes steadfastly in the feature prioritization. Why might Jessica believe in prioritization?

A. Because it ensures that all team members know that cost is the only factor in the prioritization equation.

B. Because it ensures that all team members are aware that risk never enters the equation of prioritization.

C. Because it ensures that all team members are aware that risk trumps value in the prioritization equation.

D. Because it ensures that all team members are aware of the product features most valuable to the customer.

32. George as a product owner believes steadfastly in the feature prioritization. Why might George believe in prioritization?

A. Because it ensures that the most valuable features are developed first.

B. Because it ensures that all product features get delivered in a release.

C. Because it ensures that all team members know that valuable product features will always be developed in the affinity plan.

D. Because it ensures that the local safety of all features are developed first.

33. Margaret as a product owner believes steadfastly in the feature prioritization. Why might Margaret believe in prioritization?

A. Because it facilitates a discussion helpful for post-iteration reflection.

B. Because it facilitates lessons learned on product defects.

C. Because it maximizes the earnings potential of product developers.

D. Because it facilitates an optimized and early return on investment.

34. Hanna as a product owner believes steadfastly in the feature prioritization. Why might Hanna believe in prioritization?

A. Because it helps order the closing backlog for release.

B. Because it helps order the Kanban board for task sequencing.

C. Because it helps order the iteration backlog for release planning.

D. Because it helps order the product backlog for release planning.

35. Hanna as a product owner believes steadfastly in the feature prioritization. Why might Hanna believe in prioritization?

A. Because it ranks the team members in order of velocity.

B. Because it provides for an optimized early ROI.

C. Because it provides for a local pessimum in product delivery.

D. Because it provides for value-based ranking of developer tasks.

D. Because minimal planning is involved with agile.

36. Henrietta, the head of a multi-national corporation, is considering hiring an agile team to develop a new database system. However, the agile team Henrietta is working with tells her that estimating final cost can be difficult. Why is it more difficult to estimate cost on an agile project?

A. Because market demand is difficult to predict.

B. Because agile welcomes changing scope throughout a project which will change costing.

C. Because the customer has not idea of what it will be necessary to spend to buy a valuable product.

D. Because the cost of product development is highly volatile.

37. Janet, the head of a multi-national corporation, is considering hiring an agile team to develop a new database system. However, the agile team Janet is working with tells her that estimating final cost can be difficult. Why is it more difficult to estimate cost on an agile project?

A. Because market demand is difficult to predict.

B. Because agile welcomes changing scope, which can increase or decrease the level of effort.

C. Because the cost of developers is a sunk cost.

38. Why is it more difficult to estimate cost on an agile project?

A. Because no planning is involved with agile.

B. Because agile welcomes changing scope.

C. Because the cost of developers is constantly in flux.

D. Because customers have little experience with the agile quality to cost and value triangle.

39. Peter, the head of a multi-national corporation, is considering hiring an agile team to develop a new database system. However, the agile team Peter is working with tells him that the exact cost of delivering the new database system is difficult to estimate. Why is it more difficult to estimate cost on an agile project?

A. Because of its requirement to use self-organizing teams.

B. Because the cost of developers is constantly in flux.

C. Because agile welcomes changing scope.

D. Because no planning is involved with agile.

40. Usually peer pressure has a negative connotation. Why is peer pressure viewed as an advantage of the daily stand-up meeting?

A. Because competition breeds high productivity and peer pressure has been identified by human resource experts to be the best method for increasing competition in the workplace.

B. Because in an agile project the team is dependent upon each member to provide consistent and sustainable results for the success of the project. Peer pressure in this context is a positive attribute because team members, or peers, feel responsible for providing positive results so the team can function efficiently.

C. Because peer pressure encourages team members to take huge project risks that otherwise would never transpire and an underlying theme of agile project management is risk seeking.

D. This question is incorrect. Peer pressure is not an advantage of the daily stand-up meeting.

PMI-ACP Lite Mock Exam 3 Answer Key and Explanations

1. A - During reflection or retrospectives, an agile team reserves time to reflect on the work it has completed with the objective of continuous improvement. In these self-assessment/team-assessment events, topics can include: lessons learned from successes and failures; team standards that worked, failed, or were not properly followed; and other areas of improvement. [Agile Retrospectives: Making Good Teams Great. Esther Derby, Diana Larsen, Ken Schwaber.] [Knowledge and Skills: Level 2]

2. C - Empowered teams - ones that are self-organizing and know how to solve problems with minimal management involvement - are a cornerstone of the agile methodology. An agile team feels empowered when it collectively assumes responsibility for the delivery of the product (i.e., taking ownership). [Coaching Agile Teams. Lyssa Adkins.] [Knowledge and Skills: Level 1]

3. A - The product backlog initially serves as a rough estimate of the product's requirements [Agile Estimating and Planning. Mike Cohn.] [Agile estimation]

4. A - Control limits - those which set an objective range to indicate whether a process is controlled or stabilized or defect free (e.g., within three sigmas of the mean) - may be used in an agile project. Generally, a control limit of three-sigma (s) is used on a Shewhart control chart. A sigma refers to one standard deviation. So three sigmas indicates a limit three standard deviations away from the mean in both the positive and negative direction. This applies to normal data, where a normal distribution curve has been obtained. [Lean-Agile Software Development: Achieving Enterprise Agility. Alan Shalloway, Guy Beaver, James R. Trott.] [Knowledge and Skills: Level 3]

5. C - To build trust among the team, agile believes heavily in participatory decision models where team members collaborate to make decisions. Although a team leader or scrum master will need to make some decisions individually, many decisions can be made by the team collectively. These agile principles are also known as collective ownership, self-organization, and self-discipline. In collective ownership, the team members are equally responsible for project results and are empowered to participate in decision making and problem solving processes. [Agile Retrospectives: Making Good Teams Great. Esther Derby, Diana Larsen, Ken Schwaber.] [Knowledge and Skills: Level 2]

6. D - A persona is a notional user of the system under development. Being much more detailed than actors in use case modeling where generic user names are assigned (e.g., end user), personas try to elaborate on users with detailed descriptions to provide context to the developers. Some personas have such notional details as name, address, age, income, likes and dislikes, and other specific details. [User Stories Applied: For Agile Software Development. Mike Cohn.] [Agile analysis and design]

7. D - Key soft skills negotiation qualities for the effective implementation and practice of agile are: emotional intelligence, collaboration, adaptive leadership, negotiation, conflict resolution, servant

leadership. [Coaching Agile Teams. Lyssa Adkins.] [Soft skills negotiation]

8. C - A project burndown chart is an often used information radiator to show iteration progress. It charts two series: the actual work remaining and ideal/estimated work remaining. The vertical axis is the work unit (often story points or hours) and the horizontal axis is iteration duration (typically in number of days). The ideal/estimated work series is a straight, downward sloping line originating on the vertical axis at the value of work to be completed (e.g., 20 story points) and extending to the horizontal axis (i.e., 0 story points) on the last day of the iteration. The actual series is dependent upon the agile team's productivity and the task complexity and is updated daily. The actual series is typically volatile and is not a straight line but ebbs and flows as the project team tackles the development process. [Agile Estimating and Planning. Mike Cohn.] [Agile estimation]

9. A - Dynamic Systems Development Method (DSDM) is a structured framework that emphasizes a business perspective with a heavy focus on proving the 'fitness' or marketability. Similar to scrum, DSDM has three major phases: initiating project activities, project life cycle activities, and closing project activities (i.e., similar to scrum's pre-game, game, post-game). The project life cycle has five stages: feasibility study, business study, functional model iteration, design and build iteration, and implementation. [Agile Software Development: The Cooperative Game – 2nd Edition. Alistair Cockburn.] [Knowledge and Skills: Level 2]

10. A - Effective communication is a cornerstone of agile. Communication is the act of transferring information among various parties. Communications management is a knowledge and skill area of agile that highlights this importance. PMI has several definitions regarding communications management and agile builds on top of these to add its own perspective: 1) Communications Planning: Determining the information and communication needs of the projects stakeholders 2) Information Distribution: Making needed information available to project stakeholders in a timely manner, 3) Performance Reporting: Collecting and distributing performance information. This includes status reporting, progress measurement, and forecasting, and 4) Managing Stakeholders: Managing communications to satisfy the requirements and resolve issues with project stakeholders. From an agile perspective: communication among the team is built into the process and facilitated through collocation, information radiators, daily stand-up meetings, retrospectives etc.; Although it is hoped that the product owner, customer, and user can be heavily involved with the project and also use these communication techniques, a plan for conveying information to stakeholders may be needed if this is not the case. [Agile Software Development: The Cooperative Game – 2nd Edition. Alistair Cockburn.] [Knowledge and Skills: Level 1]

11. D - Extreme Programming (XP) uses the following practices: pair programming, collective ownership, continuous integration, 40-hour week, on-site customer, coding standards, open workspace, and team rules [Agile Software Development: The Cooperative Game – 2nd Edition.

Alistair Cockburn.] [Knowledge and Skills: Level 3]

12. A - A high-performance agile team is one that is ideally collocated for osmotic communication and face-to-face interaction. However, collocation isn't always feasible in today's multinational environment. For distributed teams, several practices are available to provide the best form of effective communication in the absence of being collocated: team intranet sites, virtual team rooms, and video conferencing over e-mail when possible. Geographic separation, especially on a world-wide scale, causes the team to consider language and cultural differences, and time zone differences. [Agile Software Development: The Cooperative Game – 2nd Edition. Alistair Cockburn.] [Knowledge and Skills: Level 3]

13. D - The key characteristics of a healthy stand-up meeting include: peer pressure - the team is dependent upon each other so expectations of peers drives progress; fine-grained coordination - the team should understand the necessity for focus and working dependently; fine focus - the team should understand the need for brevity in the stand-up meeting so the team can be productive; daily commitment - the team should understand the value of daily commitments to each other and uphold those commitments; identification of obstacles - the team collectively should be aware of each other's obstacles so that the team collectively can try to resolve them. [The Art of Agile Development. James Shore.] [Communications]

14. A - When an agile team is scoring a particularly vague and unclear user story, it typically assigns it a high value knowing that it will most likely become further defined in upcoming iterations. [Agile Estimating and Planning. Mike Cohn.] [Agile estimation]

15. D - When considering whether to apply new agile practices, several internal and external factors should be considered. Internal factors include whether the project is developing new processes or products; whether the organization is collaborative and emphasizes trust, adaptability, collective ownership, and has minimal or informal project management processes; the size, location, and skills of the project team. External factors include the industry stability and customer engagement or involvement. Generally, agile is best suited to developing new processes or products for an organization that is collaborative and emphasizes trust, adaptability, collective ownership, and has minimal project management processes by an agile/project team that is relatively small in size, is collocated, and is cross-functional in skill. Additionally, agile is known to succeed in industries that are quickly adapting to disruptive technologies as opposed to industries that are stable and perhaps inflexible to adaptive approaches. And, lastly, the component of customer involvement and engagement cannot be stressed enough; the more participation, the better. [The Art of Agile Development. James Shore.] [Knowledge and Skills: Level 3]

16. C - An agile team must always face the prioritization of product features in its product backlog. From release planning to iteration planning, an agile team must prioritize the user stories/ features of its product to ensure that high-quality and high-value features are developed first to help facilitate an optimized and early return on investment (ROI). An agile team typically prioritizes requirements or user stories/features in terms of relative value and risk; value is defined by the customer (i.e., customer-value prioritization). Two common methods to prioritize product features are: MoSCoW and Kano. The MoSCoW method categorizes features into 'Must have,' 'Should have,' 'Could have,' and 'Would have' features. The Kano method categorizes features into 'Must haves (threshold),' 'Dissatisfiers,' 'Satisfiers,' and 'Delighters.' Must haves are features that are requisite. Dissatisfiers are features that adversely impact perceived value and should be eliminated. 'Satisfiers' are features that increase perceived value linearly, where the more you add the more the customer is pleased, but are not required, and 'Delighters' are features that increase perceived value exponentially to please the customer. To prioritize features based on risk, a risk-to-value matrix can be used. A risk-to-value matrix has four quadrants, with the horizontal axis having low and high value, and the vertical axis having low and high risk. User stories are assigned to one of the four categories/quadrants: low-value, low-risk; low-value, high-risk; high-value, low-risk; high-value, high-risk. A cost-to-value matrix can also be made in this manner. All prioritization in agile is 'relative,' meaning that the priority of one user story is relative to other user stories and not prioritized on a fixed scale. [Lean-Agile Software Development: Achieving Enterprise Agility. Alan Shalloway, Guy Beaver, James R. Trott.] [Knowledge and Skills: Level 1]

17. C - Agile teams typically use story points to estimate the relative size or effort of developing a user story [Agile Estimating and Planning. Mike Cohn.] [Agile estimation]

18. D - A warm, welcoming environment that promotes effective communication, innovation, and motivated team members is an important aspect to consider when designing team space. Guidelines for a better agile team space include: collocation of team members; reduction of non-essential noise/distractions; dedicated whiteboard and wall space for information radiators; space for the daily stand-up meeting and other meetings; pairing workstations; and other pleasantries like plants and comfortable furniture. [Agile Retrospectives: Making Good Teams Great. Esther Derby, Diana Larsen, Ken Schwaber.] [Communications]

19. B - The extreme programming (XP) principle of continuous integration is that code is integrated into the full code base as soon as it is built, tested, and completed. Once integrated, the code base and therefore the entire system is built and tested. Continuous integration is just one principle of XP that promotes rapid delivery of software and the early detection of integration defects. [The Art of Agile Development. James Shore.] [Product quality]

20. B - Crystal is a family of methodologies for a flexible and lightweight approach to software development. The family of methodologies is color coded to differentiate its members (e.g., clear, yellow, orange, red.) The color chosen depends on the level of effort required. On one end of the spectrum is crystal clear, which is for smaller efforts, while crystal red is for larger efforts. Regardless of color, the crystal framework is cyclical and has three fundamental processes: chartering, delivery cycles, and wrap-up. Crystal chartering includes building the team, doing an Exploratory 360, defining standards of practice for the team, and building the project plan. In the delivery cycle, the crystal team iteratively develops, integrates, tests, and releases the product in iterations that last from one week to two months. Like other agile frameworks, crystal includes collaborative events, like stand-up meetings and reflective improvement workshops. In wrap-up the team concludes the project and holds a completion ritual where the team reflects on the entire project. [Agile Software Development: The Cooperative Game – 2nd Edition. Alistair Cockburn.] [Knowledge and Skills: Level 2]

21. A - In the closing phase, the agile team completes all remaining project work. In a software project, remaining work can be such tasks as user training documentation and installation manuals. [Agile Project Management: Creating Innovative Products – 2nd Edition. Jim Highsmith.] [Knowledge and Skills: Level 1]

22. C - Value stream mapping is a lean manufacturing analysis technique adopted by agile. A value stream map may be used to analyze the flow of information or materials from origin to destination to identify areas of waste. The identified areas of waste are opportunities for process improvement. Waste can take many forms and can be remembered using the pneumonic device WIDETOM. W - waiting; I - inventory; D - defects; E - extra processing; T - transportation; O - over-production ; M - Motion. A value stream map is typically mapped or charted collaboratively with a team so it may define and view the entire process together, pinpointing areas of waste within the process. Processes that add value (processing of a part or feature) are generally referred to as "value-added" and processes that do not (e.g., waiting for a part to arrive) are generally referred to as "non value-added." Generally speaking, one wants to reduce, to the largest extent possible, the non value-added time (i.e., areas of waste). [Lean-Agile Software Development: Achieving Enterprise Agility. Alan Shalloway, Guy Beaver, James R. Trott.] [Value stream analysis]

23. C - The agile triangle includes value, quality, and constraints as its parameters. [Agile Project Management: Creating Innovative Products – 2nd Edition. Jim Highsmith.] [Knowledge and Skills: Level 1]

24. D - Osmotic communication is a concept of communication where information is shared between collocated team members unconsciously. By sharing the same work environment, team members are exposed to the same environmental sounds and other environmental input and unconsciously share a common framework that improves communication. [Agile Software Development: The Cooperative Game – 2nd Edition. Alistair Cockburn.] [Communications]

25. D - Literally thousands of decisions are made in the course of a project. Many of these decisions are made in response to problems that inevitably arise and confront the agile team. Therefore it is essential that an agile team is properly versed in problem-solving strategies, tools, and techniques. Some common problem-solving techniques include: ask it loud; revisit the problem; 5Y; sunk cost fallacy; devil's advocate; be kind, rewind; asking probing questions; and reflective/active listening. [Agile Retrospectives: Making Good Teams Great. Esther Derby, Diana Larsen, Ken Schwaber.] [Knowledge and Skills: Level 1]

26. D - Because each iteration typically produces a working product that is built and integrated and iterations are typically two to four weeks in length, there is frequent verification and validation to ensure product quality. Verification is the confirmation that a product performs as specified by a customer (e.g. as indicated by a user story) and validation is the confirmation that a product behaves as desired (i.e., meets the customer's need). Sometimes a product may be built and integrated to specification - that is, it can be verified - but it does not meet the intent of the customer - that is, it cannot be validated. [Agile Software Development: The Cooperative Game – 2nd Edition. Alistair Cockburn.] [Product quality]

27. C - Time, budget, and cost estimation is an important knowledge and skill area of agile. According to Highsmith, the nature of the agile method, whereby it welcomes changing scope, means that it lends itself well to fixed budgets and a fixed schedule because changing scope makes it difficult to estimate a total cost. Generally speaking, the budget and schedule constraints are known but before a project will commence there needs to be an agreed upon set of base product functionality defined in an initiation phase; fixing scope reduces an agile team's innovative tendency to provide improved value. For companies that are familiar with fixed-price contracts, where requirements are agreed upon before contract closing, adopting agile can be a weary initial venture. Instead, other contract vehicle types are recommended for agile efforts. These include: a general service contract for the initiation phase and separate fixed-price contracts for iterations or user stories; time-and-material contracts; not-to-exceed with fixed-fee contracts; and, incentive contracts (e.g., fixed price with incentive; cost-reimbursable with award fee). [Agile Project Management: Creating Innovative Products – 2nd Edition. Jim Highsmith.] [Knowledge and Skills: Level 1]

28. B - Servant leadership has its roots with an essay written in 1970 by Robert K Greenleaf. Greenleaf defined servant leaders as humble stewards devoted to their company and work to serve their peers, teams, and customers. In a self-organizing team, a servant leader, as Greenleaf defined it, is ideal as the team leader is an enabler, listening to the agile team's needs, removing obstacles, and providing tools or other support to promote high productivity. [Coaching Agile Teams. Lyssa Adkins.] [Soft skills negotiation]

29. D - Fixed-price contracts, although typical of traditional projects where scope is defined ahead of time, are not well suited for agile. When scope is fixed it can deter a team from exploring out-of-scope solutions that may add value to the product. Contracts suited for agile include: general service for the initial phase with fixed-price contracts for successive phases; cost-reimbursable/time and materials; not-to-exceed with fixed-fee; and a combination with incentives. [Agile Software Development: The Cooperative Game – 2nd Edition. Alistair Cockburn.] [Knowledge and Skills: Level 3]

30. D - A warm, welcoming environment that promotes effective communication, innovation, and motivated team members is an important aspect to consider when designing team space. Guidelines for a better agile team space include: collocation of team members; reduction of non-essential noise/distractions; dedicated whiteboard and wall space for information radiators; space for the daily stand-up meeting and other meetings; pairing workstations; and other pleasantries like plants and comfortable furniture. [Agile Retrospectives: Making Good Teams Great. Esther Derby, Diana Larsen, Ken Schwaber.] [Communications]

31. D - An agile team must always face the prioritization of product features in its product backlog. From release planning to iteration planning, an agile team must prioritize the user stories/ features of its product to ensure that high-quality and high-value features are developed first to help facilitate an optimized and early return on investment (ROI). An agile team typically prioritizes requirements or user stories/features in terms of relative value and risk; value is defined by the customer (i.e., customer-value prioritization). Two common methods to prioritize product features are: MoSCoW and Kano. The MoSCoW method categorizes features into 'Must have,' 'Should have,' 'Could have,' and 'Would have' features. The Kano method categorizes features into 'Must haves (threshold),' 'Dissatisfiers,' 'Satisfiers,' and 'Delighters.' Must haves are features that are requisite. Dissatisfiers are features that adversely impact perceived value and should be eliminated. 'Satisfiers' are features that increase perceived value linearly, where the more you add the more the customer is pleased, but are not required, and 'Delighters' are features that increase perceived value exponentially to please the customer. To prioritize features based on risk, a risk-to-value matrix can be used. A risk-to-value matrix has four quadrants, with the horizontal axis having low and high value, and the vertical axis having low and high risk. User stories are assigned to one of the four categories/quadrants: low-value, low-risk; low-value, high-risk; high-value, low-risk; high-value, high-risk. A cost-to-value matrix can also be made in this manner. All prioritization in agile is 'relative,' meaning that the priority of one user story is relative to other user stories and not prioritized on a fixed scale. [Lean-Agile Software Development: Achieving Enterprise Agility. Alan Shalloway, Guy Beaver, James R. Trott.] [Knowledge and Skills: Level 1]

32. A - An agile team must always face the prioritization of product features in its product backlog. From release planning to iteration planning, an agile team must prioritize the user stories/ features of its product to ensure that high-quality and high-value features are developed first to help facilitate an optimized and early return on investment (ROI). An agile team typically prioritizes requirements or user stories/features in terms of relative value and risk; value is defined by the customer (i.e., customer-value prioritization). Two common methods to prioritize product features are: MoSCoW and Kano. The MoSCoW method categorizes features into 'Must have,' 'Should have,' 'Could have,' and 'Would have' features. The Kano method categorizes features into 'Must haves (threshold),' 'Dissatisfiers,' 'Satisfiers,' and 'Delighters.' Must haves are features that are requisite. Dissatisfiers are features that adversely impact perceived value and should be eliminated. 'Satisfiers' are features that increase perceived value linearly, where the more you add the more the customer is pleased, but are not required, and 'Delighters' are features that increase perceived value exponentially to please the customer. To prioritize features based on risk, a risk-to-value matrix can be used. A risk-to-value matrix has four quadrants, with the horizontal axis having low and high value, and the vertical axis having low and high risk. User stories are assigned to one of the four categories/quadrants: low-value, low-risk; low-value, high-risk; high-value, low-risk; high-value, high-risk. A cost-to-value matrix can also be made in this manner. All prioritization in agile is 'relative,' meaning that the priority of one user story is relative to other user stories and not prioritized on a fixed scale. [Lean-Agile Software Development: Achieving Enterprise Agility. Alan Shalloway, Guy Beaver, James R. Trott.] [Knowledge and Skills: Level 1]

33. D - An agile team must always face the prioritization of product features in its product backlog. From release planning to iteration planning, an agile team must prioritize the user stories/ features of its product to ensure that high-quality and high-value features are developed first to help facilitate an optimized and early return on investment (ROI). An agile team typically prioritizes requirements or user stories/features in terms of relative value and risk; value is defined by the customer (i.e., customer-value prioritization). Two common methods to prioritize product features are: MoSCoW and Kano. The MoSCoW method categorizes features into 'Must have,' 'Should have,' 'Could have,' and 'Would have' features. The Kano method categorizes features into 'Must haves (threshold),' 'Dissatisfiers,' 'Satisfiers,' and 'Delighters.' Must haves are features that are requisite. Dissatisfiers are features that adversely impact perceived value and should be eliminated. 'Satisfiers' are features that increase perceived value linearly, where the more you add the more the customer is pleased, but are not required, and 'Delighters' are features that increase perceived value exponentially to please the customer. To prioritize features based on risk, a risk-to-value matrix can be used. A risk-to-value matrix has four quadrants, with the horizontal axis having low and high value, and the vertical axis having low and high risk. User stories are assigned to one of the four categories/quadrants: low-value, low-risk; low-value, high-risk; high-value, low-risk; high-value, high-risk. A cost-to-value matrix can also be made in this manner. All prioritization in agile is 'relative,' meaning that the priority of one user story is relative to other user stories and not prioritized on a fixed scale. [Lean-Agile Software Development: Achieving Enterprise Agility. Alan Shalloway, Guy Beaver, James R. Trott.] [Knowledge and Skills: Level 1]

34. D - An agile team must always face the prioritization of product features in its product backlog. From release planning to iteration planning, an agile team must prioritize the user stories/ features of its product to ensure that high-quality and high-value features are developed first to help facilitate an optimized and early return on investment (ROI). An agile team typically prioritizes requirements or user stories/features in terms of relative value and risk; value is defined by the customer (i.e., customer-value prioritization). Two common methods to prioritize product features are: MoSCoW and Kano. The MoSCoW method categorizes features into 'Must have,' 'Should have,' 'Could have,' and 'Would have' features. The Kano method categorizes features into 'Must haves (threshold),' 'Dissatisfiers,' 'Satisfiers,' and 'Delighters.' Must haves are features that are requisite. Dissatisfiers are features that adversely impact perceived value and should be eliminated. 'Satisfiers' are features that increase perceived value linearly, where the more you add the more the customer is pleased, but are not required, and 'Delighters' are features that increase perceived value exponentially to please the customer. To prioritize features based on risk, a risk-to-value matrix can be used. A risk-to-value matrix has four quadrants, with the horizontal axis having low and high value, and the vertical axis having low and high risk. User stories are assigned to one of the four categories/quadrants: low-value, low-risk; low-value, high-risk; high-value, low-risk; high-value, high-risk. A cost-to-value matrix can also be made in this manner. All prioritization in agile is 'relative,' meaning that the priority of one user story is relative to other user stories and not prioritized on a fixed scale. [Lean-Agile Software Development: Achieving Enterprise Agility. Alan Shalloway, Guy Beaver, James R. Trott.] [Knowledge and Skills: Level 1]

35. B - An agile team must always face the prioritization of product features in its product backlog. From release planning to iteration planning, an agile team must prioritize the user stories/ features of its product to ensure that high-quality and high-value features are developed first to help facilitate an optimized and early return on investment (ROI). An agile team typically prioritizes requirements or user stories/features in terms of relative value and risk; value is defined by the customer (i.e., customer-value prioritization). Two common methods to prioritize product features are: MoSCoW and Kano. The MoSCoW method categorizes features into 'Must have,' 'Should have,' 'Could have,' and 'Would have' features. The Kano method categorizes features into 'Must haves (threshold),' 'Dissatisfiers,' 'Satisfiers,' and 'Delighters.' Must haves are features that are requisite. Dissatisfiers are features that adversely impact perceived value and should be eliminated. 'Satisfiers' are features that increase perceived value linearly, where the more you add the more the customer is pleased, but are not required, and 'Delighters' are features that increase perceived value exponentially to please the customer. To prioritize features based on risk, a risk-to-value matrix can be used. A risk-to-value matrix has four quadrants, with the horizontal axis having low and high value, and the vertical axis having low and high risk. User stories are assigned to one of the four categories/quadrants: low-value, low-risk; low-value, high-risk; high-value, low-risk; high-value, high-risk. A cost-to-value matrix can also be made in this manner. All prioritization in agile is 'relative,' meaning that the priority of one user story is relative to other user stories and not prioritized on a fixed scale. [Lean-Agile Software Development: Achieving Enterprise Agility. Alan Shalloway, Guy Beaver, James R. Trott.] [Knowledge and Skills: Level 1]

36. B - Time, budget, and cost estimation is an important knowledge and skill area of agile. According to Highsmith, the nature of the agile method, whereby it welcomes changing scope, means that it lends itself well to fixed budgets and a fixed schedule because changing scope makes it difficult to estimate a total cost. Generally speaking, the budget and schedule constraints are known but before a project will commence there needs to be an agreed upon set of base product functionality defined in an initiation phase; fixing scope reduces an agile team's innovative tendency to provide improved value. For companies that are familiar with fixed-price contracts, where requirements are agreed upon before contract closing, adopting agile can be a weary initial venture. Instead, other contract vehicle types are recommended for agile efforts. These include: a general service contract for the initiation phase and separate fixed-price contracts for iterations or user stories; time-and-material contracts; not-to-exceed with fixed-fee contracts; and, incentive contracts (e.g., fixed price with incentive; cost-reimbursable with award fee). [Agile Project Management: Creating Innovative Products – 2nd Edition. Jim Highsmith.] [Knowledge and Skills: Level 1]

37. B - Time, budget, and cost estimation is an important knowledge and skill area of agile. According to Highsmith, the nature of the agile method, whereby it welcomes changing scope, means that it lends itself well to fixed budgets and a fixed schedule because changing scope makes it difficult to estimate a total cost. Generally speaking, the budget and schedule constraints are known but before a project will commence there needs to be an agreed upon set of base product functionality defined in an initiation phase; fixing scope reduces an agile team's innovative tendency to provide improved value. For companies that are familiar with fixed-price contracts, where requirements are agreed upon before contract closing, adopting agile can be a weary initial venture. Instead, other contract vehicle types are recommended for agile efforts. These include: a general service contract for the initiation phase and separate fixed-price contracts for iterations or user stories; time-and-material contracts; not-to-exceed with fixed-fee contracts; and, incentive contracts (e.g., fixed price with incentive; cost-reimbursable with award fee). [Agile Project Management: Creating Innovative Products – 2nd Edition. Jim Highsmith.] [Knowledge and Skills: Level 1]

38. B - Time, budget, and cost estimation is an important knowledge and skill area of agile. According to Highsmith, the nature of the agile method, whereby it welcomes changing scope, means that it lends itself well to fixed budgets and a fixed schedule because changing scope makes it difficult to estimate a total cost. Generally speaking, the budget and schedule constraints are known but before a project will commence there needs to be an agreed upon set of base product functionality defined in an initiation phase; fixing scope reduces an agile team's innovative tendency to provide improved value. For companies that are familiar with fixed-price contracts, where requirements are agreed upon before contract closing, adopting agile can be a weary initial venture. Instead, other contract vehicle types are recommended for agile efforts. These include: a general service contract for the initiation phase and separate fixed-price contracts for iterations or user stories; time-and-material contracts; not-to-exceed with fixed-fee contracts; and, incentive contracts (e.g., fixed price with incentive; cost-reimbursable with award fee). [Agile Project Management: Creating Innovative Products – 2nd Edition. Jim Highsmith.] [Knowledge and Skills: Level 1]

39. C - Time, budget, and cost estimation is an important knowledge and skill area of agile. According to Highsmith, the nature of the agile method, whereby it welcomes changing scope, means that it lends itself well to fixed budgets and a fixed schedule because changing scope makes it difficult to estimate a total cost. Generally speaking, the budget and schedule constraints are known but before a project will commence there needs to be an agreed upon set of base product functionality defined in an initiation phase; fixing scope reduces an agile team's innovative tendency to provide improved value. For companies that are familiar with fixed-price contracts, where requirements are agreed upon before contract closing, adopting agile can be a weary initial venture. Instead, other contract vehicle types are recommended for agile efforts. These include: a general service contract for the initiation phase and separate fixed-price contracts for iterations or user stories; time-and-material contracts; not-to-exceed with fixed-fee contracts; and, incentive contracts (e.g., fixed price with incentive; cost-reimbursable with award fee). [Agile Project Management: Creating Innovative Products – 2nd Edition. Jim Highsmith.] [Knowledge and Skills: Level 1]

40. B - The key characteristics of a healthy stand-up meeting include: peer pressure - the team is dependent upon each other so expectations of peers drives progress; fine-grained coordination - the team should understand the necessity for focus and working dependently; fine focus - the team should understand the need for brevity in the stand-up meeting so the team can be productive; daily commitment - the team should understand the value of daily commitments to each other and uphold those commitments; identification of obstacles - the team collectively should be aware of each other's obstacles so that the team collectively can try to resolve them. [The Art of Agile Development. James Shore.] [Communications]

PMI-ACP Lite Mock Exam 4 Practice Questions

Test Name: PMI-ACP Lite Mock Exam 4
Total Questions: 40
Correct Answers Needed to Pass:
30 (75.00%)
Time Allowed: 60 Minutes

Test Description

This is a cumulative PMI-ACP Mock Exam which can be used as a benchmark for your PMI-ACP aptitude. This practice test includes questions from all exam topic areas, including sections from Agile Tools and Techniques, and all three Agile Knowledge and Skills areas.

Test Questions

1. Wilson and the agile team he belongs to are having a discussion regarding 'stakeholder management.' Why is 'stakeholder management' an important topic of conversation for an agile team?

A. Because having engaged stakeholders that actively participate is crucial for success.

B. Because without assigning tasks and duties to stakeholders scope creep is inevitable.

C. Because managing the requirements of stakeholders is essential to keep the product backlog from expanding.

D. Because preventing the stakeholders from interfering with developers helps improve velocity.

2. Why is the presence of a product owner necessary when playing a game of planning poker?

A. Because the product owner provides an overview of user stories and answers any questions the development team may have.

B. Because the product owner must report any outliers (i.e., extremely long or short estimates) on the risk register.

C. Because the product owner must relay to the customer the range of story points assigned to each user story .

D. Because the product owner must moderate the planning poker session.

3. Patty is explaining the importance of an agile team being empowered. What does an empowered team mean?

A. A team that is self-organizing and involves the entire team and customer or user to blaze a forward trail and solve problems.

B. A team that is management-oriented and focused solely on meeting scope, cost, and schedule constraints.

C. A team that is capable of exceeding sustainable development velocities in "power" iterations to meet backlog goals.

D. A team that solves problems through the use of market research.

4. Lila, as project leader, has been discussing the importance of 'stakeholder management' with her team. Why is stakeholder management so important?

A. Because without participation from stakeholders, the chances of a successful project are optimized.

B. Because without participation from stakeholders, the team can focus on providing a valuable product that adheres to the initial project plan.

C. Because without stakeholder management, stakeholders will inevitably interfere with necessary product development.

D. Because without active participation from stakeholders, the chances of a successful project are reduced.

5. Marge as a product owner believes steadfastly in the feature prioritization. Why might Marge believe in prioritization?

A. Because without prioritization a team would not know how prepare for retrospective workshops.

B. Because without prioritization a team would not know how to gauge unit testing efforts.

C. Because without prioritization a team would not know how to estimate user story sizes.

D. Because without prioritization a team would not know in what order to develop user stories in order to optimize value delivered to the customer.

6. Which of the following responses is NOT a part of active listening?

A. Taking notes.

B. Being present and focusing your attention on the speaker.

C. Talking loudly.

D. Being silent.

7. Select a method used in agile for the purpose of prioritization.

A. Cannon

B. WIDETOM

C. WoCSoM

D. Kano

8. Which of the following responses is NOT a part of active listening?

A. Being present and focusing your attention on the speaker.

B. Closed-ended questions.

C. Being silent.

D. Taking notes.

9. Of the following, which is NOT a part of active listening?

A. Taking notes.

B. Leaving the conversation early.

C. Good body language.

D. Being silent.

10. What technology can facilitate some osmotic communication for team members that do NOT share the same workspace?

A. Instant messaging

B. Near Field Communication

C. None

D. Bluetooth

11. An agile team has just estimated the relative value of developing a user story during a game of planning poker. The following scores were played: Bob: 40; Tim: 8; Mark: 1; Ursula: 13; Yvonne: 20. According to the rules of planning poker, which two team members should defend their positions?

A. Tim and Mark

B. Ursula and Yvonne

C. Bob and Yvonne

D. Bob and Mark

12. Hillary is using a software development framework adapted specifically for agile that from the unified process (UP). Which framework is Hillary using?

A. Simple unified process (SUP)

B. Adapted unified process (AdUP)

C. Extreme unified process (EUP)

D. Agile unified process (AUP)

13. Peter's agile team is geographically dispersed throughout the world. What is one factor the team should consider when conducting its business?

A. Whether or not to consider language differences when communicating.

B. Whether or not to plan an iteration.

C. Whether or not to use a rolling look ahead plan for complex projects.

D. Whether or not to use information radiators.

14. Feedback techniques are ubiquitous in agile projects. Select the response which lists a feedback technique.

A. Timeboxing

B. Daily stand-up meeting

C. Process tree

D. Console mapping

15. Which type of risk category is typically given a lower priority when creating the risk-adjusted backlog: a) high-value, high risk or b) low-value, low risk?

A. Both are equivalent.

B. Low-value, low risk

C. High-value, high risk

D. High-severity, low-likelihood

16. What is a positive indicator that agile may be appropriate to an organization as a new project methodology?

A. That the adopting organization values strict and inflexible project management practices.

B. That the adopting organization values hierarchical decision making.

C. That the adopting organization values top-down management.

D. That the adopting organization values trust, collective ownership, and adaptability.

17. Consider the following EVM scenario and calculate the SV. The team is on week 30 of a 100 week project. Its BAC is \$100,000 and AC is \$15,000. The team estimates it is 20% complete overall and has an EV of \$20,000.

A. \$20,000

B. (\$10,000)

C. \$10,000

D. \$30,000

18. Thomas notices that his team just assigned a user story the value of 10 to indicate the relative effort it will take to develop the user story. What is Thomas and his team most likely using to estimate relative user story development effort?

A. Story coins

B. Story chapters

C. Story marks

D. Story points

19. Generally, how is an agile project estimated?

A. From both a horizontal and vertical dimension

B. From the bottom up

C. From the top down

D. Both from the top down and the bottom up

20. In agile, the "team space" is an important place that should foster effective communication. What is a guideline for promoting such an environment?

A. Collocation of team members

B. Isolation of team members

C. Rotation of team members

D. Separation of team members by function

21. As team lead, Xavier is constantly monitoring the effectiveness of communication among his team and stakeholders. What is the knowledge and skill area that deals with communication?

A. Communications management

B. Command and control

C. Stakeholder analysis

D. Brainstorming

22. If a software product is developed for multiple organizations within one industry, it can be described as:

A. Broad-spectrum software

B. Narrow-band software

C. Vertical-market software

D. Horizontal-market software

23. Jessica, as a certified agile practitioner, believes in the value of 'knowledge sharing.' Which of the following is the best definition of 'knowledge sharing?'

A. The collaborative sharing of information among all stakeholders and team members to promote a well-informed project environment.

B. The sharing of information on a need-to-know basis.

C. The sharing of information between the product owner and chief programming engineer regarding the adaptability of the development team to implement performance improvement plans.

D. The sharing of information on a just-in-time basis.

24. From the following, select a common agile framework/methodology.

A. Extreme programming (XP)

B. Peer perfect programming (3P)

C. Ultra programming (UP)

D. Paired programming (PP)

25. Becky and her agile team have just performed decomposition on several user stories and wants to prioritize them. What common technique might she and her team use to prioritize the user stories?

A. Cost-to-schedule matrix

B. Cost-to-value matrix

C. Cost-to-risk matrix

D. Cost-to-constraint matrix

26. Perry is explaining the MoSCoW technique which is often used in agile to prioritize user stories. What does the C stand for?

A. Could disrupt dependencies

B. Could have

C. Cannot have

D. Could do without

27. Bill, as the agile team lead, likes being able to demo the latest iteration of a working product to the customer. His team delivers a demo of the product every two weeks so the customer may provide feedback and perform acceptance. What type of delivery concept provides this type of regular interval feedback that is a cornerstone of agile development?

A. Iteration delivery

B. Prototype delivery

C. Demo and acceptance delivery

D. Incremental delivery

28. Why is an empowered team considered an important team attribute in agile?

A. Empowered teams remove themselves from being responsible of product quality in order to reduce association with project failure.

B. Empowered teams need extensive management involvement in order to understand customer need

C. Empowered teams remain inflexible to changing customer requirements and focus on delivering to specification.

D. Empowered teams take ownership of the product and thus have a strong focus on delivering value.

29. List the primary steps in the Crystal development process project chartering activity.

A. Building the team; Performing an Exploratory 360; Picking team conventions and practices; Building the initial project plan

B. Building the team; Performing an Exploratory 180; Picking team conventions and practices; Building the initial project plan

C. Choosing the product owner; Performing an Exploratory 360; Picking team conventions and practices; Building the initial project plan

D. Building the team; Performing an Exploratory 360; Picking story points or ideal days; Building the initial project plan

30. When is the product roadmap initially created?

A. After the first release.

B. At the beginning of a project, usually after the vision statement has been defined.

C. After the first iteration.

D. During closing as end-user documentation to understand the product

31. What is the primary input to Highsmith's agile project management adapting phase?

A. Built-in test output

B. Iteration schedule slip points

C. Feature feedback and critique

D. Scrum error analysis

32. What agile artifact outlines the project's expected rate of return?

A. Task board

B. Iteration backlog

C. Burndown chart

D. Business case

33. How are user stories or features prioritized for development in the agile methodology?

A. By difficulty

B. By value

C. By developer preference

D. By ease of implementation

34. Which of the following is NOT a typical grouping of user stories for purposes of organization?

A. By alphabetical letter

B. By relation to product feature

C. By priority

D. By logical sequence and dependency

35. Select an advantage of using an information radiator.

A. Allows for a streamlined process for changing sprint deadlines

B. Makes communication of project status less time consuming

C. Improves team dynamics by offering a place to air grievances

D. Decreases the amount of time spent in daily standup meetings

36. How might an agile team continuously improve its product?

A. By using comprehensive documentation to define team values.

B. By performing ongoing testing.

C. By performing integration testing near the end of a release.

D. By performing work breakdown structure reviews.

37. One level of planning in the agile project management methodology is release panning. Why is release planning important?

A. It helps ensure the customer and agile team understand the product vision, acceptance criteria, and high-level product release plan.

B. It helps the team understand customer portfolio risks

C. It helps the customer solidify product requirements for the release

D. It helps the agile team decompose user stories into tasks.

38. Becky, as project leader, intends on building a high-performance team. What is a practice or technique she can use to build a high performance team?

A. Making all decisions for the team

B. Having a team that is self-organizing and self-disciplined

C. Promoting competition

D. Assigning more work than can be accomplished in an iteration to set a sense of urgency

39. Calculate the Net Present Value of the following investment candidate. The initial investment cost is $1,000. The discount rate is 5%. At the end of year 1, $100 is expected. At the end of year 2, $300 is expected. At the end of year 3, $450 is expected.

A. $(220.00)

B. $(244.00)

C. $(230.00)

D. $(300.00)

40. How can a team ensure it benefits from osmotic communication?

A. By collocating its team members.

B. By purchasing its team members blue tooth headsets.

C. By isolating its team members.

D. By separating team members into functional specialties.

PMI-ACP Lite Mock Exam 4 Answer Key and Explanations

1. A - Stakeholder management is a growing topic area within strategic management that brings awareness to the importance of managing stakeholders (i.e., facilitating active participation of stakeholders and fostering a strong collaborative environment) for a project's success. Stakeholder management is typically defined in the context of guiding principles and values. R. E. Freeman's 'Managing for Stakeholders' includes 10 principles: 1) Stakeholder interests need to go together over time. 2) We need a philosophy of volunteerism – to engage stakeholders and manage relationships ourselves rather than leave it to government. 3) We need to find solutions to issues that satisfy multiple stakeholders simultaneously. 4) Everything that we do serves stakeholders. We never trade off the interests of one versus the other continuously over time. 5) We act with purpose that fulfills our commitment to stakeholders. We act with aspiration towards fulfilling our dreams and theirs. 6) We need intensive communication and dialogue with stakeholders – not just those who are friendly. 7)Stakeholders consist of real people with names and faces and children. They are complex. 8)We need to generalize the marketing approach. 9) We engage with both primary and secondary stakeholders. 10) We constantly monitor and redesign processes to make them better serve our stakeholders. Because stakeholder involvement is critical for the success of a project, where projects without active participation from stakeholders are prone to failure, stakeholder management should be a topic that every agile team knows well. [The Art of Agile Development. James Shore.] [Knowledge and Skills: Level 1]

2. A - Planning poker is based upon the wideband Delphi estimation technique. It is a consensus-based technique for estimating effort. Sometimes called scrum poker, it is a technique for a relative estimation of effort, typically in story points, to develop a user story. At a planning poker meeting, each estimator is given an identical deck of planning poker cards with a wide range of values. The Fibonacci sequence is often used for values for planning poker (i.e., 0, 1, 1, 2, 3, 5,8,etc.); another common sequence is (question mark, 0, 1/2, 1, 2, 3, 5, 8, 13, 20, 40, and 100). A planning poker meeting works as follows: 1) a moderator, not estimating, facilitates the meeting. 2) the product owner/manager provides a short overview of the user story and answers clarifying questions posed by the developers. Typically the product owner does not vote. 3) Each estimator selects an estimate of work effort by selecting a card, 4) Once everyone has selected a card, everyone overturns their card concurrently, 5) Estimators with high and low estimates are given a chance to defend positions. 6) The process repeats until there is consensus. The developer who owns the user story is typically given higher credence. [Agile Estimating and Planning. Mike Cohn.] [Agile estimation]

3. A - Empowered teams - ones that are self-organizing and know how to solve problems with minimal management involvement - are a cornerstone of the agile methodology. This is the antithesis to the classic viewpoint of the traditional project manager who is seen as someone that controls all decisions and delegates tasks to a team with little feedback. An agile team must include all members and stakeholders to make decisions, and make decisions expediently. Because it is essential that the user/customer be involved with development, it is encouraged that the user/customer is closely integrated with the agile team with collocation/on-site support being ideal. An agile team feels empowered when it collectively assumes responsibility for the delivery of the product (i.e., taking ownership). [Coaching Agile Teams. Lyssa Adkins.] [Knowledge and Skills: Level 1]

4. D - Stakeholder management is a growing topic area within strategic management that brings awareness to the importance of managing stakeholders (i.e., facilitating active participation of stakeholders and fostering a strong collaborative environment) for a project's success. Stakeholder management is typically defined in the context of guiding principles and values. R. E. Freeman's 'Managing for Stakeholders' includes 10 principles: 1) Stakeholder interests need to go together over time. 2) We need a philosophy of volunteerism – to engage stakeholders and manage relationships ourselves rather than leave it to government. 3) We need to find solutions to issues that satisfy multiple stakeholders simultaneously. 4) Everything that we do serves stakeholders. We never trade off the interests of one versus the other continuously over time. 5) We act with purpose that fulfills our commitment to stakeholders. We act with aspiration towards fulfilling our dreams and theirs. 6) We need intensive communication and dialogue with stakeholders – not just those who are friendly. 7)Stakeholders consist of real people with names and faces and children. They are complex. 8)We need to generalize the marketing approach. 9) We engage with both primary and secondary stakeholders. 10) We constantly monitor and redesign processes to make them better serve our stakeholders. Because stakeholder involvement is critical for the success of a project, where projects without active participation from stakeholders are prone to failure, stakeholder management should be a topic that every agile team knows well. [The Art of Agile Development. James Shore.] [Knowledge and Skills: Level 1]

5. D - An agile team must always face the prioritization of product features in its product backlog. From release planning to iteration planning, an agile team must prioritize the user stories/ features of its product to ensure that high-quality and high-value features are developed first to help facilitate an optimized and early return on investment (ROI). An agile team typically prioritizes requirements or user stories/features in terms of relative value and risk; value is defined by the customer (i.e., customer-value prioritization). Two common methods to prioritize product features are: MoSCoW and Kano. The MoSCoW method categorizes features into 'Must have,' 'Should have,' 'Could have,' and 'Would have' features. The Kano method categorizes features into 'Must haves (threshold),' 'Dissatisfiers,' 'Satisfiers,' and 'Delighters.' Must haves are features that are requisite. Dissatisfiers are features that adversely impact perceived value and should be eliminated. 'Satisfiers' are features that increase perceived value linearly, where the more you add the more the customer is pleased, but are not required, and 'Delighters' are features that increase perceived value exponentially to please the customer. To prioritize features based on risk, a risk-to-value matrix can be used. A risk-to-value matrix has four quadrants, with the horizontal axis having low and high value, and the vertical axis having low and high risk. User stories are assigned to one of the four categories/quadrants: low-value, low-risk; low-value, high-risk; high-value, low-risk; high-value, high-risk. A cost-to-value matrix can also be made in this manner. All prioritization in agile is 'relative,' meaning that the priority of one user story is relative to other user stories and not prioritized on a fixed scale. [Lean-Agile Software Development: Achieving Enterprise Agility. Alan Shalloway, Guy Beaver, James R. Trott.] [Knowledge and Skills: Level 1]

6. C - One communication technique to reduce misunderstanding and miscommunication is active listening. A well run agile project necessitates both good listeners and communicators, active listening helps work towards both of these necessities. The basics of active listening include: 1) Being present and focusing your attention on the speaker. 2) Taking notes instead of interrupting. 3) Paraphrasing to confirm and review what you have heard. 4) Summarizing the conversation once it has concluded for posterity. Using open ended questions, good body language, and silence can help improve listening skills. [Coaching Agile Teams. Lyssa Adkins.] [Knowledge and Skills: Level 1]

7. D - An agile team must always face the prioritization of product features in its product backlog. From release planning to iteration planning, an agile team must prioritize the user stories/ features of its product to ensure that high-quality and high-value features are developed first to help facilitate an optimized and early return on investment (ROI). An agile team typically prioritizes requirements or user stories/features in terms of relative value and risk; value is defined by the customer (i.e., customer-value prioritization). Two common methods to prioritize product features are: MoSCoW and Kano. The MoSCoW method categorizes features into 'Must have,' 'Should have,' 'Could have,' and 'Would have' features. The Kano method categorizes features into 'Must haves (threshold),' 'Dissatisfiers,' 'Satisfiers,' and 'Delighters.' Must haves are features that are requisite. Dissatisfiers are features that adversely impact perceived value and should be eliminated. 'Satisfiers' are features that increase perceived value linearly, where the more you add the more the customer is pleased, but are not required, and 'Delighters' are features that increase perceived value exponentially to please the customer. To prioritize features based on risk, a risk-to-value matrix can be used. A risk-to-value matrix has four quadrants, with the horizontal axis having low and high value, and the vertical axis having low and high risk. User stories are assigned to one of the four categories/quadrants: low-value, low-risk; low-value, high-risk; high-value, low-risk; high-value, high-risk. A cost-to-value matrix can also be made in this manner. All prioritization in agile is 'relative,' meaning that the priority of one user story is relative to other user stories and not prioritized on a fixed scale. [Lean-Agile Software Development: Achieving Enterprise Agility. Alan Shalloway, Guy Beaver, James R. Trott.] [Knowledge and Skills: Level 1]

8. B - One communication technique to reduce misunderstanding and miscommunication is active listening. A well run agile project necessitates both good listeners and communicators, active listening helps work towards both of these necessities. The basics of active listening include: 1) Being present and focusing your attention on the speaker. 2) Taking notes

instead of interrupting. 3) Paraphrasing to confirm and review what you have heard. 4) Summarizing the conversation once it has concluded for posterity. Using open ended questions, good body language, and silence can help improve listening skills. [Coaching Agile Teams. Lyssa Adkins.] [Knowledge and Skills: Level 1]

9. B - One communication technique to reduce misunderstanding and miscommunication is active listening. A well run agile project necessitates both good listeners and communicators, active listening helps work towards both of these necessities. The basics of active listening include: 1) Being present and focusing your attention on the speaker. 2) Taking notes instead of interrupting. 3) Paraphrasing to confirm and review what you have heard. 4) Summarizing the conversation once it has concluded for posterity. Using open ended questions, good body language, and silence can help improve listening skills. [Coaching Agile Teams. Lyssa Adkins.] [Knowledge and Skills: Level 1]

10. A - Video conferencing and instant messaging are technologies that can provide some level of osmotic communication. [Agile Software Development: The Cooperative Game – 2nd Edition. Alistair Cockburn.] [Communications]

11. D - Planning poker is based upon the wideband Delphi estimation technique. It is a consensus-based technique for estimating effort. Sometimes called scrum poker, it is a technique for a relative estimation of effort, typically in story points, to develop a user story. At a planning poker meeting, each estimator is given an identical deck of planning poker cards with a wide range of values. The Fibonacci sequence is often used for values for planning poker (i.e., 0, 1, 1, 2, 3, 5,8,etc.); another common sequence is (question mark, 0, 1/2, 1, 2, 3, 5, 8, 13, 20, 40, and 100). A planning poker meeting works as follows: 1) a moderator, not estimating, facilitates the meeting. 2) the product owner/manager provides a short overview of the user story and answers clarifying questions posed by the developers. Typically the product owner does not vote. 3) Each estimator selects an estimate of work effort by selecting a card, 4) Once everyone has selected a card, everyone overturns their card concurrently, 5) Estimators with high and low estimates are given a chance to defend positions. 6) The process repeats until there is consensus. The developer who owns the user story is typically given higher credence. [Agile Estimating and Planning. Mike Cohn.] [Agile estimation]

12. D - Agile Unified Process (AUP) is a simplified version of the Unified Process, or UP (UP itself is a more detailed framework for iterative and incremental software development). AUP simplifies UP for the agile framework. AUP projects use four phases: 1) inception, 2) elaboration, 3) construction, and 4) transition. At the end of each short iteration, the team delivers a working product. [Agile Software Development: The Cooperative Game – 2nd Edition. Alistair Cockburn.] [Knowledge and Skills: Level 2]

13. A - A high-performance agile team is one that is ideally collocated for osmotic communication and face-to-face interaction. However, collocation isn't always feasible in today's multinational environment. For distributed teams, several practices are available to provide the best form of effective communication in the absence of being collocated: team intranet sites, virtual team rooms, and video conferencing over e-mail when possible. Geographic separation, especially on a world-wide scale, causes the team to consider language and cultural differences, and time zone differences. [Agile Software Development: The Cooperative Game – 2nd Edition. Alistair Cockburn.] [Knowledge and Skills: Level 3]

14. B - There are several feedback techniques - techniques that facilitate constructive criticism to improve product value and quality - built into the agile process. In the classic definition, feedback is a dynamic process where past information influences the behavior of the same process in the future. Agile feedback techniques include prototyping, simulation, demonstration, evaluations, pair programming, unit testing, continuous integration, daily stand-up meetings, sprint planning. Because agile prides itself on a transparent and collaborative environment, feedback is essentially ubiquitous. [Agile Retrospectives: Making Good Teams Great. Esther Derby, Diana Larsen, Ken Schwaber.] [Knowledge and Skills: Level 1]

15. B - A risk-adjusted backlog is a product backlog organized by taking into account risk. Risk can be estimated as the product of severity/consequence and likelihood. User stories can also be positioned on a risk-to-value matrix to help prioritize them in the backlog. The risk-to-value matrix is a chart with four quadrants. Along the horizontal axis is value in ascending order. Along the vertical axis is risk in ascending order. A user story that is high risk and high value is located in the top-right corner. A user story that is low risk and high value is located in the lower-right corner. A user story that is low risk and high value is located in the lower-right corner. A user story that is low risk and low value is located in the lower-left corner. Typically a team will prioritize high-value, low-risk user stories first, followed by high-value, high-risk user stories, followed by low-value, low-risk user stories, followed by low-value, high-risk user stories. [The Art of Agile Development. James Shore.] [Risk management]

16. D - When considering whether to apply new agile practices, several internal and external factors should be considered. Internal factors include whether the project is developing new processes or products; whether the organization is collaborative and emphasizes trust, adaptability, collective ownership, and has minimal or informal project management processes; the size, location, and skills of the project team. External factors include the industry stability and customer engagement or involvement. Generally, agile is best suited to developing new processes or products for an organization that is collaborative and emphasizes trust, adaptability, collective ownership, and has minimal project management processes by an agile/project team that is relatively small in size, is collocated, and is cross-functional in skill. Additionally, agile is known to succeed in industries that are quickly adapting to disruptive technologies as opposed to industries that are stable and perhaps inflexible to adaptive approaches. And, lastly, the component of customer involvement and engagement cannot be stressed enough; the more participation, the better. [The Art of Agile Development. James Shore.] [Knowledge and Skills: Level 3]

17. B - EVM or earned value management is a management technique used to evaluate project performance with respect to cost and schedule. EVM relies on other common financial metrics like Budget At Completion (BAC), Actual Cost (AC), Planned Value (PV), Earned Value (EV), Cost Variance (CV), Schedule Variance (SV), Cost Performance Index (CPI), and Schedule Performance Index (SPI). CV and SV can be converted into performance indicators of CPI and SPI, respectively, and tracked and charted to show progress over time. PV is the planned value of work at a given time in a project; you can calculate it by multiplying the BAC by the ratio of current week/scheduled weeks (e.g., 5 weeks into a 15 week $15,000 project = $5,000 PV). EV is value of work actually completed or earned (e.g., you have completed 50% of the project by week 5 of a 15 week $15,000 project = $7,500 EV). SV is the difference between what a project has earned to date and what it was planned to earn to date (i.e., SV = EV - PV). [Agile Estimating and Planning. Mike Cohn.] [Metrics]

18. D - Agile teams typically use story points to estimate the relative size or effort of developing a user story [Agile Estimating and Planning. Mike Cohn.] [Agile estimation]

19. C - When estimating an agile project, a top-down approach is typically used. This involves high-level estimation at first, followed by more detailed estimation. [Agile Estimating and Planning. Mike Cohn.] [Agile estimation]

20. A - A warm, welcoming environment that promotes effective communication, innovation, and motivated team members is an important aspect to consider when designing team space. Guidelines for a better agile team space include: collocation of team members; reduction of non-essential noise/distractions; dedicated whiteboard and wall space for information radiators; space for the daily stand-up meeting and other meetings; pairing workstations; and other pleasantries like plants and comfortable furniture. [Agile Retrospectives: Making Good Teams Great. Esther Derby, Diana Larsen, Ken Schwaber.] [Communications]

21. A - Effective communication is a cornerstone of agile. Communication is the act of transferring information among various parties. Communications management is a knowledge and skill area of agile that highlights this importance. PMI has several definitions regarding communications management and agile builds on top of these to add its own perspective: 1) Communications Planning: Determining the information and communication needs of the projects stakeholders 2) Information Distribution: Making needed information available to project stakeholders in a timely manner, 3) Performance Reporting: Collecting and distributing performance information. This includes status reporting, progress measurement, and forecasting, and 4) Managing Stakeholders: Managing communications to satisfy the requirements and resolve issues with project stakeholders. From an agile perspective: communication among the team is built into the process and facilitated through collocation, information radiators, daily stand-up meetings, retrospectives etc.; Although it is hoped that the product owner, customer, and user can be heavily involved with the project and also use these communication techniques, a plan for conveying information to stakeholders may be needed if this is not the case. [Agile Software Development: The Cooperative Game – 2nd Edition. Alistair Cockburn.] [Knowledge and Skills: Level 1]

22. C - Vertical-market software includes solutions for many organizations within one industry (e.g., pharmaceutical software). Horizontal-market software includes solutions for many organizations in many industries (e.g., word processing software). [The Art of Agile Development. James Shore.] [Knowledge and Skills: Level 2]

23. A - In agile, effective 'knowledge sharing' is a critical factor for success. It involves the near real time communication of key information among all team members and stakeholders. To promote knowledge sharing, agile uses standard practices built into its process, such as using generalized specialists/cross functional teams, self-organizing and self-disciplined teams, collocation, daily stand-up meetings, iteration/sprint planning, release planning, pair programming and pair rotation, project retrospectives/reflection, and on-site customer support. And, of course, the sixth principle of Agile is " The most efficient and effective method of conveying information to and within a development team is face-to-face conversation." In this sense, Agile prefers and encourages collocation for all stakeholders and team members for the simple fact that face-to-face conversation is the best method of communication and, in turn, effective knowledge sharing. [Becoming Agile: ...in an imperfect world. Greg Smith, Ahmed Sidky.] [Knowledge and Skills: Level 1]

24. A - Common frameworks or methodologies used within agile include: scrum, extreme programming (XP), lean software development, crystal, feature driven development (FDD), dynamic systems development method (DSDM), agile unified process (AUP). [Agile Software Development: The Cooperative Game – 2nd Edition. Alistair Cockburn.] [Knowledge and Skills: Level 2]

25. B - In iteration planning, an agile team, collaboratively with the customer, chooses user stories to include for development. Although the user stories are prioritized in the product backlog initially during release planning, an agile team and customer should review prioritization based on progressive elaboration (i.e., gained knowledge and perspective). Prioritization is often based on value and risk and can be performed using the MoSCoW or Kano method and through the use of risk-to-value and cost-to-value matrices. An agile team performs decomposition to sub-divide user stories into more manageable tasks so that it may estimate task time. Tasks for an iteration may also be prioritized based on value, similar to how user stories are prioritized. [Lean-Agile Software Development: Achieving Enterprise Agility. Alan Shalloway, Guy Beaver, James R. Trott.] [Knowledge and Skills: Level 1]

26. B - The MoSCoW technique is commonly used in agile to prioritize user stories and create a story map. The MoSCoW technique prioritizes user stories into the following groups in descending order of priority: M - Must have; S - Should have; C - Could have; W - Would have. Must have items are those product features which are absolutely essential to develop. Should have items are product features that are not essential but have significant business value. Could have items are product features that would add some business value. Would have items are product features that have marginal business value. [User Stories Applied: For Agile Software Development. Mike Cohn.] [Agile analysis and design]

27. D - A cornerstone of Agile development is 'incremental delivery.' Incremental delivery is the frequent delivery of working products, which are successively improved, to a customer for immediate feedback and acceptance. Typically, a product is delivered at the end of each sprint or iteration for demonstration and feedback. In this feedback technique, a customer can review the product and provide updated requirements. Changed/updated/refined requirements are welcomed in the agile process to ensure the customer receives a valuable and quality product. A sprint or iteration typically lasts from two to four weeks and at the end a new and improved product is delivered, incrementally. [The Art of Agile Development. James Shore.] [Knowledge and Skills: Level 1]

28. D - Empowered teams - ones that are self-organizing and know how to solve problems with minimal management involvement - are a cornerstone of the agile methodology. An agile team feels empowered when it collectively assumes responsibility for the delivery of the product (i.e., taking ownership). [Coaching Agile Teams. Lyssa Adkins.] [Knowledge and Skills: Level 1]

29. A - The Crystal development process is cyclical/iterative. Its primary components are chartering, delivery cycles, and project wrap-up. Chartering involves creating a project charter, which can last from a few days to a few weeks. Chartering consists of four activities: 1) Building the core project team, 2) performing an Exploratory 360° assessment, 3) fine tuning the methodology, and 3) building the initial project plan. [Agile Software Development: The Cooperative Game – 2nd Edition. Alistair Cockburn.] [Agile analysis and design]

30. B - The product roadmap - owned by the product owner - serves as a high level overview of the product requirements. It is used as a tool for prioritizing features , organizing features into categories, and assigning rough time frames. Creating a product roadmap has four basic steps: 1) Identify requirements (these will become part of the product backlog), 2) Organize requirements into categories or themes, 3) Estimate relative work effort (e.g., planning poker or affinity estimation) and prioritize (value), and 4) Estimate rough time frames (estimate velocity, sprint duration, and rough release dates). [The Art of Agile Development. James Shore.] [Agile analysis and design]

31. C - In the adapting phase, the agile team encourages feedback of the latest deliverable of an iteration. From the feedback, the team adapts product features and plans for the subsequent iteration. [Agile Project Management: Creating Innovative Products – 2nd Edition. Jim Highsmith.] [Knowledge and Skills: Level 1]

32. D - Business case development is an important initial step in agile project management. The business case is a concise document that outlines the project's vision, goals, strategies for achieving goals, milestones, required investment and expected return/payback. A business case articulates the why and how a project will deliver value to a customer. [Lean-Agile Software Development: Achieving Enterprise Agility. Alan Shalloway, Guy Beaver, James R. Trott.] [Knowledge and Skills: Level 2]

33. B - User stories are prioritized based on customer value. Value is determined by return on investment, growth of team knowledge, and risk reduction. [The Art of Agile Development. James Shore.] [Planning, monitoring, and adapting]

34. A - Various grouping methods are used to organize user stories. Typical methods are: 1) Relation to a product feature (e.g., all user stories that interact with the database), 2) By logical sequence and dependency (e.g., Group 1 must be developed before Group 2 because of technological dependency), 3) By priority based on customer value. [User Stories Applied: For Agile Software Development. Mike Cohn.] [Agile analysis and design]

35. B - Information radiators improve team communication by reducing the amount of time spent explaining project status. [Agile Software Development: The Cooperative Game – 2nd Edition. Alistair Cockburn.] [Communications]

36. B - Agile project management places strong emphasis on 'continuous improvement.' Continuous improvement processes are built into the agile methodology, from customers providing feedback after each iteration to the team reserving time to reflect on its performance through retrospectives after each iteration. Ongoing unit and integration testing and keeping up with technological/industry developments also play a part in the continuous improvement process. Continuous improvement is also a key principle in the lean methodology, where a focus of removing waste from the value stream is held. [The Art of Agile Development. James Shore.] [Knowledge and Skills: Level 2]

37. A - Release planning is important because the customer and development team collaborate to create a high-level plan for product release. User stories are initially defined during release planning. The release plan typically includes a schedule that includes several iterations and an estimate for when the product will be released. The development team discusses each user story in detail to, along with the customer, assign them to the project's iterations. [The Art of Agile Development. James Shore.] [Planning, monitoring, and adapting]

38. B - Building a high-performance team is critical to any project's success. A high performance team has the right team members, is empowered, has built trust, works at a sustainable pace, has consistently high velocity/productivity, takes regular time for reflection to review work, has a team lead that removes any obstacles and provides mentoring and coaching, is self-organized and self-disciplined, and is collocated. Several management techniques can be used to build or foster a high-performance team environment, some techniques include: removing obstacles that slow down a team's performance, having high expectations of team performance, and coaching and mentoring the team to achieve its best performance. [Coaching Agile Teams. Lyssa Adkins.] [Knowledge and Skills: Level 2]

39. B - Net Present Value: A metric used to analyze the profitability of an investment or project. NPV is the difference between the present value of cash inflows and the present value of cash outflows. NPV considers the likelihood of future cash inflows that an investment or project will yield. NPV is the sum of each cash inflow/outflow for the expected duration of the investment. Each cash inflow/outflow is discounted back to its present value (PV) (i.e.,, what the money is worth in terms of today's value). NPV is the sum of all terms: NPV = Sum of [Rt/(1 + i)^t] where t = the time of the cash flow, i = the discount rate (the rate of return that could be earned on in the financial markets) , and Rt = the net cash inflow or outflow. For example, consider the following two year period. The discount rate is 5% and the initial investment cost is $500. At the end of the first year, a $200 inflow is expected. At the end of the second year, a $1,000 is expected. NPV = -500 + 200/(1.05)^1 + 1000/(1.05)^2 = ~$597. If NPV is positive, it indicates that the investment will add value to the buyer's portfolio. If NPV is negative, it will subtract value. If NPV is zero, it will neither add or subtract value. [Agile Estimating and Planning. Mike Cohn.] [Value based prioritization]

40. A - Osmotic communication is a concept of communication where information is shared between collocated team members unconsciously. By sharing the same work environment, team members are exposed to the same environmental sounds and other environmental input and unconsciously share a common framework that improves communication. [Agile Software Development: The Cooperative Game – 2nd Edition. Alistair Cockburn.] [Communications]

Knowledge Area Quiz
Planning, Monitoring, and Adapting
Practice Questions

Test Name: Knowledge Area Test: Planning, Monitoring, and Adapting
Total Questions: 15
Correct Answers Needed to Pass:
11 (73.33%)
Time Allowed: 25 Minutes

Test Description

This practice quiz specifically targets your knowledge of the Planning, Monitoring, and Adapting exam topic area.

Test Questions

1. If a team has a velocity of 20 story points and there are 83 story points remaining in the backlog and excluding all other potential constraints like increased scope, how many iterations should it take for the project team to complete the remaining story points?

   A. 6

   83

   B. 3

   C. 5

   D. 4

2. When a user story is estimated to be 0 story points, what does it indicate?

   A. That the user story costs 0 points.

   B. That the user story has no value.

   C. That the user story is an impediment to progress.

   D. That the user story takes minimal effort to design, build, and test.

3. In scrum a change report is used to document a change in scope. When is a change report typically created?

   A. During release planning

   B. Immediately after any scope change

   C. After a sprint

   D. During sprint planning

4. What does WIP stand for?

   A. Work in product

   B. Work in production

   C. Work in process

   D. Work in places

5. When is acceptance criteria defined by the customer?

   A. Only during iteration planning.

   B. When a user story is picked for an iteration.

   C. After user story definition and before coding starts.

D. Only during release planning.

6. Greg is ready to select another task for execution in the current iteration. He reviews the task and realizes that the estimated time on the task card is most likely too low. What should Greg do?

A. Select a different user story

B. Remove the card from the task board and place it in the product backlog

C. Deal with the minor inconsistency in private and work overtime to keep the iteration on schedule

D. Update the time on the task card as soon as possible

7. What two artifacts are available to agile practitioners to summarize a release plan?

A. Product vision and project data sheet

B. Project parking lot and story card layout

C. Project charter and sprint change report

D. Product vision and project charter

8. What is one type of information radiator that a scrum master uses to track and monitor team progress?

A. RFID

B. Task board

C. Gantt chart

D. Work breakdown structure (WBS)

9. Which team member should lead or facilitate the sprint review?

A. Executive sponsor

B. External facilitator

C. Product owner

D. Scrum master

10. In the agile framework, what is blitz planning?

A. Blitz planning incorporates story dependencies and involves using cards to plan a project where timeline, tasks, and story dependencies are identified and considered.

B. Blitz planning incorporates randomizing pair programmers every iteration to promote cross-functional team development.

C. Blitz planning incorporates increasing user story WIP in an iteration to determine where natural bottlenecks occur so that the team may confront them in an upcoming retrospective.

D. Blitz planning incorporates overloading an iteration with 10% more user stories than the team's current estimated velocity in order to see if the team can reach new velocity levels. The blitz serves as a motivator for the team to improve performance.

11. What is the first step agile team's take during iteration planning?

A. Aggregating similar user stories into meta-stories.

B. Decomposing large or complex user stories into smaller, more manageable user stories.

C. Aggregating dissimilar user stories into meta-stories.

D. Refactoring testing code for the upcoming iteration

12. As a developer on the agile team, Greg is beginning development on a task. Greg is at the task board and must place the task card in the correct column of the task board to update everyone of its status. In which column should Greg place the task card?

A. To do

B. Ready for testing

C. Done

D. In progress

13. In general, how can story points and value points be considered?

A. Story points represent quality and value points represent value.

B. Story points represent cost and value points represent benefit.

C. Story points represent quality and value points represent benefit.

D. Story points represent story value and value points represent product value.

14. What technique can an agile project manager use for planning in complex projects?

A. Task board plan

B. Communication plan

C. Rolling wave or rolling look ahead plan

D. Work plan

15. As project manager, David needs to facilitate a release plan meeting. What should David share and discuss in detail with the project team?

A. The project vision

B. The release and iteration vision

C. The milestone exit criteria

D. The product vision

Knowledge Area Quiz Planning, Monitoring, and Adapting Answer Key and Explanations

1. C - 83/20=4.15. Round 4.15 up to 5. 5 iterations is the best answer. [Agile Estimating and Planning. Mike Cohn.] [Planning, monitoring, and adapting]

2. D - A 0 point user story is said to be of minimal effort for a development team. [Agile Estimating and Planning. Mike Cohn.] [Planning, monitoring, and adapting]

3. C - A change report is typically authored after a sprint has completed. [Agile Project Management with Scrum. Ken Schwaber.] [Planning, monitoring, and adapting]

4. C - A lean manufacturing philosophy is to eliminate waste. One defined waste type in the lean philosophy is inventory, which is also referred to as work in process (WIP). WIP is material or parts that have started production but are not yet a finished or "done" product. Inventory is considered wasteful because it costs money to purchase, store, and maintain. One way of reducing inventory is to reduce the WIP at individual machines or servers by only moving as fast as your slowest machine or processor (the system bottleneck). Agile also strives to control its WIP through WIP limits by completing all features to a "done" state before beginning development of new features. One can think of an iteration or sprint as a process that can develop a certain amount of features. In this analogy, the WIP limit is equivalent to the sprint backlog. By maintaining a WIP limit equal to the sprint backlog, no features should be incomplete at the sprint review. [Lean-Agile Software Development: Achieving Enterprise Agility. Alan Shalloway, Guy Beaver, James R. Trott.] [Planning, monitoring, and adapting]

5. C - Acceptance criteria is typically defined in tandem with user story definition during release planning; however, acceptance criteria can also be defined during iteration planning once a story has been picked for the iteration. The one steadfast rule is that acceptance criteria must be defined before development begins. Like agile planning, the definition of acceptance criteria is constantly evolving as the conversation with the product owner matures. [The Art of Agile Development. James Shore.] [Planning, monitoring, and adapting]

6. D - Agile team members should feel free to update incorrect task time estimates as soon as possible. Team members can use current iteration progress and accrued experience to come to a new task time estimate. [Lean-Agile Software Development: Achieving Enterprise Agility. Alan Shalloway, Guy Beaver, James R. Trott.] [Planning, monitoring, and adapting]

7. B - An agile practitioner can use the project parking lot and story card layout to summarize a release plan. [Agile Estimating and Planning. Mike Cohn.] [Planning, monitoring, and adapting]

8. B - An agile team often uses a task board to monitor and control progress. A task board identifies tasks to be completed during an iteration and their progress. [Lean-Agile Software Development: Achieving Enterprise Agility. Alan Shalloway, Guy Beaver, James R. Trott.] [Planning, monitoring, and adapting]

9. C - Because the product owner is responsible for ROI and has the most knowledge on what the complete objectives are for a product, the product owner should lead the sprint review. [Agile Project Management with Scrum. Ken Schwaber.] [Planning, monitoring, and adapting]

10. A - Blitz planning incorporates story dependencies and involves using cards to plan a project where timeline, tasks, and story dependencies are identified and considered. [Agile Software Development: The Cooperative Game – 2nd Edition. Alistair Cockburn.] [Planning, monitoring, and adapting]

11. B - During iteration planning, the team follows three steps to create an iteration backlog: 1) The team decomposes large or complex user stories into multiple, smaller stories, 2) The team breaks each user story into development tasks, and 3) The team estimates the task effort or duration, typically using ideal hours. [The Art of Agile Development. James Shore.] [Planning, monitoring, and adapting]

12. D - Greg should place the task card in the 'in progress' column to signify that the task is currently being executed. [Lean-Agile Software Development: Achieving Enterprise Agility. Alan Shalloway, Guy Beaver, James R. Trott.] [Planning, monitoring, and adapting]

13. B - In general, story points can be considered as the cost of developing a user story, while value points can be considered as the benefit of developing a user story. [Agile Estimating and Planning. Mike Cohn.] [Planning, monitoring, and adapting]

14. C - In large, complex projects, agile project leaders can facilitate iteration planning by using a rolling wave or rolling look ahead plan, which involves making plans for the next few iterations at a time. [Agile Estimating and Planning. Mike Cohn.] [Planning, monitoring, and adapting]

15. D - In release planning, the agile project manager discusses the product vision with the development team in detail. This ensures that the proper requirements, acceptance criteria, and priorities are established. [The Art of Agile Development. James Shore.] [Planning, monitoring, and adapting]

PMI-ACP Lite Mock Exam 5 Practice Questions

Test Name: PMI-ACP Lite Mock Exam 5
Total Questions: 40
Correct Answers Needed to Pass:
30 (75.00%)
Time Allowed: 60 Minutes

Test Description

This is a cumulative PMI-ACP Mock Exam which can be used as a benchmark for your PMI-ACP aptitude. This practice test includes questions from all exam topic areas, including sections from Agile Tools and Techniques, and all three Agile Knowledge and Skills areas.

Test Questions

1. Calculate the return on investment of the following: Gain: $30,000; Cost: $10,000.

A. 33%

B. 200%

C. 300%

D. -50%

2. How might an agile team continuously improve?

A. By isolating team members so that they may focus on developing code without interruption.

B. By reviewing customer feedback at the end of a project.

C. By using software techniques that are outdated but functional.

D. By keeping up with industry developments in technology.

3. For a new agile project team, what is a good next step for building a high performance team?

A. Immediately establishing a daily stand-up where team members are told their roles.

B. Holding a retrospective where the project leader can assign roles to team members.

C. Taking the team out for lunch so that members can get to know one another and establish trust.

D. Calling a meeting where the project leader can assign preliminary tasks to the team.

4. During the daily scrum, Joseph, the scrum master, notices that several team members are holding disruptive side conversations. What should Joseph do?

A. Bring up the issue in the project retrospective.

B. Extend the meeting to make up for lost time.

C. Trust that as a self-organizing team, it will notice the issue and correct the problem.

D. Cancel the meeting.

5. Select a method used in agile for the purpose of prioritization.

A. MoSCoW

B. Cano

C. WIDETOM

D. Cannon

6. Becky and her agile team have just performed decomposition on several user stories and wants to prioritize them. What common technique might she and her team use to prioritize the user stories?

A. Kano

B. Cano

C. Cannon

D. Agile

7. What is a typical scrum timebox value for a sprint review meeting?

A. 4 hours

B. 8 hours

C. 16 hours

D. 24 hours

8. What type of team uses collaboration to solve problems and decides on the path forward?

A. Honored team

B. Empowered team

C. Integrated team

D. Certified team

9. Ethan as project leader, has been discussing the importance of 'stakeholder management' with his team. Why is stakeholder management so important?

A. Chances of project success are inversely related to stakeholder involvement.

B. Chances of project success are independent of stakeholder involvement.

C. Chances of project success are greatly improved with engaged stakeholders.

D. Chances of project success are greatly reduced with engaged stakeholders.

10. The general translation of the lean term "Kaizen" is

A. Change through value stream mapping

B. Change though process improvement

C. Change for the better

D. Change through the elimination of waste

11. Of the following, which is NOT a phase of Highsmith's agile project management?

A. Exploring

B. Closing

C. Envisioning

D. Planning

12. Stella and her team are using a framework where the team follows a prescriptive development process that plans and manages from the perspective of the product features. Which framework is Stella's team incorporating into its agile effort?

A. Test driven development (TDD)

B. Defect driven development (3D)

C. Feature driven development (FDD)

D. Acceptance test driven development (ATDD)

13. Paul is explaining the agile project management method to his superiors. He must describe the phases of agile project management. Which response has the correct sequence of agile phases as typically introduced by Highsmith?

A. Closing, adapting, exploring, speculating, envisioning

B. Planning, executing, initiating, monitoring and controlling, closing

C. Envisioning, speculating, exploring, adapting, closing

D. Envisioning, exploring, speculating, adapting, closing

14. Select the response that has the traditional project management phases in the proper sequence (as typically introduced).

A. Initiating, planning, executing, monitoring and controlling, closing

B. Closing, planning, initiating, executing, monitoring and controlling

C. Initiating, planning, executing, closing, monitoring and controlling

D. Planning, executing, initiating, monitoring and controlling, closing

15. Bart is using a cost-to-value matrix technique to understand the value of each feature in the eyes of the customer. What is a cost-to-value matrix an example of?

A. An WIDETOM analysis technique

B. A priority-based analysis technique

C. A constraints-based analysis technique

D. A value-based analysis technique

16. Wendy is concerned with the recent stagnant performance of her agile team. She believes it to be highly capable but stuck in a rut. What agile knowledge and skill technique might Wendy consider?

A. Coaching and mechanizing

B. Crowdsourcing and mentoring

C. Symptom and solution

D. Coaching and mentoring

17. Peter is a project leader for an agile project. He makes sure that his team always has a non-threatening environment when it needs to brainstorm. The use of a non-threatening environment is a…

A. Facilitation method

B. Asymmetric method

C. Capitulation method

D. Prescriptive method

18. How are NPV and IRR similar?

A. Both are used as financial metrics.

B. Both are used as refactoring metrics.

C. Both are used as reflection metrics.

D. Both are used as sprint metrics.

19. From the following, select a technique that promotes agile 'knowledge sharing.'

A. Separation

B. Collocation

C. Isolation

D. Sequestering

20. When value stream mapping it is important to identify areas of waste that exist in the process. The pneumonic device WIDETOM may be used to remember the different forms of muda (or waste). What does the M in WIDETOM stand for with respect to waste?

A. Make-up WIP

B. Mirroring

C. Mistake

D. Motion

21. In agile, the "team space" is an important place that should foster effective communication. What is a guideline for promoting such an environment?

A. Space for daily stand-up meetings

B. Separation of team members by function

C. Isolation of team members

D. Rotation of team members

22. What is the process called when an agile team subdivides user stories into manageable tasks?

A. Sub-tasking

B. Sub-functioning

C. Decomposition

D. Subdivision

23. What is one piece of information a stakeholder can review using a risk-based burnup chart?

A. The amount of story points remaining to complete in an iteration.

B. The amount of remaining use stories to decompose in a release.

C. The amount of defects identified to date in a release.

D. The amount of story points that will be completed in a project in a worst-case scenario.

24. Terry is currently negotiating the type of contract for her agile project with the customer's financial representative. What types of contracts are suitable for agile efforts?

A. General service for the initial phase with fixed-price contracts for successive phases; fixed-price; not-to-exceed with fixed-fee

B. General service for the initial phase with fixed-price contracts for successive phases; cost-reimbursable/time and materials; not-to-exceed with fixed-fee

C. General service for the initial phase with fixed-price contracts for successive phases; cost-reimbursable/time and materials; fixed-price

D. Fixed-price; cost-reimbursable/time and materials; not-to-exceed with fixed-fee

25. Which of the following responses is NOT a community value per the PMI agile community of practice community charter?

A. Courage

B. Honesty

C. Confident

D. Collaboration

26. According to Highsmith and his definition of adaptive leadership, what is one item a project leader can focus on for "doing agile?"

A. Quality

B. Integrity

C. Value

D. Model

27. What information radiator, similar to a burnup chart, can be used on an agile project to show total scope of items in the backlog?

A. Total scope diagram

B. Cumulative flow diagram

C. Lean flow diagram

D. Total flow diagram

28. Kyle is using a popular agile framework that emphasizes the user of information radiators such as task boards and burndown charts and includes three major phases: pre-game, game, and post-game. Which framework is Kyle most likely using?

A. Lean

B. Crystal

C. Scrum

D. XP

29. From the following, select a technique that promotes agile 'knowledge sharing.'

A. Extreme programming, extreme rotation

B. Couple programming, couple rotation

C. Pare programming, pare rotation

D. Pair programming, pair rotation

30. What topic area within strategic management helps with the facilitation of a collaborative environment where stakeholders are heavily involved in a project?

A. Brainstorming management

B. Stakeholder management

C. Teamwork management

D. Collaborating management

31. Select the response that holds one of Ron Jeffries three Cs used to help define user stories.

A. Creative

B. Collaboration

C. Customer-oriented

D. Confirmation

32. Of the following responses, which is NOT a community value per the PMI agile community of practice community charter?

A. Collaboration

B. Honesty

C. Trust

D. Weary

33. What do the three Cs mean with respect to user stories?

A. Card, collaboration, conformance

B. Card, collaboration, confirmation

C. Card, conversation, confirmation

D. Collaboration, conformance, configurable

34. Which of the following responses is a community value per the PMI agile community of practice community charter?

A. Trust

B. Collected

C. Careful

D. Commandeering

35. Select the response that holds one of Ron Jeffries three Cs used to help define user stories.

A. Conversation

B. Collaboration

C. Collection

D. Customer-focused

36. Having a high emotional intelligence is important to promote effective communication in an agile team. What is one of the seven components of emotional intelligence as defined by Higgs & Dulewicz?

A. Competitiveness

B. Introversion

C. Intuitiveness

D. Self determination

37. Randy always likes to remind himself that the agile software project he is working on is like a CAS. What does CAS stand for?

A. Cost acquisition system

B. Complex adaptive system

C. Constructive adaptive simulation

D. Complex accrual system

38. Lisa is describing the four Agile Manifesto values to her co-workers. Which response lists one of its primary values?

A. Comprehensive documentation

B. Following a plan

C. Individuals and interactions

D. Contract negotiation

39. Which of the following is a key soft skill negotiation quality?

A. Conceding

B. Controlling

C. Collaboration

D. Compromise

40. Why does an agile practitioner during a stand-up meeting state current obstacles to project progress?

A. To update the obstacle information radiator.

B. To communicate with the team obstacles that collectively it may be able to resolve.

C. To provide rationale for project delays and false starts.

D. To place blame and let upper management know where inefficiencies exist.

PMI-ACP Lite Mock Exam 5 Answer Key and Explanations

1. B - Return on Investment (ROI): A metric used to evaluate the efficiency of an investment or to compare efficiency among a number of investments. To calculate ROI, the return of an investment (i.e., the gain minus the cost) is divided by the cost of the investment. The result is usually expressed as a percentage and sometimes a ratio. The product owner is often said to be responsible for the ROI. [Agile Estimating and Planning. Mike Cohn.] [Value based prioritization]

2. D - Agile project management places strong emphasis on 'continuous improvement.' Continuous improvement processes are built into the agile methodology, from customers providing feedback after each iteration to the team reserving time to reflect on its performance through retrospectives after each iteration. Ongoing unit and integration testing and keeping up with technological/industry developments also play a part in the continuous improvement process. Continuous improvement is also a key principle in the lean methodology, where a focus of removing waste from the value stream is held. [The Art of Agile Development. James Shore.] [Knowledge and Skills: Level 2]

3. C - The BEST answer is taking the team out to lunch for bonding and trust building. The other responses include behaviors atypical of a high performance team (i.e., project leader controlling and directing too much rather than letting the self-organizing team manage itself). [Agile Retrospectives: Making Good Teams Great. Esther Derby, Diana Larsen, Ken Schwaber.] [Knowledge and Skills: Level 2]

4. C - A high-performance, self-organizing team should realize and correct the disruptive behavior. [Coaching Agile Teams. Lyssa Adkins.] [Communications]

5. A - An agile team must always face the prioritization of product features in its product backlog. From release planning to iteration planning, an agile team must prioritize the user stories/ features of its product to ensure that high-quality and high-value features are developed first to help facilitate an optimized and early return on investment (ROI). An agile team typically prioritizes requirements or user stories/features in terms of relative value and risk; value is defined by the customer (i.e., customer-value prioritization). Two common methods to prioritize product features are: MoSCoW and Kano. The MoSCoW method categorizes features into 'Must have,' 'Should have,' 'Could have,' and 'Would have' features. The Kano method categorizes features into 'Must haves (threshold),' 'Dissatisfiers,' 'Satisfiers,' and 'Delighters.' Must haves are features that are requisite. Dissatisfiers are features that adversely impact perceived value and should be eliminated. 'Satisfiers' are features that increase perceived value linearly, where the more you add the more the customer is pleased, but are not required, and 'Delighters' are features that increase perceived value exponentially to please the customer. To prioritize features based on risk, a risk-to-value matrix can be used. A risk-to-value matrix has four quadrants, with the horizontal axis having low and high value, and the vertical axis having low and high risk. User stories are assigned to one of the four categories/quadrants: low-

value, low-risk; low-value, high-risk; high-value, low-risk; high-value, high-risk. A cost-to-value matrix can also be made in this manner. All prioritization in agile is 'relative,' meaning that the priority of one user story is relative to other user stories and not prioritized on a fixed scale. [Lean-Agile Software Development: Achieving Enterprise Agility. Alan Shalloway, Guy Beaver, James R. Trott.] [Knowledge and Skills: Level 1]

6. A - In iteration planning, an agile team, collaboratively with the customer, chooses user stories to include for development. Although the user stories are prioritized in the product backlog initially during release planning, an agile team and customer should review prioritization based on progressive elaboration (i.e., gained knowledge and perspective). Prioritization is often based on value and risk and can be performed using the MoSCoW or Kano method and through the use of risk-to-value and cost-to-value matrices. An agile team performs decomposition to sub-divide user stories into more manageable tasks so that it may estimate task time. Tasks for an iteration may also be prioritized based on value, similar to how user stories are prioritized. [Lean-Agile Software Development: Achieving Enterprise Agility. Alan Shalloway, Guy Beaver, James R. Trott.] [Knowledge and Skills: Level 1]

7. A - In the agile framework scrum, sprint planning and sprint review meetings are often timeboxed at four hours. [The Art of Agile Development. James Shore.] [Planning, monitoring, and adapting]

8. B - Empowered teams - ones that are self-organizing and know how to solve problems with minimal management involvement - are a cornerstone of the agile methodology. This is the antithesis to the classic viewpoint of the traditional project manager who is seen as someone that controls all decisions and delegates tasks to a team with little feedback. An agile team must include all members and stakeholders to make decisions, and make decisions expediently. Because it is essential that the user/customer be involved with development, it is encouraged that the user/customer is closely integrated with the agile team with collocation/on-site support being ideal. An agile team feels empowered when it collectively assumes responsibility for the delivery of the product (i.e., taking ownership). [Coaching Agile Teams. Lyssa Adkins.] [Knowledge and Skills: Level 1]

9. C - Stakeholder management is a growing topic area within strategic management that brings awareness to the importance of managing stakeholders (i.e., facilitating active participation of stakeholders and fostering a strong collaborative environment) for a project's success. Stakeholder management is typically defined in the context of guiding principles and values. R. E. Freeman's 'Managing for Stakeholders' includes 10 principles: 1) Stakeholder interests need to go together over time. 2) We need a philosophy of volunteerism – to engage stakeholders and manage relationships ourselves rather than leave it to government. 3) We need to find solutions to issues that satisfy multiple stakeholders simultaneously. 4) Everything that we do serves stakeholders. We never trade off the interests of one versus the other continuously over time. 5) We act with purpose that fulfills our commitment to stakeholders. We act with aspiration towards fulfilling our dreams and theirs. 6)

We need intensive communication and dialogue with stakeholders – not just those who are friendly. 7)Stakeholders consist of real people with names and faces and children. They are complex. 8)We need to generalize the marketing approach. 9) We engage with both primary and secondary stakeholders. 10) We constantly monitor and redesign processes to make them better serve our stakeholders. Because stakeholder involvement is critical for the success of a project, where projects without active participation from stakeholders are prone to failure, stakeholder management should be a topic that every agile team knows well. [The Art of Agile Development. James Shore.] [Knowledge and Skills: Level 1]

10. C - The Japanese word "kaizen" means change for the better. [Lean-Agile Software Development: Achieving Enterprise Agility. Alan Shalloway, Guy Beaver, James R. Trott.] [Knowledge and Skills: Level 2]

11. D - The agile project management phases, in sequence, are: Envisioning, speculating, exploring, adapting, closing. [Manifesto for Agile Software Development. Agile Alliance.] [Knowledge and Skills: Level 1]

12. C - Feature driven development (FDD) uses a prescriptive model where the software development process is planned, managed, and tracked from the perspective of individual software features. FDD uses short iterations of two weeks or less to develop a set amount of features. The five step FDD process is: 1. Develop overall model; 2. Create the features list; 3. Plan by feature; 4. Design by feature; 5 Build by feature. [Agile Software Development: The Cooperative Game – 2nd Edition. Alistair Cockburn.] [Knowledge and Skills: Level 2]

13. C - The agile project management phases, in sequence of introduction, are: Envisioning, speculating, exploring, adapting, closing. It is important to note that these phases can occur simultaneously and iteratively. [Agile Project Management: Creating Innovative Products – 2nd Edition. Jim Highsmith.] [Knowledge and Skills: Level 1]

14. A - The traditional project management phases are typically introduced in the following sequence: Initiating, planning, executing, monitoring and controlling, and closing. It is important to note that monitoring and controlling happen concurrently and throughout the project life-cycle with other phases. [Agile Project Management: Creating Innovative Products – 2nd Edition. Jim Highsmith.] [Knowledge and Skills: Level 1]

15. D - Value-based analysis strives to understand how value, as defined by the customer, relates to various components of the product, like features and tasks. Features are often prioritized with prioritization based on value and risk. Prioritization can be performed using the MoSCoW or Kano method and through the use of risk-to-value and cost-to-value matrices. [Lean-Agile Software Development: Achieving Enterprise Agility. Alan Shalloway, Guy Beaver, James R. Trott.] [Knowledge and Skills: Level 2]

16. D - Coaching and mentoring within teams can be helpful for nascent agile teams and even for more experienced agile teams. Coaching and mentoring is the act of helping a person or team improve performance and achieve realistic goals. Because agile has a value of continuous improvement, coaching and mentoring is not solely for new or immature teams, but experienced ones too where coaching can help achieve higher levels of performance. The amount of coaching and mentoring an agile team needs is variable. Some newer teams will need a coach guiding the team nearly all the time while others may need a coach only for particularly challenging situations. A not uncommon scenario is to have a coach help the team collectively during sprint/iteration planning and then during the iteration help mentor individual team members. [Coaching Agile Teams. Lyssa Adkins.] [Knowledge and Skills: Level 1]

17. A - As a project leader or scrum master, effective facilitation methods are critical for building a high-performance and motivated team. Facilitation of meetings, discussions, demonstrations, etc., is a constant on an agile project. Some general facilitation methods include: using a small number of people for brainstorming events; hosting events in a non-threatening/comfortable environment; having an agenda that is shared with the group ahead of time; using open-ended questions instead of closed-ended questions; including a diverse representation to gain a broader perspective of the topic. [Agile Retrospectives: Making Good Teams Great. Esther Derby, Diana Larsen, Ken Schwaber.] [Knowledge and Skills: Level 2]

18. A - The internal rate of return (IRR) is a financial metric used to measure and compare the profitability of investments. The IRR is the "rate" that makes the net present value of all cash flows from a particular investment equal to zero. Unlike NPV which is a dollar amount (i.e., a magnitude) value, the IRR is a rate (i.e.,, a percentage). Often times, the IRR is compared against a threshold rate value to determine if the investment is a suitable risk worth implementing. For example, you might calculate an IRR to be 13% for an investment while a comparative market rate is 2%. The IRR being larger than the comparative market rate, would indicate the investment is worth pursuing. [Agile Estimating and Planning. Mike Cohn.] [Value based prioritization]

19. B - In agile, effective 'knowledge sharing' is a critical factor for success. It involves the near real time communication of key information among all team members and stakeholders. To promote knowledge sharing, agile uses standard practices built into its process, such as using generalized specialists/cross functional teams, self-organizing and self-disciplined teams, collocation, daily stand-up meetings, iteration/sprint planning, release planning, pair programming and pair rotation, project retrospectives/reflection, and on-site customer support. And, of course, the sixth principle of Agile is " The most efficient and effective method of conveying information to and within a development team is face-to-face conversation." In this sense, Agile prefers and encourages collocation for all stakeholders and team members for the simple fact that face-to-face conversation is the best method of communication and, in turn, effective knowledge sharing. [Becoming Agile: ...in an imperfect world. Greg Smith, Ahmed Sidky.] [Knowledge and Skills: Level 1]

20. D - Value stream mapping is a lean manufacturing analysis technique adopted by agile. A value stream map may be used to analyze the flow of information or materials from origin to destination to identify areas of waste. The identified areas of waste are opportunities for process improvement. Waste can take many forms and can be remembered using the pneumonic device WIDETOM. W - waiting; I - inventory; D - defects; E - extra processing; T - transportation; O - over-production ; M - Motion. A value stream map is typically mapped or charted collaboratively with a team so it may define and view the entire process together, pinpointing areas of waste within the process. Processes that add value (processing of a part or feature) are generally referred to as "value-added" and processes that do not (e.g., waiting for a part to arrive) are generally referred to as "non value-added." Generally speaking, one wants to reduce, to the largest extent possible, the non value-added time (i.e., areas of waste). [Lean-Agile Software Development: Achieving Enterprise Agility. Alan Shalloway, Guy Beaver, James R. Trott.] [Value stream analysis]

21. A - A warm, welcoming environment that promotes effective communication, innovation, and motivated team members is an important aspect to consider when designing team space. Guidelines for a better agile team space include: collocation of team members; reduction of non-essential noise/distractions; dedicated whiteboard and wall space for information radiators; space for the daily stand-up meeting and other meetings; pairing workstations; and other pleasantries like plants and comfortable furniture. [Agile Retrospectives: Making Good Teams Great. Esther Derby, Diana Larsen, Ken Schwaber.] [Communications]

22. C - In iteration planning, an agile team, collaboratively with the customer, chooses user stories to include for development. Although the user stories are prioritized in the product backlog initially during release planning, an agile team and customer should review prioritization based on progressive elaboration (i.e., gained knowledge and perspective). Prioritization is often based on value and risk and can be performed using the MoSCoW or Kano method and through the use of risk-to-value and cost-to-value matrices. An agile team performs decomposition to sub-divide user stories into more manageable tasks so that it may estimate task time. Tasks for an iteration may also be prioritized based on value, similar to how user stories are prioritized. [Lean-Agile Software Development: Achieving Enterprise Agility. Alan Shalloway, Guy Beaver, James R. Trott.] [Knowledge and Skills: Level 1]

23. D - A risk-based burnup chart tracks targeted and actual product delivery progress and also includes estimates of how likely the team is to achieve targeted value adjusted for risk. Typically, risk is shown as three different levels: best-case; most likely; and worst-case. For example, if you have a 10 iteration project and the team's current velocity is 10 story points, you can portray the chance of completing 100 story points (most likely case), the chance of completing 80 story points (worst-case), and the chance of completing 120 story points (best-case). In this way, the stakeholders get a feel for the range of risk. [The Art of Agile Development. James Shore.] [Risk management]

24. B - Fixed-price contracts, although typical of traditional projects where scope is defined ahead of time, are not well suited for agile. When scope is fixed it can deter a team from exploring out-of-scope solutions that may add value to the product. Contracts suited for agile include: general service for the initial phase with fixed-price contracts for successive phases; cost-reimbursable/time and materials; not-to-exceed with fixed-fee; and a combination with incentives. [Agile Software Development: The Cooperative Game – 2nd Edition. Alistair Cockburn.] [Knowledge and Skills: Level 3]

25. C - The following are community values of the PMI agile community of practice community charter: Vision, Servant Leadership, Trust, Collaboration, Honesty, Learning, Courage, Openness, Adaptability, Leading Change, Transparency [PMI Agile Community of Practice Community Charter. Project Management Institute.] [Knowledge and Skills: Level 1]

26. A - Highsmith defines adaptive leadership as two dimensional: Being agile and doing agile. Being agile includes focusing on cornerstones of agile project management, like incremental delivery, continuous integration, and adapting to changing requirements. Doing agile includes several activities that an agile leader must do: do less; speed-to-value, quality, and engage and inspire. [Agile Project Management: Creating Innovative Products – 2nd Edition. Jim Highsmith.] [Soft skills negotiation]

27. B - Like burnup charts, cumulative flow diagrams are information radiators that can track progress for agile projects. CFDs differ from traditional burnup charts because they convey total scope (not started, started, completed) of the entire backlog. Tracked items can be features, stories, tasks, or use cases. By tracking total scope, CFDs communicate absolute progress and give a proportional sense of project progress (e.g., On Day 14: 15% of features have been completed; 15% have been started; and, 70% have not been started). [Lean-Agile Software Development: Achieving Enterprise Agility. Alan Shalloway, Guy Beaver, James R. Trott.] [Planning, monitoring, and adapting]

28. C - Scrum is a framework that strives to facilitate the development of complex products quickly and efficiently, the adaptation of changing requirements, the delivery of working products incrementally. Scrum development includes three major phases: pre-game, game, and post-game. Scrum emphasizes the use of product and sprint backlogs, iterative development (termed "sprints"), daily stand-up meetings (termed "scrums"), sprint reviews (demos) and reflection, and the use of information radiators such as task boards and burndown charts. [Ken Schwaber. Agile Project Management with Scrum. Chapter 1.] [Knowledge and Skills: Level 2]

29. D - In agile, effective 'knowledge sharing' is a critical factor for success. It involves the near real time communication of key information among all team members and stakeholders. To promote knowledge sharing, agile uses standard practices built into its process, such as using generalized specialists/cross functional teams, self-organizing and self-disciplined teams, collocation, daily stand-up meetings, iteration/sprint planning, release planning, pair programming and pair rotation, project retrospectives/reflection, and on-site customer support. And, of course, the sixth principle of Agile is " The most efficient and effective method of conveying information to and within a development team is face-to-face conversation." In this sense, Agile prefers and encourages collocation for all stakeholders and team members for the simple fact that face-to-face conversation is the best method of communication and, in turn, effective knowledge sharing. [Becoming Agile: ...in an imperfect world. Greg Smith, Ahmed Sidky.] [Knowledge and Skills: Level 1]

30. B - Stakeholder management is a growing topic area within strategic management that brings awareness to the importance of managing stakeholders (i.e., facilitating active participation of stakeholders and fostering a strong collaborative environment) for a project's success. Stakeholder management is typically defined in the context of guiding principles and values. R. E. Freeman's 'Managing for Stakeholders' includes 10 principles: 1) Stakeholder interests need to go together over time. 2) We need a philosophy of volunteerism – to engage stakeholders and manage relationships ourselves rather than leave it to government. 3) We need to find solutions to issues that satisfy multiple stakeholders simultaneously. 4) Everything that we do serves stakeholders. We never trade off the interests of one versus the other continuously over time. 5) We act with purpose that fulfills our commitment to stakeholders. We act with aspiration towards fulfilling our dreams and theirs. 6) We need intensive communication and dialogue with stakeholders – not just those who are friendly. 7)Stakeholders consist of real people with names and faces and children. They are complex. 8)We need to generalize the marketing approach. 9) We engage with both primary and secondary stakeholders. 10) We constantly monitor and redesign processes to make them better serve our stakeholders. Because stakeholder involvement is critical for the success of a project, where projects without active participation from stakeholders are prone to failure, stakeholder management should be a topic that every agile team knows well. [The Art of Agile Development. James Shore.] [Knowledge and Skills: Level 1]

31. D - Ron Jeffries' three Cs for user story definition are card, conversation, confirmation. [User Stories Applied: For Agile Software Development. Mike Cohn.] [Planning, monitoring, and adapting]

32. D - The following are community values of the PMI agile community of practice community charter: Vision, Servant Leadership, Trust, Collaboration, Honesty, Learning, Courage, Openness, Adaptability, Leading Change, Transparency [PMI Agile Community of Practice Community Charter. Project Management Institute.] [Knowledge and Skills: Level 1]

33. C - Ron Jeffries' three Cs for user story definition are card, conversation, confirmation. [User Stories Applied: For Agile Software Development. Mike Cohn.] [Planning, monitoring, and adapting]

34. A - The following are community values of the PMI agile community of practice community charter: Vision, Servant Leadership, Trust, Collaboration, Honesty, Learning, Courage, Openness, Adaptability, Leading Change, Transparency [PMI Agile Community of Practice Community Charter. Project Management Institute.] [Knowledge and Skills: Level 1]

35. A - Ron Jeffries' three Cs for user story definition are card, conversation, confirmation. [User Stories Applied: For

Agile Software Development. Mike Cohn.] [Planning, monitoring, and adapting]

36. C - Higgs & Dulewicz (1999) defines emotional intelligence using seven components: 1) Self-awareness, 2) Emotional resilience, 3) Motivation, 4) Interpersonal sensitivity, 5) Influence, 6) Intuitiveness, and 7) Conscientiousness. [Coaching Agile Teams. Lyssa Adkins.] [Soft skills negotiation]

37. B - A complex adaptive system, or CAS, is a system composed of interacting, adaptive agents or components. The term is used in agile to remind practitioners that the development of a product is adaptive in that previous interactions, events, decisions influence future behavior. The term chaordic (a made up word blending chaotic and order) is sometimes used when describing CASs. Literature points to three key characteristics of chaordic projects: alignment and cooperation, emergence and self-organization, and learning and adaptation. [Agile Project Management: Creating Innovative Products – 2nd Edition. Jim Highsmith.] [Knowledge and Skills: Level 3]

38. C - The Agile Manifesto defines four values. The four values list primary values and secondary values, with primary values superseding secondary values. The values are 1) individuals and interactions over processes and tools, 2) working software over comprehensive documentation, 3) customer collaboration over contract negotiation, and 4) responding to change over following a plan. [Manifesto for Agile Software Development. Agile Alliance.] [Knowledge and Skills: Level 1]

39. C - Key soft skills negotiation qualities for the effective implementation and practice of agile are: emotional intelligence, collaboration, adaptive leadership, negotiation, conflict resolution, servant leadership. [Coaching Agile Teams. Lyssa Adkins.] [Soft skills negotiation]

40. B - The key characteristics of a healthy stand-up meeting include: peer pressure - the team is dependent upon each other so expectations of peers drives progress; fine-grained coordination - the team should understand the necessity for focus and working dependently; fine focus - the team should understand the need for brevity in the stand-up meeting so the team can be productive; daily commitment - the team should understand the value of daily commitments to each other and uphold those commitments; identification of obstacles - the team collectively should be aware of each other's obstacles so that the team collectively can try to resolve them. [The Art of Agile Development. James Shore.] [Communications]

PMI-ACP Lite Mock Exam 6 Practice Questions

Test Name: PMI-ACP Lite Mock Exam 6
Total Questions: 40
Correct Answers Needed to Pass:
30 (75.00%)
Time Allowed: 60 Minutes

Test Description

This is a cumulative PMI-ACP Mock Exam which can be used as a benchmark for your PMI-ACP aptitude. This practice test includes questions from all exam topic areas, including sections from Agile Tools and Techniques, and all three Agile Knowledge and Skills areas.

Test Questions

1. Xavier has just written production code and applied a test as part of the four step process of TDD. What step is Xavier performing?

A. 2nd

B. 1st

C. 4th

D. 3rd

2. Select the response that lists one of the five core risk areas that can impact a project.

A. Personnel loss

B. Configuration management

C. Release management

D. Version management

3. In agile, a business case should include which of the following topics?

A. Milestones

B. Work breakdown structure

C. Product version

D. Configuration plan

4. During the exploring phase of Highsmith's agile project management model, what goals do agile project leaders have?

A. Configuring unit testing plans

B. Helping developers to overcome obstacles, managing team interactions with product owners, customers, and stakeholders

C. Authoring feature breakdown documentation

D. Measuring task progress against task schedule

5. Pick the response which is NOT a characteristic of the agile verification process.

A. Confirms the product meets specifications and requirements.

B. Helps ensure quality.

C. Confirms the product meets user needs.

D. Performed frequently.

6. When using three-sigma as a control limit range, what characteristic must the underlying data have?

A. A normal distribution

B. A sigma distribution

C. A skewed distribution

D. A theta distribution

7. Select from the following a key soft skill negotiation quality.

A. Conflict assessment

B. Conflict identification

C. Conflict resolution

D. Conflict validation

8. In planning poker, a modified Fibonacci sequence is often used for the playing card values. Which of the following sequences is the beginning of the modified Fibonacci sequence used for planning poker?

A. 1, 3, 5, 7, 9, 11, 13

B. 0, 1, 2, 3, 5, 8, 13

C. 0, 3, 7, 11, 15, 17, 21

D. 0, 1, 1, 2, 4, 8, 16

9. Michael, in his review of estimated user story points for the upcoming iteration, finds that the project manager is artificially inflating the user story points to significantly lengthen the project period of performance in order to increase project revenue. It is a time and material contract and lengthening the period of performance would help boost Michael's parent company's profit. What should Michael do?

A. Confront the customer representative.

B. Confront Michael's project manager's boss.

C. Report the unethical and illegal conduct to the appropriate parties.

D. Confront his project manager.

10. Which of the following is a key soft skill negotiation quality?

A. Adaptive leadership

B. Agile leadership

C. Constant leadership

D. Collaborative leadership

11. What typically occurs directly after an agile team and product owner build an initial product roadmap?

A. Release planning.

B. Definition of the product vision

C. Exploratory 360.

D. Iteration planning

12. You are working on an agile team that's developing software for a major shipping company. The team has just entered Highsmith's agile project management speculation phase after completing the envisioning phase. In addition to estimating project costs, what else should be considered?

A. Project risk and accompanying mitigation strategies

B. Project schedule

C. Constraints and quality drivers

D. Project vision and scope

13. Select the response that best defines progressive elaboration.

A. Continuous planning with the expectation that velocity will increase progressively as the project progresses.

B. Continuous planning with the expectation that story point values will decrease in relation to the steep learning curve of developers.

C. Continuous planning with the expectation that plans and details will inevitably change but become more refined as the project progresses.

D. Continuous planning with the expectation that estimates of task time will become more progressive as the project evolves.

14. Lisa is describing the four Agile Manifesto values to her co-workers. Of the following, which response lists one of its primary values?

A. Comprehensive documentation

B. Processes and tools

C. Responding to change

D. Contract negotiation

15. Of the following, which is NOT a secondary agile value per the Agile Manifesto?

A. Appropriate processes and tools aid the development process

B. Documentation supports working software and appropriate processes and tools aid the development process

C. Products work as intended because of frequent delivery iterations

D. Contracts need to be negotiated and plans followed

16. How do actors - of use case modeling - and personas - of agile modeling - differ?

A. There is no difference.

B. Actor descriptions will use photographs to provide further context and define several different people for one type of user, whereas persona descriptions typically are generic and concise.

C. Actor descriptions are typically much more detailed than persona descriptions.

D. Persona descriptions will use photographs to provide further context and define several different people for one type of user, whereas actor descriptions typically are generic and concise.

17. While Bernard is discussing to Stephanie his take on the most prominent risks the project is facing, Stephanie paraphrases what Bernard is saying to confirm her interpretation. What type of listening technique is Lisa using?

A. Serial

B. Cooperative

C. Active

D. Collaborative

18. What can an agile team do to foster an innovative, collaborative, and comfortable team space?

A. Seat by team member function

B. Have plants, natural lighting, and comfortable seating available

C. Have yearly, individual performance reviews

D. Minimize team member interaction

19. EVM is a frequently used project management abbreviation. What does CPI stand for in the EVM technique?

A. Cost performance index

B. Correlated performance indicator

C. Cost performance indicator

D. Cost parametric index

20. Select the response that defines an information radiator.

A. Raw data organized into information to show data access and modification dates.

B. A highly detailed section of the agile project management waterfall plan.

C. A schema for organizing information into related datum.

D. A visual representation of project-related data to illustrate project status.

21. Select the response that lists one of the five core risk areas that can impact a project.

A. Productivity variation

B. Cost variation

C. Budget variation

D. Schedule variation

22. Erica is working for a kitchen tools manufacturing project, which is intended to make modern cooking ovens. This project is very important for the company as well as for Erica's career. In an effort to articulate agile best practices to upper management, which three parameters of the agile triangle will Erica emphasize?

A. Value, cost, constraints

B. Schedule, scope, constraints

C. Value, quality, constraints

D. Cost, quality, value

23. EVM is a frequently used project management abbreviation. What does AC stand for in the EVM technique?

A. Actual cost

B. Average cost

C. Analysis cost

D. Abbreviated cost

24. Select a method that is commonly used to help prioritize user stories.

A. Cost-to-schedule matrix

B. Cost-to-value matrix

C. Cost-to-constraint matrix

D. Cost-to-risk matrix

25. Why is an empowered team considered an important team attribute in agile?

A. Empowered teams take responsibility of the product and thus have a strong focus on delivering value.

B. Empowered teams remove themselves from being responsible of product quality in order to reduce association with project failure.

C. Empowered teams need extensive management involvement in order to understand customer need

D. Empowered teams adapt slowly to changing requirements and therefore can reduce scope-creep risk.

26. What is one method that can be used to improve communication for a team that cannot be collocated?

A. Setting up an e-mail distribution list

B. Setting up an internal memorandum system

C. Setting up a virtual team room

D. Setting up a fax machine system

27. What person in the agile framework "empowers the team to be self-organized and self-disciplined?"

A. Customer

B. Business analyst

C. Product owner

D. Project leader

28. Select a technique that promotes agile 'knowledge sharing.'

A. Couple programming

B. Pare programming

C. Pair programming

D. Duo programming

29. EVM is a frequently used project management abbreviation. How is SV calculated?

A. SV = EV - PV

B. SV = BAC - AC

C. SV = PV - EV

D. SV = BAC - PV

30. Of the following responses, which is NOT a community value per the PMI agile community of practice community charter?

A. Courage

B. Humble

C. Openness

D. Honesty

31. Which of the following is the best definition of value-based decomposition and prioritization?

A. The decomposition of iterations into intervals that are in turn prioritized by value.

B. The decomposition of story points into intervals that are in turn prioritized by value.

C. The decomposition of user stories into tasks that are in turn prioritized by value.

D. The decomposition of release plans into intervals that are in turn prioritized by value.

32. Select the response that holds one of Ron Jeffries three Cs used to help define user stories.

A. Collaboration

B. Card

C. Creative

D. Customer-driven

33. Of the three project buffer methods - square root of the sum of squares, critical chain project management method (CCPM), and halving the sum of most likely estimates - which typically provides the most adequate buffer

A. Square root of the sum of squares

B. Square of the sum of squares

C. Critical chain project management method (CCPM)

D. Halving the sum of most likely estimates

34. Jules, as an agile mentor, has been encouraging the team to spend some quality time together to build a sense of community. What is Jules doing when he provides this mentoring?

A. Motivating the team

B. Criticizing the team

C. Restructuring the team

D. Working the team

35. What agile estimation technique is sometimes conducted in silence and particularly useful for quickly estimating the relative work effort of large product backlogs?

A. Affinity estimating

B. Planning game

C. Planning poker

D. SMART

36. User stories are a common artifact across many agile frameworks. Which framework can generally be credited with their origin?

A. Crystal

B. FDD

C. Scrum

D. XP

37. Of the following responses, which is a community value per the PMI agile community of practice community charter?

A. Hasty

B. Servant Leadership

C. Curt

D. Motivating

38. Which of the following is an agile principle per the Agile Manifesto?

A. Individuals and interactions

B. Customer collaboration

C. Responding to change

D. Using working software as the primary measure of progress.

39. Lisa is describing the four Agile Manifesto values to her co-workers. Of the following, which response lists a secondary value?

A. Working software

B. Customer collaboration

C. Responding to change

D. Contract negotiation

40. Which of the following responses is NOT an Agile Manifesto value or principle regarding communication?

A. Face-to-face communication whenever possible

B. Delivering working software frequently

C. Customer collaboration over contract negotiation

D. Individuals and interactions over processes and tools

PMI-ACP Lite Mock Exam 6 Answer Key and Explanations

1. D - The TDD process has four basic steps: 1) Write a test, 2) Verify and validate the test, 3) Write product code and apply the test, 4) Refactor the product code. An example may be that a user has to enter an age value. A good test is to make sure the user data entry is a positive number and not a different type of input, like a letter (i.e., write the test). The programmer would verify that entering a letter instead of a number would cause the program to cause an exception (i.e., v&v the test). The programmer would then write product code that takes user entry for the age value (i.e., write the product code). The programmer would then run the product code and enter correct age values and incorrect age values (i.e., apply the test). If the product code is successful, the programmer would refactor the product code to improve its design. Using these four steps iteratively ensures that programmers think about how a software program might fail first and to build product code that is holistically being tested. This helps produce high quality code. [The Art of Agile Development. James Shore.] [Product quality]

2. A - The five core risk areas include: productivity variation (difference between planned and actual performance); scope creep (considerable additional requirements beyond initial agreement); specification breakdown (lack of stakeholder consensus on requirements); intrinsic schedule flaw (poor estimates of task durations), personnel loss (the loss of human resources). [The Software Project Manager's Bridge to Agility. Michele Sliger, Stacia Broderick.] [Risk management]

3. A - Business case development is an important initial step in agile project management. The business case is a concise document that outlines the project's vision, goals, strategies for achieving goals, milestones, required investment and expected return/payback. A business case articulates the why and how a project will deliver value to a customer. [Lean-Agile Software Development: Achieving Enterprise Agility. Alan Shalloway, Guy Beaver, James R. Trott.] [Knowledge and Skills: Level 2]

4. B - When conducting the exploring phase, project leaders assist developers by removing any obstacles or constraints that my impeded progress, and managing interaction with product owners, customers, and other stakeholders. [Agile Project Management: Creating Innovative Products – 2nd Edition. Jim Highsmith.] [Knowledge and Skills: Level 1]

5. C - Because each iteration typically produces a working product that is built and integrated and iterations are typically two to four weeks in length, there is frequent verification and validation to ensure product quality. Verification is the confirmation that a product performs as specified by a customer (e.g. as indicated by a user story) and validation is the confirmation that a product behaves as desired (i.e., meets the customer's need). Sometimes a product may be built and integrated to specification - that is, it can be verified - but it does not meet the intent of the customer - that is, it cannot be validated. [Agile Software Development: The

Cooperative Game – 2nd Edition. Alistair Cockburn.] [Product quality]

6. A - Control limits - those which set an objective range to indicate whether a process is controlled or stabilized or defect free (e.g., within three sigmas of the mean) - may be used in an agile project. Generally, a control limit of three-sigma (s) is used on a Shewhart control chart. A sigma refers to one standard deviation. So three sigmas indicates a limit three standard deviations away from the mean in both the positive and negative direction. This applies to normal data, where a normal distribution curve has been obtained. [Lean-Agile Software Development: Achieving Enterprise Agility. Alan Shalloway, Guy Beaver, James R. Trott.] [Knowledge and Skills: Level 3]

7. C - Key soft skills negotiation qualities for the effective implementation and practice of agile are: emotional intelligence, collaboration, adaptive leadership, negotiation, conflict resolution, servant leadership. [Coaching Agile Teams. Lyssa Adkins.] [Soft skills negotiation]

8. B - The Fibonacci sequence begins with 0 and 1 and every successive number is the sum of the previous two numbers. Therefore the Fibonacci sequence begins 0, 1, 1, 2, 3, 5, 8, 13, etc. In planning poker, a 1 is removed because it is redundant. [Agile Estimating and Planning. Mike Cohn.] [Agile estimation]

9. C - The PMI Code of Ethics and Professional Conduct states that it is mandatory for a project manager to: inform yourself about and uphold the policies, rules, regulations, and laws that govern your work, including professional and volunteer activities; report unethical or illegal conduct to appropriate parties and, if necessary, to those affected by the misconduct; ensure that any allegations of misconduct or illegal activity are substantiated and file only complaints that are supported by facts; never take part or help someone else take part in illegal activities. [PMI Code of Ethics and Professional Conduct. Project Management Institute.] [Knowledge and Skills: Level 2]

10. A - Key soft skills negotiation qualities for the effective implementation and practice of agile are: emotional intelligence, collaboration, adaptive leadership, negotiation, conflict resolution, servant leadership. [Coaching Agile Teams. Lyssa Adkins.] [Soft skills negotiation]

11. A - The product roadmap - owned by the product owner - serves as a high level overview of the product requirements. It is used as a tool for prioritizing features , organizing features into categories, and assigning rough time frames. Creating a product roadmap has four basic steps: 1) Identify requirements (these will become part of the product backlog), 2) Organize requirements into categories or themes, 3) Estimate relative work effort (e.g., planning poker or affinity estimation) and prioritize (value), and 4) Estimate rough time frames (estimate velocity, sprint duration, and rough release dates). [The Art of Agile Development. James Shore.] [Agile analysis and design]

12. A - The focus in the speculation phase is on estimating iteration and release plans, defining feature breakdown, developing a rough project plan, considering project risk and risk mitigation strategies, and estimating project costs. [Agile Project

Management: Creating Innovative Products – 2nd Edition. Jim Highsmith.] [Knowledge and Skills: Level 1]

13. C - Progressive elaboration is continuous planning with the expectation that project plans and details will change but become more refined as the project progresses. [Agile Estimating and Planning. Mike Cohn.] [Agile analysis and design]

14. C - The Agile Manifesto defines four values. The four values list primary values and secondary values, with primary values superseding secondary values. The values are 1) individuals and interactions over processes and tools, 2) working software over comprehensive documentation, 3) customer collaboration over contract negotiation, and 4) responding to change over following a plan. [Manifesto for Agile Software Development. Agile Alliance.] [Knowledge and Skills: Level 1]

15. C - The agile secondary values include: documentation of software, processes and tools, contract negotiation, and following project plans. [Manifesto for Agile Software Development. Agile Alliance.] [Knowledge and Skills: Level 1]

16. D - A persona is a notional user of the system under development. Being much more detailed than actors in use case modeling where generic user names are assigned (e.g., end user), personas try to elaborate on users with detailed descriptions to provide context to the developers. Some personas have such notional details as name, address, age, income, likes and dislikes, and other specific details. [User Stories Applied: For Agile Software Development. Mike Cohn.] [Agile analysis and design]

17. C - One communication technique to reduce misunderstanding and miscommunication is active listening. A well run agile project necessitates both good listeners and communicators, active listening helps work towards both of these necessities. The basics of active listening include: 1) Being present and focusing your attention on the speaker. 2) Taking notes instead of interrupting. 3) Paraphrasing to confirm and review what you have heard. 4) Summarizing the conversation once it has concluded for posterity. Using open ended questions, good body language, and silence can help improve listening skills. [Coaching Agile Teams. Lyssa Adkins.] [Knowledge and Skills: Level 1]

18. B - A warm, welcoming environment that promotes effective communication, innovation, and motivated team members is an important aspect to consider when designing team space. Guidelines for a better agile team space include: collocation of team members; reduction of non-essential noise/distractions; dedicated whiteboard and wall space for information radiators; space for the daily stand-up meeting and other meetings; pairing workstations; and other pleasantries like plants and comfortable furniture. [Agile Retrospectives: Making Good Teams Great. Esther Derby, Diana Larsen, Ken Schwaber.] [Communications]

19. A - EVM or earned value management is a management technique used to evaluate project performance with respect to cost and schedule. EVM relies on other common financial metrics like Budget At Completion (BAC), Actual Cost (AC), Planned Value (PV), Earned Value (EV), Cost Variance (CV), Schedule Variance

(SV), Cost Performance Index (CPI), and Schedule Performance Index (SPI). [Agile Estimating and Planning. Mike Cohn.] [Metrics]

20. D - An information radiator is a visual representation of project status data. [Agile Software Development: The Cooperative Game – 2nd Edition. Alistair Cockburn.] [Communications]

21. A - The five core risk areas include: productivity variation (difference between planned and actual performance); scope creep (considerable additional requirements beyond initial agreement); specification breakdown (lack of stakeholder consensus on requirements); intrinsic schedule flaw (poor estimates of task durations), personnel loss (the loss of human resources). [The Software Project Manager's Bridge to Agility. Michele Sliger, Stacia Broderick.] [Risk management]

22. C - The agile triangle includes value, quality, and constraints as its parameters. [Agile Project Management: Creating Innovative Products – 2nd Edition. Jim Highsmith.] [Knowledge and Skills: Level 1]

23. A - EVM or earned value management is a management technique used to evaluate project performance with respect to cost and schedule. EVM relies on other common financial metrics like Budget At Completion (BAC), Actual Cost (AC), Planned Value (PV), Earned Value (EV), Cost Variance (CV), Schedule Variance (SV), Cost Performance Index (CPI), and Schedule Performance Index (SPI). [Agile Estimating and Planning. Mike Cohn.] [Metrics]

24. B - An agile team must always face the prioritization of product features in its product backlog. From release planning to iteration planning, an agile team must prioritize the user stories/ features of its product to ensure that high-quality and high-value features are developed first to help facilitate an optimized and early return on investment (ROI). An agile team typically prioritizes requirements or user stories/features in terms of relative value and risk; value is defined by the customer (i.e., customer-value prioritization). Two common methods to prioritize product features are: MoSCoW and Kano. The MoSCoW method categorizes features into 'Must have,' 'Should have,' 'Could have,' and 'Would have' features. The Kano method categorizes features into 'Must haves (threshold),' 'Dissatisfiers,' 'Satisfiers,' and 'Delighters.' Must haves are features that are requisite. Dissatisfiers are features that adversely impact perceived value and should be eliminated. 'Satisfiers' are features that increase perceived value linearly, where the more you add the more the customer is pleased, but are not required, and 'Delighters' are features that increase perceived value exponentially to please the customer. To prioritize features based on risk, a risk-to-value matrix can be used. A risk-to-value matrix has four quadrants, with the horizontal axis having low and high value, and the vertical axis having low and high risk. User stories are assigned to one of the four categories/quadrants: low-value, low-risk; low-value, high-risk; high-value, low-risk; high-value, high-risk. A cost-to-value matrix can also be made in this manner. All prioritization in agile is 'relative,' meaning that the priority of one user story is relative to other user stories and not prioritized on a fixed scale. [Lean-Agile Software Development: Achieving

Enterprise Agility. Alan Shalloway, Guy Beaver, James R. Trott.] [Knowledge and Skills: Level 1]

25. A - Empowered teams - ones that are self-organizing and know how to solve problems with minimal management involvement - are a cornerstone of the agile methodology. An agile team feels empowered when it collectively assumes responsibility for the delivery of the product (i.e., taking ownership). [Coaching Agile Teams. Lyssa Adkins.] [Knowledge and Skills: Level 1]

26. C - A high-performance agile team is one that is ideally collocated for osmotic communication and face-to-face interaction. However, collocation isn't always feasible in today's multinational environment. For distributed teams, several practices are available to provide the best form of effective communication in the absence of being collocated: team intranet sites, virtual team rooms, and video conferencing over e-mail when possible. Geographic separation, especially on a world-wide scale, causes the team to consider language and cultural differences, and time zone differences. [The Art of Agile Development. James Shore.] [Knowledge and Skills: Level 2]

27. D - A common misconception in agile is that an agile team does not need a leader. In fact, all agile teams need a leader, but the way in which the leader leads is fundamentally different than the typical traditional project manager/project leader method. Some have theorized that this misconception stems from the desired 'self-organizing' quality of the agile team. And although the 'self-organizing' agile team is empowered to take ownership and responsibility of the product and make some decisions itself, it nevertheless requires a leader to help provide guidance, mentoring, coaching, problem solving, and decision making. Some key aspects required of an agile leader include: empowering team members to decide what standard agile practices and methods it will use; allowing the team to be self-organized and self-disciplined; empowering the team members to make decisions collaboratively with the customer; inspire the team to be innovative and explore new ideas and technology capabilities; be a champion of and articulate the product vision to team members so it will be motivated to accomplish the overall objective; remove any obstacles and solve any problems the team may face in its effort; communicate and endorse the values and principles of agile project management to stakeholders that may be unfamiliar with agile; ensure that all stakeholders, including business managers and developers, are collaborating effectively; and, be able to adapt the leadership style to the working environment to ensure that the agile values and principles are effectively upheld. [The Art of Agile Development. James Shore.] [Knowledge and Skills: Level 1]

28. C - In agile, effective 'knowledge sharing' is a critical factor for success. It involves the near real time communication of key information among all team members and stakeholders. To promote knowledge sharing, agile uses standard practices built into its process, such as using generalized specialists/cross functional teams, self-organizing and self-disciplined teams, collocation, daily stand-up meetings, iteration/sprint planning, release planning, pair programming and pair rotation, project retrospectives/reflection, and on-site customer support. And, of course, the sixth principle of Agile is " The most efficient and effective method of conveying information to and within a development team is face-to-face conversation." In this sense, Agile prefers and encourages collocation for all stakeholders and team members for the simple fact that face-to-face conversation is the best method of communication and, in turn, effective knowledge sharing. [Becoming Agile: ...in an imperfect world. Greg Smith, Ahmed Sidky.] [Knowledge and Skills: Level 1]

29. A - EVM or earned value management is a management technique used to evaluate project performance with respect to cost and schedule. EVM relies on other common financial metrics like Budget At Completion (BAC), Actual Cost (AC), Planned Value (PV), Earned Value (EV), Cost Variance (CV), Schedule Variance (SV), Cost Performance Index (CPI), and Schedule Performance Index (SPI). SV is the difference between what a project has earned to date and what it was planned to earn to date (i.e., SV = EV - PV). [Agile Estimating and Planning. Mike Cohn.] [Metrics]

30. B - The following are community values of the PMI agile community of practice community charter: Vision, Servant Leadership, Trust, Collaboration, Honesty, Learning, Courage, Openness, Adaptability, Leading Change, Transparency [PMI Agile Community of Practice Community Charter. Project Management Institute.] [Knowledge and Skills: Level 1]

31. C - In iteration planning, an agile team, collaboratively with the customer, chooses user stories to include for development. Although the user stories are prioritized in the product backlog initially during release planning, an agile team and customer should review prioritization based on progressive elaboration (i.e., gained knowledge and perspective). Prioritization is often based on value and risk and can be performed using the MoSCoW or Kano method and through the use of risk-to-value and cost-to-value matrices. An agile team performs decomposition to sub-divide user stories into more manageable tasks so that it may estimate task time. Tasks for an iteration may also be prioritized based on value, similar to how user stories are prioritized. [Lean-Agile Software Development: Achieving Enterprise Agility. Alan Shalloway, Guy Beaver, James R. Trott.] [Knowledge and Skills: Level 1]

32. B - Ron Jeffries' three Cs for user story definition are card, conversation, confirmation. [User Stories Applied: For Agile Software Development. Mike Cohn.] [Planning, monitoring, and adapting]

33. A - The agile practitioner should follow several rules of thumb when estimating a project buffer: 1) Only use a buffer if the project has more than 10 user stories, 2) The square root of the sum of squares method has shown to provide the most accurate buffer, 3) the estimate buffer should be at least 20% of the total project duration, 4) In the absence of sufficient data. like worst case scenario estimates, you can use the halving of most likely estimates to estimate a project buffer. [Agile Estimating and Planning. Mike Cohn.] [Agile estimation]

34. A - Having a motivated team is essential for any project, regardless of whether it is agile or not. Motivated teams work together better, have strong productivity, and exceed expectations. Some simple steps to increase motivation are 1) spending quality time together; where team members get to know one another on a personal level to build a sense of community, 2) providing feedback, mentoring and coaching; where team members are congratulated and thanked on jobs well done and also mentored or coached to improve in skill and capability, and 3) empowerment; where the team is empowered to make many key decisions which, along the way, builds trust and shows that leadership believes in the capabilities of the team. [The Art of Agile Development. James Shore.] [Knowledge and Skills: Level 1]

35. A - Affinity estimating is a method to predict the work effort, typically in story points, of developing a user story. It is particularly useful for large product backlogs. Although several methods exist, the basic affinity estimating model involves sizing user stories on a scale from small to large. The scale can be a Fibonacci sequence or t-shirt sizes and is typically taped to a wall in a large conference room. Participants then attach their user stories to the wall as estimates. It is often done in silence and has several iterations until the user stories have been estimated. [The Art of Agile Development. James Shore.] [Agile estimation]

36. D - XP is generally considered to be the originator of user stories. [User Stories Applied: For Agile Software Development. Mike Cohn.] [Knowledge and Skills: Level 2]

37. B - The following are community values of the PMI agile community of practice community charter: Vision, Servant Leadership, Trust, Collaboration, Honesty, Learning, Courage, Openness, Adaptability, Leading Change, Transparency [PMI Agile Community of Practice Community Charter. Project Management Institute.] [Knowledge and Skills: Level 1]

38. D - The Agile Manifesto defines 12 supporting principles. Agile principles include 1) Our highest priority is to satisfy the customer through early and continuous delivery of valuable software. 2) Welcome changing requirements, even late in development. Agile processes harness change for the customer's competitive advantage. 3) Deliver working software frequently, from a couple of weeks to a couple of months, with preference to the shorter timescale. 4) Business people and developers must work together daily throughout the project. 5) Build projects around motivated individuals. Give them the environment and support they need, and trust them to get the job done. 6) The most efficient and effective method of conveying information to and within a development team is face-to-face conversation. 7) Working software is the primary measure of progress. 8) Agile processes promote sustainable development. The sponsors, developers, and users should be able to maintain a constant pace indefinitely. 9) Continuous attention to technical excellence and good design enhances agility. 10) Simplicity--the art of maximizing the amount of work not done--is essential. 11) The best architectures, requirements, and designs emerge from self-organizing teams. 12) At regular intervals, the team reflects on how to become more effective, then tunes and adjusts its behavior accordingly. [Manifesto for Agile Software Development. Agile Alliance.] [Knowledge and Skills: Level 1]

39. D - The Agile Manifesto defines four values. The four values list primary values and secondary values, with primary values superseding secondary values. The values are 1) individuals and interactions over processes and tools, 2) working software over comprehensive documentation, 3) customer collaboration over contract negotiation, and 4) responding to change over following a plan. [Manifesto for Agile Software Development. Agile Alliance.] [Knowledge and Skills: Level 1]

40. B - The Agile Manifesto developed by the Agile Alliance covers 4 values and 12 principles. The four values are: 1) individuals and interactions over processes and tools, 2) working software over comprehensive documentation, 3) customer collaboration over contract negotiation, and 4) responding to change over following a plan. The 12 principles are: 1) focusing on satisfying the customer, 2) welcoming change, 3) delivering working software frequently, 4) ensuring that business people and developers work together, 5) motivating the individuals involved in development, 6) using face-to-face communication whenever possible, 7) working software as the primary measure of progress, 8) maintaining a constant pace of development, 9) paying continuous attention to technical excellence and good design, 10) aiming for simplicity, 11) using self-organizing teams, and 12) regularly reflecting on how to become more effective. [Manifesto for Agile Software Development. Agile Alliance.] [Communications]

Knowledge Area Quiz Agile Estimation Practice Questions

Test Name: Knowledge Area Test: Agile Estimation
Total Questions: 15
Correct Answers Needed to Pass: 11 (73.33%)
Time Allowed: 25 Minutes

Test Description

This practice quiz specifically targets your knowledge of the Agile Estimation exam topic area.

Test Questions

1. Often times during release planning user stories are categorized and organized by theme. Which of the following agile artifact is often used to show organization and progress of user stories by theme?

   A. Theme parking garage

   B. Theme runway

   C. Story theme chart

   D. Parking lot chart

2. What is a project buffer?

   A. Extra time added to each time-boxed value for a task to account for delays, obstacles, and other unforeseen issues to help predict an accurate project completion date.

   B. Extra time added to the beginning of a project to account for team discovery

   C. Extra time added to the end of a project to account for delays, obstacles, and other unforeseen issues to help predict an accurate completion date.

   D. Extra time added throughout a project to account for reflection workshops

3. On a burndown chart, two series are typically charted. Select the response that lists those two series (also referred to as lines).

   A. The net and gross work remaining

   B. The actual and ideal work remaining

   C. The estimated and ideal work remaining

   D. The actual and net work remaining

4. What is a story point?

   A. Fixed unit of testing effort.

   B. Dynamic unit of testing effort.

   C. Dynamic unit of development effort.

   D. Fixed unit of development effort.

5. In agile estimating and planning, what is 'incremental' revenue?

   A. Revenue retained through the development of new product features or services that prevent existing customers from stopping use of the existing product.

B. New revenue realized through the sales of products or services to new customers.

C. Additional revenue realized through the sales of new product features or services to existing customers.

D. New revenue found in a hidden value stream.

6. What is affinity estimating?

A. A method to estimate time to market.

B. A method to estimate user story work effort.

C. A method to estimate customer reaction to product features.

D. Another name for planning poker.

7. When estimating the relative work effort to develop user stories, agile teams have both ideal days and story points as a method for estimation. What should agile teams be weary of doing with these methods?

A. Using both estimate methods simultaneously in a project.

B. Using ideal days too early in a project

C. Forgetting to convert both methods into story velocity for a common basis of estimation

D. Using story points too early in a project

8. How can an agile team estimate the relative size of developing a user story?

A. Using story points

B. Using decomposition

C. Using velocity

D. Using aggregation

9. How are planning poker and affinity estimating similar?

A. They are both methods used in agile to estimate task difficulty.

B. They are both methods used in agile to estimate risk.

C. They are both methods used in agile to estimate value.

D. They are both methods used in agile for relative sizing of the work effort involved for developing user stories.

10. Kyle's team just completed a sprint. The team had estimated that it could complete 45 story points, but only completed 30 story points in the sprint. How many story points would be a safe estimate for to estimate for the next sprint?

A. 45

B. 30

C. 50

D. 40

11. Besides using story points to estimate the relative size of a user story, how else may an agile team estimate user story size?

A. Using exact time-boxing

B. Using ideal days

C. Using heuristics

D. Using ideal velocity

12. When is it appropriate to estimate tasks for an iteration?

A. Both during iteration planning and during the iteration itself

B. Only during release planning

C. During the iteration

D. During iteration planning

13. In agile estimating and planning, what is 'new' revenue?

A. New revenue found in a hidden value stream.

B. Additional revenue realized through the sales of new product features or services to existing customers.

C. Revenue retained through the development of new product features or services that prevent existing customers from stopping use of the existing product.

D. New revenue realized through the sales of products or services to new customers.

14. Name an agile planning technique used to estimate the point value of a user story.

A. Planning poker

B. Texas Hold'Em

C. Narrowband Delphi

D. Delphi narrowband

15. What agile estimation technique is conducted using a deck of cards for quickly estimating the relative work effort of developing user stories in a product backlog?

A. Affinity estimation

B. Planning poker

C. SMART

D. Planning game

Knowledge Area Quiz
Agile Estimation
Answer Key and Explanations

1. D - A parking lot chart is an agile artifact used to organize and categorize user stories by theme. A parking lot chart typically includes the name of the identified themes, the number of stories and story points it includes, and a progress chart to show the completion percentage of story points. For example, a parking lot chart could have a theme of 'database' with 6 user stories worth 80 story points at a 50% completion. A 50% completion would indicate that 40 story points had been completed, but NOT necessarily that 3 stories had been completed because not all stories are equivalent in effort. [Agile Estimating and Planning. Mike Cohn.] [Agile estimation]

2. C - A project buffer is extra time added to the end of a project to account for delays, obstacles, and other unforeseen issues to help predict an accurate completion date. A project buffer can be estimated using several methods. Three commonly used methods are 1) square root of the sum of squares method, 2) Critical chain project management method (CCPM), 3) halving the sum of most likely estimates . The square root of the sum of squares method involves finding a local safety for all tasks, squaring all the local safeties, summing these squares, and then finding the square root of the sum. The Critical chain project management method (CCPM) is the sum of half the local safeties of all tasks. The local safety is the difference between the 50% confidence estimate and the 90% confidence estimate. The halving the sum of most likely estimates method involves adding all the most likely estimates and dividing by two. [Agile Estimating and Planning. Mike Cohn.] [Agile estimation]

3. B - A project burndown chart is an often used information radiator to show iteration progress. It charts two series: the actual work remaining and ideal/estimated work remaining. The vertical axis is the work unit (often story points or hours) and the horizontal axis is iteration duration (typically in number of days). The ideal/estimated work series is a straight, downward sloping line originating on the vertical axis at the value of work to be completed (e.g., 20 story points) and extending to the horizontal axis (i.e., 0 story points) on the last day of the iteration. The actual series is dependent upon the agile team's productivity and the task complexity and is updated daily. The actual series is typically volatile and is not a straight line but ebbs and flows as the project team tackles the development process. [Agile Estimating and Planning. Mike Cohn.] [Agile estimation]

4. D - A story point is a fixed unit of development effort. It is used in the relative sizing of user stories to estimate work effort involved with development. Story points are not time-based, meaning [Agile Estimating and Planning. Mike Cohn.] [Agile estimation]

5. C - Additional revenue is revenue realized through the sales of new product features or services to existing customers. [Agile Estimating and Planning. Mike Cohn.] [Agile estimation]

6. B - Affinity estimating is a method to predict the work effort, typically in story points, of developing a user story. It is particularly useful for large product

backlogs. Although several methods exist, the basic affinity estimating method involves sizing user stories on a scale from small to large. The scale can be a Fibonacci sequence or t-shirt sizes and is typically taped to a wall in a large conference room. Participants then attach their user stories to the wall as estimates. It is often done in silence and has several iterations until the user stories have been estimated. [The Art of Agile Development. James Shore.] [Agile estimation]

7. A - Agile teams should agree to one method of estimation, either story points or ideal days, as both use different units of measurement and can lead to confusion. [Agile Estimating and Planning. Mike Cohn.] [Agile estimation]

8. A - Agile teams typically use story points to estimate the relative size or effort of developing a user story [Agile Estimating and Planning. Mike Cohn.] [Agile estimation]

9. D - Both planning poker and affinity estimation are agile techniques used to size the work effort of developing user stories. [Agile Estimating and Planning. Mike Cohn.] [Agile estimation]

10. B - Estimating how many user story points a team can complete in a sprint/iteration should be based upon its previous iterations, if possible. If Kyle's team estimated 45 story points in its first sprint but completed only 30 story points, it would be wise to estimate no more than 30 for its next sprint/iteration. [Agile Estimating and Planning. Mike Cohn.] [Agile estimation]

11. B - Instead of using story points, agile teams may estimate the relative sizes of user stories using ideal days. Ideal days represents the amount of days - uninterrupted by meetings, personal life, non-working days, or any other delays, obstacles or distractions - that it would take a single person to build, test, and release the user story, relative to other user stories in the backlog. [Agile Estimating and Planning. Mike Cohn.] [Agile estimation]

12. A - It is appropriate to estimate tasks both during iteration planning and throughout the iteration. [Agile Estimating and Planning. Mike Cohn.] [Agile estimation]

13. D - New revenue is revenue realized through the sales of products or services to new customers. [Agile Estimating and Planning. Mike Cohn.] [Agile estimation]

14. A - Planning poker is a common agile estimation technique used to estimate the relative point value of a user story. [Agile Estimating and Planning. Mike Cohn.] [Agile estimation]

15. B - Planning poker is based upon the wideband Delphi estimation technique. It is a consensus-based technique for estimating effort. Sometimes called scrum poker, it is a technique for a relative estimation of effort, typically in story points, to develop a user story. At a planning poker meeting, each estimator is given an identical deck of planning poker cards with a wide range of values. The Fibonacci sequence is often used for values for planning poker (i.e., 0, 1, 1, 2, 3, 5,8,etc.); another common sequence is (question mark, 0, 1/2, 1, 2, 3, 5, 8, 13, 20, 40, and 100). A planning poker meeting works as follows: 1) a moderator, not estimating, facilitates the meeting. 2) the product owner/manager provides a short overview of the user story and answers clarifying questions posed by the developers. Typically the product owner does not vote. 3) Each estimator selects an estimate of work effort by selecting a card, 4) Once everyone has selected a card, everyone overturns their card concurrently, 5) Estimators with high and low estimates are given a chance to defend positions. 6) The process repeats until there is consensus. The developer who owns the user story is typically given higher credence. [Agile Estimating and Planning. Mike Cohn.] [Agile estimation]

PMI-ACP Lite Mock Exam 7 Practice Questions

Test Name: PMI-ACP Lite Mock Exam 7
Total Questions: 40
Correct Answers Needed to Pass:
30 (75.00%)
Time Allowed: 60 Minutes

Test Description

This is a cumulative PMI-ACP Mock Exam which can be used as a benchmark for your PMI-ACP aptitude. This practice test includes questions from all exam topic areas, including sections from Agile Tools and Techniques, and all three Agile Knowledge and Skills areas.

Test Questions

1. Which of the following responses is NOT an Agile Manifesto value or principle regarding communication?

A. Working software over welcoming change

B. Face-to-face communication whenever possible

C. Individuals and interactions over processes and tools

D. Customer collaboration over contract negotiation

2. In a self-assessment or reflection event, what is a likely topic a team will focus on?

A. Product owner incompatibilities

B. Lessons learned from mistakes

C. Customer inconsistencies in requirements

D. The programmer who authored the most bugs

3. In a self-assessment or reflection event, what is a likely topic a team will focus on?

A. Team standards that worked

B. Product owner risks

C. The programmer who authored the most bugs

D. Customer inconsistencies in requirements

4. Bob has recently started an agile project where he is to be the project leader. What should Bob aspire to be as agile leader?

A. Someone who disregards any innovative thought that is outside the project scope.

B. Someone who promotes a competitive environment to increase efficiency among the team.

C. Someone who makes all team decisions without team consultation.

D. Someone who builds trust in the team and encourages it to explore new ideas and technology.

5. Before starting an agile project, Hank always likes his team to review the Agile Manifesto. One of his favorite principles regards the Agile Manifesto's preferred method of communication. Can you help Hank correctly identify the preferred communication method?

A. Customer value communication

B. Customer quality communication

C. Face-to-face communication

D. Simplicity communication

6. Of the following, select the best adjective that describes an agile team's project and quality standards.

A. Customer-defined

B. Team-defined

C. ISO 9001-defined

D. Project lead-defined

7. EVM is a frequently used project management abbreviation. How is CV calculated?

A. CV = EV - AC

B. CV = BAC - EV - AC

C. CV = BAC - AC - EV

D. CV = AC - EV

8. If the NPV of an investment is below zero, what does that indicate to the potential buyer?

A. That it would subtract value from the buyer's portfolio.

B. That it would neither add to nor subtract value from the buyer's portfolio.

C. That it would add value to the buyer's portfolio.

D. None of the above.

9. Which of the following is an agile 'feedback technique for product?'

A. Kanban analysis

B. Cycle retention

C. Constructive planning

D. Iteration planning

10. What delivery concept does agile pride itself on and having a definition of "frequent delivery of working products, which are successively improved, to a customer for immediate feedback and acceptance?"

A. Iterative delivery

B. Sprint delivery

C. Incremental delivery

D. Cyclical delivery

11. What daily meeting often uses timeboxing to ensure it lasts no longer than fifteen minutes?

A. Daily task board update

B. Daily risk meeting

C. Daily stand-up meetings/Daily scrum

D. Daily defect meeting

12. What else besides sound input does osmotic communication include?

A. Visual information input

B. ESP

C. Data logs

D. E-mail

13. What is one reason to have a motivated team on an agile project?

A. Improve teamwork and collaboration

B. Meet expectations

C. Decrease productivity

D. Maintain velocity

14. Randy is in the middle of performing a risk-based spike task to understand how the upgrade to Windows 8 required by the customer will impact the user interface. What is one reason Randy would perform a risk-based spike task?

A. Manage idle time.

B. Manage risk and reduce uncertainty.

C. Eliminate the need for further risk management.

D. Decrease the likelihood of upgrade localization.

15. What must a scrum team define before beginning a project so that it may know when a feature has been fully developed and in a state of readiness for shipping?

A. Its definition of delivery readiness.

B. Its definition of releasability.

C. Its definition of done in concert with the product owner

D. Its definition of shipability.

16. Select an advantage of using an information radiator.

A. Improves development skills for junior software programmers

B. Decreases team morale

C. Improves team communication

D. Increases competition among team members to improve productivity

17. What is an advantage of continuous integration, as practiced in XP?

A. Decreases the need for testing

B. Decreases the need for team communication and collaboration

C. Supports the detection of early defects with any software integration.

D. Decreases the need for customer feedback

18. Select a technique that promotes agile 'knowledge sharing.'

A. Retrospectives

B. Defect inspection

C. Introspectives

D. Roadmap retrospective

19. Which of the following is an agile principle per the Agile Manifesto?

A. Test-driven development

B. Defect reduction

C. Focus on product value

D. Using self-organizing teams.

20. In agile, a business case should include which of the following topics?

A. Initial velocity estimate

B. Defect threshold

C. Project standards

D. Rate of return

21. In agile, the "team space" is an important place that should foster effective communication. What is a guideline for promoting such an environment?

A. Large swaths of blank wall space devoid of project information

B. Plants, natural lighting, and comfortable seating

C. Seating by team member function

D. Minimized team member interaction

22. What typically occurs directly before an agile team and product owner will work on developing an initial product roadmap?

A. Definition of the product backlog.

B. Definition of the product vision

C. Definition of the iteration duration.

D. Release planning.

23. Communicating using open ended questions, like "What did you think of the agile seminar?" instead of closed questions, like "Did you enjoy the agile seminar?" are encouraged to improve team collaboration. Which communication technique encourages using open ended questions?

A. Active

B. Gesture

C. Reactive

D. Mime

24. Which of the following is an agile principle per the Agile Manifesto?

A. Teams and interactions

B. Delivering incremental change

C. Delivering comprehensive documentation

D. Delivering working software frequently.

25. Of the following, which is an agile principle per the Agile Manifesto?

A. Delivering comprehensive documentation

B. Delivering incremental change

C. Ensuring that business people and developers hold daily retrospective meetings

D. Ensuring that business people and developers work together.

26. Why is an empowered team considered an important team attribute in agile?

A. Empowered teams solve problems collectively and thus share a focus on delivering value

B. Empowered teams remain inflexible to changing customer requirements and focus on delivering to specification.

C. Empowered teams need extensive management involvement in order to understand customer need

D. Empowered teams remove themselves from being responsible of product quality in order to reduce association with project failure.

27. Gabe is the financial executive for an upcoming project that is slated to use agile. In terms of estimating time, budget, and cost for an agile effort, what does Gabe typically have defined?

A. Time and cost

B. Budget and cost

C. Cost

D. Budget and time

28. What person in the agile framework "inspires the team to be innovative and to try new technologies?"

A. Project leader

B. Product tester

C. Product owner

D. Customer

29. Help Gilbert select key principles of lean software development.

A. Designing for the sub-system, deciding early and delivering on time

B. Designing for the whole system (i.e., seeing the whole), deciding late and delivering fast

C. Designing for the whole system, deciding late, and delivering once

D. Designing holistically, deciding early and delivering on time

30. What person in the agile framework "removes any obstacles the team faces in its path?"

A. Developer

B. Project leader

C. Tester

D. Customer

31. As an agile certified practitioner, Harry has just entered the exploring phase of Highsmith's agile project management model. What is Harry and his team mostly performing during this phase?

A. Designing, building, and testing of product features

B. Facilitating project vision kaizen

C. Developing risk mitigation strategies

D. Assessing project risk

32. What is the second step of the ATDD four step process?

A. Discuss

B. Develop

C. Distill

D. Demo

33. Being a strong facilitator is required for a project leader or scrum master. Which of the following is a facilitation method used by a project leader?

A. Using a single discipline or expertise for brainstorming events

B. Dismissing poor ideas at brainstorming events immediately

C. Using non-threatening and creative environments

D. Using a large number of people for brainstorming events

34. What is the first step of the ATDD four step process?

A. Distill

B. Demo

C. Discuss

D. Develop

35. What is the third step of the ATDD four step process?

A. Develop

B. Discuss

C. Demo

D. Distill

36. Select a technique used for value-based analysis?

A. MoSCoW

B. SMART

C. WIDETOM

D. inVEsT

37. According to Highsmith and his definition of adaptive leadership, what is one item a project leader can do for "doing agile?"

A. Do less

B. Do value first

C. Do more

D. Do continuous integration

38. Jerry is reviewing an agile artifact that explains the why and how a project will deliver value to a customer. Which artifact is Jerry most likely reviewing?

A. Business case

B. Burndown chart

C. Value stream map

D. Task board

39. Jill and her agile team are authoring a document required by local law regulations. This type of conformance is known as

A. Accreditation compliance

B. Regulatory compliance

C. Fail-safe compliance

D. Documentation compliance

40. Reba and the agile team she belongs to are having a discussion regarding 'stakeholder management.' What is 'stakeholder management?'

A. The management or facilitation of a work environment where all stakeholders are actively involved throughout the project.

B. The management or caging of stakeholder expectations to prevent scope creep.

C. The management or facilitation of a work environment where developers can assign tasks to stakeholders.

D. Managing the problems that stakeholders present throughout the project.

PMI-ACP Lite Mock Exam 7 Answer Key and Explanations

1. A - The Agile Manifesto developed by the Agile Alliance covers 4 values and 12 principles. The four values are: 1) individuals and interactions over processes and tools, 2) working software over comprehensive documentation, 3) customer collaboration over contract negotiation, and 4) responding to change over following a plan. The 12 principles are: 1) focusing on satisfying the customer, 2) welcoming change, 3) delivering working software frequently, 4) ensuring that business people and developers work together, 5) motivating the individuals involved in development, 6) using face-to-face communication whenever possible, 7) working software as the primary measure of progress, 8) maintaining a constant pace of development, 9) paying continuous attention to technical excellence and good design, 10) aiming for simplicity, 11) using self-organizing teams, and 12) regularly reflecting on how to become more effective. [Manifesto for Agile Software Development. Agile Alliance.] [Communications]

2. B - During reflection or retrospectives, an agile team reserves time to reflect on the work it has completed with the objective of continuous improvement. In these self-assessment/team-assessment events, topics can include: lessons learned from successes and failures; team standards that worked, failed, or were not properly followed; and other areas of improvement. [Agile Retrospectives: Making Good Teams Great. Esther Derby, Diana Larsen, Ken Schwaber.] [Knowledge and Skills: Level 2]

3. A - During reflection or retrospectives, an agile team reserves time to reflect on the work it has completed with the objective of continuous improvement. In these self-assessment/team-assessment events, topics can include: lessons learned from successes and failures; team standards that worked, failed, or were not properly followed; and other areas of improvement. [Agile Retrospectives: Making Good Teams Great. Esther Derby, Diana Larsen, Ken Schwaber.] [Knowledge and Skills: Level 2]

4. D - A common misconception in agile is that an agile team does not need a leader. In fact, all agile teams need a leader, but the way in which the leader leads is fundamentally different than the typical traditional project manager/project leader method. Some have theorized that this misconception stems from the desired 'self-organizing' quality of the agile team. And although the 'self-organizing' agile team is empowered to take ownership and responsibility of the product and make some decisions itself, it nevertheless requires a leader to help provide guidance, mentoring, coaching, problem solving, and decision making. Some key aspects required of an agile leader include: empowering team members to decide what standard agile practices and methods it will use; allowing the team to be self-organized and self-disciplined; empowering the team members to make decisions collaboratively with the customer; inspire the team to be innovative and explore new ideas and technology capabilities; be a champion of and articulate the product vision to team members so it will be motivated to accomplish the overall objective; remove any obstacles and solve any problems the team may face in its effort; communicate and endorse the values and principles of agile project management

to stakeholders that may be unfamiliar with agile; ensure that all stakeholders, including business managers and developers, are collaborating effectively; and, be able to adapt the leadership style to the working environment to ensure that the agile values and principles are effectively upheld. [The Art of Agile Development. James Shore.] [Knowledge and Skills: Level 1]

5. C - The Agile Manifesto developed by the Agile Alliance covers 4 values and 12 principles. The four values are: 1) individuals and interactions over processes and tools, 2) working software over comprehensive documentation, 3) customer collaboration over contract negotiation, and 4) responding to change over following a plan. The 12 principles are: 1) focusing on satisfying the customer, 2) welcoming change, 3) delivering working software frequently, 4) ensuring that business people and developers work together, 5) motivating the individuals involved in development, 6) using face-to-face communication whenever possible, 7) working software as the primary measure of progress, 8) maintaining a constant pace of development, 9) paying continuous attention to technical excellence and good design, 10) aiming for simplicity, 11) using self-organizing teams, and 12) regularly reflecting on how to become more effective. [Manifesto for Agile Software Development. Agile Alliance.] [Communications]

6. B - All agile efforts have project and quality standards that the team defines collaboratively at the beginning of an effort and refines collaboratively throughout the effort. Project and quality standards help an agile team with team cohesion and provide a structure, albeit one that can adapt as the project evolves, to promote a self-disciplined environment. There is no 'one size fits all' standards definition in agile; because every project is different, it has been shown that the team should define which project and quality standards it should hold itself against and strive to conform to those standards while also being open to adapting those standards throughout the project to optimize performance and delivered value. Project standards can range from where the daily stand-up meeting is located and how long each participant has to share his or her progress and challenges to highly specific software coding styles, methods for test-driven development, and what the team's definition of 'done-done' means. [Agile Software Development: The Cooperative Game – 2nd Edition. Alistair Cockburn.] [Knowledge and Skills: Level 1]

7. A - EVM or earned value management is a management technique used to evaluate project performance with respect to cost and schedule. EVM relies on other common financial metrics like Budget At Completion (BAC), Actual Cost (AC), Planned Value (PV), Earned Value (EV), Cost Variance (CV), Schedule Variance (SV), Cost Performance Index (CPI), and Schedule Performance Index (SPI). CV is the difference between what a project has earned to date and cost to date (i.e., CV = EV - AC). AC is the actual cost the project has incurred to date. [Agile Estimating and Planning. Mike Cohn.] [Metrics]

8. A - Net Present Value: A metric used to analyze the profitability of an investment or project. NPV is the difference between the present value of cash inflows and the present value of cash outflows. NPV considers the likelihood of future cash

inflows that an investment or project will yield. NPV is the sum of each cash inflow/outflow for the expected duration of the investment. Each cash inflow/outflow is discounted back to its present value (PV) (i.e.,, what the money is worth in terms of today's value). NPV is the sum of all terms: NPV = Sum of [Rt/(1 + i)^t] where t = the time of the cash flow, i = the discount rate (the rate of return that could be earned on in the financial markets) , and Rt = the net cash inflow or outflow. For example, consider the following two year period. The discount rate is 5% and the initial investment cost is $500. At the end of the first year, a $200 inflow is expected. At the end of the second year, a $1,000 is expected. NPV = -500 + 200/(1.05)^1 + 1000/(1.05)^2 = ~$597. If NPV is positive, it indicates that the investment will add value to the buyer's portfolio. If NPV is negative, it will subtract value. If NPV is zero, it will neither add or subtract value. [Agile Estimating and Planning. Mike Cohn.] [Value based prioritization]

9. D - There are several feedback techniques - techniques that facilitate constructive criticism to improve product value and quality - built into the agile process. In the classic definition, feedback is a dynamic process where past information influences the behavior of the same process in the future. Agile feedback techniques include prototyping, simulation, demonstration, evaluations, pair programming, unit testing, continuous integration, daily stand-up meetings, sprint planning. Because agile prides itself on a transparent and collaborative environment, feedback is essentially ubiquitous. [Agile Retrospectives: Making Good Teams Great. Esther Derby, Diana Larsen, Ken Schwaber.] [Knowledge and Skills: Level 1]

10. C - A cornerstone of Agile development is 'incremental delivery.' Incremental delivery is the frequent delivery of working products, which are successively improved, to a customer for immediate feedback and acceptance. Typically, a product is delivered at the end of each sprint or iteration for demonstration and feedback. In this feedback technique, a customer can review the product and provide updated requirements. Changed/updated/refined requirements are welcomed in the agile process to ensure the customer receives a valuable and quality product. A sprint or iteration typically lasts from two to four weeks and at the end a new and improved product is delivered, incrementally. [The Art of Agile Development. James Shore.] [Knowledge and Skills: Level 1]

11. C - The use of a stop watch is sometimes used in the daily stand-up meeting to ensure that the meeting is brief and productive. Typically, a stand-up meeting should last no longer than 15 minutes (i.e., a 15 minute timebox). [The Art of Agile Development. James Shore.] [Communications]

12. A - Osmotic communication includes picking up sensory input of sound, sight or vision, smell and other shared workspace environmental conditions. [Agile Software Development: The Cooperative Game – 2nd Edition. Alistair Cockburn.] [Communications]

13. A - Having a motivated team is essential for any project, regardless of whether it is agile or not. Motivated teams work together better, have strong productivity, and exceed expectations. Some simple steps to increase motivation are 1) spending quality time together; where team members get to know one another on a personal level to build a sense of community, 2) providing feedback, mentoring and coaching; where team members are congratulated and thanked on jobs well done and also mentored or coached to improve in skill and capability, and 3) empowerment; where the team is empowered to make many key decisions which, along the way, builds trust and shows that leadership believes in the capabilities of the team. [The Art of Agile Development. James Shore.] [Knowledge and Skills: Level 1]

14. B - Risked-based spike is a risk management technique and is often thought of as a task. A risked-based spike is a task used to gain knowledge in an area of uncertainty to reduce risk. For example, a development team may need to understand how migrating from Windows 7 to Windows 8 may impact the look and feel of the interface. Risked-based spikes typically are included in iteration planning directly before a the task that holds the uncertainty. [The Art of Agile Development. James Shore.] [Risk management]

15. C - Because a cornerstone of the scrum framework in agile is to 'always have a product that you could theoretically ship,' it is important for the team and product owner to have a definition of 'done' or what criteria is necessary to consider user features or functionality in a state of finality. [Coaching Agile Teams. Lyssa Adkins.] [Product quality]

16. C - Information radiators improve team communication. [Agile Software Development: The Cooperative Game – 2nd Edition. Alistair Cockburn.] [Communications]

17. C - The extreme programming (XP) principle of continuous integration is that code is integrated into the full code base as soon as it is built, tested, and completed. Once integrated, the code base and therefore the entire system is built and tested. Continuous integration is just one principle of XP that promotes rapid delivery of software and the early detection of integration defects. [The Art of Agile Development. James Shore.] [Product quality]

18. A - In agile, effective 'knowledge sharing' is a critical factor for success. It involves the near real time communication of key information among all team members and stakeholders. To promote knowledge sharing, agile uses standard practices built into its process, such as using generalized specialists/cross functional teams, self-organizing and self-disciplined teams, collocation, daily stand-up meetings, iteration/sprint planning, release planning, pair programming and pair rotation, project retrospectives/reflection, and on-site customer support. And, of course, the sixth principle of Agile is " The most efficient and effective method of conveying information to and within a development team is face-to-face conversation." In this sense, Agile prefers and encourages collocation for all stakeholders and team members for the simple fact that face-to-face conversation is the best method of communication and, in turn, effective knowledge sharing. [Becoming Agile: ...in an imperfect world. Greg Smith, Ahmed Sidky.] [Knowledge and Skills: Level 1]

19. D - The Agile Manifesto defines 12 supporting principles. Agile principles include 1) Our highest priority is to satisfy the customer through early and continuous delivery of valuable software. 2) Welcome changing requirements, even late in development. Agile processes harness change for the customer's competitive advantage. 3) Deliver working software frequently, from a couple of weeks to a couple of months, with preference to the shorter timescale. 4) Business people and developers must work together daily throughout the project. 5) Build projects around motivated individuals. Give them the environment and support they need, and trust them to get the job done. 6) The most efficient and effective method of conveying information to and within a development team is face-to-face conversation. 7) Working software is the primary measure of progress. 8) Agile processes promote sustainable development. The sponsors, developers, and users should be able to maintain a constant pace indefinitely. 9) Continuous attention to technical excellence and good design enhances agility. 10) Simplicity--the art of maximizing the amount of work not done--is essential. 11) The best architectures, requirements, and designs emerge from self-organizing teams. 12) At regular intervals, the team reflects on how to become more effective, then tunes and adjusts its behavior accordingly. [Manifesto for Agile Software Development. Agile Alliance.] [Knowledge and Skills: Level 1]

20. D - Business case development is an important initial step in agile project management. The business case is a concise document that outlines the project's vision, goals, strategies for achieving goals, milestones, required investment and expected return/payback. A business case articulates the why and how a project will deliver value to a customer. [Lean-Agile Software Development: Achieving Enterprise Agility. Alan Shalloway, Guy Beaver, James R. Trott.] [Knowledge and Skills: Level 2]

21. B - A warm, welcoming environment that promotes effective communication, innovation, and motivated team members is an important aspect to consider when designing team space. Guidelines for a better agile team space include: collocation of team members; reduction of non-essential noise/distractions; dedicated whiteboard and wall space for information radiators; space for the daily stand-up meeting and other meetings; pairing workstations; and other pleasantries like plants and comfortable furniture. [Agile Retrospectives: Making Good Teams Great. Esther Derby, Diana Larsen, Ken Schwaber.] [Communications]

22. B - The product roadmap - owned by the product owner - serves as a high level overview of the product requirements. It is used as a tool for prioritizing features , organizing features into categories, and assigning rough time frames. Creating a product roadmap has four basic steps: 1) Identify requirements (these will become part of the product backlog), 2) Organize requirements into categories or themes, 3) Estimate relative work effort (e.g., planning poker or affinity estimation) and prioritize (value), and 4) Estimate rough time frames (estimate velocity, sprint duration, and rough release dates). [The Art of Agile Development. James Shore.] [Agile analysis and design]

23. A - One communication technique to reduce misunderstanding and miscommunication is active listening. A well run agile project necessitates both good listeners and communicators, active listening helps work towards both of these necessities. The basics of active listening include: 1) Being present and focusing your attention on the speaker. 2) Taking notes instead of interrupting. 3) Paraphrasing to confirm and review what you have heard. 4) Summarizing the conversation once it has concluded for posterity. Using open ended questions, good body language, and silence can help improve listening skills. [Coaching Agile Teams. Lyssa Adkins.] [Knowledge and Skills: Level 1]

24. D - The Agile Manifesto defines 12 supporting principles. Agile principles include 1) Our highest priority is to satisfy the customer through early and continuous delivery of valuable software. 2) Welcome changing requirements, even late in development. Agile processes harness change for the customer's competitive advantage. 3) Deliver working software frequently, from a couple of weeks to a couple of months, with preference to the shorter timescale. 4) Business people and developers must work together daily throughout the project. 5) Build projects around motivated individuals. Give them the environment and support they need, and trust them to get the job done. 6) The most efficient and effective method of conveying information to and within a development team is face-to-face conversation. 7) Working software is the primary measure of progress. 8) Agile processes promote sustainable development. The sponsors, developers, and users should be able to maintain a constant pace indefinitely. 9) Continuous attention to technical excellence and good design enhances agility. 10) Simplicity--the art of maximizing the amount of work not done--is essential. 11) The best architectures, requirements, and designs emerge from self-organizing teams. 12) At regular intervals, the team reflects on how to become more effective, then tunes and adjusts its behavior accordingly. [Manifesto for Agile Software Development. Agile Alliance.] [Knowledge and Skills: Level 1]

25. D - The Agile Manifesto defines 12 supporting principles. Agile principles include 1) Our highest priority is to satisfy the customer through early and continuous delivery of valuable software. 2) Welcome changing requirements, even late in development. Agile processes harness change for the customer's competitive advantage. 3) Deliver working software frequently, from a couple of weeks to a couple of months, with preference to the shorter timescale. 4) Business people and developers must work together daily throughout the project. 5) Build projects around motivated individuals. Give them the environment and support they need, and trust them to get the job done. 6) The most efficient and effective method of conveying information to and within a development team is face-to-face conversation. 7) Working software is the primary measure of progress. 8) Agile processes promote sustainable development. The sponsors, developers, and users should be able to maintain a constant pace indefinitely. 9) Continuous attention to technical excellence and good design enhances agility. 10) Simplicity--the art of maximizing the amount of work not done--is essential. 11) The best architectures, requirements, and designs emerge from self-organizing teams. 12) At regular intervals, the team reflects on how to become more effective, then tunes and adjusts its behavior accordingly. [Manifesto for Agile Software Development. Agile Alliance.] [Knowledge and Skills: Level 1]

26. A - Empowered teams - ones that are self-organizing and know how to solve problems with minimal management involvement - are a cornerstone of the agile methodology. An agile team feels empowered when it collectively assumes responsibility for the delivery of the product (i.e., taking ownership). [Coaching Agile Teams. Lyssa Adkins.] [Knowledge and Skills: Level 1]

27. D - Time, budget, and cost estimation is an important knowledge and skill area of agile. According to Highsmith, the nature of the agile method, whereby it welcomes changing scope, means that it lends itself well to fixed budgets and a fixed schedule because changing scope makes it difficult to estimate a total cost. Generally speaking, the budget and schedule constraints are known but before a project will commence there needs to be an agreed upon set of base product functionality defined in an initiation phase; fixing scope reduces an agile team's innovative tendency to provide improved value. For companies that are familiar with fixed-price contracts, where requirements are agreed upon before contract closing, adopting agile can be a weary initial venture. Instead, other contract vehicle types are recommended for agile efforts. These include: a general service contract for the initiation phase and separate fixed-price contracts for iterations or user stories; time-and-material contracts; not-to-exceed with fixed-fee contracts; and, incentive contracts (e.g., fixed price with incentive; cost-reimbursable with award fee). [Agile Project Management: Creating Innovative Products – 2nd Edition. Jim Highsmith.] [Knowledge and Skills: Level 1]

28. A - A common misconception in agile is that an agile team does not need a leader. In fact, all agile teams need a leader, but the way in which the leader leads is fundamentally different than the typical traditional project manager/project leader method. Some have theorized that this misconception stems from the desired 'self-organizing' quality of the agile team. And although the 'self-organizing' agile team is empowered to take ownership and responsibility of the product and make some decisions itself, it nevertheless requires a leader to help provide guidance, mentoring, coaching, problem solving, and decision making. Some key aspects required of an agile leader include: empowering team members to decide what standard agile practices and methods it will use; allowing the team to be self-organized and self-disciplined; empowering the team members to make decisions collaboratively with the customer; inspire the team to be innovative and explore new ideas and technology capabilities; be a champion of and articulate the product vision to team members so it will be motivated to accomplish the overall objective; remove any obstacles and solve any problems the team may face in its effort; communicate and endorse the values and principles of agile project management to stakeholders that may be unfamiliar with agile; ensure that all stakeholders, including business managers and developers, are collaborating effectively; and, be able to adapt the leadership style to the working environment to ensure that the agile values and principles are effectively upheld. [The Art of Agile Development. James Shore.] [Knowledge and Skills: Level 1]

29. B - The principles of lean software development are: Eliminate waste; Amplify learning; Decide as late as possible; Deliver as fast as possible; Empower the team; Build integrity in; See the whole. [Lean-Agile Software Development: Achieving Enterprise Agility. Alan Shalloway, Guy Beaver, James R. Trott.] [Knowledge and Skills: Level 2]

30. B - A common misconception in agile is that an agile team does not need a leader. In fact, all agile teams need a leader, but the way in which the leader leads is fundamentally different than the typical traditional project manager/project leader method. Some have theorized that this misconception stems from the desired 'self-organizing' quality of the agile team. And although the 'self-organizing' agile team is empowered to take ownership and responsibility of the product and make some decisions itself, it nevertheless requires a leader to help provide guidance, mentoring, coaching, problem solving, and decision making. Some key aspects required of an agile leader include: empowering team members to decide what standard agile practices and methods it will use; allowing the team to be self-organized and self-disciplined; empowering the team members to make decisions collaboratively with the customer; inspire the team to be innovative and explore new ideas and technology capabilities; be a champion of and articulate the product vision to team members so it will be motivated to accomplish the overall objective; remove any obstacles and solve any problems the team may face in its effort; communicate and endorse the values and principles of agile project management to stakeholders that may be unfamiliar with agile; ensure that all stakeholders, including business managers and developers, are collaborating effectively; and, be able to adapt the leadership style to the working environment to ensure that the agile values and principles are effectively upheld. [The Art of Agile Development. James Shore.] [Knowledge and Skills: Level 1]

31. A - In the exploring phase, the agile team focuses on designing, building, and testing product features. This occurs within useful increments to the customer. [Agile Project Management: Creating Innovative Products – 2nd Edition. Jim Highsmith.] [Knowledge and Skills: Level 1]

32. C - Acceptance Test Driven Development (ATDD) is similar to Test-driven development (TDD) in that it requires programmers to create tests first before any product code. The tests in ATDD are aimed at confirming features/behaviors that the intended software will have. The iterative cycle of ATDD with its four steps can be remembered as the four Ds: 1) Discuss, 2) Distill, 3) Develop, and 4) Demo. 1) Discuss: The agile team and customer or business stakeholder discuss a user story in detail. Talking about the expected behaviors the user story should have and what it should not. 2) The development team takes those items learned from the discussion and distills them into tests that will verify and validate those behaviors. The distillation process is where the entire team should have a good understanding of what "done" (or completed) means for a user story. That is, what the acceptance criteria are. 3) After distillation, the team develops the test code and product code to implement the product features. 4) Once the product features have been developed, the team demonstrates them to the customer or business stakeholders for feedback. [Lean-Agile Software Development: Achieving Enterprise Agility. Alan Shalloway, Guy Beaver, James R. Trott.] [Product quality]

33. C - As a project leader or scrum master, effective facilitation methods are critical for building a high-performance and motivated team. Facilitation of meetings, discussions, demonstrations, etc., is a constant on an agile project. Some general facilitation methods include: using a small number of people for brainstorming events; hosting events in a non-threatening/comfortable environment; having an agenda that is shared with the group ahead of time; using open-ended questions instead of closed-ended questions; including a diverse representation to gain a broader perspective of the topic. [Agile Retrospectives: Making Good Teams Great. Esther Derby, Diana Larsen, Ken Schwaber.] [Knowledge and Skills: Level 2]

34. C - Acceptance Test Driven Development (ATDD) is similar to Test-driven development (TDD) in that it requires programmers to create tests first before any product code. The tests in ATDD are aimed at confirming features/behaviors that the intended software will have. The iterative cycle of ATDD with its four steps can be remembered as the four Ds: 1) Discuss, 2) Distill, 3) Develop, and 4) Demo. 1) Discuss: The agile team and customer or business stakeholder discuss a user story in detail. Talking about the expected behaviors the user story should have and what it should not. 2) The development team takes those items learned from the discussion and distills them into tests that will verify and validate those behaviors. The distillation process is where the entire team should have a good understanding of what "done" (or completed) means for a user story. That is, what the acceptance criteria are. 3) After distillation, the team develops the test code and product code to implement the product features. 4) Once the product features have been developed, the team demonstrates them to the customer or business stakeholders for feedback. [Lean-Agile Software Development: Achieving Enterprise Agility. Alan Shalloway, Guy Beaver, James R. Trott.] [Product quality]

35. A - Acceptance Test Driven Development (ATDD) is similar to Test-driven development (TDD) in that it requires programmers to create tests first before any product code. The tests in ATDD are aimed at confirming features/behaviors that the intended software will have. The iterative cycle of ATDD with its four steps can be remembered as the four Ds: 1) Discuss, 2) Distill, 3) Develop, and 4) Demo. 1) Discuss: The agile team and customer or business stakeholder discuss a user story in detail. Talking about the expected behaviors the user story should have and what it should not. 2) The development team takes those items learned from the discussion and distills them into tests that will verify and validate those behaviors. The distillation process is where the entire team should have a good understanding of what "done" (or completed) means for a user story. That is, what the acceptance criteria are. 3) After distillation, the team develops the test code and product code to implement the product features. 4) Once the product features have been developed, the team demonstrates them to the customer or business stakeholders for feedback. [Lean-Agile Software Development: Achieving

Enterprise Agility. Alan Shalloway, Guy Beaver, James R. Trott.] [Product quality]

36. A - Value-based analysis strives to understand how value, as defined by the customer, relates to various components of the product, like features and tasks. Features are often prioritized with prioritization based on value and risk. Prioritization can be performed using the MoSCoW or Kano method and through the use of risk-to-value and cost-to-value matrices. [Lean-Agile Software Development: Achieving Enterprise Agility. Alan Shalloway, Guy Beaver, James R. Trott.] [Knowledge and Skills: Level 2]

37. A - Highsmith defines adaptive leadership as two dimensional: Being agile and doing agile. Being agile includes focusing on cornerstones of agile project management, like incremental delivery, continuous integration, and adapting to changing requirements. Doing agile includes several activities that an agile leader must do: do less; speed-to-value, quality, and engage and inspire. [Agile Project Management: Creating Innovative Products – 2nd Edition. Jim Highsmith.] [Soft skills negotiation]

38. A - Business case development is an important initial step in agile project management. The business case is a concise document that outlines the project's vision, goals, strategies for achieving goals, milestones, required investment and expected return/payback. A business case articulates the why and how a project will deliver value to a customer. [Lean-Agile Software Development: Achieving Enterprise Agility. Alan Shalloway, Guy Beaver, James R. Trott.] [Knowledge and Skills: Level 2]

39. B - Although in agile project management, it is generally practiced to generate minimal documentation to support the project, some specific documents, like those required by regulatory bodies need to be created to comply with local and federal law. [Agile Project Management: Creating Innovative Products – 2nd Edition. Jim Highsmith.] [Knowledge and Skills: Level 3]

40. A - Stakeholder management is a growing topic area within strategic management that brings awareness to the importance of managing stakeholders (i.e., facilitating active participation of stakeholders and fostering a strong collaborative environment) for a project's success. Stakeholder management is typically defined in the context of guiding principles and values. R. E. Freeman's 'Managing for Stakeholders' includes 10 principles: 1) Stakeholder interests need to go together over time. 2) We need a philosophy of volunteerism – to engage stakeholders and manage relationships ourselves rather than leave it to government. 3) We need to find solutions to issues that satisfy multiple stakeholders simultaneously. 4) Everything that we do serves stakeholders. We never trade off the interests of one versus the other continuously over time. 5) We act with purpose that fulfills our commitment to stakeholders. We act with aspiration towards fulfilling our dreams and theirs. 6) We need intensive communication and dialogue with stakeholders – not just those who are friendly. 7)Stakeholders consist of real people with names and faces and children. They are complex. 8)We need to generalize the marketing approach. 9) We engage with both primary and secondary stakeholders. 10) We constantly monitor and redesign processes to make them better serve our stakeholders. Because stakeholder involvement is critical for the success of a project, where projects without active participation from stakeholders are prone to failure, stakeholder management should be a topic that every agile team knows well. [The Art of Agile Development. James Shore.] [Knowledge and Skills: Level 1]

PMI-ACP Lite Mock Exam 8 Practice Questions

Test Name: PMI-ACP Lite Mock Exam 8
Total Questions: 40
Correct Answers Needed to Pass:
30 (75.00%)
Time Allowed: 60 Minutes

Test Description

This is a cumulative PMI-ACP Mock Exam which can be used as a benchmark for your PMI-ACP aptitude. This practice test includes questions from all exam topic areas, including sections from Agile Tools and Techniques, and all three Agile Knowledge and Skills areas.

Test Questions

1. Which of the following is NOT a secondary agile value per the Agile Manifesto?

A. Contracts need to be negotiated and plans followed

B. Documentation supports working software and appropriate processes and tools aid the development process

C. Appropriate processes and tools aid the development process

D. Stakeholders must interact effectively to create business value

2. When working with a task board, in which column should a developer find a task that has NOT yet started?

A. In progress

B. Done

C. To do

D. Ready for testing

3. Calculate the return on investment of the following: Gain: $5,000; Cost: $10,000.

A. 50%

B. -67%

C. -40%

D. -50%

4. Greg has just finished completed a task. He wants to update the team and other stakeholders about the progress of the task. In which column of the task board should Greg place the task card?

A. Done

B. To do

C. Ready for testing

D. In progress

5. Paul as the product owner, likes being able to provide constructive criticism to the agile team regarding its latest iteration of a product. Although Paul has other opportunities to provide feedback, this particular type occurs after the delivery of a new product associated with the end of a sprint or iteration. What type of delivery concept provides this type of customer feedback?

A. Incremental delivery

B. Done done delivery

C. Acceptance test delivery

D. Model delivery

6. Value stream mapping is an example of a

A. Defect technique

B. Process analysis technique

C. Done done technique

D. Code refactoring technique

7. Of the following, which is NOT a part of active listening?

A. Being silent.

B. Being present and focusing your attention on the speaker.

C. Open ended questions.

D. Talking loudly.

8. Joy, as an agile team leader, is noticing that her daily stand-up meetings are lasting well long of the suggested 15 minutes. What can she do to ensure meetings stay brief and productive?

A. Ask team members to cancel daily stand-up meetings in favor for a weekly two hour meeting.

B. Wait to handle any issues that take longer than a few minutes to discuss after the daily stand-up meeting has concluded.

C. Dissuade team members from sharing pertinent progress information to keep the meetings brief.

D. Downplay or ignore shared information that she feels is inconsequential so team members will, via osmotic communication, feel disinclined to share at daily stand-ups.

9. Frank is using a software tool to sketch a prototype of a web site for the customer to review. The prototype will include the layout, content, and some functionality. What type of prototype is Frank using?

A. Model

B. Wireframe

C. Simulated

D. Draft

10. Which agile framework emphasizes the importance of an "on-site customer?"

A. HUP

B. AUP

C. XP

D. DSDM

11. As a product owner, Hanna believes in the value of 'incremental delivery.' Why might Hanna see value in incremental delivery?

A. As product owner, she can choose to pair program during the delivery demonstration to remove defects.

B. As product owner, she can choose which developers are working on the project.

C. As product owner, she can refactor the code herself.

D. As product owner, she can review the state of the product and provide feedback.

12. How often does iteration planning occur?

A. Before each iteration

B. During an iteration

C. During daily planning

D. After each iteration

13. When does planning for a release take place?

A. During iteration planning

B. During daily planning

C. During closing

D. During release planning

14. Hector is using a risk-to-value matrix technique to understand the value of each feature according to the customer. What is a risk-to-value matrix an example of?

A. A constraints-based analysis technique

B. An IDEF-0 analysis technique

C. A value-based analysis technique

D. A quality-based analysis technique

15. As agile team leader, Stacey intends to schedule a brainstorming session to generate ideas that may help solve some of the team's current issues. Which of the following is NOT a good brainstorming technique that Stacey should use?

A. Having an engaging and experienced facilitator lead the brainstorming session.

B. Use closed-ended questions to keep on schedule.

C. Having a multi-disciplinary/diverse group so that many different perspectives are available.

D. Sending participants preparatory material, so they know what to expect and what is expected of them.

16. When is an iteration backlog created?

A. During the project vision workshop

B. During iteration planning

C. During reflection meetings

D. During release planning

17. EVM is a frequently used project management abbreviation. What does EV stand for in the EVM technique?

A. Earned verification

B. Earned variation

C. Earned validation

D. Earned value

18. What earned value management (EVM) variable captures the total project budget?

A. Net present value (NPV)

B. Budget at completion (BAC)

C. Earned value (EV)

D. Project budget (PB)

19. What technology can facilitate some osmotic communication for team members that do NOT share the same workspace?

A. Video conferencing

B. None

C. Mail

D. E-mail

20. Although face-to-face communication is preferred in agile projects, other types of communication may substitute in the absence of collocated team members. Which of the following is NOT a satisfactory substitute for face-to-face communication?

A. Postal mail

B. Video conferencing

C. Instant messaging

D. E-mail

21. Which of the following is an agile 'feedback technique for product?'

A. Prototyping

B. Defect reduction plan

C. Waterfalling

D. E-mailing

22. Of the following, which is a key soft skill negotiation quality?

A. Collaboration intelligence

B. Emotional adaptation

C. Capitulation

D. Collaboration

23. What is the perfect amount of coaching and mentoring for an agile team so that it may improve its performance?

A. Coaching and mentoring is unnecessary within agile project management.

B. Continuous and pervasive coaching and mentoring.

C. It varies depending on the needs of the team and size of the organization.

D. Minimal to reduce distracting the development team.

24. What is a product backlog?

A. A list of the product features to be developed in a sprint.

B. A list of all product features to be developed in a release.

C. A list of the product features to be developed in an iteration.

D. A list of possible product features to be developed in an iteration.

25. When estimating time, budget and cost for agile projects, what constraints are generally known by the customer?

A. Cost

B. Time and budget

C. Time and cost

D. Budget and cost

26. When defining an iteration length, what details should a team focus on?

A. Delivering valuable chunks of product functionality, story definition and development, and customer acceptance of stories.

B. Delivering valuable chunks of untested code, expected task complexity, and customer acceptance of stories.

C. Average team velocity, financial calendar quarter schedule, and the build, test, design process.

D. Delivering valuable chunks of untested code, story definition and development, and customer acceptance of stories.

27. Jules is describing the SMART acronym used for task analysis in an agile seminar. What does the M stand for?

A. Miserly

B. Moore's Law

C. Measurable

D. Mandatory

28. Which of the following is NOT a characteristic of agile project management?

A. Focus on business priorities

B. Incremental development of products and services

C. Focus on customer value

D. Use of baselines for schedule and budget control

29. What person in the agile framework "empowers the team to make decisions collaboratively with the customer?"

A. Product owner

B. Business analyst

C. Project leader

D. Customer

30. Nathan intends to schedule a brainstorming session to generate ideas that may help solve some of the team's current issues. Which of the following is a good brainstorming technique that Nathan should use?

A. Sending participants preparatory material, so they know what to expect and what is expected of them.

B. Encouraging criticism early and often to prevent poorly thought out ideas entering the conversation as technical debt.

C. Hosting the meeting in the typical Monday morning conference room that is usually only available to certain team members.

D. Having a single-discipline/homogenous group so that the team can communicate more effectively.

31. Of the following, which is an agile principle per the Agile Manifesto?

A. Encouraging customer collaboration

B. Welcoming processes and tools

C. Encouraging working software

D. Welcoming change.

32. What is a common communication technique that may help teams reduce miscommunication and misunderstanding?

A. Active listening

B. Passive listening

C. Engaged listening

D. Focused listening

33. You have been tasked to serve as an agile project leader for a new online camp reservation system. What agile manifesto-influenced tactic will you apply as project leader?

A. Ignoring lessons learned because they are unlikely to occur again

B. Strict team oversight and delegation of tasks

C. Employing the waterfall development method

D. Conveying information to the customer about iteration progress

34. According to the PMI Code, what should be done with any allegations of misconduct or illegal activity?

A. Ensure that they are comprehensive.

B. Ensure that they are substantiated.

C. Ensure that they are filed with the appropriate parties immediately.

D. Ensure that they are properly outlined.

35. Of the following responses, which is a community value per the PMI agile community of practice community charter?

A. Transparency

B. Enthralled

C. Flexible

D. Endurance

36. What popular agile game is available for a team that wants to estimate the relative effort of developing user stories using story points?

A. Card planning

B. Planning poker

C. Planning cards

D. Planning game

37. Select a technique used for value-based analysis?

A. SMART

B. Cano

C. inVEsT

D. Kano

38. Nathan and his team are in the midst of iteration planning. How does the team prioritize and select the features to be developed in the forthcoming iteration?

A. By quality and cost

B. By value and velocity

C. By priority and market research

D. By velocity and market research

39. Peter, Jacob, Ralph, Brandy, and Sue have just voted in a planning poker meeting. Peter voted a 1, Jacob a 2, Ralph a 3, Brandy a 2, and Sue an 8. What should the team do next?

A. Take the mode as the estimate (2).

B. Use 3.2 as the estimate.

C. Err on the side of caution and use 8 as the estimate.

D. Have Peter and Sue explain their votes and repeat the voting process.

40. Ralph is describing the INVEST acronym used for user story development in an agile practitioner seminar. What does the E in INVEST stand for?

A. Easy

B. Error proof

C. Erratum

D. Estimable

PMI-ACP Lite Mock Exam 8 Answer Key and Explanations

1. D - The agile secondary values include: documentation of software, processes and tools, contract negotiation, and following project plans. [Manifesto for Agile Software Development. Agile Alliance.] [Knowledge and Skills: Level 1]

2. C - Tasks that have not yet started should be located in the 'to do' column. [Lean-Agile Software Development: Achieving Enterprise Agility. Alan Shalloway, Guy Beaver, James R. Trott.] [Planning, monitoring, and adapting]

3. D - Return on Investment (ROI): A metric used to evaluate the efficiency of an investment or to compare efficiency among a number of investments. To calculate ROI, the return of an investment (i.e., the gain minus the cost) is divided by the cost of the investment. The result is usually expressed as a percentage and sometimes a ratio. The product owner is often said to be responsible for the ROI. [Agile Estimating and Planning. Mike Cohn.] [Value based prioritization]

4. C - Greg should place the task card in the 'ready for testing' column. All tasks must go through a testing or verification process to ensure quality is built into the development process. Typically, completed tasks are moved to the 'Ready for testing' column. Testing is then executed by the project testers and the customer. It is important to note that some tasks on the task board will not have specific verification or testing criteria. These tasks don't go in the 'Ready for testing' column but still need to be verified and are often placed in a 'To verify' column. [Lean-Agile Software Development: Achieving Enterprise Agility. Alan Shalloway, Guy Beaver, James R. Trott.] [Planning, monitoring, and adapting]

5. A - A cornerstone of Agile development is 'incremental delivery.' Incremental delivery is the frequent delivery of working products, which are successively improved, to a customer for immediate feedback and acceptance. Typically, a product is delivered at the end of each sprint or iteration for demonstration and feedback. In this feedback technique, a customer can review the product and provide updated requirements. Changed/updated/refined requirements are welcomed in the agile process to ensure the customer receives a valuable and quality product. A sprint or iteration typically lasts from two to four weeks and at the end a new and improved product is delivered, incrementally. [The Art of Agile Development. James Shore.] [Knowledge and Skills: Level 1]

6. B - Value stream mapping is a collaborative process analysis technique where a diverse team depicts/maps a process to identify where waste occurs and where improvements can be made. It is an example of a process analysis technique. Like value stream mapping, process mapping is also used to map a process to identify bottlenecks (places where processing slows and inventory can build). [Lean-Agile Software Development: Achieving Enterprise Agility. Alan Shalloway, Guy Beaver, James R. Trott.] [Knowledge and Skills: Level 2]

7. D - One communication technique to reduce misunderstanding and miscommunication is active listening. A well run agile project necessitates both

good listeners and communicators, active listening helps work towards both of these necessities. The basics of active listening include: 1) Being present and focusing your attention on the speaker. 2) Taking notes instead of interrupting. 3) Paraphrasing to confirm and review what you have heard. 4) Summarizing the conversation once it has concluded for posterity. Using open ended questions, good body language, and silence can help improve listening skills. [Coaching Agile Teams. Lyssa Adkins.] [Knowledge and Skills: Level 1]

8. B - Issues that take longer than a few minutes to resolve in a daily stand-up meeting should be tabled and resolved between the appropriate parties after the daily stand-up meeting has concluded. This ensures that the meetings are brief and productive. [The Art of Agile Development. James Shore.] [Communications]

9. B - In the agile design process, prototypes help the customer understand current design state. Three common types of prototypes are HTML, paper (i.e., sketches), and wireframes. A wireframe is a sketch of a user interface, identifying its content, layout, functionality, is usually black and white, and excludes detailed pictures or graphics. A wireframe can be created on paper, whiteboards, or using software. [Agile Estimating and Planning. Mike Cohn.] [Agile analysis and design]

10. C - XP primary principles include: collective ownership, continuous integration, energized work, shared workspaces, and an on-site customer. [The Art of Agile Development. James Shore.] [Knowledge and Skills: Level 3]

11. D - A cornerstone of Agile development is 'incremental delivery.' Incremental delivery is the frequent delivery of working products, which are successively improved, to a customer for immediate feedback and acceptance. Typically, a product is delivered at the end of each sprint or iteration for demonstration and feedback. In this feedback technique, a customer can review the product and provide updated requirements. Changed/updated/refined requirements are welcomed in the agile process to ensure the customer receives a valuable and quality product. A sprint or iteration typically lasts from two to four weeks and at the end a new and improved product is delivered, incrementally. [The Art of Agile Development. James Shore.] [Knowledge and Skills: Level 1]

12. A - Iteration planning occurs before every iteration [The Art of Agile Development. James Shore.] [Planning, monitoring, and adapting]

13. D - Planning for a release occurs during release planning. [The Art of Agile Development. James Shore.] [Planning, monitoring, and adapting]

14. C - Value-based analysis strives to understand how value, as defined by the customer, relates to various components of the product, like features and tasks. Features are often prioritized with prioritization based on value and risk. Prioritization can be performed using the MoSCoW or Kano method and through the use of risk-to-value and cost-to-value matrices. [Lean-Agile Software Development: Achieving Enterprise Agility. Alan Shalloway, Guy Beaver, James R. Trott.] [Knowledge and Skills: Level 2]

15. B - A successful brainstorming event should strive to consider the following points - Host the meeting in a neutral and comfortable environment - Have an engaging and experienced facilitator lead the event - Send participants an overview, with goals, schedule, and what ground rules, beforehand - Have a multi-disciplinary/diverse team to get a broader perspective - Delay any criticism that may stifle idea generation. [Agile Retrospectives: Making Good Teams Great. Esther Derby, Diana Larsen, Ken Schwaber.] [Knowledge and Skills: Level 1]

16. B - An agile team creates the iteration backlog during iteration planning [The Art of Agile Development. James Shore.] [Planning, monitoring, and adapting]

17. D - EVM or earned value management is a management technique used to evaluate project performance with respect to cost and schedule. EVM relies on other common financial metrics like Budget At Completion (BAC), Actual Cost (AC), Planned Value (PV), Earned Value (EV), Cost Variance (CV), Schedule Variance (SV), Cost Performance Index (CPI), and Schedule Performance Index (SPI). [Agile Estimating and Planning. Mike Cohn.] [Metrics]

18. B - EVM or earned value management is a management technique used to evaluate project performance with respect to cost and schedule. EVM relies on other common financial metrics like Budget At Completion (BAC), Actual Cost (AC), Planned Value (PV), Earned Value (EV), Cost Variance (CV), Schedule Variance (SV), Cost Performance Index (CPI), and Schedule Performance Index (SPI). BAC is the total project budget. [Agile Estimating and Planning. Mike Cohn.] [Knowledge and Skills: Level 3]

19. A - Video conferencing and instant messaging are technologies that can provide some level of osmotic communication. [Agile Software Development: The Cooperative Game – 2nd Edition. Alistair Cockburn.] [Communications]

20. A - Video conferencing, e-mail and instant messaging are technologies that can provide some level of communication in the absence of face-to-face communication. [Agile Software Development: The Cooperative Game – 2nd Edition. Alistair Cockburn.] [Communications]

21. A - There are several feedback techniques - techniques that facilitate constructive criticism to improve product value and quality - built into the agile process. In the classic definition, feedback is a dynamic process where past information influences the behavior of the same process in the future. Agile feedback techniques include prototyping, simulation, demonstration, evaluations, pair programming, unit testing, continuous integration, daily stand-up meetings, sprint planning. Because agile prides itself on a transparent and collaborative environment, feedback is essentially ubiquitous. [Agile Retrospectives: Making Good Teams Great. Esther Derby, Diana Larsen, Ken Schwaber.] [Knowledge and Skills: Level 1]

22. D - Key soft skills negotiation qualities for the effective implementation and practice of agile are: emotional intelligence, collaboration, adaptive leadership, negotiation, conflict resolution, servant leadership. [Coaching Agile Teams. Lyssa Adkins.] [Soft skills negotiation]

23. C - Coaching and mentoring within teams can be helpful for nascent agile teams and even for more experienced agile teams. Coaching and mentoring is the act of helping a person or team improve performance and achieve realistic goals. Because agile has a value of continuous improvement, coaching and mentoring is not solely for new or immature teams, but experienced ones too where coaching can help achieve higher levels of performance. The amount of coaching and mentoring an agile team needs is variable. Some newer teams will need a coach guiding the team nearly all the time while others may need a coach only for particularly challenging situations. A not uncommon scenario is to have a coach help the team collectively during sprint/iteration planning and then during the iteration help mentor individual team members. [Coaching Agile Teams. Lyssa Adkins.] [Knowledge and Skills: Level 1]

24. B - The product backlog is a comprehensive list of all product features to be developed in an iteration. [Lean-Agile Software Development: Achieving Enterprise Agility. Alan Shalloway, Guy Beaver, James R. Trott.] [Agile analysis and design]

25. B - Time, budget, and cost estimation is an important knowledge and skill area of agile. According to Highsmith, the nature of the agile method, whereby it welcomes changing scope, means that it lends itself well to fixed budgets and a fixed schedule because changing scope makes it difficult to estimate a total cost. Generally speaking, the budget and schedule constraints are known but before a project will commence there needs to be an agreed upon set of base product functionality defined in an initiation phase; fixing scope reduces an agile team's innovative tendency to provide improved value. For companies that are familiar with fixed-price contracts, where requirements are agreed upon before contract closing, adopting agile can be a weary initial venture. Instead, other contract vehicle types are recommended for agile efforts. These include: a general service contract for the initiation phase and separate fixed-price contracts for iterations or user stories; time-and-material contracts; not-to-exceed with fixed-fee contracts; and, incentive contracts (e.g., fixed price with incentive; cost-reimbursable with award fee). [Agile Project Management: Creating Innovative Products – 2nd Edition. Jim Highsmith.] [Knowledge and Skills: Level 1]

26. A - When defining the length of iterations, the team should consider how it will deliver valuable chunks of product functionality, the definition and development of user stories, and the acceptance of user stories by customers. [Agile Estimating and Planning. Mike Cohn.] [Planning, monitoring, and adapting]

27. C - The acronym SMART (specific, measurable, achievable, relevant, and time-boxed) helps the agile practitioner remember the characteristics of a well-defined task. S – Specific tasks are ones that clearly contribute to the development of a user story. It should not be vague. M – Measurable tasks are ones that the team and customer can verify. A - Achievable tasks are ones that developers may realistically implement and understand. R - Relevant tasks are ones that unequivocally add value to the user story. T - Timeboxed tasks are ones that can have an estimate assigned of the amount of effort or time needed for development. [Agile Retrospectives: Making Good Teams Great. Esther Derby, Diana Larsen, Ken Schwaber.] [Planning, monitoring, and adapting]

28. D - Key characteristics of agile project management include: continuous improvement, cross-functional teams, short iterations, an incremental approach, and business priorities and customer value. [The Art of Agile Development. James Shore.] [Knowledge and Skills: Level 1]

29. C - A common misconception in agile is that an agile team does not need a leader. In fact, all agile teams need a leader, but the way in which the leader leads is fundamentally different than the typical traditional project manager/project leader method. Some have theorized that this misconception stems from the desired 'self-organizing' quality of the agile team. And although the 'self-organizing' agile team is empowered to take ownership and responsibility of the product and make some decisions itself, it nevertheless requires a leader to help provide guidance, mentoring, coaching, problem solving, and decision making. Some key aspects required of an agile leader include: empowering team members to decide what standard agile practices and methods it will use; allowing the team to be self-organized and self-disciplined; empowering the team members to make decisions collaboratively with the customer; inspire the team to be innovative and explore new ideas and technology capabilities; be a champion of and articulate the product vision to team members so it will be motivated to accomplish the overall objective; remove any obstacles and solve any problems the team may face in its effort; communicate and endorse the values and principles of agile project management to stakeholders that may be unfamiliar with agile; ensure that all stakeholders, including business managers and developers, are collaborating effectively; and, be able to adapt the leadership style to the working environment to ensure that the agile values and principles are effectively upheld. [The Art of Agile Development. James Shore.] [Knowledge and Skills: Level 1]

30. A - A successful brainstorming event should strive to consider the following points - Host the meeting in a neutral and comfortable environment - Have an engaging and experienced facilitator lead the event - Send participants an overview, with goals, schedule, and what ground rules, beforehand - Have a multi-disciplinary/diverse team to get a broader perspective - Delay any criticism that may stifle idea generation. [Agile Retrospectives: Making Good Teams Great. Esther Derby, Diana Larsen, Ken Schwaber.] [Knowledge and Skills: Level 1]

31. D - The Agile Manifesto defines 12 supporting principles. Agile principles include 1) Our highest priority is to satisfy the customer through early and continuous delivery of valuable software. 2) Welcome changing requirements, even late in development. Agile processes harness change for the customer's competitive advantage. 3) Deliver working software frequently, from a couple of weeks to a couple of months, with preference to the shorter timescale. 4) Business people and developers must work together daily throughout the project. 5) Build projects around motivated individuals. Give them the environment and support they need, and trust them to get the job done. 6) The most efficient and effective method of conveying information to and within a development team is face-to-face conversation. 7) Working software is the primary measure of progress. 8) Agile processes promote sustainable development. The sponsors, developers, and users should be able to maintain a constant pace indefinitely. 9) Continuous attention to technical excellence and good design enhances agility. 10) Simplicity--the art of maximizing the amount of work not done--is essential. 11) The best architectures, requirements, and designs emerge from self-organizing teams. 12) At regular intervals, the team reflects on how to become more effective, then tunes and adjusts its behavior accordingly. [Manifesto for Agile Software Development. Agile Alliance.] [Knowledge and Skills: Level 1]

32. A - One communication technique to reduce misunderstanding and miscommunication is active listening. A well run agile project necessitates both good listeners and communicators, active listening helps work towards both of these necessities. The basics of active listening include: 1) Being present and focusing your attention on the speaker. 2) Taking notes instead of interrupting. 3) Paraphrasing to confirm and review what you have heard. 4) Summarizing the conversation once it has concluded for posterity. Using open ended questions, good body language, and silence can help improve listening skills. [Coaching Agile Teams. Lyssa Adkins.] [Knowledge and Skills: Level 1]

33. D - Customer collaboration over contract negotiation as an agile value and focusing on satisfying the customer as an agile principle indicates that conveying information to the customer about iteration progress is the best choice. The Agile Manifesto defines four values and 12 supporting principles. The values are 1) individuals and interactions over processes and tools, 2) working software over comprehensive documentation, 3) customer collaboration over contract negotiation, and 4) responding to change over following a plan. Agile principles include 1) focusing on satisfying the customer, 2) welcoming change, 3) delivering working software frequently, 4) ensuring that business people and developers work together, 5) motivating the individuals involved in development, 6) using face-to-face communication whenever possible, 7) using working software as the primary measure of progress, 8) maintaining a constant pace of development, 9) paying continuous attention to technical excellence and good design, 10) aiming for simplicity, 11) using self-organizing teams, and 12) regularly reflecting on how to become more effective. [Manifesto for Agile Software Development. Agile Alliance.] [Knowledge and Skills: Level 1]

34. B - The PMI Code of Ethics and Professional Conduct states that it is mandatory for a project manager to: inform yourself about and uphold the policies, rules, regulations, and laws that govern your work, including professional and volunteer activities; report unethical or illegal conduct to appropriate parties and, if necessary, to those affected by the misconduct; ensure that any allegations of misconduct or illegal activity are substantiated and file only complaints that are supported by facts; never take part or help someone else take part in illegal activities. [PMI Code of Ethics and Professional Conduct. Project Management Institute.] [Knowledge and Skills: Level 2]

35. A - The following are community values of the PMI agile community of practice community charter: Vision, Servant Leadership, Trust, Collaboration, Honesty, Learning, Courage, Openness, Adaptability, Leading Change, Transparency [PMI Agile Community of Practice Community Charter. Project Management Institute.] [Knowledge and Skills: Level 1]

36. B - Planning poker is a popular agile game used to estimate the relative work effort of developing a user story. Each team member has a deck of cards with various numbered values which he or she can draw from to "play (showing one card)" to indicate an estimated point value of developing a user story. [Coaching Agile Teams. Lyssa Adkins.] [Knowledge and Skills: Level 3]

37. D - Value-based analysis strives to understand how value, as defined by the customer, relates to various components of the product, like features and tasks. Features are often prioritized with prioritization based on value and risk. Prioritization can be performed using the MoSCoW or Kano method and through the use of risk-to-value and cost-to-value matrices. [Lean-Agile Software Development: Achieving Enterprise Agility. Alan Shalloway, Guy Beaver, James R. Trott.] [Knowledge and Skills: Level 2]

38. B - When a team performs iteration planning, it prioritizes features or user stories to develop in the forthcoming iteration by priority and velocity. The most valuable user stories are typically developed first and the team's estimated velocity helps plan how many user stories or features should be developed in the iteration. [The Art of Agile Development. James Shore.] [Planning, monitoring, and adapting]

39. D - Planning poker is based upon the wideband Delphi estimation technique. It is a consensus-based technique for estimating effort. Sometimes called scrum poker, it is a technique for a relative estimation of effort, typically in story points, to develop a user story. At a planning poker meeting, each estimator is given an identical deck of planning poker cards with a wide range of values. The Fibonacci sequence is often used for values for planning poker (i.e., 0, 1, 1, 2, 3, 5,8,etc.); another common sequence is (question mark, 0, 1/2, 1, 2, 3, 5, 8, 13, 20, 40, and 100). A planning poker meeting works as follows: 1) a moderator, not estimating, facilitates the meeting. 2) the product owner/manager provides a short overview of the user story and answers clarifying questions posed by the developers. Typically the product owner does not vote. 3) Each estimator selects an estimate of work effort by selecting a card, 4) Once everyone has selected a card, everyone overturns their card concurrently, 5) Estimators with high and low estimates are given a chance to defend positions. 6) The process repeats until there is consensus. The developer who owns the user story is typically given higher credence. [Agile Estimating and Planning. Mike Cohn.] [Agile estimation]

40. D - The acronym INVEST (independent, negotiable, valuable, estimable, small, and testable) helps the agile practitioner remember the characteristics of a good user story. I – Independent stories can be developed in any order and avoid dependencies which can make development more complex. N – Negotiable user stories mean that both the customer and developer should feel free to analyze and adapt a user story to meet customer needs. V – A valuable user story describes how the product feature will provide value to the customer. E – Estimable user stories are ones that developers can readily estimate the effort or duration required for developing them. S- Small user stories are ones that take about two to five days of work to implement. T - Testable user stories are ones that can be verified according to acceptance criteria to ensure value. [Agile Retrospectives: Making Good Teams Great. Esther Derby, Diana Larsen, Ken Schwaber.] [Planning, monitoring, and adapting]

Knowledge Area Quiz
Agile Analysis and Design
Practice Questions

Test Name: Knowledge Area Test: Agile Analysis and Design
Total Questions: 15
Correct Answers Needed to Pass:
11 (73.33%)
Time Allowed: 25 Minutes

Test Description

This practice quiz specifically targets your knowledge of the Agile Analysis and Design exam topic area.

Test Questions

1. In agile modeling, what is a persona?

   A. A made up personality used for facilitating the daily stand-up meeting

   B. An assigned personality used in reflection workshops.

   C. A notional user of the system under development.

   D. A method to describe the customer's personality for the day so the team may adapt to his or her feedback in the most effective way

2. What is a theme in the context of agile development?

   A. A set of related topics for the retrospective.

   B. A set of related programmer tasks.

   C. A set of related topics for scrum review.

   D. A set of related user stories.

3. Of the following, select the response which holds the three aspects of a user story.

   A. Written description; conversations; and testing criteria

   B. Spoken dialogue; written rationale; and done done criteria

   C. Spoken description; written dialogue; and testing criteria

   D. Spoken description; collaborative dialogue; and testing criteria

4. During iteration planning the team is having a difficult time interpreting the customer's intent of the user story. What should the team do?

   A. Collaborate with the customer to clarify the user story.

   B. Discuss among the product development team.

   C. Conduct several spike tasks.

   D. Research the domain.

5. Code refactoring allows for

A. Restructuring of test code to update unit test code without changing external behavior.

B. Restructuring of source code to update external functionality and internal behavior.

C. Restructuring of source code to update external functionality without changing internal behavior.

D. Restructuring of source code to update internal code without changing external behavior.

6. The customer is off site this week but insists on seeing a working prototype of the design so that she may provide feedback. What is a suitable prototype method to use?

A. Whiteboard

B. Chart paper

C. HTML or other portable software solution

D. Paper

7. What is the agile story map essentially equivalent to in traditional project management?

A. The product list

B. The product requirements

C. The project plan

D. The project schedule

8. In agile parlance, what does progressive elaboration refer to?

A. Continuous planning with the expectation that plans and details will inevitably change but become more refined as the project progresses.

B. Continuous planning with the expectation that velocity will increase progressively as the project progresses.

C. Continuous planning with the expectation that estimates of task time will become more progressive as the project evolves.

D. Continuous planning with the expectation that story point values will decrease in relation to the steep learning curve of developers.

9. What are prototypes and how are they used in projects?

A. Prototypes are not used in projects.

B. Prototypes are initial schedules used in a rolling wave plan.

C. Prototypes are relatively low cost, low risk methods to share a design concept for stakeholder feedback.

D. Prototypes are user stories in draft format awaiting acceptance to the product backlog.

10. What is rolling wave planning and how does it relate to progressive elaboration?

A. Rolling wave planning involves planning for an entire release at the beginning of a project. Progressive elaboration assumes that while customer requirements may change, they will not impact the initial rolling wave plan.

B. Rolling wave planning involves a retrospective review of plans from the previous two iterations. Momentum from these two iterations , typically interpreted as velocity, form a 'prediction wave' which can be used to plan the next iteration. Progressive elaboration assumes that the wave will grow in power as the project progresses.

C. Rolling wave planning involves planning in waves or phases. Only the next few iterations are planned in detail and iterations more distant are planned only at a high-level. Progressive elaboration is continuous planning that assumes that details and requirements will be better refined later and will be incorporated into the planning process at the appropriate time.

D. Rolling wave planning and progressive elaboration are both antiquated traditional project management planning techniques.

11. Of the following, which user story is NOT closed?

A. A camper can sign up for a trip.

B. A camper can navigate the webpage.

C. A camper can review a detailed trip itinerary.

D. A camper can cancel a trip.

12. In which agile project management methodology does chartering play a significant role?

A. TDD

B. Crystal

C. XP

D. FDD

13. What is the purpose of the Exploratory 360 assessment?

A. To define the core project team

B. To assess project soundness in terms of business value and feasibility

C. To conduct an introspective reflection on the team makeup

D. To define a project mission and vision

14. What is the ideal duration range for developing a user story?

A. 1 to 2 sprints

B. 1 to 2 iterations

C. 2 to 5 days

D. 15 days

15. Select the technique that is commonly used to create a story map?

A. MoSCoW

B. MoSTyN

C. MoNTO

D. MoNTauK

Knowledge Area Quiz
Agile Analysis and Design
Answer Key and Explanations

1. C - A persona is a notional user of the system under development. Being much more detailed than actors in use case modeling where generic user names are assigned (e.g., end user), personas try to elaborate on users with detailed descriptions to provide context to the developers. Some personas have such notional details as name, address, age, income, likes and dislikes, and other specific details. [User Stories Applied: For Agile Software Development. Mike Cohn.] [Agile analysis and design]

2. D - A theme, in the context of agile development, is a set of related user stories. [User Stories Applied: For Agile Software Development. Mike Cohn.] [Agile analysis and design]

3. A - A user story is composed of the following three aspects: 1) A written description of the story; 2) Conversations about the story (think verbal, rather than written here); and, 3) Tests that convey when a story can be accepted or complete. [User Stories Applied: For Agile Software Development. Mike Cohn.] [Agile analysis and design]

4. A - Because agile emphasizes customer collaboration, the team should simply collaborate with the customer to clarify the user story. [User Stories Applied: For Agile Software Development. Mike Cohn.] [Agile analysis and design]

5. D - Code refactoring is method of improving working source code to make it more efficient, readable, extensible, maintainable and less complex. Through refactoring one is able to restructure source code modifying internal code without changing the external behavior. [Agile Retrospectives: Making Good Teams Great. Esther Derby, Diana Larsen, Ken Schwaber.] [Agile analysis and design]

6. C - HTML and other software based solutions are ideal for presenting prototypes to customers, especially when off site. Software based prototypes are dynamic, graphic capable, and portable. [Agile Software Development: The Cooperative Game – 2nd Edition. Alistair Cockburn.] [Agile analysis and design]

7. C - In agile, the story map is essentially the project plan. It orders the user stories/product features into logical themes to serve as a plan for development. [User Stories Applied: For Agile Software Development. Mike Cohn.] [Agile analysis and design]

8. A - Progressive elaboration is continuous planning with the expectation that project plans and details will change but become more refined as the project progresses. [Agile Estimating and Planning. Mike Cohn.] [Agile analysis and design]

9. C - Prototypes are low cost, low risk methods to portray a design idea to a customer in order to obtain feedback before development. Although time consuming and having cost, prototypes can help save later costs that may occur if a design is not modeled beforehand to obtain feedback and fails to meet customer expectations. [Agile Software Development: The Cooperative Game – 2nd Edition.

Alistair Cockburn.] [Agile analysis and design]

10. C - Rolling wave planning (or rolling look ahead planning) involves planning in waves or phases and is especially useful for large, complex projects. Only the next few iterations are planned in detail and iterations more distant are planned only at a high-level. Progressive elaboration is continuous planning that assumes that details and requirements will be better refined later and will be incorporated into the planning process at the appropriate time. [Agile Estimating and Planning. Mike Cohn.] [Agile analysis and design]

11. B - The best answer is "A camper can navigate the webpage" because it is an activity that has no clear end point. The other selections include activities that have a clear end point. [User Stories Applied: For Agile Software Development. Mike Cohn.] [Agile analysis and design]

12. B - The Crystal development process is cyclical/iterative. Its primary components are chartering, delivery cycles, and project wrap-up. Chartering involves creating a project charter, which can last from a few days to a few weeks. Chartering consists of four activities: 1) Building the core project team, 2) performing an Exploratory 360° assessment, 3) fine tuning the methodology, and 3) building the initial project plan. [Agile Software Development: The Cooperative Game – 2nd Edition. Alistair Cockburn.] [Agile analysis and design]

13. B - The executive sponsor conducts the Exploratory 360° assessment to assess the business case of the project. Several dimensions are explored: business value, requirements, domain area, and technology impacts. Based on the results the team adjusts the Crystal methodology to the need or, in some cases, the project may be cancelled if serious issues are discovered. [Agile Software Development: The Cooperative Game – 2nd Edition. Alistair Cockburn.] [Agile analysis and design]

14. C - The ideal development duration range for a user story is 2 to 5 days. [User Stories Applied: For Agile Software Development. Mike Cohn.] [Agile analysis and design]

15. A - The MoSCoW technique is commonly used in agile to prioritize user stories and create a story map. The MoSCoW technique prioritizes user stories into the following groups in descending order of priority: M - Must have; S - Should have; C - Could have; W - Would have. Must have items are those product features which are absolutely essential to develop. Should have items are product features that are not essential but have significant business value. Could have items are product features that would add some business value. Would have items are product features that have marginal business value. [User Stories Applied: For Agile Software Development. Mike Cohn.] [Agile analysis and design]

PMI-ACP Lite Mock Exam 9 Practice Questions

Test Name: PMI-ACP Lite Mock Exam 9
Total Questions: 40
Correct Answers Needed to Pass:
30 (75.00%)
Time Allowed: 60 Minutes

Test Description

This is a cumulative PMI-ACP Mock Exam which can be used as a benchmark for your PMI-ACP aptitude. This practice test includes questions from all exam topic areas, including sections from Agile Tools and Techniques, and all three Agile Knowledge and Skills areas.

Test Questions

1. Andy and his team are in the middle of iteration planning. The team has identified from one user story eight required tasks. Approximately how long should each task take to develop or execute?

A. Exactly one hour

B. Less than two hours

C. Between four hours and two days

D. Five business days

2. Henry and his agile team have just made a group decision about how many features to build, test, and integrate in the upcoming sprint. What type of decision making model is it when a team makes decisions collaboratively?

A. Exclusive

B. Participatory

C. Inclusive

D. Merit

3. What occurs during the initiating phase of traditional project management?

A. Comparing actual vs. planned work

B. Detailed project planning

C. Execution of the project plan

D. Definition of the business objectives

4. Select the last phase of Jim Highsmith's agile project management model.

A. Exploring

B. Speculating

C. Adapting

D. Closing

5. Which is NOT a phase of Highsmith's agile project management?

A. Envisioning

B. Closing

C. Exploring

D. Initiating

6. Peter and Zach work together on an agile project as software developers. Because Peter and Zach are collocated they are often aware of each other's daily progress without speaking directly to one another. What are Peter and Zach benefiting from?

A. Kanban communication

B. Extra sensory perception

C. Osmotic communication

D. Chaordic communication

7. Frank is using an agile framework that emphasizes using a strict business perspective. Which framework is Frank most likely using?

A. Static systems development method (SSDM)

B. Extreme systems development method (XSDM)

C. Dynamic systems development method (DSDM)

D. Dynamic product development method (DPDM)

8. Servant leadership is a desirable feature for a team leader in agile. What is the best short description of servant leadership?

A. A translator.

B. A task driver.

C. An enabler.

D. An interpreter.

9. On a burndown chart, how does the charted 'actual work accomplished' series appear?

A. As a straight, downward sloping line

B. Typically as a non-linear line that reflects the ebbs and flows of development

C. As a curved, downward sloping line

D. As a straight, upward sloping line

10. Which framework often leveraged in agile heavily emphasizes continuous improvement?

A. Extreme software development

B. Kaizen value development

C. Lean software development

D. Extreme unified process (EUP)

11. Which framework uses the following four phases: 1. inception, 2. elaboration, 3. construction, 4. transition?

A. Simple unified process (SUP)

B. Extreme unified process (EUP)

C. Agile unified process (AUP)

D. Adapted unified process (AdUP)

12. Perry is about to prioritize user stories to develop a story map with her agile team. What technique is commonly used to do so?

A. ToRonTO

B. BoSToN

C. MoSCoW

D. HaMBurG

13. Two of the Agile Manifesto's four core values cover communication values. Select these values from the list.

A. Face-to-face communication whenever possible and continuous improvement

B. Face-to-face communication whenever possible and self-organizing teams

C. Individuals and interactions over processes and tools, and customer collaboration over contract negotiation

D. Face-to-face communication whenever possible and ensuring that business people and developers work together

14. Chris is serving as a scrum master for a local software company. In the envisioning phase of Jim Highsmith's agile project management model, Chris and his team will focus on which of the following items?

A. Specification of iterations and release plans

B. Detailed project plan

C. Project vision, scope and requirements, and project schedule

D. Feature breakdown structure

15. Select the correct definition of the Critical chain project management method (CCPM) used in estimating a project buffer.

A. Half the squared sum of the 50% confidence estimate for all tasks

B. Sum the 50% confidence estimate for all tasks

C. Half the sum of the total safety time for all the tasks in a project

D. Find the square root of half the 50% confidence estimate for all tasks

16. A healthy stand-up meeting has several characteristics. Select the response that lists a majority of these characteristics.

A. Fine-grained coordination, a fine focus, lengthy discussion

B. Fine-grained coordination, a fine focus, and daily commitment

C. Fine-grained coordination, daily commitment, and short iterations

D. Fine-grained coordination, peer pressure, and a safety net

17. Select the best adjective that describes an agile team's project and quality standards.

A. Tailorable

B. Firm

C. Set

D. Inelastic

18. Define Cohn's square root of the sum of squares method that is often used to calculate a project buffer.

A. First find the 90% confidence level value of all tasks. Next, sum the square of these values. Finally, find the square root of the sum.

B. First find the 10% confidence level value of all tasks. Next, sum the square of these values. Finally, find the square root of the sum.

C. First find the local pessimum value of all tasks. Next, sum the square of these values. Finally, find the square root of the sum.

D. First find the local safety value of all tasks. Next, sum the square of these values. Finally, find the square root of the sum.

19. Select the best adjective that describes an agile team's project and quality standards.

A. Static

B. Fixed

C. Adaptable

D. Rigid

20. Of the following, select the best adjective that describes an agile team's project and quality standards.

A. Fixed

B. Static

C. Rigid

D. Adjustable

21. How does the project trade-off matrix classify the constraints of scope, cost, and schedule?

A. Fixed, flexible or accept

B. Fixed, flexible or closed

C. Fixed, formed, or closed

D. Fixed, floating, or accept

22. Highsmith has indicated that a particular type of contract is suitable for the agile method. Which type of contract does Highsmith indicate?

A. Fixed-value

B. Fixed-cost

C. Fixed-budget and fixed-schedule

D. Fixed-price

23. Select the response that lists contract types suited for agile development.

A. General service for the initial phase with fixed-price contracts for successive phases; cost-reimbursable/time and materials; not-to-exceed with fixed-fee

B. General service for the initial phase with fixed-price contracts for successive phases; cost-reimbursable/time and materials; fixed-price

C. Fixed-price; cost-reimbursable/ time and materials; not-to-exceed with fixed-fee

D. General service for the initial phase with fixed-price contracts for successive phases; fixed-price; not-to-exceed with fixed-fee

24. Define the concept of "timebox" as used in task definition.

A. Setting a range of acceptable story points that the team may accomplish within a set time period.

B. Setting a range of acceptable tasks that the team may accomplish within a set time period.

C. Setting an estimated and realistic duration for how long a task will take to perform.

D. Setting a strict, time requirement for the duration of task performance.

25. According to Highsmith, the agile project management approach is suitable for what type of contract?

A. Fixed-budget

B. Fixed-schedule

C. Fixed-price

D. Fixed-budget and fixed-schedule

26. Jill, as project lead, has been using mentoring to help coach her team to improve its performance. What is Jill doing when she provides mentoring?

A. Leading the team

B. Motivating the team

C. Criticizing the team

D. Reforming the team

27. Select the best definition of velocity.

A. A measure of the number of user story points or stories completed per iteration.

B. A measure of the number of user story points planned per release.

C. A measure of the number of user story points planned for an iteration.

D. A measure of the number of user story points completed per day.

28. Harry is the financial executive for an upcoming project that is slated to use agile. In terms of estimating time, budget, and cost for an agile effort, what does Harry typically have defined?

A. Time and cost

B. Cost

C. Budget and cost

D. Budget and time

29. Of the following, which is an agile principle per the Agile Manifesto?

A. Defect reduction

B. Regularly reflection on how to become more effective.

C. Focus on product value

D. Test-driven development

30. What person in the agile framework "ensures that all stakeholders, including business managers and developers, are collaborating effectively?"

A. Iteration planner

B. Product owner

C. Customer

D. Project leader

31. Which of the following responses best defines active listening?

A. Focusing your full attention on a speaker.

B. Focusing your full attention to any inconsistencies in the speaker's argument.

C. Focusing your full attention on what to say next in the conversation.

D. Focusing your full attention on environmental surroundings.

32. Lisa is describing the four Agile Manifesto values to her co-workers. Of the following, which response lists one of its primary values?

A. Following a plan

B. Working software

C. Comprehensive documentation

D. Processes and tools

33. The Agile Manifesto includes 12 principles. Which selection is the correct principle outlining the Agile Manifesto's communication preference?

A. Face-to-face communication whenever possible

B. Osmotic communication

C. Near Field Communication

D. Group-think communication

34. Chris is reviewing a long, descriptive document about his agile project that is required by local regulations. This type of conformance to local law is known as

A. Regulatory compliance

B. Forced compliance

C. Documentation compliance

D. Certification compliance

35. Having a high emotional intelligence is important to promote effective communication in an agile team. Which of the following\ is one of the seven components of emotional intelligence as defined by Higgs & Dulewicz?

A. Interpersonal gamesmanship

B. Influence

C. Fortitude

D. Emotional numbness

36. Where does the agile methodology technique of "stand-up" meeting get its name?

A. From the fact that team members must stand-up to challenges presented to them in the previous sprint

B. From the fact that all team members are encouraged to physically stand-up during the meeting to ensure for the meeting's efficiency.

C. From the fact that a team member must physically stand-up when called upon by the project leader to present yesterday's progress.

D. From the fact that team members must stand-up or present exploratory ideas to the team to determine project feasibility

37. Henry and Vicky are developers on an agile project. Many times Vicky is aware of Henry's daily situation without speaking directly with him and can help him problem solve if needed. What are Henry and Vicky benefiting from?

A. Entropic communication

B. Osmotic communication

C. Chaordic communication

D. Active listening

38. Kyle and his agile team have taken a user story that it estimates to be of average difficulty to develop and assigned it a value of 10. Now Kyle and his team must estimate the relative size or effort of other user stories in the backlog relative to this average user story. What unit is the value of 10 most likely in?

A. Function points

B. Use case points

C. Task points

D. Story points

39. Select from the following types of contracts, the one most suited for the agile framework.

A. General service contract for the initial phase with separate fixed-schedule contracts for each iteration.

B. General service contract for the initial phase with separate fixed-price contracts for each iteration.

C. Specific service contract for the initial phase with separate fixed-price contracts for each iteration.

D. Specific service contract for the initial phase with separate fixed-schedule contracts for each iteration.

40. Quimby has recently started an agile project where she is to be the project leader. What should Quimby aspire to be as agile leader?

A. Someone who constantly criticizes team members so that they are aware of their defects and can improve their performance.

B. Someone who inspires the team to focus on customer and product quality and value through an open and transparent development environment where the team is self-organizing and self-disciplined.

C. Someone that drives the team to maximum and unsustainable performance levels to exceed customer expectations.

D. Someone who inspires the team to focus on schedule, cost, and scope in a top-down, decision making development environment.

PMI-ACP Lite Mock Exam 9 Answer Key and Explanations

1. C - User stories or features are first assigned to iterations during release planning. The user stories are features are then decomposed into tasks during iteration planning so that the tasks may be assigned to specific developers. To help manage planning and monitoring, a rule of thumb for estimating task duration is that each task should take approximately four hours to two days of development work. [The Art of Agile Development. James Shore.] [Planning, monitoring, and adapting]

2. B - To build trust among the team, agile believes heavily in participatory decision models where team members collaborate to make decisions. Although a team leader or scrum master will need to make some decisions individually, many decisions can be made by the team collectively. These agile principles are also known as collective ownership, self-organization, and self-discipline. In collective ownership, the team members are equally responsible for project results and are empowered to participate in decision making and problem solving processes. [Agile Retrospectives: Making Good Teams Great. Esther Derby, Diana Larsen, Ken Schwaber.] [Knowledge and Skills: Level 2]

3. D - Definition of business objectives occurs during the initiating phase in a traditional project management effort. [Manifesto for Agile Software Development. Agile Alliance.] [Knowledge and Skills: Level 1]

4. D - Jim Highsmith's agile project management model consists of the following five phases: Envisioning, speculating, exploring, adapting, and closing. [Agile Project Management: Creating Innovative Products – 2nd Edition. Jim Highsmith.] [Knowledge and Skills: Level 1]

5. D - The agile project management phases, in sequence, are: Envisioning, speculating, exploring, adapting, closing. [Manifesto for Agile Software Development. Agile Alliance.] [Knowledge and Skills: Level 1]

6. C - Osmotic communication is a concept of communication where information is shared between collocated team members unconsciously. By sharing the same work environment, team members are exposed to the same environmental sounds and other environmental input and unconsciously share a common framework that improves communication. [Agile Software Development: The Cooperative Game – 2nd Edition. Alistair Cockburn.] [Communications]

7. C - Scrum is a framework that strives to facilitate the development of complex products quickly and efficiently, the adaptation of changing requirements, the delivery of working products incrementally. Scrum development includes three major phases: pre-game, game, and post-game. Scrum emphasizes the use of product and sprint backlogs, iterative development (termed "sprints"), daily stand-up meetings (termed "scrums"), sprint reviews (demos) and reflection, and the use of information radiators such as task boards and burndown charts. [Ken Schwaber. Agile Project Management with Scrum. Chapter 1.] [Knowledge and Skills: Level 2]

8. C - Servant leadership has its roots with an essay written in 1970 by Robert K Greenleaf. Greenleaf defined servant leaders as humble stewards devoted to their company and work to serve their peers, teams, and customers. In a self-organizing team, a servant leader, as Greenleaf defined it, is ideal as the team leader is an enabler, listening to the agile team's needs, removing obstacles, and providing tools or other support to promote high productivity. [Coaching Agile Teams. Lyssa Adkins.] [Soft skills negotiation]

9. B - A project burndown chart is an often used information radiator to show iteration progress. It charts two series: the actual work remaining and ideal/estimated work remaining. The vertical axis is the work unit (often story points or hours) and the horizontal axis is iteration duration (typically in number of days). The ideal/estimated work series is a straight, downward sloping line originating on the vertical axis at the value of work to be completed (e.g., 20 story points) and extending to the horizontal axis (i.e., 0 story points) on the last day of the iteration. The actual series is dependent upon the agile team's productivity and the task complexity and is updated daily. The actual series is typically volatile and is not a straight line but ebbs and flows as the project team tackles the development process. [Agile Estimating and Planning. Mike Cohn.] [Agile estimation]

10. C - Agile project management places strong emphasis on 'continuous improvement.' Continuous improvement processes are built into the agile methodology, from customers providing feedback after each iteration to the team reserving time to reflect on its performance through retrospectives after each iteration. Ongoing unit and integration testing and keeping up with technological/industry developments also play a part in the continuous improvement process. Continuous improvement is also a key principle in the lean methodology, where a focus of removing waste from the value stream is held. [The Art of Agile Development. James Shore.] [Knowledge and Skills: Level 2]

11. C - Agile Unified Process (AUP) is a simplified version of the Unified Process, or UP (UP itself is a more detailed framework for iterative and incremental software development). AUP simplifies UP for the agile framework. AUP projects use four phases: 1) inception, 2) elaboration, 3) construction, and 4) transition. At the end of each short iteration, the team delivers a working product. [Agile Software Development: The Cooperative Game – 2nd Edition. Alistair Cockburn.] [Knowledge and Skills: Level 2]

12. C - The MoSCoW technique is commonly used in agile to prioritize user stories and create a story map. The MoSCoW technique prioritizes user stories into the following groups in descending order of priority: M - Must have; S - Should have; C - Could have; W - Would have. Must have items are those product features which are absolutely essential to develop. Should have items are product features that are not essential but have significant business value. Could have items are product features that would add some business value. Would have items are product features that have marginal business value. [User Stories Applied: For Agile Software Development. Mike Cohn.] [Agile analysis and design]

13. C - The Agile Manifesto developed by the Agile Alliance covers 4 values and 12 principles. The four values are: 1) individuals and interactions over processes and tools, 2) working software over comprehensive documentation, 3) customer collaboration over contract negotiation, and 4) responding to change over following a plan. The 12 principles are: 1) focusing on satisfying the customer, 2) welcoming change, 3) delivering working software frequently, 4) ensuring that business people and developers work together, 5) motivating the individuals involved in development, 6) using face-to-face communication whenever possible, 7) working software as the primary measure of progress, 8) maintaining a constant pace of development, 9) paying continuous attention to technical excellence and good design, 10) aiming for simplicity, 11) using self-organizing teams, and 12) regularly reflecting on how to become more effective. [Manifesto for Agile Software Development. Agile Alliance.] [Communications]

14. C - The focus in the envisioning phase is on project vision, scope (and requirements), project schedule, and assembling a project team. [Agile Project Management: Creating Innovative Products – 2nd Edition. Jim Highsmith.] [Knowledge and Skills: Level 1]

15. C - A project buffer is extra time added to the end of a project to account for delays, obstacles, and other unforeseen issues to help predict an accurate completion date. A project buffer can be estimated using several methods. Three commonly used methods are 1) square root of the sum of squares method, 2) Critical chain project management method (CCPM), 3) halving the sum of most likely estimates . The square root of the sum of squares method involves finding a local safety for all tasks, squaring all the local safeties, summing these squares, and then finding the square root of the sum. The Critical chain project management method (CCPM) is the sum of half the local safeties of all tasks. The local safety is the difference between the 50% confidence estimate and the 90% confidence estimate. The halving the sum of most likely estimates method involves adding all the most likely estimates and dividing by two. [Agile Estimating and Planning. Mike Cohn.] [Agile estimation]

16. B - The key characteristics of a healthy stand-up meeting include: peer pressure - the team is dependent upon each other so expectations of peers drives progress; fine-grained coordination - the team should understand the necessity for focus and working dependently; fine focus - the team should understand the need for brevity in the stand-up meeting so the team can be productive; daily commitment - the team should understand the value of daily commitments to each other and uphold those commitments; identification of obstacles - the team collectively should be aware of each other's obstacles so that the team collectively can try to resolve them. [The Art of Agile Development. James Shore.] [Communications]

17. A - All agile efforts have project and quality standards that the team defines collaboratively at the beginning of an effort and refines collaboratively throughout the effort. Project and quality standards help an agile team with team cohesion and provide a structure, albeit one that can adapt as the project evolves, to promote a self-disciplined environment. There is no 'one size fits all' standards definition in agile;

because every project is different, it has been shown that the team should define which project and quality standards it should hold itself against and strive to conform to those standards while also being open to adapting those standards throughout the project to optimize performance and delivered value. Project standards can range from where the daily stand-up meeting is located and how long each participant has to share his or her progress and challenges to highly specific software coding styles, methods for test-driven development, and what the team's definition of 'done-done' means. [Agile Software Development: The Cooperative Game – 2nd Edition. Alistair Cockburn.] [Knowledge and Skills: Level 1]

18. D - A project buffer is extra time added to the end of a project to account for delays, obstacles, and other unforeseen issues to help predict an accurate completion date. A project buffer can be estimated using several methods. Three commonly used methods are 1) square root of the sum of squares method, 2) Critical chain project management method (CCPM), 3) halving the sum of most likely estimates . The square root of the sum of squares method involves finding a local safety for all tasks, squaring all the local safeties, summing these squares, and then finding the square root of the sum. The Critical chain project management method (CCPM) is the sum of half the local safeties of all tasks. The local safety is the difference between the 50% confidence estimate and the 90% confidence estimate. The halving the sum of most likely estimates method involves adding all the most likely estimates and dividing by two. [Agile Estimating and Planning. Mike Cohn.] [Agile estimation]

19. C - All agile efforts have project and quality standards that the team defines collaboratively at the beginning of an effort and refines collaboratively throughout the effort. Project and quality standards help an agile team with team cohesion and provide a structure, albeit one that can adapt as the project evolves, to promote a self-disciplined environment. There is no 'one size fits all' standards definition in agile; because every project is different, it has been shown that the team should define which project and quality standards it should hold itself against and strive to conform to those standards while also being open to adapting those standards throughout the project to optimize performance and delivered value. Project standards can range from where the daily stand-up meeting is located and how long each participant has to share his or her progress and challenges to highly specific software coding styles, methods for test-driven development, and what the team's definition of 'done-done' means. [Agile Software Development: The Cooperative Game – 2nd Edition. Alistair Cockburn.] [Knowledge and Skills: Level 1]

20. D - All agile efforts have project and quality standards that the team defines collaboratively at the beginning of an effort and refines collaboratively throughout the effort. Project and quality standards help an agile team with team cohesion and provide a structure, albeit one that can adapt as the project evolves, to promote a self-disciplined environment. There is no 'one size fits all' standards definition in agile; because every project is different, it has been shown that the team should define which project and quality standards it should hold itself against and strive to conform to those standards while also being open to adapting those standards throughout the project to optimize performance and delivered value. Project standards can range from where the daily stand-up meeting is located and how long each participant has to share his or her progress and challenges to highly specific software coding styles, methods for test-driven development, and what the team's definition of 'done-done' means. [Agile Software Development: The Cooperative Game – 2nd Edition. Alistair Cockburn.] [Knowledge and Skills: Level 1]

21. A - The project trade-off matrix classifies the constraints of scope, schedule, and cost as fixed, flexible, or accept. [Agile Project Management: Creating Innovative Products – 2nd Edition. Jim Highsmith.] [Planning, monitoring, and adapting]

22. C - Time, budget, and cost estimation is an important knowledge and skill area of agile. According to Highsmith, the nature of the agile method, whereby it welcomes changing scope, means that it lends itself well to fixed budgets and a fixed schedule because changing scope makes it difficult to estimate a total cost. Generally speaking, the budget and schedule constraints are known but before a project will commence there needs to be an agreed upon set of base product functionality defined in an initiation phase; fixing scope reduces an agile team's innovative tendency to provide improved value. For companies that are familiar with fixed-price contracts, where requirements are agreed upon before contract closing, adopting agile can be a weary initial venture. Instead, other contract vehicle types are recommended for agile efforts. These include: a general service contract for the initiation phase and separate fixed-price contracts for iterations or user stories; time-and-material contracts; not-to-exceed with fixed-fee contracts; and, incentive contracts (e.g., fixed price with incentive; cost-reimbursable with award fee). [Agile Project Management: Creating Innovative Products – 2nd Edition. Jim Highsmith.] [Knowledge and Skills: Level 1]

23. A - Fixed-price contracts, although typical of traditional projects where scope is defined ahead of time, are not well suited for agile. When scope is fixed it can deter a team from exploring out-of-scope solutions that may add value to the product. Contracts suited for agile include: general service for the initial phase with fixed-price contracts for successive phases; cost-reimbursable/time and materials; not-to-exceed with fixed-fee; and a combination with incentives. [Agile Software Development: The Cooperative Game – 2nd Edition. Alistair Cockburn.] [Knowledge and Skills: Level 3]

24. C - Timeboxing is a realistic estimate or expectation of how long an action, task, or event will take to perform. Some tasks cannot be performed in the initial timeboxed estimate and are good candidates for reevaluation and possibly further decomposition into more tasks. [The Art of Agile Development. James Shore.] [Planning, monitoring, and adapting]

25. D - Time, budget, and cost estimation is an important knowledge and skill area of agile. According to Highsmith, the nature of the agile method, whereby it welcomes changing scope, means that it lends itself well to fixed budgets and a fixed schedule because changing scope makes it difficult to estimate a total cost. Generally speaking, the budget and schedule constraints are known but before a project will commence there needs to be an agreed upon set of base product functionality defined in an initiation phase; fixing scope reduces an agile team's innovative tendency to provide improved value. For companies that are familiar with fixed-price contracts, where requirements are agreed upon before contract closing, adopting agile can be a weary initial venture. Instead, other contract vehicle types are recommended for agile efforts. These include: a general service contract for the initiation phase and separate fixed-price contracts for iterations or user stories; time-and-material contracts; not-to-exceed with fixed-fee contracts; and, incentive contracts (e.g., fixed price with incentive; cost-reimbursable with award fee). [Agile Project Management: Creating Innovative Products – 2nd Edition. Jim Highsmith.] [Knowledge and Skills: Level 1]

26. B - Having a motivated team is essential for any project, regardless of whether it is agile or not. Motivated teams work together better, have strong productivity, and exceed expectations. Some simple steps to increase motivation are 1) spending quality time together; where team members get to know one another on a personal level to build a sense of community, 2) providing feedback, mentoring and coaching; where team members are congratulated and thanked on jobs well done and also mentored or coached to improve in skill and capability, and 3) empowerment; where the team is empowered to make many key decisions which, along the way, builds trust and shows that leadership believes in the capabilities of the team. [The Art of Agile Development. James Shore.] [Knowledge and Skills: Level 1]

27. A - Velocity is a measure of the number of user story points or stories completed by a team per iteration. An agile team can use its previous velocity recordings as a method of estimating how many user story points it may complete in the next iteration. [Agile Estimating and Planning. Mike Cohn.] [Agile estimation]

28. D - Time, budget, and cost estimation is an important knowledge and skill area of agile. According to Highsmith, the nature of the agile method, whereby it welcomes changing scope, means that it lends itself well to fixed budgets and a fixed schedule because changing scope makes it difficult to estimate a total cost. Generally speaking, the budget and schedule constraints are known but before a project will commence there needs to be an agreed upon set of base product functionality defined in an initiation phase; fixing scope reduces an agile team's innovative tendency to provide improved value. For companies that are familiar with fixed-price contracts, where requirements are agreed upon before contract closing, adopting agile can be a weary initial venture. Instead, other contract vehicle types are recommended for agile efforts. These include: a general service contract for the initiation phase and separate fixed-price contracts for iterations or user stories; time-and-material contracts; not-to-exceed with fixed-fee contracts; and, incentive contracts (e.g., fixed price with incentive; cost-reimbursable with award fee). [Agile Project Management: Creating Innovative Products – 2nd Edition. Jim Highsmith.] [Knowledge and Skills: Level 1]

29. B - The Agile Manifesto defines 12 supporting principles. Agile principles include 1) Our highest priority is to satisfy the customer through early and continuous delivery of valuable software. 2) Welcome changing requirements, even late in development. Agile processes harness change for the customer's competitive advantage. 3) Deliver working software frequently, from a couple of weeks to a couple of months, with preference to the shorter timescale. 4) Business people and developers must work together daily throughout the project. 5) Build projects around motivated individuals. Give them the environment and support they need, and trust them to get the job done. 6) The most efficient and effective method of conveying information to and within a development team is face-to-face conversation. 7) Working software is the primary measure of progress. 8) Agile processes promote sustainable development. The sponsors, developers, and users should be able to maintain a constant pace indefinitely. 9) Continuous attention to technical excellence and good design enhances agility. 10) Simplicity--the art of maximizing the amount of work not done--is essential. 11) The best architectures, requirements, and designs emerge from self-organizing teams. 12) At regular intervals, the team reflects on how to become more effective, then tunes and adjusts its behavior accordingly. [Manifesto for Agile Software Development. Agile Alliance.] [Knowledge and Skills: Level 1]

30. D - A common misconception in agile is that an agile team does not need a leader. In fact, all agile teams need a leader, but the way in which the leader leads is fundamentally different than the typical traditional project manager/project leader method. Some have theorized that this misconception stems from the desired 'self-organizing' quality of the agile team. And although the 'self-organizing' agile team is empowered to take ownership and responsibility of the product and make some decisions itself, it nevertheless requires a leader to help provide guidance, mentoring, coaching, problem solving, and decision making. Some key aspects required of an agile leader include: empowering team members to decide what standard agile practices and methods it will use; allowing the team to be self-organized and self-disciplined; empowering the team members to make decisions collaboratively with the customer; inspire the team to be innovative and explore new ideas and technology capabilities; be a champion of and articulate the product vision to team members so it will be motivated to accomplish the overall objective; remove any obstacles and solve any problems the team may face in its effort; communicate and endorse the values and principles of agile project management to stakeholders that may be unfamiliar with agile; ensure that all stakeholders, including business managers and developers, are collaborating effectively; and, be able to adapt the leadership style to the working environment to ensure that the agile values and principles are effectively upheld. [The Art of Agile Development. James Shore.] [Knowledge and Skills: Level 1]

31. A - One communication technique to reduce misunderstanding and miscommunication is active listening. A well run agile project necessitates both good listeners and communicators, active listening helps work towards both of these necessities. The basics of active listening include: 1) Being present and focusing your attention on the speaker. 2) Taking notes instead of interrupting. 3) Paraphrasing to confirm and review what you have heard. 4) Summarizing the conversation once it has concluded for posterity. Using open ended questions, good body language, and silence can help improve listening skills. [Coaching

Agile Teams. Lyssa Adkins.] [Knowledge and Skills: Level 1]

32. B - The Agile Manifesto defines four values. The four values list primary values and secondary values, with primary values superseding secondary values. The values are 1) individuals and interactions over processes and tools, 2) working software over comprehensive documentation, 3) customer collaboration over contract negotiation, and 4) responding to change over following a plan. [Manifesto for Agile Software Development. Agile Alliance.] [Knowledge and Skills: Level 1]

33. A - The Agile Manifesto developed by the Agile Alliance covers 4 values and 12 principles. The four values are: 1) individuals and interactions over processes and tools, 2) working software over comprehensive documentation, 3) customer collaboration over contract negotiation, and 4) responding to change over following a plan. The 12 principles are: 1) focusing on satisfying the customer, 2) welcoming change, 3) delivering working software frequently, 4) ensuring that business people and developers work together, 5) motivating the individuals involved in development, 6) using face-to-face communication whenever possible, 7) working software as the primary measure of progress, 8) maintaining a constant pace of development, 9) paying continuous attention to technical excellence and good design, 10) aiming for simplicity, 11) using self-organizing teams, and 12) regularly reflecting on how to become more effective. [Manifesto for Agile Software Development. Agile Alliance.] [Communications]

34. A - Although in agile project management, it is generally practiced to generate minimal documentation to support the project, some specific documents, like those required by regulatory bodies need to be created to comply with local and federal law. [Agile Project Management: Creating Innovative Products – 2nd Edition. Jim Highsmith.] [Knowledge and Skills: Level 3]

35. B - Higgs & Dulewicz (1999) defines emotional intelligence using seven components: 1) Self-awareness, 2) Emotional resilience, 3) Motivation, 4) Interpersonal sensitivity, 5) Influence, 6) Intuitiveness, and 7) Conscientiousness. [Coaching Agile Teams. Lyssa Adkins.] [Soft skills negotiation]

36. B - The term "stand-up" originates from the fact that ALL team members are encouraged to stand during the meeting to promote meeting efficiency. The theory is that by physically standing no one will get comfortable enough to waste valuable time. [The Art of Agile Development. James Shore.] [Communications]

37. B - Osmotic communication is a concept of communication where information is shared between collocated team members unconsciously. By sharing the same work environment, team members are exposed to the same environmental sounds and other environmental input and unconsciously share a common framework that improves communication. [Agile Software Development: The Cooperative Game – 2nd Edition. Alistair Cockburn.] [Communications]

38. D - Agile teams typically use story points to estimate the relative size or effort of developing a user story [Agile Estimating and Planning. Mike Cohn.] [Agile estimation]

39. B - Time, budget, and cost estimation is an important knowledge and skill area of agile. According to Highsmith, the nature of the agile method, whereby it welcomes changing scope, means that it lends itself well to fixed budgets and a fixed schedule because changing scope makes it difficult to estimate a total cost. Generally speaking, the budget and schedule constraints are known but before a project will commence there needs to be an agreed upon set of base product functionality defined in an initiation phase; fixing scope reduces an agile team's innovative tendency to provide improved value. For companies that are familiar with fixed-price contracts, where requirements are agreed upon before contract closing, adopting agile can be a weary initial venture. Instead, other contract vehicle types are recommended for agile efforts. These include: a general service contract for the initiation phase and separate fixed-price contracts for iterations or user stories; time-and-material contracts; not-to-exceed with fixed-fee contracts; and, incentive contracts (e.g., fixed price with incentive; cost-reimbursable with award fee). [Agile Project Management: Creating Innovative Products – 2nd Edition. Jim Highsmith.] [Knowledge and Skills: Level 1]

40. B - A common misconception in agile is that an agile team does not need a leader. In fact, all agile teams need a leader, but the way in which the leader leads is fundamentally different than the typical traditional project manager/project leader method. Some have theorized that this misconception stems from the desired 'self-organizing' quality of the agile team. And although the 'self-organizing' agile team is empowered to take ownership and responsibility of the product and make some decisions itself, it nevertheless requires a leader to help provide guidance, mentoring, coaching, problem solving, and decision making. Some key aspects required of an agile leader include: empowering team members to decide what standard agile practices and methods it will use; allowing the team to be self-organized and self-disciplined; empowering the team members to make decisions collaboratively with the customer; inspire the team to be innovative and explore new ideas and technology capabilities; be a champion of and articulate the product vision to team members so it will be motivated to accomplish the overall objective; remove any obstacles and solve any problems the team may face in its effort; communicate and endorse the values and principles of agile project management to stakeholders that may be unfamiliar with agile; ensure that all stakeholders, including business managers and developers, are collaborating effectively; and, be able to adapt the leadership style to the working environment to ensure that the agile values and principles are effectively upheld. [The Art of Agile Development. James Shore.] [Knowledge and Skills: Level 1]

Knowledge Area Quiz
Product Quality
Practice Questions

Test Name: Knowledge Area Test: Product Quality
Total Questions: 15
Correct Answers Needed to Pass:
11 (73.33%)
Time Allowed: 25 Minutes

Test Description

This practice quiz specifically targets your knowledge of the Product Quality exam topic area.

Test Questions

1. What project artifact is helpful for testers performing an exploratory test? The artifact gives a brief overview of product functionality.

   A. The project roadmap.

   B. The project vision.

   C. The project charter.

   D. The project data sheet.

2. How are test-driven development and acceptance test-driven development similar?

   A. Both strategies involve writing unit tests that never fail to help software development.

   B. They are one and the same strategy, but called by different names based on the agile framework being used.

   C. Both strategies involve writing product code before test code.

   D. Both strategies involve writing test code before product code.

3. How often is code typically integrated on an XP effort?

   A. At least once per day

   B. Once per iteration

   C. Once per release

   D. Immediately before release

4. Select the best definition 'done.'

   A. A team defined term that indicates when a user story point is completed.

   B. A team defined term that indicates when a project is successfully completed.

   C. A team and product owner defined term that indicates when a feature or product is considered to be completed and ready for shipping.

   D. A team defined term that indicates when a scrum has completed for the day.

5. In agile, what is meant by frequent verification and validation?

A. Because of its tendency to release working products in short time increments, verification and validation take place frequently.

B. Because of its tendency to reuse old programming software, verification and validation take place frequently.

C. Because customer requirements are constantly changing, frequent verification and validation is the only means to ensure the work breakdown structure.

D. Because working products are released only at the end of a project, verification and validation take place frequently.

6. Being continuously integrated theoretically means

A. Having integrated but incomplete units of source code.

B. Having a working product ready to ship at any time.

C. Having semi-working functionality at any time.

D. Having integrated but untested source code.

7. Kyle is performing a type of test that is done throughout an agile project and on the completed product. In his testing, Kyle is trying to uncover any software bugs or system design faults that may not have been identified in typical unit testing. What type of testing is Kyle performing?

A. Refactor testing

B. Exploratory testing

C. Assimilation testing

D. Interface testing

8. What does TDD stand for in agile parlance?

A. Top-down design

B. Test-design development

C. Test-driven development

D. Test-driven design

9. A product owner specifies in acceptance criteria that a user feature provide extreme excitement to the end user. However, when reviewing the feature in the sprint demo, the product owner complains the feature does not provide the extreme excitement she wanted. Why might this type of reaction occur?

A. Because the iteration ended before the programmers could get the desired excitability for the feature.

B. Because extreme excitement is not easily testable.

C. Because the programmers failed to read the story card properly.

D. Because the product owner changed her mind.

10. The commit build process includes what type of testing?

A. Unit and spike

B. Exploratory and spike

C. Unit and exploratory

D. Unit and integration

11. Following the XP principle of continuous integration, when is completed code integrated into the code base?

A. Immediately.

B. At the end of the release.

C. At iteration intervals to synchronize configuration management.

D. At the end of the sprint.

12. Jerry on an XP influenced agile team has just completed coding a new feature. When should he integrate the new code into the code base?

A. At the end of the release.

B. At the end of the sprint.

C. At iteration intervals to synchronize configuration management.

D. Immediately.

13. What is an advantage of continuous integration, as practiced in XP?

A. Supports rapid delivery of working software

B. Decreases the need for testing

C. Decreases the need for customer feedback

D. Decreases the need for team communication and collaboration

14. TDD has four basic steps. What is the first step in TDD?

A. Verify and validate that the test fails

B. Write product code and apply the test

C. Refactor the product code

D. Write test code that will fail

15. Sarah is explaining to Hanson the similarities between test-driven development and acceptance test-driven development. Can you help her identify a similarity?

A. Both strategies involve using an inversion model to refactor old software code.

B. Both techniques involve using a cyclical, four-step process.

C. Both strategies are for the Visual Basic programming language only.

D. Both strategies are for the C# programming language only.

Knowledge Area Quiz
Product Quality
Answer Key and Explanations

1. C - A project charter provides a brief overview of product functionality and serves as a guide for testers performing exploratory testing. [Lean-Agile Software Development: Achieving Enterprise Agility. Alan Shalloway, Guy Beaver, James R. Trott.] [Product quality]

2. D - Acceptance Test Driven Development (ATDD) is similar to Test-driven development (TDD) in that it requires programmers to create tests first before any product code. The tests in ATDD are aimed at confirming features/behaviors that the intended software will have. The iterative cycle of ATDD with its four steps can be remembered as the four Ds: 1) Discuss, 2) Distill, 3) Develop, and 4) Demo. 1) Discuss: The agile team and customer or business stakeholder discuss a user story in detail. Talking about the expected behaviors the user story should have and what it should not. 2) The development team takes those items learned from the discussion and distills them into tests that will verify and validate those behaviors. The distillation process is where the entire team should have a good understanding of what "done" (or completed) means for a user story. That is, what the acceptance criteria are. 3) After distillation, the team develops the test code and product code to implement the product features. 4) Once the product features have been developed, the team demonstrates them to the customer or business stakeholders for feedback. [Lean-Agile Software Development: Achieving Enterprise Agility. Alan Shalloway, Guy Beaver, James R. Trott.] [Product quality]

3. A - An XP project typically integrates code at least once per day. [The Art of Agile Development. James Shore.] [Product quality]

4. C - Because a cornerstone of the scrum framework in agile is to 'always have a product that you could theoretically ship,' it is important for the team and product owner to have a definition of 'done' or what criteria is necessary to consider user features or functionality in a state of finality. [Coaching Agile Teams. Lyssa Adkins.] [Product quality]

5. A - Because each iteration typically produces a working product that is built and integrated and iterations are typically two to four weeks in length, there is frequent verification and validation to ensure product quality. Verification is the confirmation that a product performs as specified by a customer (e.g. as indicated by a user story) and validation is the confirmation that a product behaves as desired (i.e., meets the customer's need). Sometimes a product may be built and integrated to specification - that is, it can be verified - but it does not meet the intent of the customer - that is, it cannot be validated. [Agile Software Development: The Cooperative Game – 2nd Edition. Alistair Cockburn.] [Product quality]

6. B - Being continuously integrated theoretically means having a working product ready to ship at any time. [The Art of Agile Development. James Shore.] [Product quality]

7. B - Regular exploratory testing is encouraged to improve product quality. Typically, exploratory testing is performed on completed product software to test the system design for any bugs and to identify any new features that may add value to the customer. Exploratory testing should cover what a developer is unable to anticipate through the course of normal unit testing. A project charter is often used as a general overview of the product that exploratory testers use for testing guidance. [The Art of Agile Development. James Shore.] [Product quality]

8. C - Test-driven development, or TDD, is an agile methodology that has software developers develop automated software tests before developing software that implements product features. This helps ensure quality as each bit of feature software is tested individually to remove bugs and improve performance before it is integrated with the final product. [The Art of Agile Development. James Shore.] [Product quality]

9. B - The BEST answer is because the acceptance criteria is too vague (remember the T of INVEST for defining good user stories) and cannot be easily tested. [The Art of Agile Development. James Shore.] [Product quality]

10. D - The commit build process includes both unit and integration testing. [The Art of Agile Development. James Shore.] [Product quality]

11. A - The extreme programming (XP) principle of continuous integration is that code is integrated into the full code base as soon as it is built, tested, and completed. Once integrated, the code base and therefore the entire system is built and tested. Continuous integration is just one principle of XP that promotes rapid delivery of software and the early detection of integration defects. [The Art of Agile Development. James Shore.] [Product quality]

12. D - The extreme programming (XP) principle of continuous integration is that code is integrated into the full code base as soon as it is built, tested, and completed. Once integrated, the code base and therefore the entire system is built and tested. Continuous integration is just one principle of XP that promotes rapid delivery of software and the early detection of integration defects. [The Art of Agile Development. James Shore.] [Product quality]

13. A - The extreme programming (XP) principle of continuous integration is that code is integrated into the full code base as soon as it is built, tested, and completed. Once integrated, the code base and therefore the entire system is built and tested. Continuous integration is just one principle of XP that promotes rapid delivery of software and the early detection of integration defects. [The Art of Agile Development. James Shore.] [Product quality]

14. D - The TDD process has four basic steps: 1) Write a test, 2) Verify and validate the test, 3) Write product code and apply the test, 4) Refactor the product code. An example may be that a user has to enter an age value. A good test is to make sure the user data entry is a positive number and not a different type of input, like a letter (i.e., write the test). The programmer would

verify that entering a letter instead of a number would cause the program to cause an exception (i.e., v&v the test). The programmer would then write product code that takes user entry for the age value (i.e., write the product code). The programmer would then run the product code and enter correct age values and incorrect age values (i.e., apply the test). If the product code is successful, the programmer would refactor the product code to improve its design. Using these four steps iteratively ensures that programmers think about how a software program might fail first and to build product code that is holistically being tested. This helps produce high quality code. [The Art of Agile Development. James Shore.] [Product quality]

15. B - Acceptance Test Driven Development (ATDD) is similar to Test-driven development (TDD) in that it requires programmers to create tests first before any product code. The tests in ATDD are aimed at confirming features/behaviors that the intended software will have. The iterative cycle of ATDD with its four steps can be remembered as the four Ds: 1) Discuss, 2) Distill, 3) Develop, and 4) Demo. 1) Discuss: The agile team and customer or business stakeholder discuss a user story in detail. Talking about the expected behaviors the user story should have and what it should not. 2) The development team takes those items learned from the discussion and distills them into tests that will verify and validate those behaviors. The distillation process is where the entire team should have a good understanding of what "done" (or completed) means for a user story. That is, what the acceptance criteria are. 3) After distillation, the team develops the test code and product code to implement the product features. 4) Once the product features have been developed, the team demonstrates them to the customer or business stakeholders for feedback. [Lean-Agile Software Development: Achieving Enterprise Agility. Alan Shalloway, Guy Beaver, James R. Trott.] [Product quality]

PMI-ACP Lite Mock Exam 10 Practice Questions

Test Name: PMI-ACP Lite Mock Exam 10
Total Questions: 40
Correct Answers Needed to Pass: 30 (75.00%)
Time Allowed: 60 Minutes

Test Description

This is a cumulative PMI-ACP Mock Exam which can be used as a benchmark for your PMI-ACP aptitude. This practice test includes questions from all exam topic areas, including sections from Agile Tools and Techniques, and all three Agile Knowledge and Skills areas.

Test Questions

1. Select from the following types of contracts, the one most suited for the agile framework.

A. Fixed-cost

B. General service contract for the initial phase with separate fixed-schedule contracts for each user story.

C. Time-and-vendor

D. Not-to-exceed with fixed-fee

2. In a retrospective, a good facilitator always remembers to 'set the stage.' What does set the stage mean?

A. Generating insights

B. Creating a safe environment that is open and honest

C. Deciding what to do

D. Gathering data

3. Jules, as an agile mentor, has been empowering the team to make many key decisions. What is Jules doing when he provides this empowerment?

A. Refactoring the team

B. Guiding the team

C. Reforming the team

D. Motivating the team

4. Select the best definition of an 'empowered team.'

A. A team that relies on external leadership to show it the path forward.

B. A team that is told what to do and how to do it.

C. A team that takes ownership of a product and is collectively responsible for its delivery.

D. A team that solves problems through the use of market research.

5. It is Hank's turn in the daily stand-up meeting. He starts reviewing what he has achieved since the last meeting, continues with what he plans to achieve before the next meeting, and then rambles for 15 minutes about the minutiae of technical obstacles to his progress. How is Hank hurting the agile team's progress?

A. Hank is not hurting the team's progress, but, in fact, improving it by comprehensively covering all pertinent talking points of the stand-up meeting.

B. Hank should open first with the discussion regarding technical obstacles as this is what will impact team performance the most.

C. Hank should start first with what he plans to achieve before the next meeting before discussing what he has achieved since the last meeting.

D. Hank is spending too much time discussing the obstacles he is facing with the team. The team should confront Hank that any obstacles that cannot be discussed in a few minutes should be tabled for later discussion with the appropriate stakeholders.

6. As agile team leader, Stacey intends to schedule a brainstorming session to generate ideas that may help solve some of the team's current issues. Which of the following is NOT a good brainstorming technique that Stacey should use?

A. Having a single-discipline/homogenous group so that the team can communicate more effectively.

B. Having a multi-disciplinary/diverse group so that many different perspectives are available.

C. Sending participants preparatory material, so they know what to expect and what is expected of them.

D. Delaying any criticism that may hamper idea generation.

7. As agile team leader, Stacey intends to schedule a brainstorming session to generate ideas that may help solve some of the team's current issues. Which of the following is NOT a good brainstorming technique that Stacey should use?

A. Delaying any criticism that may hamper idea generation.

B. Sending participants preparatory material, so they know what to expect and what is expected of them.

C. Having a multi-disciplinary/diverse group so that many different perspectives are available.

D. Ignore team members that she feels provide little value.

8. As agile team leader, Stacey intends to schedule a brainstorming session to generate ideas that may help solve some of the team's current issues. Which of the following is NOT a good brainstorming technique that Stacey should use?

A. Having a multi-disciplinary/diverse group so that many different perspectives are available.

B. Sending participants preparatory material, so they know what to expect and what is expected of them.

C. Delaying any criticism that may hamper idea generation.

D. Split the team into competitive factions to promote a sense of urgency.

9. As agile team leader, Nathan intends to schedule a brainstorming session to generate ideas that may help solve some of the team's current issues. Which of the following is a good brainstorming technique that Nathan should use?

A. Having a single-discipline/homogenous group so that the team can communicate more effectively.

B. Leaving participants in the dark until the day of the meeting to add an element of surprise.

C. Encouraging criticism early and often to prevent poorly thought out ideas entering the conversation as technical debt.

D. Having an engaging and experienced facilitator lead the brainstorming session.

10. Stacey intends to schedule a brainstorming session to generate ideas that may help solve some of the team's current issues. Which of the following is NOT a good brainstorming technique that Stacey should use?

A. Having an engaging and experienced facilitator lead the brainstorming session.

B. Sending participants preparatory material, so they know what to expect and what is expected of them.

C. Hosting the meeting in a neutral and comfortable environment.

D. Picking a reserved team member as facilitator.

11. As agile team leader, Stacey intends to schedule a brainstorming session to generate ideas that may help solve some of the team's current issues. Which of the following is NOT a good brainstorming technique that Stacey should use?

A. Hosting the meeting in a neutral and comfortable environment.

B. Allow only the dominant personalities to contribute.

C. Having an engaging and experienced facilitator lead the brainstorming session.

D. Sending participants preparatory material, so they know what to expect and what is expected of them.

12. As an agile certified practitioner, Roger extols the virtue of fine-grained communication in the daily stand-up meeting. How is fine-grained communication an indicator of a healthy stand-up meeting?

A. Having fine-grained coordination during a stand-up meeting indicates that the team understands how important it is to have a sharp, inter-dependent focus for the duration of the meeting.

B. Having fine-grained coordination during a stand-up meeting indicates that each team member is solely focused on his or her own obstacles and uninterested in other team members' progress or obstacles.

C. Having fine-grained coordination during a stand-up meeting indicates a lack of defects and well tested and integrated code.

D. Having fine-grained coordination during a stand-up meeting is a false indicator of a healthy stand-up meeting. The team should have a broad focus to remain open to innovative ideas from other sectors of industry.

13. Henry is using the MoSCoW technique to understand the value of each feature according to the customer. What is MoSCoW an example of?

A. A constraints-based analysis technique

B. A priority-based analysis technique

C. A value-based analysis technique

D. An WIDETOM analysis technique

14. Which of the following is the best definition of coaching and mentoring?

A. Guiding a team or person to improve performance.

B. Helping a person or team collaborate with one another.

C. Helping a person or team prioritize features in the backlog.

D. Helping a person or team come up with new ideas.

15. Which of the following is the best definition of coaching and mentoring?

A. Helping a person or team improve performance and reach goals.

B. Helping a person or team communicate with one another.

C. Helping a person or team prioritize features in the backlog.

D. Helping a person or team come up with new ideas.

16. Pick the response that best compares and contrasts verification and validation.

A. Both are methods to confirm product quality. Verification confirms the product meets specified requirements. Validation confirms the product meets the holistic intent of the customer.

B. Both are methods to confirm product quality. Verification confirms the product meets specified requirements. Validation confirms the product meets the holistic intent of the customer.

C. Both are methods to increase product value. Verification confirms new features to be added. Validation confirms the new features were built correctly.

D. Both are methods to confirm product scope. Verification confirms product features are in scope. Validation confirms no product features are out of scope.

17. Which of the following is the best definition of coaching and mentoring?

A. Helping a person or team come up with new ideas.

B. Helping a person or team prioritize features in the backlog.

C. Providing guidance and direction to a person or group in an effort to improve performance.

D. Helping a person or team work together effectively.

18. Christy is confused about the purpose of a product roadmap. She asks Thomas, her project manager, to identify a benefit of a product roadmap to help her understand a product roadmaps purpose. Select the benefit of a product roadmap.

A. Helps facilitate iteration development.

B. Helps facilitate prioritization of features.

C. Helps facilitate reflection meetings.

D. Helps facilitate daily stand-up meetings.

19. Susan is concerned with the recent stagnant performance of her agile team. She believes it to be highly capable but the team seems to be lacking a desire to improve. What agile knowledge and skill technique might Susan consider?

A. Coaching and mentoring

B. Symptom and solution

C. Coaching and meeting

D. Consolidating and mentoring

20. Clare is concerned with the recent stagnant performance of her agile team. She believes it to be highly capable but the team does not seem to be focused on improving over its current level. What agile knowledge and skill technique might Clare consider?

A. Coaching and meeting

B. Profiteering and gamesmanship

C. Consolidating and mentoring

D. Coaching and mentoring

21. According to Highsmith, Agile project management differs from traditional project management in what four fundamental ways?

A. High-level project scope, multiple iterations of product development, teams are self-organizing, extensive customer involvement

B. High-level project scope, multiple iterations of product development, teams are delegated tasks from the top-down, extensive customer involvement

C. High-level project scope, multiple iterations of product development, teams are self-organizing, minimized customer involvement

D. High-precision project scope, multiple iterations of product development, teams are self-organizing, extensive customer involvement

22. A risk-to-value chart may be used to help prioritize user stories in the product backlog. Select the type of user-story that is typically given low priority in the backlog?

A. High-value, high-risk

B. Low-value, high-risk

C. High-value, low-risk

D. Low-value, low-risk

23. Theresa and her agile team are planning an iteration that holds several tasks with high risk. What is one method that Theresa and her team can use to reduce risk?

A. Hold a Kaizen event.

B. Hold a risk-mitigation reflection workshop.

C. Hold a value stream mapping event.

D. Perform risk-based spike tasks.

24. If an agile team is 'playing' a game of poker for estimation, what game is it mostly playing?

A. Planning poker

B. Two-card poker

C. Affinity poker

D. Hold'Em poker

25. Esther is concerned with the recent stagnant performance of her agile team. She believes it to be highly capable but the team is stuck at an average level of performance. What agile knowledge and skill technique might Esther consider?

A. Capturing and mentoring

B. Incentive and profit

C. Coaching and mentoring

D. Coaching and mobilizing

26. As agile team leader, Stacey intends to schedule a brainstorming session to generate ideas that may help solve some of the team's current issues. Which of the following is NOT a good brainstorming technique that Stacey should use?

A. Hosting the meeting in a neutral and comfortable environment.

B. Encouraging criticism early and often to prevent poorly thought out ideas entering the conversation as technical debt.

C. Delaying any criticism that may hamper idea generation.

D. Having an engaging and experienced facilitator lead the brainstorming session.

27. As agile team leader, Stacey intends to schedule a brainstorming session to generate ideas that may help solve some of the team's current issues. Which of the following is NOT a good brainstorming technique that Stacey should use?

A. Trust that the team will be self-organizing and facilitate the event itself.

B. Having an engaging and experienced facilitator lead the brainstorming session.

C. Delaying any criticism that may hamper idea generation.

D. Hosting the meeting in a neutral and comfortable environment.

28. A common metric used in agile is velocity. What is velocity?

A. A measure of the number of user story points or stories completed per iteration.

B. A measure of the number of user story points completed per release.

C. A measure of the number of user story points completed per day.

D. A measure of the number of iteration plans completed per iteration.

29. As agile team leader, Nathan intends to schedule a brainstorming session to generate ideas that may help solve some of the team's current issues. Which of the following is a good brainstorming technique that Nathan should use?

A. Encouraging criticism early and often to prevent poorly thought out ideas entering the conversation as technical debt.

B. Having a multi-disciplinary/diverse group so that many different perspectives are available.

C. Picking a reserved team member as facilitator.

D. Hosting the meeting in the typical Monday morning conference room that is usually only available to certain team members.

30. What types of topics does an agile team cover when it performs reflection?

A. How to stop the customer from changing requirements

B. How to encourage team members to work overtime to maintain project schedule

C. How to reinforce successful practices

D. How to discourage any newly tried successful practice that the team did not agree to during project chartering

31. What person in the agile framework "empowers the team to work collaboratively?"

A. Project leader

B. Scrum member

C. Business analyst

D. Product owner

32. Victor, as an agile leader, practices with an adaptive leadership style. What are the two dimensions Highsmith uses to define adaptive leadership?

A. Practicing agile and playing agile

B. Living agile and breathing agile

C. Being agile and doing agile

D. Thinking agile and living agile

33. Of the following, which is a common communication technique that may help teams improve their collaboration and understanding?

A. Passive listening

B. Engaged listening

C. Active listening

D. Focused listening

34. Harry's agile team failed to complete a user story in its most recent iteration. What should Harry and his team do?

A. Finish the user story over the weekend or other downtime.

B. Collaborate with the customer to determine if and when the user story should be completed.

C. Remove the user story from the project.

D. Immediately add the user story to the top of the next iteration's backlog.

35. Which of the following is NOT a typical grouping of user stories for purposes of organization?

A. By relation to product feature

B. By priority

C. By authoring date

D. By logical sequence and dependency

36. How may variance and trend analysis be incorporated into an agile project?

A. In iteration review meetings

B. In a release plan

C. In formal risk review meetings

D. In a retrospective

37. Greg is pleased when the customer and project testers test his most recently developed feature, find that it passes acceptance criteria, and integrate it into the product. In which column should Greg now place the associated task card?

A. To do

B. Done

C. In progress

D. Ready for testing

38. If an agile team sets a feature WIP limit of four for its sprint, how many features may be simultaneously developed during the sprint?

A. No more than one.

B. No more than two.

C. No more than eight.

D. No more than four.

39. How does acceptance test-driven software help define "done?"

A. In the demo step of the ATDD process, the agile team demonstrates the product to business stakeholders who, in turn, provide feedback on how close the team is to "done."

B. In the discuss step of the ATDD process, developers and business stakeholders explore expected behavior of the user story. If the behavior is met, the user story is "done."

C. In the develop step of the ATDD process, developers develop the expected behavior of the product with the intent of meeting the acceptance criteria. At this point, the user story is "done."

D. In the distill step of the ATDD process, developers and business stakeholders identify acceptance criteria for a user story. If the acceptance criteria are well-defined, the user story is "done."

40. Jane is explaining to her agile team that only the customer can define when the team is "done" with a user story. Which process step of ATDD is where the team will find out if it is "done?"

A. In the discuss step of the ATDD process, developers and business stakeholders explore expected behavior of the user story. If the behavior is met, the user story is "done."

B. In the demo step of the ATDD process, the agile team demonstrates the product to business stakeholders who, in turn, provide feedback on whether the team is to "done."

C. In the develop step of the ATDD process, developers develop the expected behavior of the product with the intent of meeting the acceptance criteria. At this point, the user story is "done."

D. In the distill step of the ATDD process, developers and business stakeholders identify acceptance criteria for a user story. If the acceptance criteria are well-defined, the user story is "done."

PMI-ACP Lite Mock Exam 10 Answer Key and Explanations

1. D - Time, budget, and cost estimation is an important knowledge and skill area of agile. According to Highsmith, the nature of the agile method, whereby it welcomes changing scope, means that it lends itself well to fixed budgets and a fixed schedule because changing scope makes it difficult to estimate a total cost. Generally speaking, the budget and schedule constraints are known but before a project will commence there needs to be an agreed upon set of base product functionality defined in an initiation phase; fixing scope reduces an agile team's innovative tendency to provide improved value. For companies that are familiar with fixed-price contracts, where requirements are agreed upon before contract closing, adopting agile can be a weary initial venture. Instead, other contract vehicle types are recommended for agile efforts. These include: a general service contract for the initiation phase and separate fixed-price contracts for iterations or user stories; time-and-material contracts; not-to-exceed with fixed-fee contracts; and, incentive contracts (e.g., fixed price with incentive; cost-reimbursable with award fee). [Agile Project Management: Creating Innovative Products – 2nd Edition. Jim Highsmith.] [Knowledge and Skills: Level 1]

2. B - Setting the stage for a retrospective means creating a safe environment that is open and honest. [Agile Retrospectives: Making Good Teams Great. Esther Derby, Diana Larsen, Ken Schwaber.] [Planning, monitoring, and adapting]

3. D - Having a motivated team is essential for any project, regardless of whether it is agile or not. Motivated teams work together better, have strong productivity, and exceed expectations. Some simple steps to increase motivation are 1) spending quality time together; where team members get to know one another on a personal level to build a sense of community, 2) providing feedback, mentoring and coaching; where team members are congratulated and thanked on jobs well done and also mentored or coached to improve in skill and capability, and 3) empowerment; where the team is empowered to make many key decisions which, along the way, builds trust and shows that leadership believes in the capabilities of the team. [The Art of Agile Development. James Shore.] [Knowledge and Skills: Level 1]

4. C - Empowered teams - ones that are self-organizing and know how to solve problems with minimal management involvement - are a cornerstone of the agile methodology. An agile team feels empowered when it collectively assumes responsibility for the delivery of the product (i.e., taking ownership). [Coaching Agile Teams. Lyssa Adkins.] [Knowledge and Skills: Level 1]

5. D - Issues that take longer than a few minutes to resolve in a daily stand-up meeting should be tabled and resolved between the appropriate parties after the daily stand-up meeting has concluded. This ensures that the meetings are brief and productive. [The Art of Agile Development. James Shore.] [Communications]

6. A - A successful brainstorming event should strive to consider the following points - Host the meeting in a neutral and comfortable environment - Have an engaging and experienced facilitator lead

the event - Send participants an overview, with goals, schedule, and what ground rules, beforehand - Have a multi-disciplinary/diverse team to get a broader perspective - Delay any criticism that may stifle idea generation. [Agile Retrospectives: Making Good Teams Great. Esther Derby, Diana Larsen, Ken Schwaber.] [Knowledge and Skills: Level 1]

7. D - A successful brainstorming event should strive to consider the following points - Host the meeting in a neutral and comfortable environment - Have an engaging and experienced facilitator lead the event - Send participants an overview, with goals, schedule, and what ground rules, beforehand - Have a multi-disciplinary/diverse team to get a broader perspective - Delay any criticism that may stifle idea generation. [Agile Retrospectives: Making Good Teams Great. Esther Derby, Diana Larsen, Ken Schwaber.] [Knowledge and Skills: Level 1]

8. D - A successful brainstorming event should strive to consider the following points - Host the meeting in a neutral and comfortable environment - Have an engaging and experienced facilitator lead the event - Send participants an overview, with goals, schedule, and what ground rules, beforehand - Have a multi-disciplinary/diverse team to get a broader perspective - Delay any criticism that may stifle idea generation. [Agile Retrospectives: Making Good Teams Great. Esther Derby, Diana Larsen, Ken Schwaber.] [Knowledge and Skills: Level 1]

9. D - A successful brainstorming event should strive to consider the following points - Host the meeting in a neutral and comfortable environment - Have an engaging and experienced facilitator lead the event - Send participants an overview, with goals, schedule, and what ground rules, beforehand - Have a multi-disciplinary/diverse team to get a broader perspective - Delay any criticism that may stifle idea generation. [Agile Retrospectives: Making Good Teams Great. Esther Derby, Diana Larsen, Ken Schwaber.] [Knowledge and Skills: Level 1]

10. D - A successful brainstorming event should strive to consider the following points - Host the meeting in a neutral and comfortable environment - Have an engaging and experienced facilitator lead the event - Send participants an overview, with goals, schedule, and what ground rules, beforehand - Have a multi-disciplinary/diverse team to get a broader perspective - Delay any criticism that may stifle idea generation. [Agile Retrospectives: Making Good Teams Great. Esther Derby, Diana Larsen, Ken Schwaber.] [Knowledge and Skills: Level 1]

11. B - A successful brainstorming event should strive to consider the following points - Host the meeting in a neutral and comfortable environment - Have an engaging and experienced facilitator lead the event - Send participants an overview, with goals, schedule, and what ground rules, beforehand - Have a multi-disciplinary/diverse team to get a broader perspective - Delay any criticism that may stifle idea generation. [Agile Retrospectives: Making Good Teams Great. Esther Derby, Diana Larsen, Ken Schwaber.] [Knowledge and Skills: Level 1]

12. A - The key characteristics of a healthy stand-up meeting include: peer pressure - the team is dependent upon each other so

expectations of peers drives progress; fine-grained coordination - the team should understand the necessity for focus and working dependently; fine focus - the team should understand the need for brevity in the stand-up meeting so the team can be productive; daily commitment - the team should understand the value of daily commitments to each other and uphold those commitments; identification of obstacles - the team collectively should be aware of each other's obstacles so that the team collectively can try to resolve them. [The Art of Agile Development. James Shore.] [Communications]

13. C - Value-based analysis strives to understand how value, as defined by the customer, relates to various components of the product, like features and tasks. Features are often prioritized with prioritization based on value and risk. Prioritization can be performed using the MoSCoW or Kano method and through the use of risk-to-value and cost-to-value matrices. [Lean-Agile Software Development: Achieving Enterprise Agility. Alan Shalloway, Guy Beaver, James R. Trott.] [Knowledge and Skills: Level 2]

14. A - Coaching and mentoring within teams can be helpful for nascent agile teams and even for more experienced agile teams. Coaching and mentoring is the act of helping a person or team improve performance and achieve realistic goals. [Coaching Agile Teams. Lyssa Adkins.] [Knowledge and Skills: Level 1]

15. A - Coaching and mentoring within teams can be helpful for nascent agile teams and even for more experienced agile teams. Coaching and mentoring is the act of helping a person or team improve performance and achieve realistic goals. [Coaching Agile Teams. Lyssa Adkins.] [Knowledge and Skills: Level 1]

16. B - Because each iteration typically produces a working product that is built and integrated and iterations are typically two to four weeks in length, there is frequent verification and validation to ensure product quality. Verification is the confirmation that a product performs as specified by a customer (e.g. as indicated by a user story) and validation is the confirmation that a product behaves as desired (i.e., meets the customer's need). Sometimes a product may be built and integrated to specification - that is, it can be verified - but it does not meet the intent of the customer - that is, it cannot be validated. [Agile Software Development: The Cooperative Game – 2nd Edition. Alistair Cockburn.] [Product quality]

17. C - Coaching and mentoring within teams can be helpful for nascent agile teams and even for more experienced agile teams. Coaching and mentoring is the act of helping a person or team improve performance and achieve realistic goals. [Coaching Agile Teams. Lyssa Adkins.] [Knowledge and Skills: Level 1]

18. B - The product roadmap - owned by the product owner - serves as a high level overview of the product requirements. It is used as a tool for prioritizing features , organizing features into categories, and assigning rough time frames. Creating a product roadmap has four basic steps: 1) Identify requirements (these will become part of the product backlog), 2) Organize requirements into categories or themes, 3) Estimate relative work effort (e.g., planning poker or affinity estimation) and prioritize (value), and 4) Estimate rough time frames (estimate velocity, sprint duration, and rough release dates). [The Art of Agile Development. James Shore.] [Agile analysis and design]

19. A - Coaching and mentoring within teams can be helpful for nascent agile teams and even for more experienced agile teams. Coaching and mentoring is the act of helping a person or team improve performance and achieve realistic goals. Because agile has a value of continuous improvement, coaching and mentoring is not solely for new or immature teams, but experienced ones too where coaching can help achieve higher levels of performance. The amount of coaching and mentoring an agile team needs is variable. Some newer teams will need a coach guiding the team nearly all the time while others may need a coach only for particularly challenging situations. A not uncommon scenario is to have a coach help the team collectively during sprint/iteration planning and then during the iteration help mentor individual team members. [Coaching Agile Teams. Lyssa Adkins.] [Knowledge and Skills: Level 1]

20. D - Coaching and mentoring within teams can be helpful for nascent agile teams and even for more experienced agile teams. Coaching and mentoring is the act of helping a person or team improve performance and achieve realistic goals. Because agile has a value of continuous improvement, coaching and mentoring is not solely for new or immature teams, but experienced ones too where coaching can help achieve higher levels of performance. The amount of coaching and mentoring an agile team needs is variable. Some newer teams will need a coach guiding the team nearly all the time while others may need a coach only for particularly challenging situations. A not uncommon scenario is to have a coach help the team collectively during sprint/iteration planning and then during the iteration help mentor individual team members. [Coaching Agile Teams. Lyssa Adkins.] [Knowledge and Skills: Level 1]

21. A - Agile project management differs fundamentally from traditional project management in the following ways: High-level project scope, multiple iterations of product development, teams are self-organizing, extensive customer involvement. [Manifesto for Agile Software Development. Agile Alliance.] [Knowledge and Skills: Level 1]

22. B - A risk-adjusted backlog is a product backlog organized by taking into account risk. Risk can be estimated as the product of severity/consequence and likelihood. User stories can also be positioned on a risk-to-value matrix to help prioritize them in the backlog. The risk-to-value matrix is a chart with four quadrants. Along the horizontal axis is value in ascending order. Along the vertical axis is risk in ascending order. A user story that is high risk and high value is located in the top-right corner. A user story that is low risk and high value is located in the lower-right corner. A user story that is low risk and high value is located in the lower-right corner. A user story that is low risk and low value is located in the lower-left corner. Typically a team will prioritize high-value, low-risk user stories first, followed by high-value, high-risk user stories, followed by low-value, low-risk user stories, followed by low-value, high-risk user stories. [The Art of Agile

Development. James Shore.] [Risk management]

23. D - Risked-based spike is a risk management technique and is often thought of as a task. A risked-based spike is a task used to gain knowledge in an area of uncertainty to reduce risk. For example, a development team may need to understand how migrating from Windows 7 to Windows 8 may impact the look and feel of the interface. Risked-based spikes typically are included in iteration planning directly before a the task that holds the uncertainty. [The Art of Agile Development. James Shore.] [Risk management]

24. A - Planning poker is based upon the wideband Delphi estimation technique. It is a consensus-based technique for estimating effort. Sometimes called scrum poker, it is a technique for a relative estimation of effort, typically in story points, to develop a user story. At a planning poker meeting, each estimator is given an identical deck of planning poker cards with a wide range of values. The Fibonacci sequence is often used for values for planning poker (i.e., 0, 1, 1, 2, 3, 5,8,etc.); another common sequence is (question mark, 0, 1/2, 1, 2, 3, 5, 8, 13, 20, 40, and 100). A planning poker meeting works as follows: 1) a moderator, not estimating, facilitates the meeting. 2) the product owner/manager provides a short overview of the user story and answers clarifying questions posed by the developers. Typically the product owner does not vote. 3) Each estimator selects an estimate of work effort by selecting a card, 4) Once everyone has selected a card, everyone overturns their card concurrently, 5) Estimators with high and low estimates are given a chance to defend positions. 6) The process repeats until there is consensus. The developer who owns the user story is typically given higher credence. [Agile Estimating and Planning. Mike Cohn.] [Agile estimation]

25. C - Coaching and mentoring within teams can be helpful for nascent agile teams and even for more experienced agile teams. Coaching and mentoring is the act of helping a person or team improve performance and achieve realistic goals. Because agile has a value of continuous improvement, coaching and mentoring is not solely for new or immature teams, but experienced ones too where coaching can help achieve higher levels of performance. The amount of coaching and mentoring an agile team needs is variable. Some newer teams will need a coach guiding the team nearly all the time while others may need a coach only for particularly challenging situations. A not uncommon scenario is to have a coach help the team collectively during sprint/iteration planning and then during the iteration help mentor individual team members. [Coaching Agile Teams. Lyssa Adkins.] [Knowledge and Skills: Level 1]

26. B - A successful brainstorming event should strive to consider the following points - Host the meeting in a neutral and comfortable environment - Have an engaging and experienced facilitator lead the event - Send participants an overview, with goals, schedule, and what ground rules, beforehand - Have a multi-disciplinary/diverse team to get a broader perspective - Delay any criticism that may stifle idea generation. [Agile Retrospectives: Making Good Teams Great. Esther Derby, Diana Larsen, Ken Schwaber.] [Knowledge and Skills: Level 1]

27. A - A successful brainstorming event should strive to consider the following points - Host the meeting in a neutral and comfortable environment - Have an engaging and experienced facilitator lead the event - Send participants an overview, with goals, schedule, and what ground rules, beforehand - Have a multi-disciplinary/diverse team to get a broader perspective - Delay any criticism that may stifle idea generation. [Agile Retrospectives: Making Good Teams Great. Esther Derby, Diana Larsen, Ken Schwaber.] [Knowledge and Skills: Level 1]

28. A - Velocity is a measure of the number of user story points or stories completed per iteration. An agile team can use its previous velocity values as a method of estimating how many user story points it may complete in the next iteration. [Agile Estimating and Planning. Mike Cohn.] [Metrics]

29. B - A successful brainstorming event should strive to consider the following points - Host the meeting in a neutral and comfortable environment - Have an engaging and experienced facilitator lead the event - Send participants an overview, with goals, schedule, and what ground rules, beforehand - Have a multi-disciplinary/diverse team to get a broader perspective - Delay any criticism that may stifle idea generation. [Agile Retrospectives: Making Good Teams Great. Esther Derby, Diana Larsen, Ken Schwaber.] [Knowledge and Skills: Level 1]

30. C - During reflection an agile team takes a break after completing an iteration to pause and contemplate about its performance. Topics include: lessons learned from successes and failures, such as programming methods that were highly efficient or inefficient; how to reinforce successful practices, such as new testing standard practices; how to discourage negative practices, like straying from team approved coding standards in order to make an iteration deadline. [Agile Software Development: The Cooperative Game – 2nd Edition. Alistair Cockburn.] [Planning, monitoring, and adapting]

31. A - A common misconception in agile is that an agile team does not need a leader. In fact, all agile teams need a leader, but the way in which the leader leads is fundamentally different than the typical traditional project manager/project leader method. Some have theorized that this misconception stems from the desired 'self-organizing' quality of the agile team. And although the 'self-organizing' agile team is empowered to take ownership and responsibility of the product and make some decisions itself, it nevertheless requires a leader to help provide guidance, mentoring, coaching, problem solving, and decision making. Some key aspects required of an agile leader include: empowering team members to decide what standard agile practices and methods it will use; allowing the team to be self-organized and self-disciplined; empowering the team members to make decisions collaboratively with the customer; inspire the team to be innovative and explore new ideas and technology capabilities; be a champion of and articulate the product vision to team members so it will be motivated to accomplish the overall objective; remove any obstacles and solve any problems the team may face in its effort; communicate and endorse the values and principles of agile project management to stakeholders that may be unfamiliar with agile; ensure that all stakeholders, including business managers and developers, are collaborating effectively; and, be able to adapt the leadership style to the working environment to ensure that the agile values and principles are effectively upheld. [The Art of Agile Development. James Shore.] [Knowledge and Skills: Level 1]

32. C - Highsmith defines adaptive leadership as two dimensional: Being agile and doing agile. Being agile includes focusing on cornerstones of agile project management, like incremental delivery, continuous integration, and adapting to changing requirements. Doing agile includes several activities that an agile leader must do: do less; speed-to-value, quality, and engage and inspire. [Agile Project Management: Creating Innovative Products – 2nd Edition. Jim Highsmith.] [Soft skills negotiation]

33. C - One communication technique to reduce misunderstanding and miscommunication is active listening. A well run agile project necessitates both good listeners and communicators, active listening helps work towards both of these necessities. The basics of active listening include: 1) Being present and focusing your attention on the speaker. 2) Taking notes instead of interrupting. 3) Paraphrasing to confirm and review what you have heard. 4) Summarizing the conversation once it has concluded for posterity. Using open ended questions, good body language, and silence can help improve listening skills. [Coaching Agile Teams. Lyssa Adkins.] [Knowledge and Skills: Level 1]

34. B - The team should meet with the customer to determine if and when the use story should be completed. [Agile Estimating and Planning. Mike Cohn.] [Planning, monitoring, and adapting]

35. C - Various grouping methods are used to organize user stories. Typical methods are: 1) Relation to a product feature (e.g., all user stories that interact with the database), 2) By logical sequence and dependency (e.g., Group 1 must be developed before Group 2 because of technological dependency), 3) By priority based on customer value. [User Stories Applied: For Agile Software Development. Mike Cohn.] [Agile analysis and design]

36. A - Unlike traditional project management methods that evaluate risk and variance and trends in formal meetings, agile incorporates risk analysis and variance and trend analysis into iteration review meetings. Risk and variance and trend analysis may be performed in agile using information radiators, like a risk burndown chart, and the use of traditional earned value management (EVM) to measure cost and schedule variance (CV and SV, respectively). [Agile Estimating and Planning. Mike Cohn.] [Knowledge and Skills: Level 3]

37. B - The 'done' column holds tasks that have been completely developed, tested or verified, and integrated into the product and require no further attention. The 'done' column should not hold incomplete tasks, but ones that are truly completed. [Lean-Agile Software Development: Achieving Enterprise Agility. Alan Shalloway, Guy Beaver, James R. Trott.] [Planning, monitoring, and adapting]

38. D - A lean manufacturing philosophy is to eliminate waste. One defined waste type in the lean philosophy is inventory, which is also referred to as work in process (WIP).

WIP is material or parts that have started production but are not yet a finished or "done" product. Inventory is considered wasteful because it costs money to purchase, store, and maintain. One way of reducing inventory is to reduce the WIP at individual machines or servers by only moving as fast as your slowest machine or processor (the system bottleneck). Agile also strives to control its WIP through WIP limits by completing all features to a "done" state before beginning development of new features. One can think of an iteration or sprint as a process that can develop a certain amount of features. In this analogy, the WIP limit is equivalent to the sprint backlog. By maintaining a WIP limit equal to the sprint backlog, no features should be incomplete at the sprint review. [Lean-Agile Software Development: Achieving Enterprise Agility. Alan Shalloway, Guy Beaver, James R. Trott.] [Planning, monitoring, and adapting]

39. A - Acceptance Test Driven Development (ATDD) is similar to Test-driven development (TDD) in that it requires programmers to create tests first before any product code. The tests in ATDD are aimed at confirming features/behaviors that the intended software will have. The iterative cycle of ATDD with its four steps can be remembered as the four Ds: 1) Discuss, 2) Distill, 3) Develop, and 4) Demo. 1) Discuss: The agile team and customer or business stakeholder discuss a user story in detail. Talking about the expected behaviors the user story should have and what it should not. 2) The development team takes those items learned from the discussion and distills them into tests that will verify and validate those behaviors. The distillation process is where the entire team should have a good understanding of what "done" (or completed) means for a user story. That is, what the acceptance criteria are. 3) After distillation, the team develops the test code and product code to implement the product features. 4) Once the product features have been developed, the team demonstrates them to the customer or business stakeholders for feedback. [Lean-Agile Software Development: Achieving Enterprise Agility. Alan Shalloway, Guy Beaver, James R. Trott.] [Product quality]

40. B - Acceptance Test Driven Development (ATDD) is similar to Test-driven development (TDD) in that it requires programmers to create tests first before any product code. The tests in ATDD are aimed at confirming features/behaviors that the intended software will have. The iterative cycle of ATDD with its four steps can be remembered as the four Ds: 1) Discuss, 2) Distill, 3) Develop, and 4) Demo. 1) Discuss: The agile team and customer or business stakeholder discuss a user story in detail. Talking about the expected behaviors the user story should have and what it should not. 2) The development team takes those items learned from the discussion and distills them into tests that will verify and validate those behaviors. The distillation process is where the entire team should have a good understanding of what "done" (or completed) means for a user story. That is, what the acceptance criteria are. 3) After distillation, the team develops the test code and product code to implement the product features. 4) Once the product features have been developed, the team demonstrates them to the customer or business stakeholders for feedback. [Lean-Agile Software Development: Achieving

Enterprise Agility. Alan Shalloway, Guy Beaver, James R. Trott.] [Product quality]

Knowledge Area Quiz
Soft Skills Negotiation
Practice Questions

Test Name: Knowledge Area Test: Soft Skills Negotiation
Total Questions: 15
Correct Answers Needed to Pass:
11 (73.33%)
Time Allowed: 25 Minutes

Test Description

This practice quiz specifically targets your knowledge of the Soft Skills Negotiation exam topic area.

Test Questions

1. Which of the following best defines collaboration?

   A. Working as a team to overcome conflict.

   B. Working individually to achieve objectives.

   C. Working and communicating as a team to achieve objectives.

   D. Working independently to achieve personal goals.

2. Which of the following best defines conflict resolution?

   A. The facilitation of resolving conflict among team members.

   B. The facilitation of acceptance test-driven development conflicts.

   C. The facilitation of test-driven development conflicts.

   D. The facilitation of resolving conflicting code integration.

3. Which of the following is the best definition of emotional intelligence?

   A. Being aware and in control of your emotions.

   B. Being aware of team members' emotions.

   C. Being aware of your emotions.

   D. Being in control of team members' emotions.

4. Having a high emotional intelligence is important to promote effective communication in an agile team. Which of the following\ is one of the seven components of emotional intelligence as defined by Higgs & Dulewicz?

   A. Self determination

   B. Self-awareness

   C. Introversion

   D. Competitiveness

5. According to Highsmith, what two dimensions help define 'adaptive leadership?'

A. Adaptive agility and anticipatory agility

B. Being agile and practicing agile

C. Being agile and doing agile

D. Adaptive agility and prescriptive agility

6. Which of the following best defines conflict resolution?

A. Resolving team member and customer communication issues.

B. Resolving conflict among team members.

C. Removing problematic team members.

D. Resolving issues of standard compliance among team members.

7. Which of the following summarizes principles, leadership, and teams in the agile framework?

A. Leaders manage teams and teams manage principles.

B. Leaders manage teams under established principles.

C. Teams manage principles and leaders.

D. Leaders manage principles and principles manage teams.

8. Which of the following best defines negotiation?

A. Holding reflection workshops to remove any obstacles from team processes and practices.

B. Holding discussions to come to agreement between two or more parties.

C. Having the customer define expectations of software deliverables.

D. Adapting to change in team dynamics through constant collaboration.

9. What is one effective way to improve collaboration in an agile effort?

A. Through the strict adherence of e-mail for communication.

B. Through isolation of team members.

C. Through the use of pair programming.

D. Through the seating of team members by function.

10. Which of the following is the best definition of servant leadership?

A. Listening to your team and providing it with the support it needs to be productive.

B. Leading team members by example.

C. Removing the customer as an obstacle to the development team.

D. Listening to your customer and translating requirements into specifications.

11. Rachel is explaining the concept of emotional intelligence to key stakeholders. Which of the following is the best definition of emotional intelligence?

A. Being aware of and in control of team members' emotions.

B. Being aware and in control of your emotions and aware of your team members' emotions.

C. Being aware of your emotions and aware of team members' emotions.

D. Being aware of team members' emotions.

12. High emotional intelligence is a desired quality in an agile team member. Which response is the best definition of emotional intelligence?

A. Being aware of team members' emotions.

B. Being aware of your emotions.

C. Being in control of team members' emotions.

D. Being aware and in control of your emotions.

13. Why is having a high emotional intelligence a desired quality of an agile team member?

A. It encourages motivation.

B. It promotes effective collaboration.

C. It eliminates the likelihood of overworked team members.

D. It ensures having passionate team members.

14. Rachel, as scrum master, is explaining the need for high emotional intelligence among team members. Why is high emotional intelligence desired?

A. It helps facilitate effective collaboration.

B. It helps instill passion among team members.

C. It helps facilitate team reflection.

D. It eliminates the likelihood of overworked team members.

15. Henry is explaining the concept of servant leadership to key stakeholders. Which of the following is the best definition of servant leadership?

A. Being attentive to the needs of the scrum master.

B. Being aware of team members' emotions.

C. Being attentive to the needs of your team.

D. Being attentive to the needs of the product owner.

Knowledge Area Quiz
Soft Skills Negotiation
Answer Key and Explanations

1. C - Collaboration is a key soft skill negotiation skill. It involves working in groups to create ideas, solve problems, and produce solutions. [Coaching Agile Teams. Lyssa Adkins.] [Soft skills negotiation]

2. A - Conflict resolution is a key soft skill negotiation skill. It involves applying proper leadership techniques to resolve and diffuse any conflict between team members or other stakeholders. [Coaching Agile Teams. Lyssa Adkins.] [Soft skills negotiation]

3. A - Having a high emotional intelligence means self-awareness, control over your own emotions, and being attentive to other team members' emotions. A high emotional intelligence allows team members to collaborate effectively. [Coaching Agile Teams. Lyssa Adkins.] [Soft skills negotiation]

4. B - Higgs & Dulewicz (1999) defines emotional intelligence using seven components: 1) Self-awareness, 2) Emotional resilience, 3) Motivation, 4) Interpersonal sensitivity, 5) Influence, 6) Intuitiveness, and 7) Conscientiousness. [Coaching Agile Teams. Lyssa Adkins.] [Soft skills negotiation]

5. C - Highsmith defines adaptive leadership as two dimensional: Being agile and doing agile. Being agile includes focusing on cornerstones of agile project management, like incremental delivery, continuous integration, and adapting to changing requirements. Doing agile includes several activities that an agile leader must do: do less; speed-to-value, quality, and engage and inspire. [Agile Project Management: Creating Innovative Products – 2nd Edition. Jim Highsmith.] [Soft skills negotiation]

6. B - Conflict resolution is a key soft skill negotiation skill. It involves applying proper leadership techniques to resolve and diffuse any conflict between team members or other stakeholders. [Coaching Agile Teams. Lyssa Adkins.] [Soft skills negotiation]

7. D - In high performance teams, leaders manage the principles and principles manage the teams. [Becoming Agile: ...in an imperfect world. Greg Smith, Ahmed Sidky.] [Soft skills negotiation]

8. B - Negotiation is a key soft skill negotiation skill. It involves discussion or conversation to work towards a common understanding between two parties. [Coaching Agile Teams. Lyssa Adkins.] [Soft skills negotiation]

9. C - Pair programming is an effective method for improving team collaboration. [Agile Retrospectives: Making Good Teams Great. Esther Derby, Diana Larsen, Ken Schwaber.] [Soft skills negotiation]

10. A - Servant leadership has its roots with an essay written in 1970 by Robert K Greenleaf. Greenleaf defined servant leaders as humble stewards devoted to their company and work to serve their peers, teams, and customers. In a self-organizing team, a servant leader, as Greenleaf defined it, is ideal as the team leader is an enabler, listening to the agile team's needs, removing

obstacles, and providing tools or other support to promote high productivity. [Coaching Agile Teams. Lyssa Adkins.] [Soft skills negotiation]

11. B - Having a high emotional intelligence means self-awareness, control over your own emotions, and being attentive to other team members' emotions. A high emotional intelligence allows team members to collaborate effectively. [Coaching Agile Teams. Lyssa Adkins.] [Soft skills negotiation]

12. D - Having a high emotional intelligence means self-awareness, control over your own emotions, and being attentive to other team members' emotions. A high emotional intelligence allows team members to collaborate effectively. [Coaching Agile Teams. Lyssa Adkins.] [Soft skills negotiation]

13. B - Having a high emotional intelligence means self-awareness, control over your own emotions, and being attentive to other team members' emotions. A high emotional intelligence allows team members to collaborate effectively. [Coaching Agile Teams. Lyssa Adkins.] [Soft skills negotiation]

14. A - Having a high emotional intelligence means self-awareness, control over your own emotions, and being attentive to other team members' emotions. A high emotional intelligence allows team members to collaborate effectively. [Coaching Agile Teams. Lyssa Adkins.] [Soft skills negotiation]

15. C - Servant leadership has its roots with an essay written in 1970 by Robert K Greenleaf. Greenleaf defined servant leaders as humble stewards devoted to their company and work to serve their peers, teams, and customers. In a self-organizing team, a servant leader, as Greenleaf defined it, is ideal as the team leader is an enabler, listening to the agile team's needs, removing obstacles, and providing tools or other support to promote high productivity. [Coaching Agile Teams. Lyssa Adkins.] [Soft skills negotiation]

PMI-ACP Lite Mock Exam 11 Practice Questions

Test Name: PMI-ACP Lite Mock Exam 11
Total Questions: 40
Correct Answers Needed to Pass: 30 (75.00%)
Time Allowed: 60 Minutes

Test Description

This is a cumulative PMI-ACP Mock Exam which can be used as a benchmark for your PMI-ACP aptitude. This practice test includes questions from all exam topic areas, including sections from Agile Tools and Techniques, and all three Agile Knowledge and Skills areas.

Test Questions

1. In release planning, where does an agile team typically record acceptance criteria for a user story?

A. On the product data sheet

B. On the back of user story cards

C. In the user story Excel database

D. On the user story acceptance criteria information radiator

2. Yvonne and her agile team have just been hired by an independent company to develop a cutting edge software project. Yvonne and her team should comply with the organization's code of ethics and conduct. What is this type of compliance known as?

A. Incentive compliance

B. Organization compliance

C. Facility compliance

D. Commissioned compliance

3. Feedback techniques are ubiquitous in agile projects. Select the response which lists a feedback technique.

A. Iteration

B. Increment

C. Sprint

D. Demo / demonstration

4. Ernie knows that feedback techniques are ubiquitous in agile projects. Which of the following lists an agile 'feedback technique for product?'

A. Iteration

B. Release planning

C. Increment

D. Sprint

5. Select a technique that promotes agile 'knowledge sharing.'

A. Incremental planning

B. Integer planning

C. Iteration planning

D. Interval planning

6. When agile team members make decisions collaboratively and take ownership of a product, what is the decision model known as?

A. Command

B. Managerial

C. Participatory

D. Individual

7. Lisa is describing the four Agile Manifesto values to her co-workers. Of the following, which response lists a secondary value?

A. Responding to change

B. Comprehensive documentation

C. Working software

D. Individuals and interactions

8. Wendy has been given a deck of cards for an upcoming agile planning meeting. In the meeting Wendy is to use the cards for estimating the work effort involved with developing user stories. What agile estimation technique is Wendy applying?

A. Planning poker

B. Infinity estimation

C. Poker affinity

D. Affinity estimation

9. Peter is estimating the relative work effort of user stories at a meeting. The meeting is taking place in a large conference room with a Fibonacci scale attached to the wall. A facilitator asks the participants to size their user stories by attaching them to appropriate places on the scale using their best judgment. This estimation is performed mostly in silence. What type of estimation technique is Peter using?

A. Poker affinity

B. Planning poker

C. Infinity estimation

D. Affinity estimating

10. Select the best adjective that describes an agile team's project and quality standards.

A. Stiff

B. Inflexible

C. Unbending

D. Evolving

11. Select the best adjective that describes an agile team's project and quality standards.

A. Fluid

B. Inflexible

C. Stiff

D. Unbending

12. Barry and his agile team just completed an iteration. The team has reserved a block of time to devote to reviewing its performance in the iteration. What is this agile principle called?

A. Iteration speculation

B. Information burnup

C. Information burndown

D. Reflection

13. Denise is concerned about how effective her agile team is at communicating with key stakeholders. What is the agile knowledge and skill area that concerns itself with communications among team members and stakeholders?

A. Collaboration management

B. Information flow management

C. Communications management

D. Marketing

14. Jack is explaining the advantages of using information radiators to a new agile recruit. Help Jack select an advantage of using an information radiator.

A. Information radiators allow key information to be obscured from the customer.

B. Information radiators allow only the project leader to review project status.

C. Information radiators allow only certain team members to review project status.

D. Information radiators allow all team members and stakeholders to review project status.

15. Calculate the Net Present Value of the following investment candidate. The initial investment cost is $1,000. The discount rate is 10%. At the end of year 1, $150 is expected. At the end of year 2, $300 is expected. At the end of year 3, $550 is expected.

A. $202

B. $0

C. ($202)

D. $2,000

16. Consider the following EVM scenario and calculate the CV. The team is on week 30 of a 100 week project. Its BAC is $100,000 and AC is $15,000. The team estimates it is 20% complete overall and has an EV of $20,000.

A. ($5,000)

B. $5,000

C. $0

D. $10,000

17. Calculate the IRR for the following one year investment. The initial investment cost is \$600. The expected income in year 1 is \$720.

A. 10%

B. 20%

C. 15.00%

D. -20%

18. Calculate the IRR for the following one year investment. The initial investment cost is \$400. The expected income in year 1 is \$440.

A. 7.38%

B. 15%

C. 10%

D. 5%

19. David is explaining the advantages of using information radiators to a new agile recruit. Help David select an advantage of using an information radiator.

A. Information radiators increase the need for other more lengthy forms of communication, like e-mail, so promote more team communication.

B. Information radiators improve coding compliance.

C. Information radiators decrease the need for other more lengthy forms of communication, like e-mail.

D. Information radiators decrease the need for continuous integration.

20. Kyle is explaining the advantages of using information radiators to a new agile recruit. Help Kyle select an advantage of using an information radiator.

A. Information radiators decrease coding defects.

B. Information radiators simplify communication.

C. Information radiators increase coding compliance.

D. Information radiators decrease the need for unit testing.

21. In agile, the "team space" is an important place that should foster effective communication. Of the following, which is a guideline for promoting such an environment?

A. Infrequent updates of information radiators

B. Fluorescent lighting

C. Use of headphones so developers can drown out background noise

D. Reduction of non-essential noise and distractions

22. In agile, the "team space" is an important place that should foster effective communication. What is a guideline for promoting such an environment?

A. Use of headphones so developers can drown out background noise

B. Fluorescent lighting

C. Infrequent updates of information radiators

D. Pairing or sharing workstations

23. What are the three fundamental processes in the crystal framework?

A. Chartering, delivery cycles, wrap-up

B. Negotiating, delivering, closing

C. Initiating, developing, closing

D. Envisioning, speculating, adapting

24. Which of the following is an agile 'feedback technique for product?'

A. Pair programming

B. In-stream refactoring

C. Negative feedback loop

D. Kanban filtering

25. Which of the following is an agile 'feedback technique for product?'

A. Negative feedback loop

B. In-stream refactoring

C. Kanban filtering

D. Unit testing

26. An agile team has decided to use an experienced agile practitioner and facilitator to help it reach an improved level of performance. What knowledge and skill area is this practitioner providing to the team?

A. Coaching and mentoring

B. Envisioning and elaborating

C. Incentive and profit

D. Coaching and mobilizing

27. Which of the following responses is a community value per the PMI agile community of practice community charter?

A. Intrepid

B. Cautious

C. Vision

D. Nurturing

28. When value stream mapping it is important to identify areas of waste that exist in the process. The pneumonic device WIDETOM may be used to remember the different forms of muda (or waste). What does the O in WIDETOM stand for with respect to waste?

A. Over-zealous

B. Over-production

C. Over-precipitate

D. Over-puncture

29. Having a high emotional intelligence is important to promote effective communication in an agile team. What is one of the seven components of emotional intelligence as defined by Higgs & Dulewicz?

A. Empathy

B. Clairvoyance

C. Self-awareness

D. Intrepidness

30. Select the response that lists one of the five core risk areas that can impact a project.

A. Intrinsic budgeting flaw

B. Intrinsic productivity flaw

C. Intrinsic costing flaw

D. Intrinsic schedule flaw

31. Of the following, select a method used in agile for the purpose of prioritization.

A. INVEST

B. MoCWoS

C. MoSCoW

D. SMART

32. When is the best time for an agile team to define the project and quality standards it will use?

A. At the beginning of an effort

B. After the first iteration

C. During the first retrospective workshop

D. After the first release

33. Becky, as project leader, intends on building a high-performance team. What is a practice or technique she can use to build a high performance team?

A. Collocating the team

B. Isolating team members for focus

C. Criticizing team members openly

D. Promoting competition

34. How does a product backlog change over a project?

A. It does not and should not be expected to change.

B. It becomes less defined as the project progresses.

C. It evolves to capture the most recent requirements of the customer.

D. It is static with requirements remaining fixed until the release.

35. How does the lean manufacturing concept of kanban reduce the impact of work in process bottlenecks?

A. It does not reduce bottlenecks. Bottlenecks are an inevitable by-product of any manufacturing system.

B. Through root cause analysis using 5Y

C. By being a just-in-time scheduling system.

D. Through weekly kaizen events.

36. How does velocity play into the iteration plan?

A. It helps the team predict duration of the daily stand-up meetings during the iteration.

B. It helps the team predict customer value.

C. It helps the team determine how many user stories may be developed in the forthcoming iteration.

D. It helps the team predict task durations or timeboxing values.

37. Gerald, an agile developer, is at a planning event where the relative effort of developing user stories of a large product backlog is to be estimated. The team is to assign user stories to various t-shirt sizes (small, medium, large, extra-large) that indicate the development effort. The planning event is efficient and the user stories are estimated quickly. What type of planning event is Gerald most likely attending?

A. T-shirt estimating

B. Affinity estimating

C. Relative estimating

D. Infinity estimating

38. If Lyle's agile team only plans for two to three iterations and keeps iterations further removed loosely planned. What type of planning technique is Lyle's agile team using?

A. Rolling wave planning

B. Progressive wave planning

C. Progressive elaboration

D. Release planning

39. In the XP principle of continuous integration, what happens with new code before it is integrated into the production code base?

A. It is reviewed by the customer.

B. It is postfactored to add extra lines of code for redundancy.

C. It is extensively tested.

D. It is converted to the target environment coding language.

40. What role does the project plan serve in the agile method?

A. It serves as a binding contract for the project stakeholders' legal department.

B. It serves as a rigid specification of all activities and product features.

C. It serves as a highly detailed requirements document.

D. It serves as a cursory artifact to describe features and delivery deadlines, but does not include detailed tasks, activities, or processes.

PMI-ACP Lite Mock Exam 11 Answer Key and Explanations

1. B - During release planning, acceptance criteria are typically recorded on the backs of user story cards. Agile team testers will use this acceptance criteria in their verification tests. [The Art of Agile Development. James Shore.] [Planning, monitoring, and adapting]

2. B - Compliance with a company's code of ethics and professional conduct is standard practice in agile. [PMI Agile Community of Practice Community Charter. Project Management Institute.] [Knowledge and Skills: Level 3]

3. D - There are several feedback techniques - techniques that facilitate constructive criticism to improve product value and quality - built into the agile process. In the classic definition, feedback is a dynamic process where past information influences the behavior of the same process in the future. Agile feedback techniques include prototyping, simulation, demonstration, evaluations, pair programming, unit testing, continuous integration, daily stand-up meetings, sprint planning. Because agile prides itself on a transparent and collaborative environment, feedback is essentially ubiquitous. [Agile Retrospectives: Making Good Teams Great. Esther Derby, Diana Larsen, Ken Schwaber.] [Knowledge and Skills: Level 1]

4. B - There are several feedback techniques - techniques that facilitate constructive criticism to improve product value and quality - built into the agile process. In the classic definition, feedback is a dynamic process where past information influences the behavior of the same process in the future. Agile feedback techniques include prototyping, simulation, demonstration, evaluations, pair programming, unit testing, continuous integration, daily stand-up meetings, sprint planning. Because agile prides itself on a transparent and collaborative environment, feedback is essentially ubiquitous. [Agile Retrospectives: Making Good Teams Great. Esther Derby, Diana Larsen, Ken Schwaber.] [Knowledge and Skills: Level 1]

5. C - In agile, effective 'knowledge sharing' is a critical factor for success. It involves the near real time communication of key information among all team members and stakeholders. To promote knowledge sharing, agile uses standard practices built into its process, such as using generalized specialists/cross functional teams, self-organizing and self-disciplined teams, collocation, daily stand-up meetings, iteration/sprint planning, release planning, pair programming and pair rotation, project retrospectives/reflection, and on-site customer support. And, of course, the sixth principle of Agile is " The most efficient and effective method of conveying information to and within a development team is face-to-face conversation." In this sense, Agile prefers and encourages collocation for all stakeholders and team members for the simple fact that face-to-face conversation is the best method of communication and, in turn, effective knowledge sharing. [Becoming Agile: ...in an imperfect world. Greg Smith, Ahmed Sidky.] [Knowledge and Skills: Level 1]

6. C - To build trust among the team, agile believes heavily in participatory decision models where team members collaborate to make decisions. Although a team leader or

scrum master will need to make some decisions individually, many decisions can be made by the team collectively. These agile principles are also known as collective ownership, self-organization, and self-discipline. In collective ownership, the team members are equally responsible for project results and are empowered to participate in decision making and problem solving processes. [Agile Retrospectives: Making Good Teams Great. Esther Derby, Diana Larsen, Ken Schwaber.] [Knowledge and Skills: Level 2]

7. B - The Agile Manifesto defines four values. The four values list primary values and secondary values, with primary values superseding secondary values. The values are 1) individuals and interactions over processes and tools, 2) working software over comprehensive documentation, 3) customer collaboration over contract negotiation, and 4) responding to change over following a plan. [Manifesto for Agile Software Development. Agile Alliance.] [Knowledge and Skills: Level 1]

8. A - Planning poker is based upon the wideband Delphi estimation technique. It is a consensus-based technique for estimating effort. Sometimes called scrum poker, it is a technique for a relative estimation of effort, typically in story points, to develop a user story. At a planning poker meeting, each estimator is given an identical deck of planning poker cards with a wide range of values. The Fibonacci sequence is often used for values for planning poker (i.e., 0, 1, 1, 2, 3, 5,8,etc.); another common sequence is (question mark, 0, 1/2, 1, 2, 3, 5, 8, 13, 20, 40, and 100). A planning poker meeting works as follows: 1) a moderator, not estimating, facilitates the meeting. 2) the product owner/manager provides a short overview of the user story and answers clarifying questions posed by the developers. Typically the product owner does not vote. 3) Each estimator selects an estimate of work effort by selecting a card, 4) Once everyone has selected a card, everyone overturns their card concurrently, 5) Estimators with high and low estimates are given a chance to defend positions. 6) The process repeats until there is consensus. The developer who owns the user story is typically given higher credence. [Agile Estimating and Planning. Mike Cohn.] [Agile estimation]

9. D - Affinity estimating is a method to predict the work effort, typically in story points, of developing a user story. It is particularly useful for large product backlogs. Although several methods exist, the basic affinity estimating model involves sizing user stories on a scale from small to large. The scale can be a Fibonacci sequence or t-shirt sizes and is typically taped to a wall in a large conference room. Participants then attach their user stories to the wall as estimates. It is often done in silence and has several iterations until the user stories have been estimated. [The Art of Agile Development. James Shore.] [Agile estimation]

10. D - All agile efforts have project and quality standards that the team defines collaboratively at the beginning of an effort and refines collaboratively throughout the effort. Project and quality standards help an agile team with team cohesion and provide a structure, albeit one that can adapt as the project evolves, to promote a self-disciplined environment. There is no 'one size fits all' standards definition in agile; because every project is different, it has been shown that the team should define which project and quality standards it should hold itself against and strive to conform to those standards while also being open to adapting those standards throughout the project to optimize performance and delivered value. Project standards can range from where the daily stand-up meeting is located and how long each participant has to share his or her progress and challenges to highly specific software coding styles, methods for test-driven development, and what the team's definition of 'done-done' means. [Agile Software Development: The Cooperative Game – 2nd Edition. Alistair Cockburn.] [Knowledge and Skills: Level 1]

11. A - All agile efforts have project and quality standards that the team defines collaboratively at the beginning of an effort and refines collaboratively throughout the effort. Project and quality standards help an agile team with team cohesion and provide a structure, albeit one that can adapt as the project evolves, to promote a self-disciplined environment. There is no 'one size fits all' standards definition in agile; because every project is different, it has been shown that the team should define which project and quality standards it should hold itself against and strive to conform to those standards while also being open to adapting those standards throughout the project to optimize performance and delivered value. Project standards can range from where the daily stand-up meeting is located and how long each participant has to share his or her progress and challenges to highly specific software coding styles, methods for test-driven development, and what the team's definition of 'done-done' means. [Agile Software Development: The Cooperative Game – 2nd Edition. Alistair Cockburn.] [Knowledge and Skills: Level 1]

12. D - During reflection an agile team takes a break after completing an iteration to pause and contemplate about its performance. Topics include: lessons learned from successes and failures, such as programming methods that were highly efficient or inefficient; how to reinforce successful practices, such as new testing standard practices; how to discourage negative practices, like straying from team approved coding standards in order to make an iteration deadline. [Agile Software Development: The Cooperative Game – 2nd Edition. Alistair Cockburn.] [Planning, monitoring, and adapting]

13. C - Effective communication is a cornerstone of agile. Communication is the act of transferring information among various parties. Communications management is a knowledge and skill area of agile that highlights this importance. PMI has several definitions regarding communications management and agile builds on top of these to add its own perspective: 1) Communications Planning: Determining the information and communication needs of the projects stakeholders 2) Information Distribution: Making needed information available to project stakeholders in a timely manner, 3) Performance Reporting: Collecting and distributing performance information. This includes status reporting, progress measurement, and forecasting, and 4) Managing Stakeholders: Managing communications to satisfy the requirements and resolve issues with project stakeholders. From an agile perspective: communication among the team is built into the process and facilitated through collocation, information radiators, daily stand-up meetings, retrospectives etc.; Although it is hoped that the product owner, customer, and user can be heavily involved with the project and also use these communication techniques, a plan for conveying information to stakeholders may be needed if this is not the case. [Agile Software Development: The Cooperative Game – 2nd Edition. Alistair Cockburn.] [Knowledge and Skills: Level 1]

14. D - Information radiators reduce lengthy communication, allow for all team members and stakeholders to review project status throughout a project, and reduce the need of other more time-consuming communication methods, like e-mails or memorandums. [Agile Software Development: The Cooperative Game – 2nd Edition. Alistair Cockburn.] [Communications]

15. C - Net Present Value: A metric used to analyze the profitability of an investment or project. NPV is the difference between the present value of cash inflows and the present value of cash outflows. NPV considers the likelihood of future cash inflows that an investment or project will yield. NPV is the sum of each cash inflow/outflow for the expected duration of the investment. Each cash inflow/outflow is discounted back to its present value (PV) (i.e.,, what the money is worth in terms of today's value). NPV is the sum of all terms: NPV = Sum of [Rt/(1 + i)^t] where t = the time of the cash flow, i = the discount rate (the rate of return that could be earned on in the financial markets) , and Rt = the net cash inflow or outflow. For example, consider the following two year period. The discount rate is 5% and the initial investment cost is $500. At the end of the first year, a $200 inflow is expected. At the end of the second year, a $1,000 is expected. NPV = -500 + 200/(1.05)^1 + 1000/(1.05)^2 = ~$597. If NPV is positive, it indicates that the investment will add value to the buyer's portfolio. If NPV is negative, it will subtract value. If NPV is zero, it will neither add or subtract value. [Agile Estimating and Planning. Mike Cohn.] [Value based prioritization]

16. B - EVM or earned value management is a management technique used to evaluate project performance with respect to cost and schedule. EVM relies on other common financial metrics like Budget At Completion (BAC), Actual Cost (AC), Planned Value (PV), Earned Value (EV), Cost Variance (CV), Schedule Variance (SV), Cost Performance Index (CPI), and Schedule Performance Index (SPI). CV and SV can be converted into performance indicators of CPI and SPI, respectively, and tracked and charted to show progress over time. EV is value of work actually completed or earned (e.g., you have completed 50% of the project by week 5 of a 15 week $15,000 project = $7,500 EV). CV is the difference between what a project has earned to date and cost to date (i.e., CV = EV - AC). AC is the actual cost the project has incurred to date. [Agile Estimating and Planning. Mike Cohn.] [Metrics]

17. B - The internal rate of return (IRR) is a financial metric used to measure and compare the profitability of investments. The IRR is the "rate" that makes the net present value of all cash flows from a particular investment equal to zero. Unlike NPV which is a dollar amount (i.e., a magnitude) value, the IRR is a rate (i.e.,, a percentage). Often times, the IRR is compared against a threshold rate value to determine if the investment is a suitable risk worth implementing. For example, you might calculate an IRR to be 13% for an investment while a comparative market rate is 2%. The IRR being larger than the comparative market rate, would indicate the investment is worth pursuing. [Agile Estimating and Planning. Mike Cohn.] [Value based prioritization]

18. C - The internal rate of return (IRR) is a financial metric used to measure and compare the profitability of investments. The IRR is the "rate" that makes the net present value of all cash flows from a particular investment equal to zero. Unlike NPV which is a dollar amount (i.e., a magnitude) value, the IRR is a rate (i.e.,, a percentage). Often times, the IRR is compared against a threshold rate value to determine if the investment is a suitable risk worth implementing. For example, you might calculate an IRR to be 13% for an investment while a comparative market rate is 2%. The IRR being larger than the comparative market rate, would indicate the investment is worth pursuing. [Agile Estimating and Planning. Mike Cohn.] [Value based prioritization]

19. C - Information radiators reduce lengthy communication, allow for all team members and stakeholders to review project status throughout a project, and reduce the need of other more time-consuming communication methods, like e-mails or memorandums. [Agile Software Development: The Cooperative Game – 2nd Edition. Alistair Cockburn.] [Communications]

20. B - Information radiators reduce lengthy communication, allow for all team members and stakeholders to review project status throughout a project, and reduce the need of other more time-consuming communication methods, like e-mails or memorandums. [Agile Software Development: The Cooperative Game – 2nd Edition. Alistair Cockburn.] [Communications]

21. D - A warm, welcoming environment that promotes effective communication, innovation, and motivated team members is an important aspect to consider when designing team space. Guidelines for a better agile team space include: collocation of team members; reduction of non-essential noise/distractions; dedicated whiteboard and wall space for information radiators; space for the daily stand-up meeting and other meetings; pairing workstations; and other pleasantries like plants and comfortable furniture. [Agile Retrospectives: Making Good Teams Great. Esther Derby, Diana Larsen, Ken Schwaber.] [Communications]

22. D - A warm, welcoming environment that promotes effective communication, innovation, and motivated team members is an important aspect to consider when designing team space. Guidelines for a better agile team space include: collocation of team members; reduction of non-essential noise/distractions; dedicated whiteboard and wall space for information radiators; space for the daily stand-up meeting and other meetings; pairing workstations; and other pleasantries like plants and comfortable furniture. [Agile Retrospectives: Making Good Teams Great. Esther Derby, Diana Larsen, Ken Schwaber.] [Communications]

23. A - Crystal is a family of methodologies for a flexible and lightweight approach to software development. The family of methodologies is color coded to differentiate its members (e.g., clear, yellow, orange, red.) The color chosen depends on the level of effort required. On one end of the spectrum is crystal clear, which is for smaller efforts, while crystal red is for larger efforts. Regardless of color, the crystal framework is cyclical and has three fundamental processes: chartering, delivery cycles, and wrap-up. Crystal chartering includes building the team, doing an Exploratory 360, defining standards of practice for the team, and building the project plan. In the delivery cycle, the crystal team iteratively develops, integrates, tests, and releases the product in iterations that last from one week to two months. Like other agile frameworks, crystal includes collaborative events, like stand-up meetings and reflective improvement workshops. In wrap-up the team concludes the project and holds a completion ritual where the team reflects on the entire project. [Agile Software Development: The Cooperative Game – 2nd Edition. Alistair Cockburn.] [Knowledge and Skills: Level 2]

24. A - There are several feedback techniques - techniques that facilitate constructive criticism to improve product value and quality - built into the agile process. In the classic definition, feedback is a dynamic process where past information influences the behavior of the same process in the future. Agile feedback techniques include prototyping, simulation, demonstration, evaluations, pair programming, unit testing, continuous integration, daily stand-up meetings, sprint planning. Because agile prides itself on a transparent and collaborative environment, feedback is essentially ubiquitous. [Agile Retrospectives: Making Good Teams Great. Esther Derby, Diana Larsen, Ken Schwaber.] [Knowledge and Skills: Level 1]

25. D - There are several feedback techniques - techniques that facilitate constructive criticism to improve product value and quality - built into the agile process. In the classic definition, feedback is a dynamic process where past information influences the behavior of the same process in the future. Agile feedback techniques include prototyping, simulation, demonstration, evaluations, pair programming, unit testing, continuous integration, daily stand-up meetings, sprint planning. Because agile prides itself on a transparent and collaborative environment, feedback is essentially ubiquitous. [Agile Retrospectives: Making Good Teams Great. Esther Derby, Diana Larsen, Ken Schwaber.] [Knowledge and Skills: Level 1]

26. A - Coaching and mentoring within teams can be helpful for nascent agile teams and even for more experienced agile teams. Coaching and mentoring is the act of helping a person or team improve performance and achieve realistic goals. Because agile has a value of continuous improvement, coaching and mentoring is not solely for new or immature teams, but experienced ones too where coaching can help achieve higher levels of performance. The amount of coaching and mentoring an agile team needs is variable. Some newer teams will need a coach guiding the team nearly all the time while others may need a coach only for particularly challenging situations. A not uncommon scenario is to have a coach help the team collectively during sprint/iteration planning and then

during the iteration help mentor individual team members. [Coaching Agile Teams. Lyssa Adkins.] [Knowledge and Skills: Level 1]

27. C - The following are community values of the PMI agile community of practice community charter: Vision, Servant Leadership, Trust, Collaboration, Honesty, Learning, Courage, Openness, Adaptability, Leading Change, Transparency [PMI Agile Community of Practice Community Charter. Project Management Institute.] [Knowledge and Skills: Level 1]

28. B - Value stream mapping is a lean manufacturing analysis technique adopted by agile. A value stream map may be used to analyze the flow of information or materials from origin to destination to identify areas of waste. The identified areas of waste are opportunities for process improvement. Waste can take many forms and can be remembered using the pneumonic device WIDETOM. W - waiting; I - inventory; D - defects; E - extra processing; T - transportation; O - over-production ; M - Motion. A value stream map is typically mapped or charted collaboratively with a team so it may define and view the entire process together, pinpointing areas of waste within the process. Processes that add value (processing of a part or feature) are generally referred to as "value-added" and processes that do not (e.g., waiting for a part to arrive) are generally referred to as "non value-added." Generally speaking, one wants to reduce, to the largest extent possible, the non value-added time (i.e., areas of waste). [Lean-Agile Software Development: Achieving Enterprise Agility. Alan Shalloway, Guy Beaver, James R. Trott.] [Value stream analysis]

29. C - Higgs & Dulewicz (1999) defines emotional intelligence using seven components: 1) Self-awareness, 2) Emotional resilience, 3) Motivation, 4) Interpersonal sensitivity, 5) Influence, 6) Intuitiveness, and 7) Conscientiousness. [Coaching Agile Teams. Lyssa Adkins.] [Soft skills negotiation]

30. D - The five core risk areas include: productivity variation (difference between planned and actual performance); scope creep (considerable additional requirements beyond initial agreement); specification breakdown (lack of stakeholder consensus on requirements); intrinsic schedule flaw (poor estimates of task durations), personnel loss (the loss of human resources). [The Software Project Manager's Bridge to Agility. Michele Sliger, Stacia Broderick.] [Risk management]

31. C - An agile team must always face the prioritization of product features in its product backlog. From release planning to iteration planning, an agile team must prioritize the user stories/ features of its product to ensure that high-quality and high-value features are developed first to help facilitate an optimized and early return on investment (ROI). An agile team typically prioritizes requirements or user stories/features in terms of relative value and risk; value is defined by the customer (i.e., customer-value prioritization). Two common methods to prioritize product features are: MoSCoW and Kano. The MoSCoW method categorizes features into 'Must have,' 'Should have,' 'Could have,' and 'Would have' features. The Kano method categorizes features into 'Must haves (threshold),' 'Dissatisfiers,' 'Satisfiers,' and 'Delighters.' Must haves are features that are requisite. Dissatisfiers are features that adversely impact perceived value and should be eliminated. 'Satisfiers' are features that increase perceived value linearly, where the more you add the more the customer is pleased, but are not required, and 'Delighters' are features that increase perceived value exponentially to please the customer. To prioritize features based on risk, a risk-to-value matrix can be used. A risk-to-value matrix has four quadrants, with the horizontal axis having low and high value, and the vertical axis having low and high risk. User stories are assigned to one of the four categories/quadrants: low-value, low-risk; low-value, high-risk; high-value, low-risk; high-value, high-risk. A cost-to-value matrix can also be made in this manner. All prioritization in agile is 'relative,' meaning that the priority of one user story is relative to other user stories and not prioritized on a fixed scale. [Lean-Agile Software Development: Achieving Enterprise Agility. Alan Shalloway, Guy Beaver, James R. Trott.] [Knowledge and Skills: Level 1]

32. A - All agile efforts have project and quality standards that the team defines collaboratively at the beginning of an effort and refines collaboratively throughout the effort. Project and quality standards help an agile team with team cohesion and provide a structure, albeit one that can adapt as the project evolves, to promote a self-disciplined environment. There is no 'one size fits all' standards definition in agile; because every project is different, it has been shown that the team should define which project and quality standards it should hold itself against and strive to conform to those standards while also being open to adapting those standards throughout the project to optimize performance and delivered value. Project standards can range from where the daily stand-up meeting is located and how long each participant has to share his or her progress and challenges to highly specific software coding styles, methods for test-driven development, and what the team's definition of 'done-done' means. [Agile Software Development: The Cooperative Game – 2nd Edition. Alistair Cockburn.] [Knowledge and Skills: Level 1]

33. A - Building a high-performance team is critical to any project's success. A high performance team has the right team members, is empowered, has built trust, works at a sustainable pace, has consistently high velocity/productivity, takes regular time for reflection to review work, has a team lead that removes any obstacles and provides mentoring and coaching, is self-organized and self-disciplined, and is collocated. Several management techniques can be used to build or foster a high-performance team environment, some techniques include: removing obstacles that slow down a team's performance, having high expectations of team performance, and coaching and mentoring the team to achieve its best performance. [Coaching Agile Teams. Lyssa Adkins.] [Knowledge and Skills: Level 2]

34. C - The product backlog is a comprehensive list of all product features to be developed in an iteration. It is an evolving document and changes to adapt to customer requirements. As the project progresses, project features in the backlog become better defined as the customer understands product need more completely. [Lean-Agile Software Development: Achieving Enterprise Agility. Alan

Shalloway, Guy Beaver, James R. Trott.] [Agile analysis and design]

35. C - Kanban is a just-in-time (JIT) scheduling system for inventory control. Production processes only execute if there is a demand signal for the part being processed. Carefully controlling inventory in this manner ensures that no machine is producing unnecessary/unordered parts. A machine will only send a demand signal if it has the capacity to perform the manufacturing immediately. Therefore, inventory (or WIP) will not backup or bottleneck at machines because the demand signal for inventory is highly controlled and based on processing speeds and absolute need. [Lean-Agile Software Development: Achieving Enterprise Agility. Alan Shalloway, Guy Beaver, James R. Trott.] [Planning, monitoring, and adapting]

36. C - The team uses its velocity to pick the number of user stories to develop in the upcoming iteration. [The Art of Agile Development. James Shore.] [Planning, monitoring, and adapting]

37. B - Affinity estimating is a method to predict the work effort, typically in story points, of developing a user story. It is particularly useful for large product backlogs. Although several methods exist, the basic affinity estimating model involves sizing user stories on a scale from small to large. The scale can be a Fibonacci sequence or t-shirt sizes and is typically taped to a wall in a large conference room. Participants then attach their user stories to the wall as estimates. It is often done in silence and has several iterations until the user stories have been estimated. [The Art of Agile Development. James Shore.] [Agile estimation]

38. A - Rolling wave planning (or rolling look ahead planning) involves planning in waves or phases and is especially useful for large, complex projects. Only the next few iterations are planned in detail and iterations more distant are planned only at a high-level. Progressive elaboration is continuous planning that assumes that details and requirements will be better refined later and will be incorporated into the planning process at the appropriate time. [Agile Estimating and Planning. Mike Cohn.] [Agile analysis and design]

39. C - The extreme programming (XP) principle of continuous integration is that code is integrated into the full code base as soon as it is built, tested, and completed. Once integrated, the code base and therefore the entire system is built and tested. Continuous integration is just one principle of XP that promotes rapid delivery of software and the early detection of integration defects. [The Art of Agile Development. James Shore.] [Product quality]

40. D - The agile project plan serves an initial outline to describe general features and capabilities and includes a rough project schedule to forecast milestones; however, an agile project plan is constantly changing and expected to change as customer requirements evolve. [Agile Project Management: Creating Innovative Products – 2nd Edition. Jim Highsmith.] [Knowledge and Skills: Level 1]

Knowledge Area Quiz Value Based Prioritization Practice Questions

Test Name: Knowledge Area Test: Value Based Prioritization
Total Questions: 15
Correct Answers Needed to Pass: 11 (73.33%)
Time Allowed: 25 Minutes

Test Description

This practice quiz specifically targets your knowledge of the Value Based Prioritization exam topic area.

Test Questions

1. Which of the following best defines Minimally Marketable Feature (MMF)?

   A. A feature that has minimal NPV and a marketable IRR.

   B. A feature that is relatively simple and will return value.

   C. A feature that returns the most value to a customer.

   D. A feature that has minimal IRR and a marketable NPV.

2. Which of the following best defines customer-value prioritization?

   A. Prioritization of features based on product owner affinity.

   B. Prioritization of features based on shareholder-value.

   C. Prioritization of features based on product owner need.

   D. Prioritization of features based on customer-value.

3. Select the best definition of net present value (NPV).

   A. A metric used to evaluate the speed of an investment.

   B. A metric used to evaluate the profitability of an investment.

   C. A metric used to evaluate the velocity of an investment.

   D. A metric used to evaluate the interest of an investment.

4. Which of the following is a key responsibility of the product owner according to the scrum philosophy?

   A. Pair programming assignments

   B. Velocity

   C. Return on investment

   D. Quality control

5. Which of the following best defines relative ranking/prioritization?

A. The ordering of a list of items based on a project-manager's definition of priority.

B. The ordering of a list of items based on NPV.

C. The ordering of a list of items based on NPV.

D. The ordering of a list of items based on a team-defined definition of priority.

6. Select the best definition of return on investment (ROI).

A. A metric used to evaluate the speed of an investment.

B. A metric used to evaluate the efficiency of an investment.

C. A metric used to evaluate the velocity of an investment.

D. A metric used to evaluate the interest of an investment.

7. Calculate the return on investment of the following: Gain: $25,000; Cost: $10,000.

A. 75%

B. -150%

C. 150%

D. 125%

8. Which of the following best defines the Internal Rate of Return (IRR)?

A. A metric used to evaluate the interest of an investment.

B. A metric used to evaluate the capacity of an investment.

C. A metric used to evaluate the measure of an investment.

D. A metric used to evaluate the profitability of an investment.

9. When performing value based prioritization, what is the term for a product feature that is relatively simple or small and is expected to return value.

A. Minimally Advertised Feature (MAF)

B. Minimally Marketable Feature (MMF)

C. Simple Value Feature (SVF)

D. Small Value Feature (SVF)

10. Calculate the IRR for the following one year investment. The initial investment cost is $500. The expected income in year 1 is $550.

A. 10%

B. 15%

C. 5%

D. 7.38%

11. Based on the following IRRs, and based on IRR alone without considering other

financial metrics, which of the following investments would you pick first to pursue?

A. 8%

B. 9%

C. 10%

D. 5.00%

12. According to the pareto rule:

A. 80% of value-focused market research can be explained by 20% of the target population.

B. 80% of the value derives from 20% of the work.

C. 80% of defects occur during the first 20% of the total project schedule.

D. 20% of the value derives from 80% of the work.

13. What are the key elements considered when prioritizing user stories?

A. Value, risk, and difficulty

B. Value, cost, and difficulty

C. Value, risk, and expedience

D. Value, cost, and risk

14. Calculate the IRR for the following one year investment. The initial investment cost is $500. The expected income in year 1 is $550.

A. 15%

B. 5%

C. 7.38%

D. 10%

15. Calculate the return on investment of the following: Gain: $10,000; Cost: $10,000.

A. 50%

B. 33%

C. -50%

D. 0%

Knowledge Area Quiz
Value Based Prioritization
Answer Key and Explanations

1. B - A Minimal Marketable Feature (MMF) is a software feature or product feature that is both minimal and marketable. 'Minimal' taking the meaning of simple and small or not complex. 'Marketable' taking the meaning of having some value, whether it is revenue generating or cost saving, that can be marketed or sold. [The Art of Agile Development. James Shore.] [Value based prioritization]

2. D - Customer-value prioritization is a method for relative prioritization of product features based on customer-value for ordering the product backlog. When ordering the product backlog, it is also important to consider other aspects (e.g., associated risk, dependencies, etc.,) of features. [The Art of Agile Development. James Shore.] [Value based prioritization]

3. B - Net Present Value: A metric used to analyze the profitability of an investment or project. NPV is the difference between the present value of cash inflows and the present value of cash outflows. NPV considers the likelihood of future cash inflows that an investment or project will yield. NPV is the sum of each cash inflow/outflow for the expected duration of the investment. Each cash inflow/outflow is discounted back to its present value (PV) (i.e.,, what the money is worth in terms of today's value). NPV is the sum of all terms: NPV = Sum of [Rt/(1 + i)^t] where t = the time of the cash flow, i = the discount rate (the rate of return that could be earned on in the financial markets) , and Rt = the net cash inflow or outflow. For example, consider the following two year period. The discount rate is 5% and the initial investment cost is $500. At the end of the first year, a $200 inflow is expected. At the end of the second year, a $1,000 is expected. NPV = -500 + 200/(1.05)^1 + 1000/(1.05)^2 = ~$597. If NPV is positive, it indicates that the investment will add value to the buyer's portfolio. If NPV is negative, it will subtract value. If NPV is zero, it will neither add or subtract value. [Agile Estimating and Planning. Mike Cohn.] [Value based prioritization]

4. C - One of the key responsibilities of the product owner is the return on investment. [Coaching Agile Teams. Lyssa Adkins.] [Value based prioritization]

5. D - Relative ranking/prioritization involves ordering a list of items (e.g., user stories, epics, tasks, defects, etc.,) based on a team-defined definition of priority. [The Art of Agile Development. James Shore.] [Value based prioritization]

6. B - Return on Investment (ROI): A metric used to evaluate the efficiency of an investment or to compare efficiency among a number of investments. To calculate ROI, the return of an investment (i.e., the gain minus the cost) is divided by the cost of the investment. The result is usually expressed as a percentage and sometimes a ratio. The product owner is often said to be responsible for the ROI. [Agile Estimating and Planning. Mike Cohn.] [Value based prioritization]

7. C - Return on Investment (ROI): A metric used to evaluate the efficiency of an investment or to compare efficiency among a number of investments. To calculate ROI,

the return of an investment (i.e., the gain minus the cost) is divided by the cost of the investment. The result is usually expressed as a percentage and sometimes a ratio. The product owner is often said to be responsible for the ROI. [Agile Estimating and Planning. Mike Cohn.] [Value based prioritization]

8. D - The internal rate of return (IRR) is a financial metric used to measure and compare the profitability of investments. The IRR is the "rate" that makes the net present value of all cash flows from a particular investment equal to zero. Unlike NPV which is a dollar amount (i.e., a magnitude) value, the IRR is a rate (i.e.,, a percentage). Often times, the IRR is compared against a threshold rate value to determine if the investment is a suitable risk worth implementing. For example, you might calculate an IRR to be 13% for an investment while a comparative market rate is 2%. The IRR being larger than the comparative market rate, would indicate the investment is worth pursuing. [Agile Estimating and Planning. Mike Cohn.] [Value based prioritization]

9. B - A Minimal Marketable Feature (MMF) is a software feature or product feature that is both minimal and marketable. 'Minimal' taking the meaning of simple and small or not complex. 'Marketable' taking the meaning of having some value, whether it is revenue generating or cost saving, that can be marketed or sold. [The Art of Agile Development. James Shore.] [Value based prioritization]

10. A - The internal rate of return (IRR) is a financial metric used to measure and compare the profitability of investments. The IRR is the "rate" that makes the net present value of all cash flows from a particular investment equal to zero. Unlike NPV which is a dollar amount (i.e., a magnitude) value, the IRR is a rate (i.e.,, a percentage). Often times, the IRR is compared against a threshold rate value to determine if the investment is a suitable risk worth implementing. For example, you might calculate an IRR to be 13% for an investment while a comparative market rate is 2%. The IRR being larger than the comparative market rate, would indicate the investment is worth pursuing. [Agile Estimating and Planning. Mike Cohn.] [Value based prioritization]

11. C - The internal rate of return (IRR) is a financial metric used to measure and compare the profitability of investments. The IRR is the "rate" that makes the net present value of all cash flows from a particular investment equal to zero. Unlike NPV which is a dollar amount (i.e., a magnitude) value, the IRR is a rate (i.e.,, a percentage). Often times, the IRR is compared against a threshold rate value to determine if the investment is a suitable risk worth implementing. For example, you might calculate an IRR to be 13% for an investment while a comparative market rate is 2%. The IRR being larger than the comparative market rate, would indicate the investment is worth pursuing. [Agile Estimating and Planning. Mike Cohn.] [Value based prioritization]

12. B - The pareto rule stipulates that 80% of value derives from 20% of the work. [Lean-Agile Software Development: Achieving Enterprise Agility. Alan Shalloway, Guy Beaver, James R. Trott.] [Value based prioritization]

13. D - Value, cost, and risk are key elements to consider when prioritizing user stories. [Agile Estimating and Planning. Mike Cohn.] [Value based prioritization]

14. D - The internal rate of return (IRR) is a financial metric used to measure and compare the profitability of investments. The IRR is the "rate" that makes the net present value of all cash flows from a particular investment equal to zero. Unlike NPV which is a dollar amount (i.e., a magnitude) value, the IRR is a rate (i.e.,, a percentage). Often times, the IRR is compared against a threshold rate value to determine if the investment is a suitable risk worth implementing. For example, you might calculate an IRR to be 13% for an investment while a comparative market rate is 2%. The IRR being larger than the comparative market rate, would indicate the investment is worth pursuing. [Agile Estimating and Planning. Mike Cohn.] [Value based prioritization]

15. D - Return on Investment (ROI): A metric used to evaluate the efficiency of an investment or to compare efficiency among a number of investments. To calculate ROI, the return of an investment (i.e., the gain minus the cost) is divided by the cost of the investment. The result is usually expressed as a percentage and sometimes a ratio. The product owner is often said to be responsible for the ROI. [Agile Estimating and Planning. Mike Cohn.] [Value based prioritization]

PMI-ACP Lite Mock Exam 12 Practice Questions

Test Name: PMI-ACP Lite Mock Exam 12
Total Questions: 40
Correct Answers Needed to Pass: 30 (75.00%)
Time Allowed: 60 Minutes

Test Description

This is a cumulative PMI-ACP Mock Exam which can be used as a benchmark for your PMI-ACP aptitude. This practice test includes questions from all exam topic areas, including sections from Agile Tools and Techniques, and all three Agile Knowledge and Skills areas.

Test Questions

1. What does a wireframe help an agile team accomplish?

A. It serves as a method to track team defects.

B. It serves as an archive for the user stories.

C. It serves as a prototype to facilitate customer feedback.

D. It serves as a decision gate for the customer to approve or disapprove moving to the next project phase.

2. Taking a cue from lean, what does agile do with respect to WIP?

A. It tries to reduce WIP.

B. It tries to completely eliminate WIP.

C. It tries to steadily increase WIP.

D. It tries to exponentially increase WIP.

3. Ralph is describing the INVEST acronym used for user story development in an agile practitioner seminar. What does the I in INVEST stand for?

A. Independent

B. Incremental

C. Iteration

D. Innovative

4. Which agile document holds a list of all product features to be developed in the project?

A. Product backlog

B. Task backlog

C. Sprint backlog

D. Iteration backlog

5. Gerald, as the product owner, likes being able to provide immediate feedback to the agile team regarding the latest iteration of a product. Although Gerald has other opportunities to provide feedback, this particular type occurs at frequent, set intervals. What type of delivery concept provides this type of customer feedback?

A. Incremental delivery

B. Iteration delivery

C. Demo delivery

D. Daily stand-up delivery

6. Which agile framework uses the planning game to prioritize features based on user stories and release requirements?

A. DSDM

B. Lean

C. Scrum

D. XP

7. Which of the following is a process analysis technique.

A. Value stream mapping

B. Kanban board

C. Iteration plan

D. Product roadmap

8. Ethan and his team are using a value stream map to identify waste and opportunities for improvement in a business process. Value stream mapping is an example of a

A. Process analysis technique

B. Iteration plan

C. Product roadmap

D. Kanban board

9. Ethan and his team just highlighted two processes that each have a lead time an order of magnitude more than any other processes in the system. When an agile team uses value stream mapping like Ethan's team it is an example of a

A. Product roadmap

B. Kanban board

C. Process analysis technique

D. Iteration plan

10. Which level of agile planning helps estimate when a product will be ready for release?

A. Sprint planning

B. Crystal planning

C. Iteration planning

D. Release planning

11. What topic area within strategic management helps with the facilitation of a collaborative environment where stakeholders are engaged?

A. Kanban management

B. Constraint management

C. Stakeholder management

D. Negotiation management

12. Select the type of delivery most associated with agile.

A. Iterative delivery

B. Sprint delivery

C. Just-in-time delivery

D. Incremental delivery

13. What must a scrum team and product owner define so that it may know when a user story has been completed?

A. Its definition of done.

B. Its definition of closing.

C. Its definition of completion.

D. Its definition of conclusion.

14. What must a scrum team define to help it identify when a user story has been completed?

A. Its definition of done in concert with the product owner

B. Its definition of finalization.

C. Its definition of acceptance.

D. Its definition of decision gates.

15. What is one reason to have a motivated team on an agile project?

A. Meet expectations

B. Decrease working hours

C. Maintain velocity

D. Exceed expectations

16. Select a common agile problem-solving technique.

A. Economy of scale

B. 3Y

C. Meta-analysis

D. Be kind, rewind

17. Opie, as the product owner, likes being able to review a new version of a working product at set, short intervals. What type of delivery concept provides this type of customer feedback?

A. Lead time delivery

B. Reflection delivery

C. Incremental delivery

D. JIT delivery

18. What agile artifact outlines the project's milestones?

A. Product roadmap

B. Product backlog

C. Business case

D. Kanban board

19. Help Jill select the correct agile delivery concept where a product is delivered and demonstrated at set intervals to the product owner to receive feedback?

A. Sprint delivery

B. Incremental delivery

C. Kanban delivery

D. Iterative delivery

20. What is another name for planning poker?

A. Iteration poker

B. Scrum poker

C. Kanban poker

D. Sprint poker

21. Not all agile efforts succeed the first time, what is a common cause of failure?

A. Lack of an onsite agile mentor or coach or promoter.

B. Lack of a proper portfolio analysis.

C. Lack of an onsite development strategy.

D. Lack of an onsite software protocol.

22. Not all agile efforts succeed the first time, what is a common cause of failure?

A. Lack of the adopting culture to support strict top-down decision making approaches.

B. Lack of the adopting culture to support a waterfall development method.

C. Lack of the adopting culture to support change.

D. Lack of the adopting culture to support strict requirements management definition.

23. Often during planning poker, the agile team begins with a reference point user story as a basis for subsequent estimates. What size of user story is typically used as a reference point?

A. Small

B. Extra large

C. Medium

D. Large

24. Match the most appropriate crystal family member to the notional project efforts. A) Crystal clear, B) Crystal red; 1) Small effort, 2) Large effort

A. Small effort: crystal clear; Large effort: crystal red

B. Either family member is appropriate.

C. Large effort: crystal clear; Small effort: crystal red

D. Small effort: crystal red; Large effort: crystal clear

25. Which of the following responses is NOT a community value per the PMI agile community of practice community charter?

A. Motivating

B. Adaptability

C. Transparency

D. Leading Change

26. Ursula is the financial executive for an upcoming project that is slated to use agile. In terms of estimating time, budget, and cost for an agile effort, what does Ursula typically have defined?

A. Budget and cost

B. Time and cost

C. Time and budget

D. Cost

27. Luna is concerned with the recent stagnant performance of her agile team. She believes it to be highly capable but in need of some outside, unbiased direction. What agile knowledge and skill technique might Luna consider?

A. Coaching and root cause analysis

B. Coaching and mentoring

C. Knowledge building and mentoring

D. Symptom and solution

28. Ursula and her team are scheduled to hold a reflective improvement workshop the next business day. Which agile project management methodology is the team most likely applying?

A. Feature Driven Development

B. Kanban Visual Management

C. Lean Software Development

D. Crystal

29. Select a common agile framework/methodology.

A. Lean software development

B. Toyota Production System (TPS)

C. Lean thinking

D. Lean manufacturing

30. As agile team leader, Nathan intends to schedule a brainstorming session to generate ideas that may help solve some of the team's current issues. Which of the following is a good brainstorming technique that Nathan should use?

A. Hosting the meeting in a neutral and comfortable environment.

B. Picking a reserved team member as facilitator.

C. Having a single-discipline/homogenous group so that the team can communicate more effectively.

D. Leaving participants in the dark until the day of the meeting to add an element of surprise.

31. Jake, as an agile leader, knows that adaptive leadership is an important leadership quality. What are the two dimensions Highsmith uses to define adaptive leadership?

A. Being agile and doing agile

B. Thinking agile and practicing agile

C. Coaching agile and practicing agile

D. Living agile and breathing agile

32. Hank is estimating how many days it will take him as an agile developer to build, test, and release a user story without any interruptions relative to other user stories in the backlog. What agile estimation method is Hank using?

A. Day stories

B. Ideal story days

C. Story points

D. Ideal days

33. Select a common agile problem-solving technique.

A. Devil's advocate

B. Double coincidence of want

C. Cause factoring

D. Localization

34. In agile, the "team space" is an important place that should foster effective communication. Of the following, which is a guideline for promoting such an environment?

A. The use of cubicle walls to give privacy

B. Non-opening windows

C. Dedicated wall space for information radiators

D. Loud background noise

35. A risk-to-value chart may be used to help prioritize user stories in the product backlog. Select the type of user-story that is typically given top priority in the backlog?

A. Low-value, low-risk

B. High-value, low-risk

C. High-value, high-risk

D. Low-value, high-risk

36. Which agile framework emphasizes that the team should speak a common language?

A. Crystal

B. Scrum

C. Agile unified process (AUP)

D. XP

37. Select the response that is NOT an advantage of using an information radiator.

A. Makes it easy for all team members to track progress

B. Makes communication less time consuming

C. Increases the efficiency of software developers

D. Improves team communication

38. After weeks of sharing the same office space and having desks that are collocated, it's almost as if Bob, an agile developer, can understand Rick, an agile colleague, without having to speak with him directly. What type of communication are Rick and Bob benefiting from?

A. Chaordic communication

B. Active listening

C. Osmotic communication

D. Entropic communication

39. Value stream mapping, where an agile team and customer chart processes and activities of a value stream to identify waste and makes collaborative decisions on which waste areas to focus on for improvement, is an example of:

A. A risk-based decision model

B. A participatory decision model

C. A preemptive decision model

D. An assessment decision model

40. In agile and other project management styles, team motivation is a critical factor for success. What is one method to improve team motivation?

A. Making sure the development team strictly adheres to the project plan.

B. Providing an environment where team members make all the decisions.

C. Providing a non-collaborative environment.

D. Providing coaching.

PMI-ACP Lite Mock Exam 12 Answer Key and Explanations

1. C - In the agile design process, prototypes help the customer understand current design state. Three common types of prototypes are HTML, paper (i.e., sketches), and wireframes. A wireframe is a sketch of a user interface, identifying its content, layout, functionality, is usually black and white, and excludes detailed pictures or graphics. A wireframe can be created on paper, whiteboards, or using software. [Agile Estimating and Planning. Mike Cohn.] [Agile analysis and design]

2. A - Like lean, agile efforts try to reduce WIP to a manageable and sustainable level. [Lean-Agile Software Development: Achieving Enterprise Agility. Alan Shalloway, Guy Beaver, James R. Trott.] [Planning, monitoring, and adapting]

3. A - The acronym INVEST (independent, negotiable, valuable, estimable, small, and testable) helps the agile practitioner remember the characteristics of a good user story. I – Independent stories can be developed in any order and avoid dependencies which can make development more complex. N – Negotiable user stories mean that both the customer and developer should feel free to analyze and adapt a user story to meet customer needs. V – A valuable user story describes how the product feature will provide value to the customer. E – Estimable user stories are ones that developers can readily estimate the effort or duration required for developing them. S- Small user stories are ones that take about two to five days of work to implement. T - Testable user stories are ones that can be verified according to acceptance criteria to ensure value. [Agile Retrospectives: Making Good Teams Great. Esther Derby, Diana Larsen, Ken Schwaber.] [Planning, monitoring, and adapting]

4. A - The product backlog is a comprehensive list of all product features to be developed in an iteration. It is an evolving document and changes to adapt to customer requirements. As the project progresses, project features in the backlog become better defined as the customer understands product need more completely. [Lean-Agile Software Development: Achieving Enterprise Agility. Alan Shalloway, Guy Beaver, James R. Trott.] [Agile analysis and design]

5. A - A cornerstone of Agile development is 'incremental delivery.' Incremental delivery is the frequent delivery of working products, which are successively improved, to a customer for immediate feedback and acceptance. Typically, a product is delivered at the end of each sprint or iteration for demonstration and feedback. In this feedback technique, a customer can review the product and provide updated requirements. Changed/updated/refined requirements are welcomed in the agile process to ensure the customer receives a valuable and quality product. A sprint or iteration typically lasts from two to four weeks and at the end a new and improved product is delivered, incrementally. [The Art of Agile Development. James Shore.] [Knowledge and Skills: Level 1]

6. D - Extreme programming (XP) uses the planning game to prioritize features based on user stories and release requirements. [The Art of Agile Development. James Shore.] [Knowledge and Skills: Level 3]

7. A - Value stream mapping is a collaborative process analysis technique where a diverse team depicts/maps a process to identify where waste occurs and where improvements can be made. It is an example of a process analysis technique. Like value stream mapping, process mapping is also used to map a process to identify bottlenecks (places where processing slows and inventory can build). [Lean-Agile Software Development: Achieving Enterprise Agility. Alan Shalloway, Guy Beaver, James R. Trott.] [Knowledge and Skills: Level 2]

8. A - Value stream mapping is a collaborative process analysis technique where a diverse team depicts/maps a process to identify where waste occurs and where improvements can be made. It is an example of a process analysis technique. Like value stream mapping, process mapping is also used to map a process to identify bottlenecks (places where processing slows and inventory can build). [Lean-Agile Software Development: Achieving Enterprise Agility. Alan Shalloway, Guy Beaver, James R. Trott.] [Knowledge and Skills: Level 2]

9. C - Value stream mapping is a collaborative process analysis technique where a diverse team depicts/maps a process to identify where waste occurs and where improvements can be made. It is an example of a process analysis technique. Like value stream mapping, process mapping is also used to map a process to identify bottlenecks (places where processing slows and inventory can build). [Lean-Agile Software Development: Achieving Enterprise Agility. Alan Shalloway, Guy Beaver, James R. Trott.] [Knowledge and Skills: Level 2]

10. D - Release planning helps the customer and agile team determine what should be developed during each project timeframe or phase, and when a product will ideally be ready for release. [The Art of Agile Development. James Shore.] [Planning, monitoring, and adapting]

11. C - Stakeholder management is a growing topic area within strategic management that brings awareness to the importance of managing stakeholders (i.e., facilitating active participation of stakeholders and fostering a strong collaborative environment) for a project's success. Stakeholder management is typically defined in the context of guiding principles and values. R. E. Freeman's 'Managing for Stakeholders' includes 10 principles: 1) Stakeholder interests need to go together over time. 2) We need a philosophy of volunteerism – to engage stakeholders and manage relationships ourselves rather than leave it to government. 3) We need to find solutions to issues that satisfy multiple stakeholders simultaneously. 4) Everything that we do serves stakeholders. We never trade off the interests of one versus the other continuously over time. 5) We act with purpose that fulfills our commitment to stakeholders. We act with aspiration towards fulfilling our dreams and theirs. 6) We need intensive communication and dialogue with stakeholders – not just those who are friendly. 7)Stakeholders consist of real people with names and faces and children. They are complex. 8)We need to generalize the marketing approach. 9) We engage with both primary and secondary stakeholders. 10) We constantly monitor and redesign processes to make them better

serve our stakeholders. Because stakeholder involvement is critical for the success of a project, where projects without active participation from stakeholders are prone to failure, stakeholder management should be a topic that every agile team knows well. [The Art of Agile Development. James Shore.] [Knowledge and Skills: Level 1]

12. D - A cornerstone of Agile development is 'incremental delivery.' Incremental delivery is the frequent delivery of working products, which are successively improved, to a customer for immediate feedback and acceptance. Typically, a product is delivered at the end of each sprint or iteration for demonstration and feedback. In this feedback technique, a customer can review the product and provide updated requirements. Changed/updated/refined requirements are welcomed in the agile process to ensure the customer receives a valuable and quality product. A sprint or iteration typically lasts from two to four weeks and at the end a new and improved product is delivered, incrementally. [The Art of Agile Development. James Shore.] [Knowledge and Skills: Level 1]

13. A - Because a cornerstone of the scrum framework in agile is to 'always have a product that you could theoretically ship,' it is important for the team and product owner to have a definition of 'done' or what criteria is necessary to consider user features or functionality in a state of finality. [Coaching Agile Teams. Lyssa Adkins.] [Product quality]

14. A - Because a cornerstone of the scrum framework in agile is to 'always have a product that you could theoretically ship,' it is important for the team and product owner to have a definition of 'done' or what criteria is necessary to consider user features or functionality in a state of finality. [Coaching Agile Teams. Lyssa Adkins.] [Product quality]

15. D - Having a motivated team is essential for any project, regardless of whether it is agile or not. Motivated teams work together better, have strong productivity, and exceed expectations. Some simple steps to increase motivation are 1) spending quality time together; where team members get to know one another on a personal level to build a sense of community, 2) providing feedback, mentoring and coaching; where team members are congratulated and thanked on jobs well done and also mentored or coached to improve in skill and capability, and 3) empowerment; where the team is empowered to make many key decisions which, along the way, builds trust and shows that leadership believes in the capabilities of the team. [The Art of Agile Development. James Shore.] [Knowledge and Skills: Level 1]

16. D - Literally thousands of decisions are made in the course of a project. Many of these decisions are made in response to problems that inevitably arise and confront the agile team. Therefore it is essential that an agile team is properly versed in problem-solving strategies, tools, and techniques. Some common problem-solving techniques include: ask it loud; revisit the problem; 5Y; sunk cost fallacy; devil's advocate; be kind, rewind; asking probing questions; and reflective/active listening. [Agile Retrospectives: Making Good Teams Great. Esther Derby, Diana Larsen, Ken Schwaber.] [Knowledge and Skills: Level 1]

17. C - A cornerstone of Agile development is 'incremental delivery.' Incremental delivery is the frequent delivery of working products, which are successively improved, to a customer for immediate feedback and acceptance. Typically, a product is delivered at the end of each sprint or iteration for demonstration and feedback. In this feedback technique, a customer can review the product and provide updated requirements. Changed/updated/refined requirements are welcomed in the agile process to ensure the customer receives a valuable and quality product. A sprint or iteration typically lasts from two to four weeks and at the end a new and improved product is delivered, incrementally. [The Art of Agile Development. James Shore.] [Knowledge and Skills: Level 1]

18. C - Business case development is an important initial step in agile project management. The business case is a concise document that outlines the project's vision, goals, strategies for achieving goals, milestones, required investment and expected return/payback. A business case articulates the why and how a project will deliver value to a customer. [Lean-Agile Software Development: Achieving Enterprise Agility. Alan Shalloway, Guy Beaver, James R. Trott.] [Knowledge and Skills: Level 2]

19. B - A cornerstone of Agile development is 'incremental delivery.' Incremental delivery is the frequent delivery of working products, which are successively improved, to a customer for immediate feedback and acceptance. Typically, a product is delivered at the end of each sprint or iteration for demonstration and feedback. In this feedback technique, a customer can review the product and provide updated requirements. Changed/updated/refined requirements are welcomed in the agile process to ensure the customer receives a valuable and quality product. A sprint or iteration typically lasts from two to four weeks and at the end a new and improved product is delivered, incrementally. [The Art of Agile Development. James Shore.] [Knowledge and Skills: Level 1]

20. B - Planning poker is based upon the wideband Delphi estimation technique. It is a consensus-based technique for estimating effort. Sometimes called scrum poker, it is a technique for a relative estimation of effort, typically in story points, to develop a user story. At a planning poker meeting, each estimator is given an identical deck of planning poker cards with a wide range of values. The Fibonacci sequence is often used for values for planning poker (i.e., 0, 1, 1, 2, 3, 5,8,etc.). A planning poker meeting works as follows: 1) a moderator, not estimating, facilitates the meeting. 2) the product owner/manager provides a short overview of the user story and answers clarifying questions posed by the developers. Typically the product owner does not vote. 3) Each estimator selects an estimate of work effort by selecting a card, 4) Once everyone has selected a card, everyone overturns their card concurrently, 5) Estimators with high and low estimates are given a chance to defend positions. 6) The process repeats until there is consensus. The developer who owns the user story is typically given higher credence. [Agile Estimating and Planning. Mike Cohn.] [Agile estimation]

21. A - The top 12 causes of agile failure (failure modes) according to Aaron Sanders: 1. A checkbook commitment doesn't automatically cause organizational change or support. 2. Culture doesn't support change. 3. Culture does not have retrospectives or performs them poorly. 4. Standards and quality are lost in a race to project closing. 5.Lack of collaboration in planning. 6.None or too many Product Owners. 7. Poor project leadership or scrum master that doesn't place trust in the team and allow it to be self-organizing and self-disciplined. 8.No on-site agile promoter or coach. 9.Lack of a well built, high-performance team. 10. Accrued technical debt if strict testing standards are not upheld. 11.Culture maintains traditional performance appraisals where individuals are honored and the team aspect is lost. 12. A reversion to the traditional or 'old-way' of doing business occurs because change is hard. [Coaching Agile Teams. Lyssa Adkins.] [Knowledge and Skills: Level 3]

22. C - The top 12 causes of agile failure (failure modes) according to Aaron Sanders: 1. A checkbook commitment doesn't automatically cause organizational change or support. 2. Culture doesn't support change. 3. Culture does not have retrospectives or performs them poorly. 4. Standards and quality are lost in a race to project closing. 5.Lack of collaboration in planning. 6.None or too many Product Owners. 7. Poor project leadership or scrum master that doesn't place trust in the team and allow it to be self-organizing and self-disciplined. 8.No on-site agile promoter or coach. 9.Lack of a well built, high-performance team. 10. Accrued technical debt if strict testing standards are not upheld. 11.Culture maintains traditional performance appraisals where individuals are honored and the team aspect is lost. 12. A reversion to the traditional or 'old-way' of doing business occurs because change is hard. [Coaching Agile Teams. Lyssa Adkins.] [Knowledge and Skills: Level 3]

23. C - The reference point user story for planning poker is typically a medium or average size user story. Estimators can use the reference point to make relative estimations. [Agile Estimating and Planning. Mike Cohn.] [Agile estimation]

24. A - Crystal is a family of methodologies for a flexible and lightweight approach to software development. The family of methodologies is color coded to differentiate its members (e.g., clear, yellow, orange, red.) The color chosen depends on the level of effort required. On one end of the spectrum is crystal clear, which is for smaller efforts, while crystal red is for larger efforts. Regardless of color, the crystal framework is cyclical and has three fundamental processes: chartering, delivery cycles, and wrap-up. Crystal chartering includes building the team, doing an Exploratory 360, defining standards of practice for the team, and building the project plan. In the delivery cycle, the crystal team iteratively develops, integrates, tests, and releases the product in iterations that last from one week to two months. Like other agile frameworks, crystal includes collaborative events, like stand-up meetings and reflective improvement workshops. In wrap-up the team concludes the project and holds a completion ritual where the team reflects on the entire project. [Agile Software Development: The Cooperative Game – 2nd Edition. Alistair Cockburn.] [Knowledge and Skills: Level 2]

25. A - The following are community values of the PMI agile community of practice community charter: Vision, Servant Leadership, Trust, Collaboration, Honesty, Learning, Courage, Openness, Adaptability, Leading Change, Transparency [PMI Agile Community of Practice Community

Charter. Project Management Institute.] [Knowledge and Skills: Level 1]

26. C - Time, budget, and cost estimation is an important knowledge and skill area of agile. According to Highsmith, the nature of the agile method, whereby it welcomes changing scope, means that it lends itself well to fixed budgets and a fixed schedule because changing scope makes it difficult to estimate a total cost. Generally speaking, the budget and schedule constraints are known but before a project will commence there needs to be an agreed upon set of base product functionality defined in an initiation phase; fixing scope reduces an agile team's innovative tendency to provide improved value. For companies that are familiar with fixed-price contracts, where requirements are agreed upon before contract closing, adopting agile can be a weary initial venture. Instead, other contract vehicle types are recommended for agile efforts. These include: a general service contract for the initiation phase and separate fixed-price contracts for iterations or user stories; time-and-material contracts; not-to-exceed with fixed-fee contracts; and, incentive contracts (e.g., fixed price with incentive; cost-reimbursable with award fee). [Agile Project Management: Creating Innovative Products – 2nd Edition. Jim Highsmith.] [Knowledge and Skills: Level 1]

27. B - Coaching and mentoring within teams can be helpful for nascent agile teams and even for more experienced agile teams. Coaching and mentoring is the act of helping a person or team improve performance and achieve realistic goals. Because agile has a value of continuous improvement, coaching and mentoring is not solely for new or immature teams, but experienced ones too where coaching can help achieve higher levels of performance. The amount of coaching and mentoring an agile team needs is variable. Some newer teams will need a coach guiding the team nearly all the time while others may need a coach only for particularly challenging situations. A not uncommon scenario is to have a coach help the team collectively during sprint/iteration planning and then during the iteration help mentor individual team members. [Coaching Agile Teams. Lyssa Adkins.] [Knowledge and Skills: Level 1]

28. D - Reflective improvement workshops are a cornerstone of the Crystal methodology. While all agile methodologies incorporate reflection into their standard practices, Crystal terms the practice 'reflective improvement workshops.' [Agile Software Development: The Cooperative Game – 2nd Edition. Alistair Cockburn.] [Planning, monitoring, and adapting]

29. A - Common frameworks or methodologies used within agile include: scrum, extreme programming (XP), lean software development, crystal, feature driven development (FDD), dynamic systems development method (DSDM), agile unified process (AUP). [Agile Software Development: The Cooperative Game – 2nd Edition. Alistair Cockburn.] [Knowledge and Skills: Level 2]

30. A - A successful brainstorming event should strive to consider the following points - Host the meeting in a neutral and comfortable environment - Have an engaging and experienced facilitator lead the event - Send participants an overview, with goals, schedule, and what ground rules, beforehand - Have a multi-disciplinary/diverse team to get a broader perspective - Delay any criticism that may stifle idea generation. [Agile Retrospectives: Making Good Teams Great. Esther Derby, Diana Larsen, Ken Schwaber.] [Knowledge and Skills: Level 1]

31. A - Highsmith defines adaptive leadership as two dimensional: Being agile and doing agile. Being agile includes focusing on cornerstones of agile project management, like incremental delivery, continuous integration, and adapting to changing requirements. Doing agile includes several activities that an agile leader must do: do less; speed-to-value, quality, and engage and inspire. [Agile Project Management: Creating Innovative Products – 2nd Edition. Jim Highsmith.] [Soft skills negotiation]

32. D - Instead of using story points, agile teams may estimate the relative sizes of user stories using ideal days. Ideal days represents the amount of days - uninterrupted by meetings, personal life, non-working days, or any other delays, obstacles or distractions - that it would take a single person to build, test, and release the user story, relative to other user stories in the backlog. [Agile Estimating and Planning. Mike Cohn.] [Agile estimation]

33. A - Literally thousands of decisions are made in the course of a project. Many of these decisions are made in response to problems that inevitably arise and confront the agile team. Therefore it is essential that an agile team is properly versed in problem-solving strategies, tools, and techniques. Some common problem-solving techniques include: ask it loud; revisit the problem; 5Y; sunk cost fallacy; devil's advocate; be kind, rewind; asking probing questions; and reflective/active listening. [Agile Retrospectives: Making Good Teams Great. Esther Derby, Diana Larsen, Ken Schwaber.] [Knowledge and Skills: Level 1]

34. C - A warm, welcoming environment that promotes effective communication, innovation, and motivated team members is an important aspect to consider when designing team space. Guidelines for a better agile team space include: collocation of team members; reduction of non-essential noise/distractions; dedicated whiteboard and wall space for information radiators; space for the daily stand-up meeting and other meetings; pairing workstations; and other pleasantries like plants and comfortable furniture. [Agile Retrospectives: Making Good Teams Great. Esther Derby, Diana Larsen, Ken Schwaber.] [Communications]

35. B - A risk-adjusted backlog is a product backlog organized by taking into account risk. Risk can be estimated as the product of severity/consequence and likelihood. User stories can also be positioned on a risk-to-value matrix to help prioritize them in the backlog. The risk-to-value matrix is a chart with four quadrants. Along the horizontal axis is value in ascending order. Along the vertical axis is risk in ascending order. A user story that is high risk and high value is located in the top-right corner. A user story that is low risk and high value is located in the lower-right corner. A user story that is low risk and high value is located in the lower-right corner. A user story that is low risk and low value is located in the lower-left corner. Typically a team will prioritize high-value, low-risk user stories first, followed by high-value, high-risk user stories, followed by low-value, low-risk user stories, followed by low-value, high-risk user stories. [The Art of Agile

Development. James Shore.] [Risk management]

36. B - Scrum emphasizes, in part, the following principles: always have a product you can theoretically ship, speak a common language, and continuously test the product as you build it. [Agile Project Management with Scrum. Ken Schwaber.] [Knowledge and Skills: Level 3]

37. C - Information radiators do not increase the efficiency of software developers. The use of information radiators on an agile project offer several advantages. They reduce lengthy communication, allow for all team members and stakeholders to review project status throughout a project, and reduce the need of other more time-consuming communication methods, like e-mails or memorandums. [Agile Software Development: The Cooperative Game – 2nd Edition. Alistair Cockburn.] [Communications]

38. C - Osmotic communication is a concept of communication where information is shared between collocated team members unconsciously. By sharing the same work environment, team members are exposed to the same environmental sounds and other environmental input and unconsciously share a common framework that improves communication. [Agile Software Development: The Cooperative Game – 2nd Edition. Alistair Cockburn.] [Communications]

39. B - To build trust among the team, agile believes heavily in participatory decision models where team members collaborate to make decisions. Although a team leader or scrum master will need to make some decisions individually, many decisions can be made by the team collectively. These agile principles are also known as collective ownership, self-organization, and self-discipline. In collective ownership, the team members are equally responsible for project results and are empowered to participate in decision making and problem solving processes. [Agile Retrospectives: Making Good Teams Great. Esther Derby, Diana Larsen, Ken Schwaber.] [Knowledge and Skills: Level 2]

40. D - Having a motivated team is essential for any project, regardless of whether it is agile or not. Motivated teams work together better, have strong productivity, and exceed expectations. Some simple steps to increase motivation are 1) spending quality time together; where team members get to know one another on a personal level to build a sense of community, 2) providing feedback, mentoring and coaching; where team members are congratulated and thanked on jobs well done and also mentored or coached to improve in skill and capability, and 3) empowerment; where the team is empowered to make many key decisions which, along the way, builds trust and shows that leadership believes in the capabilities of the team. [The Art of Agile Development. James Shore.] [Knowledge and Skills: Level 1]

Knowledge Area Quiz
Risk Management
Practice Questions

Test Name: Knowledge Area Test: Risk Management
Total Questions: 15
Correct Answers Needed to Pass: 11 (73.33%)
Time Allowed: 25 Minutes

Test Description

This practice quiz specifically targets your knowledge of the Risk Management exam topic area.

Test Questions

1. What type of activity does a team have on the ready should a risk happen to strike?

A. Contingency

B. Reserve

C. Spike

D. B plan

2. How might a manager use a burndown chart and team velocity to manage risks with respect to a sustainable pace of development?

A. A burndown chart is not used to manage risks on an agile project. Instead it is used to chart the progress of a team with respect to completing assigned work.

B. A manager may use a risk burndown chart by taking the team's risk burndown velocity and forecasting when all risks will be completely mitigated.

C. A manager may use a risk burndown chart by taking the team's risk burndown velocity and forecasting when all risks will be completely eliminated.

D. A manager may use a burndown chart to determine whether a team is under or over committing to an iteration base on the team's velocity prediction.

3. When is a risk audit typically performed on an agile project?

A. During the retrospective.

B. After a release.

C. After an iteration during an iteration review meeting.

D. After release planning.

4. James and his agile team are reviewing a chart that shows the risk severity over time of their current project. What information radiator is James looking at?

A. Severity graph

B. Severity burndown graph

C. Risk burndown graph

D. Impact graph

5. Besides prioritizing a backlog in terms of relative value, how else is it commonly prioritized?

A. By relative market share

B. By relative complexity

C. By relative risk

D. By relative temporal complexity

6. Rupert is reviewing a chart that shows different expectations of story point completion for an entire project based on risk. What is Rupert reviewing?

A. A risk-based burnup chart.

B. A burndown chart.

C. A risk-adjusted burndown chart.

D. A burnup chart.

7. Two software developers, Ron and Peter, are having a disagreement about the best way to approach a technical problem. What is an appropriate agile methodology for exploring potential solutions?

A. Using project burndown charts where Ron and Peter can review who has completed the most story points.

B. Using risk based task estimates to determine whose approach introduces the least amount of risk.

C. Using spike solutions where Ron and Peter each explore their respective solution to evaluate efficacy.

D. Using collective ownership coding where Ron and Peter code on solution together integrating both ideas.

8. Risks are common to all projects big and small. What can be said of risk mitigation?

A. Risk mitigation involves making risks transparent so that it is evident to all stakeholders when a project will become intractable.

B. Risk mitigation involves reducing the impact of risks whether or not they occur.

C. Risk mitigation involves eliminating risks completely.

D. Risk mitigation involves containing and transferring risk to low value features.

9. What is the frequency of risk management on an agile project?

A. At the end of a release

B. During release planning

C. At the end of an iteration

D. Continuously

10. Choose the best definition of a risk-based spike task.

A. An exploratory task conducted immediately before another task that holds uncertainty to reduce risk.

B. An exploratory task conducted immediately before a questionable user story to determine its feasibility.

C. A potentially risky task conducted with extreme caution to determine market feasibility.

D. An exploratory task conducted immediately before an epic to decompose it into more manageable development sizes.

11. What type of risk is generally managed in the agile methodology?

A. Qualitative and quantitative

B. Mitigative

C. Quantitative

D. Qualitative

12. How is risk monitored and controlled in agile projects?

A. Through team building exercises.

B. Through information radiators, daily stand-up meetings, iteration reviews, and iteration retrospectives

C. Through comprehensive documentation.

D. Risk is not monitored and controlled on agile projects.

13. Select the response that lists one of the five core risk areas that can impact a project.

A. Iteration slip

B. Failure to adapt

C. Scope creep

D. Backlog creep

14. Which of the following is the best definition of a risk burndown graph?

A. A chart that tracks risk impact over time.

B. A chart that tracks risk management over time.

C. A chart that tracks risk severity over time.

D. A chart that tracks risk severity over time.

15. Mark is reviewing the upcoming user stories for the next iteration. He notices that there will be a few tasks with high uncertainty Why might Mark want to use risk-based spike tasks in this scenario?

A. To convey to the product owner the extreme complexity of the user story.

B. To understand the impacts of the high risk tasks.

C. To understand the nature of the development team when performing under risk.

D. To convey to the scrum master the extreme complexity of the user story.

Knowledge Area Quiz
Risk Management
Answer Key and Explanations

1. A - A contingency activity is an activity ready for implementation to reduce risk impact should a risk occur. [The Art of Agile Development. James Shore.] [Risk management]

2. D - A project manager may use a burndown chart and a team's velocity to make sure the team is not under or over committing to an iteration. A sustainable pace of development is an important facet of agile project planning and risk management. [The Art of Agile Development. James Shore.] [Risk management]

3. C - A risk audit is typically performed in the iteration review after each iteration. [The Art of Agile Development. James Shore.] [Risk management]

4. C - A risk burndown chart is a risk management technique used to track project risk over time. It allows stakeholders to quickly review project risk management performance (e.g., increasing, decreasing, and by how much) over time. Severity (a product of impact and probability) is charted along the vertical axis with time on the horizontal axis. Impact typically takes a value from 0 to 5 in increasing order of risk and probability/likelihood typically takes a value from 0 to 5 in increasing order of probability. In this example, the worst severity a risk could have is 25 (5 x 5 = 25) and the least harmful severity a risk could have is 0. The agile team and customer/product owner identifies its risks and assigns severity values in a risk register and tracks those values over time. Ideally, risk severity will decrease over time. [The Art of Agile Development. James Shore.] [Risk management]

5. C - A risk-adjusted backlog is a product backlog organized by taking into account risk. Risk can be estimated as the product of severity/consequence and likelihood. User stories can also be positioned on a risk-to-value matrix to help prioritize them in the backlog. The risk-to-value matrix is a chart with four quadrants. Along the horizontal axis is value in ascending order. Along the vertical axis is risk in ascending order. A user story that is high risk and high value is located in the top-right corner. A user story that is low risk and high value is located in the lower-right corner. A user story that is low risk and high value is located in the lower-right corner. A user story that is low risk and low value is located in the lower-left corner. Typically a team will prioritize high-value, low-risk user stories first, followed by high-value, high-risk user stories, followed by low-value, low-risk user stories, followed by low-value, high-risk user stories. [The Art of Agile Development. James Shore.] [Risk management]

6. A - A risk-based burnup chart tracks targeted and actual product delivery progress and also includes estimates of how likely the team is to achieve targeted value adjusted for risk. Typically, risk is shown as three different levels: best-case; most likely; and worst-case. For example, if you have a 10 iteration project and the team's current velocity is 10 story points, you can portray the chance of completing 100 story points (most likely case), the chance of completing 80 story points (worst-case), and the chance

of completing 120 story points (best-case). In this way, the stakeholders get a feel for the range of risk. [The Art of Agile Development. James Shore.] [Risk management]

7. C - A spike solution is a simple software program used to explore and evaluate potential solutions. Ron and Peter can both develop spike solutions to help form their debate. [The Art of Agile Development. James Shore.] [Risk management]

8. B - Generally, risk mitigation is thought of as the reduction of the impact whether or not the risk occurs. [The Art of Agile Development. James Shore.] [Risk management]

9. D - Risk is continuously monitored on an agile project through information radiators, daily stand-up meetings, iteration reviews, and iteration retrospectives. [The Art of Agile Development. James Shore.] [Risk management]

10. A - Risked-based spike is a risk management technique and is often thought of as a task. A risked-based spike is a task used to gain knowledge in an area of uncertainty to reduce risk. For example, a development team may need to understand how migrating from Windows 7 to Windows 8 may impact the look and feel of the interface. Risked-based spikes typically are included in iteration planning directly before a the task that holds the uncertainty. [The Art of Agile Development. James Shore.] [Risk management]

11. D - The agile methodology generally deals with qualitative risks. NOT quantitative. [The Art of Agile Development. James Shore.] [Risk management]

12. B - The BEST answer is through information radiators, daily stand-up meetings, iteration reviews, and iteration retrospectives. In other words, risk is monitored and controlled throughout an agile project and in many different ways. [The Art of Agile Development. James Shore.] [Risk management]

13. C - The five core risk areas include: productivity variation (difference between planned and actual performance); scope creep (considerable additional requirements beyond initial agreement); specification breakdown (lack of stakeholder consensus on requirements); intrinsic schedule flaw (poor estimates of task durations), personnel loss (the loss of human resources). [The Software Project Manager's Bridge to Agility. Michele Sliger, Stacia Broderick.] [Risk management]

14. D - A risk burndown chart is a risk management technique used to track project risk over time. It allows stakeholders to quickly review project risk management performance (e.g., increasing, decreasing, and by how much) over time. Severity (a product of impact and probability) is charted along the vertical axis with time on the horizontal axis. Impact typically takes a value from 0 to 5 in increasing order of risk and probability/likelihood typically takes a value from 0 to 5 in increasing order of probability. In this example, the worst severity a risk could have is 25 (5 x 5 = 25) and the least harmful severity a risk could have is 0. The agile team and customer/product owner identifies its risks and assigns severity values in a risk register and tracks those values over time. Ideally, risk severity will decrease over time. [The Art of Agile Development. James Shore.] [Risk management]

15. B - Risked-based spike is a risk management technique and is often thought of as a task. A risked-based spike is a task used to gain knowledge in an area of uncertainty to reduce risk. For example, a development team may need to understand how migrating from Windows 7 to Windows 8 may impact the look and feel of the interface. Risked-based spikes typically are included in iteration planning directly before a the task that holds the uncertainty. [The Art of Agile Development. James Shore.] [Risk management]

PMI-ACP Lite Mock Exam 13 Practice Questions

Test Name: PMI-ACP Lite Mock Exam 13
Total Questions: 40
Correct Answers Needed to Pass:
30 (75.00%)
Time Allowed: 60 Minutes

Test Description

This is a cumulative PMI-ACP Mock Exam which can be used as a benchmark for your PMI-ACP aptitude. This practice test includes questions from all exam topic areas, including sections from Agile Tools and Techniques, and all three Agile Knowledge and Skills areas.

Test Questions

1. In agile and other project management styles, team motivation is a critical factor for success. What is one method to improve team motivation?

   A. Making sure the development team strictly adheres to the project plan.

   B. Empowering the team to make many important decisions.

   C. Providing an authoritative leadership where all decisions are made for the team.

   D. Providing an environment where team members make all the decisions.

2. Calculate the IRR for the following one year investment. The initial investment cost is $300. The expected income in year 1 is $390.

   A. 25%

   B. 30%

   C. 20%

   D. 40%

3. Calculate the return on investment of the following: Gain: $10,000; Cost: $15,000.

   A. -50%

   B. -33%

   C. 33%

   D. 20%

4. In agile and other project management styles, team motivation is a critical factor for success. What is one method to improve team motivation?

   A. Providing an environment where team members make all the decisions.

   B. Empowering the team.

   C. Making sure the development team strictly adheres to the project plan.

   D. Providing strong leadership and making all decisions so the team can focus on productivity.

5. Which of the following is the best definition of communications management?

A. Managing communication between all stakeholders and team members to promote effective conveyance of necessary information.

B. Managing communication between a few key stakeholders to promote effective conveyance of necessary information.

C. Managing communication between the team to reduce team conflict and inefficiencies.

D. Managing communication between the team and stakeholders to prevent development delays.

6. Mike, as the product owner, likes being able to provide immediate feedback to the agile team regarding the latest version of a product. Although Mike has other opportunities to provide feedback, like in the daily stand-up meeting and during iteration planning, this particular type occurs after the delivery of a new product which occurs at frequent, set intervals. What type of delivery concept provides this type of customer feedback?

A. Iteration delivery

B. Defect reduction delivery

C. Prototype delivery

D. Incremental delivery

7. In XP, the best role for the customer is which of the following?

A. Developing task timebox estimates.

B. Managing pair programming assignments.

C. Managing team conflict.

D. Writing well-defined user stories.

8. Which of the following is the best definition of 'stakeholder management?'

A. Facilitating active participation of stakeholders.

B. Assigning tasks and other activities to stakeholders.

C. Managing the number of requirement changes requested by stakeholders.

D. Managing the problems that stakeholders present throughout the project.

9. Peter, as project leader, has spoken with his agile team about 'stakeholder management.' What is 'stakeholder management?'

A. Assigning responsibilities to stakeholders.

B. The fostering of a collaborative environment where stakeholders actively participate.

C. Managing the number of scope changes requested by stakeholders.

D. Managing the myriad problems that stakeholders present throughout the project.

10. If a project team member identifies a new risk, what is a good next step?

A. Ignoring it to bring it up at the next sprint review.

B. Marking it on the risk register.

C. Immediately creating a contingency plan and adding it to the contingency plan document.

D. Immediately calling it to the team's attention to discuss its impact.

11. Adrienne is concerned about her agile team's communication with key stakeholders. What is the agile knowledge and skill area that concerns itself with effective communication?

A. Inventory management

B. Dynamic management

C. Communications management

D. Materials flow management

12. What is the objective value of NPV when finding the IRR?

A. Minimum marketable feature (MMF)

B. Zero

C. Minimum threshold value

D. Maximum threshold value

13. What does the M stand for in the user prioritization technique called MoSCoW?

A. Make sure to have

B. Must have

C. May have

D. Might have

14. What is one reason to have a motivated team on an agile project?

A. Meet expectations

B. Maintain velocity

C. Improve productivity

D. Decrease productivity

15. From the following, select a technique that promotes agile 'knowledge sharing.'

A. Scrum planning

B. Sprint planning

C. Scrimmage planning

D. Melee planning

16. Hank and his agile team are defining what it means when a feature is to be considered finished and theoretically ready for delivery. What is Hank and his agile team working on?

A. Its definition of releasability.

B. Its definition of shipability.

C. Its definition of done in concert with the product owner

D. Its definition of delivery readiness.

17. Meghan, as team leader, wants to design a comfortable, collaborative team space for her agile project. What can she do as a basic guideline?

A. Have plants, natural lighting, and comfortable seating available

B. Have yearly, individual performance reviews

C. Seat by team member function

D. Minimize team member interaction

18. Bob is an agile practitioner and works on a team that employs the Crystal methodology. His team has just started building the project charter. How long should Bob expect project chartering to last?

A. From four to eight hours.

B. A few months.

C. A few hours.

D. From a few days to a few weeks.

19. The agile development model consists of which of the following characteristics?

A. An inflexible requirements definition process

B. Development consists of multiple iterations

C. Minimized customer feedback

D. Five distinct phases

20. In agile, the "team space" is an important place that should foster effective communication. What is a guideline for promoting such an environment?

A. Dedicated whiteboard

B. Large swaths of blank wall space devoid of project information

C. Minimized team member interaction

D. Seating by team member function

21. An agile team has included a more experienced agile practitioner to help it reach an improved level of performance. What knowledge and skill area is this practitioner providing to the team?

A. Coaching and mentoring

B. Consolidating and mentoring

C. Speculating and closing

D. Coaching and meeting

22. Drew and his pair programming partner Steve are working on a new piece of software. As they build the software feature, what should Steve and Drew be sure to perform to ensure quality?

A. Mirroring.

B. Rapid reflection.

C. Unit testing.

D. Conversion testing.

23. Jan is looking at an important agile document that includes the project vision and success criteria. What document is Jan most likely reviewing?

A. Mission statement

B. Project charter

C. Team virtual page

D. Statement of work

24. Anna is concerned with the recent stagnant performance of her agile team. She believes it to be highly capable but the team seems to be in a bit of a malaise. What agile knowledge and skill technique might Anna consider?

A. Coaching and mentoring

B. Symptom and solution

C. Capturing and mentoring

D. Coaching and mobilizing

25. Vikki, as project leader, empowers her team to make some decisions. This helps to build trust and invigorates the team to improve productivity. What is Vikki doing when she empowers the team?

A. Mobilizing the team

B. Motivating the team

C. Refactoring the team

D. Working the team

26. Select a technique used for value-based analysis?

A. Cano

B. MoCWoS

C. SMART

D. Cost-to-value matrix

27. Which scrum meeting is often timeboxed to four hours?

A. Daily scrum

B. Release plan meeting

C. Affinity planning meeting

D. Sprint review meeting

28. Ginny is concerned with the recent stagnant performance of her agile team. She believes it to be highly capable but without any direction. What agile knowledge and skill technique might Ginny consider?

A. Knowledge building and mentoring

B. Symptom and solution

C. Coaching and mentoring

D. Coaching and servicing

29. Which of the following is an agile principle per the Agile Manifesto?

A. Motivating the customer

B. Motivating the external stakeholders

C. Motivating the internal stakeholders

D. Motivating the individuals involved in development.

30. How much time should be devoted to each user story in planning poker?

A. 10 minutes

B. 8 minutes.

C. Whatever it takes to come to consensus

D. Two to three minutes

31. Ralph is describing the INVEST acronym used for user story development in an agile practitioner seminar. What does the N in INVEST stand for?

A. New

B. Navigable

C. Negotiable

D. Narrow

32. Peter is a software developer on an agile project. He is pair programming with Paul. On one particular day, Paul's body language unconsciously communicated to Peter that Paul was having an especially difficult time with developing a user story. What type of communication did Peter use to understand Paul's difficulty?

A. Virtual communication

B. Near Field Communication

C. Osmotic communication

D. XP pair programming communication

33. What does the Japanese term 'Kanban' translate to in English?

A. Fool proofing a system

B. Continuous improvement

C. Billboard or signboard

D. Stop on a defect

34. Although a shared workspace is best to promote osmotic communication, separated team members may also enjoy some osmotic communication through the use of aiding technology. Pick among the listed technologies the one that helps to provide some level of osmotic communication.

A. E-mail

B. Near Field Communication

C. Bluetooth

D. Instant messaging

35. Becky, as project leader, intends on building a high-performance team. What is a practice or technique she can use to build a high performance team?

A. Removing any obstacles

B. Assigning more work than can be accomplished in an iteration to set a sense of urgency

C. Using overtime to incentivize the team to delivery early

D. Never pausing to reflect on performance until the end of the project

36. Jim has just finished building, testing, and integrating a feature in an iteration that has a WIP limit of four for features. How many other features could be in the middle of development on Jim's team?

A. No more than five.

B. No more than four.

C. No more than three.

D. No more than two.

37. Frankie has just finished building, testing, and integrating a feature in an iteration that has a WIP limit of ten for features. How many other features could be in the middle of development on Frankie's team?

A. No more than 11.

B. No more than nine.

C. No more than 10.

D. No more than five.

38. Don's agile team just finished building, testing, and releasing 1 user story point in its most recent 3 week iteration. What is the team's velocity?

A. 1

B. 1/3

C. 5

D. 3

39. Harry and the agile team he belongs to are having a discussion regarding 'stakeholder management.' What is 'stakeholder management?'

A. The management of stakeholder interactions to promote a safe and collaborative environment where stakeholders are actively engaged in the project.

B. The management of stakeholder tasks, duties, and responsibilities.

C. The management and organization of stakeholder feature requirements.

D. The management of stakeholder interactions to promote an environment where developers can develop without interaction with stakeholders.

40. Barry, as the product owner, prefers defining acceptance criteria during iteration planning rather than during release planning to take advantage of progressive elaboration. Is there anything wrong with this agile style?

A. Yes, acceptance criteria should be defined well in advance of iteration planning.

B. Yes, acceptance criteria should always be defined during release planning.

C. No, acceptance criteria for a user story may be defined as late as during iteration planning just so long as it is defined before coding begins.

D. No, acceptance criteria for a user story may be defined as late as just prior to the sprint demo just so long as it is ready for qualifying as 'done.'

PMI-ACP Lite Mock Exam 13 Answer Key and Explanations

1. B - Having a motivated team is essential for any project, regardless of whether it is agile or not. Motivated teams work together better, have strong productivity, and exceed expectations. Some simple steps to increase motivation are 1) spending quality time together; where team members get to know one another on a personal level to build a sense of community, 2) providing feedback, mentoring and coaching; where team members are congratulated and thanked on jobs well done and also mentored or coached to improve in skill and capability, and 3) empowerment; where the team is empowered to make many key decisions which, along the way, builds trust and shows that leadership believes in the capabilities of the team. [The Art of Agile Development. James Shore.] [Knowledge and Skills: Level 1]

2. B - The internal rate of return (IRR) is a financial metric used to measure and compare the profitability of investments. The IRR is the "rate" that makes the net present value of all cash flows from a particular investment equal to zero. Unlike NPV which is a dollar amount (i.e., a magnitude) value, the IRR is a rate (i.e.,, a percentage). Often times, the IRR is compared against a threshold rate value to determine if the investment is a suitable risk worth implementing. For example, you might calculate an IRR to be 13% for an investment while a comparative market rate is 2%. The IRR being larger than the comparative market rate, would indicate the investment is worth pursuing. [Agile Estimating and Planning. Mike Cohn.] [Value based prioritization]

3. B - Return on Investment (ROI): A metric used to evaluate the efficiency of an investment or to compare efficiency among a number of investments. To calculate ROI, the return of an investment (i.e., the gain minus the cost) is divided by the cost of the investment. The result is usually expressed as a percentage and sometimes a ratio. The product owner is often said to be responsible for the ROI. [Agile Estimating and Planning. Mike Cohn.] [Value based prioritization]

4. B - Having a motivated team is essential for any project, regardless of whether it is agile or not. Motivated teams work together better, have strong productivity, and exceed expectations. Some simple steps to increase motivation are 1) spending quality time together; where team members get to know one another on a personal level to build a sense of community, 2) providing feedback, mentoring and coaching; where team members are congratulated and thanked on jobs well done and also mentored or coached to improve in skill and capability, and 3) empowerment; where the team is empowered to make many key decisions which, along the way, builds trust and shows that leadership believes in the capabilities of the team. [The Art of Agile Development. James Shore.] [Knowledge and Skills: Level 1]

5. A - Effective communication is a cornerstone of agile. Communication is the act of transferring information among various parties. Communications management is a knowledge and skill area of agile that highlights this importance. PMI has several definitions regarding communications management and agile builds on top of these to add its own

perspective: 1) Communications Planning: Determining the information and communication needs of the projects stakeholders 2) Information Distribution: Making needed information available to project stakeholders in a timely manner, 3) Performance Reporting: Collecting and distributing performance information. This includes status reporting, progress measurement, and forecasting, and 4) Managing Stakeholders: Managing communications to satisfy the requirements and resolve issues with project stakeholders. From an agile perspective: communication among the team is built into the process and facilitated through collocation, information radiators, daily stand-up meetings, retrospectives etc.; Although it is hoped that the product owner, customer, and user can be heavily involved with the project and also use these communication techniques, a plan for conveying information to stakeholders may be needed if this is not the case. [Agile Software Development: The Cooperative Game – 2nd Edition. Alistair Cockburn.] [Knowledge and Skills: Level 1]

6. D - A cornerstone of Agile development is 'incremental delivery.' Incremental delivery is the frequent delivery of working products, which are successively improved, to a customer for immediate feedback and acceptance. Typically, a product is delivered at the end of each sprint or iteration for demonstration and feedback. In this feedback technique, a customer can review the product and provide updated requirements. Changed/updated/refined requirements are welcomed in the agile process to ensure the customer receives a valuable and quality product. A sprint or iteration typically lasts from two to four weeks and at the end a new and improved product is delivered, incrementally. [The Art of Agile Development. James Shore.] [Knowledge and Skills: Level 1]

7. D - The best role for a customer in XP of the available choices is to write well-defined user stories. [User Stories Applied: For Agile Software Development. Mike Cohn.] [Agile analysis and design]

8. A - Stakeholder management is a growing topic area within strategic management that brings awareness to the importance of managing stakeholders (i.e., facilitating active participation of stakeholders and fostering a strong collaborative environment) for a project's success. Stakeholder management is typically defined in the context of guiding principles and values. R. E. Freeman's 'Managing for Stakeholders' includes 10 principles: 1) Stakeholder interests need to go together over time. 2) We need a philosophy of volunteerism – to engage stakeholders and manage relationships ourselves rather than leave it to government. 3) We need to find solutions to issues that satisfy multiple stakeholders simultaneously. 4) Everything that we do serves stakeholders. We never trade off the interests of one versus the other continuously over time. 5) We act with purpose that fulfills our commitment to stakeholders. We act with aspiration towards fulfilling our dreams and theirs. 6) We need intensive communication and dialogue with stakeholders – not just those who are friendly. 7)Stakeholders consist of real people with names and faces and children. They are complex. 8)We need to generalize the marketing approach. 9) We engage with both primary and secondary stakeholders. 10) We constantly monitor and redesign processes to make them better serve our stakeholders. Because stakeholder involvement is critical for the success of a project, where projects without active participation from stakeholders are prone to failure, stakeholder management should be a topic that every agile team knows well. [The Art of Agile Development. James Shore.] [Knowledge and Skills: Level 1]

9. B - Stakeholder management is a growing topic area within strategic management that brings awareness to the importance of managing stakeholders (i.e., facilitating active participation of stakeholders and fostering a strong collaborative environment) for a project's success. Stakeholder management is typically defined in the context of guiding principles and values. R. E. Freeman's 'Managing for Stakeholders' includes 10 principles: 1) Stakeholder interests need to go together over time. 2) We need a philosophy of volunteerism – to engage stakeholders and manage relationships ourselves rather than leave it to government. 3) We need to find solutions to issues that satisfy multiple stakeholders simultaneously. 4) Everything that we do serves stakeholders. We never trade off the interests of one versus the other continuously over time. 5) We act with purpose that fulfills our commitment to stakeholders. We act with aspiration towards fulfilling our dreams and theirs. 6) We need intensive communication and dialogue with stakeholders – not just those who are friendly. 7)Stakeholders consist of real people with names and faces and children. They are complex. 8)We need to generalize the marketing approach. 9) We engage with both primary and secondary stakeholders. 10) We constantly monitor and redesign processes to make them better serve our stakeholders. Because stakeholder involvement is critical for the success of a project, where projects without active participation from stakeholders are prone to failure, stakeholder management should be a topic that every agile team knows well. [The Art of Agile Development. James Shore.] [Knowledge and Skills: Level 1]

10. D - The BEST answer is to bring the newly identified risk to the team's attention and to discuss its impact. [The Art of Agile Development. James Shore.] [Risk management]

11. C - Effective communication is a cornerstone of agile. Communication is the act of transferring information among various parties. Communications management is a knowledge and skill area of agile that highlights this importance. PMI has several definitions regarding communications management and agile builds on top of these to add its own perspective: 1) Communications Planning: Determining the information and communication needs of the projects stakeholders 2) Information Distribution: Making needed information available to project stakeholders in a timely manner, 3) Performance Reporting: Collecting and distributing performance information. This includes status reporting, progress measurement, and forecasting, and 4) Managing Stakeholders: Managing communications to satisfy the requirements and resolve issues with project stakeholders. From an agile perspective: communication among the team is built into the process and facilitated through collocation, information radiators, daily stand-up meetings, retrospectives etc.; Although it is hoped that the product owner, customer, and user can be heavily involved with the project and also use these communication techniques, a plan for conveying information to stakeholders may be needed if this is not the case. [Agile Software Development: The Cooperative Game – 2nd Edition. Alistair Cockburn.] [Knowledge and Skills: Level 1]

12. B - The internal rate of return (IRR) is a financial metric used to measure and compare the profitability of investments. The IRR is the "rate" that makes the net present value of all cash flows from a particular investment equal to zero. Unlike NPV which is a dollar amount (i.e., a magnitude) value, the IRR is a rate (i.e.,, a percentage). Often times, the IRR is compared against a threshold rate value to determine if the investment is a suitable risk worth implementing. For example, you might calculate an IRR to be 13% for an investment while a comparative market rate is 2%. The IRR being larger than the comparative market rate, would indicate the investment is worth pursuing. [Agile Estimating and Planning. Mike Cohn.] [Value based prioritization]

13. B - The MoSCoW technique is commonly used in agile to prioritize user stories and create a story map. The MoSCoW technique prioritizes user stories into the following groups in descending order of priority: M - Must have; S - Should have; C - Could have; W - Would have. Must have items are those product features which are absolutely essential to develop. Should have items are product features that are not essential but have significant business value. Could have items are product features that would add some business value. Would have items are product features that have marginal business value. [User Stories Applied: For Agile Software Development. Mike Cohn.] [Agile analysis and design]

14. C - Having a motivated team is essential for any project, regardless of whether it is agile or not. Motivated teams work together better, have strong productivity, and exceed expectations. Some simple steps to increase motivation are 1) spending quality time together; where team members get to know one another on a personal level to build a sense of community, 2) providing feedback, mentoring and coaching; where team members are congratulated and thanked on jobs well done and also mentored or coached to improve in skill and capability, and 3) empowerment; where the team is empowered to make many key decisions which, along the way, builds trust and shows that leadership believes in the capabilities of the team. [The Art of Agile Development. James Shore.] [Knowledge and Skills: Level 1]

15. B - In agile, effective 'knowledge sharing' is a critical factor for success. It involves the near real time communication of key information among all team members and stakeholders. To promote knowledge sharing, agile uses standard practices built into its process, such as using generalized specialists/cross functional teams, self-organizing and self-disciplined teams, collocation, daily stand-up meetings, iteration/sprint planning, release planning, pair programming and pair rotation, project retrospectives/reflection, and on-site customer support. And, of course, the sixth principle of Agile is " The most efficient and effective method of conveying information to and within a development team is face-to-face conversation." In this sense, Agile prefers and encourages collocation for all stakeholders and team members for the simple fact that face-to-face conversation is the best method of communication and, in turn, effective knowledge sharing. [Becoming Agile: ...in an imperfect world. Greg Smith, Ahmed Sidky.] [Knowledge and Skills: Level 1]

16. C - Because a cornerstone of the scrum framework in agile is to 'always have a product that you could theoretically ship,' it is important for the team and product owner to have a definition of 'done' or what criteria is necessary to consider user features or functionality in a state of finality. [Coaching Agile Teams. Lyssa Adkins.] [Product quality]

17. A - A warm, welcoming environment that promotes effective communication, innovation, and motivated team members is an important aspect to consider when designing team space. Guidelines for a better agile team space include: collocation of team members; reduction of non-essential noise/distractions; dedicated whiteboard and wall space for information radiators; space for the daily stand-up meeting and other meetings; pairing workstations; and other pleasantries like plants and comfortable furniture. [Agile Retrospectives: Making Good Teams Great. Esther Derby, Diana Larsen, Ken Schwaber.] [Communications]

18. D - The Crystal development process is cyclical/iterative. Its primary components are chartering, delivery cycles, and project wrap-up. Chartering involves creating a project charter, which can last from a few days to a few weeks. Chartering consists of four activities: 1) Building the core project team, 2) performing an Exploratory 360° assessment, 3) fine tuning the methodology, and 3) building the initial project plan. [Agile Software Development: The Cooperative Game – 2nd Edition. Alistair Cockburn.] [Agile analysis and design]

19. B - The agile development process has multiple iterations that focus on specific product features, encourages heavy customer feedback, and is adaptive to changing customer requirements. [Agile Project Management: Creating Innovative Products – 2nd Edition. Jim Highsmith.] [Knowledge and Skills: Level 1]

20. A - A warm, welcoming environment that promotes effective communication, innovation, and motivated team members is an important aspect to consider when designing team space. Guidelines for a better agile team space include: collocation of team members; reduction of non-essential noise/distractions; dedicated whiteboard and wall space for information radiators; space for the daily stand-up meeting and other meetings; pairing workstations; and other pleasantries like plants and comfortable furniture. [Agile Retrospectives: Making Good Teams Great. Esther Derby, Diana Larsen, Ken Schwaber.] [Communications]

21. A - Coaching and mentoring within teams can be helpful for nascent agile teams and even for more experienced agile teams. Coaching and mentoring is the act of helping a person or team improve performance and achieve realistic goals. Because agile has a value of continuous improvement, coaching and mentoring is not solely for new or immature teams, but experienced ones too where coaching can help achieve higher levels of performance. The amount of coaching and mentoring an agile team needs is variable. Some newer teams will need a coach guiding the team nearly all the time while others may need a coach only for particularly challenging situations. A not uncommon scenario is to have a coach help the team collectively during sprint/iteration planning and then during the iteration help mentor individual team members. [Coaching Agile Teams. Lyssa Adkins.] [Knowledge and Skills: Level 1]

22. C - The extreme programming (XP) principle of continuous integration is that code is integrated into the full code base as soon as it is built, tested, and completed. Once integrated, the code base and therefore the entire system is built and tested. Continuous integration is just one principle of XP that promotes rapid delivery of software and the early detection of integration defects. [The Art of Agile Development. James Shore.] [Product quality]

23. B - The project charter is an important governing document that requires all stakeholder participation. Although experts recommend it not be longer than a page in length, creating a project charter can be challenging, as all stakeholders must participate and come to a consensus. Three key elements should be included in a project charter: vision, mission, and success criteria. Vision is the 'why' or rationale of a project. Mission is the 'what' of the project and describes what the team will accomplish to reach the vision. Success criteria are management metrics that define 'how' the project will be deemed successful. [Lean-Agile Software Development: Achieving Enterprise Agility. Alan Shalloway, Guy Beaver, James R. Trott.] [Knowledge and Skills: Level 2]

24. A - Coaching and mentoring within teams can be helpful for nascent agile teams and even for more experienced agile teams. Coaching and mentoring is the act of helping a person or team improve performance and achieve realistic goals. Because agile has a value of continuous improvement, coaching and mentoring is not solely for new or immature teams, but experienced ones too where coaching can help achieve higher levels of performance. The amount of coaching and mentoring an agile team needs is variable. Some newer teams will need a coach guiding the team nearly all the time while others may need a coach only for particularly challenging situations. A not uncommon scenario is to have a coach help the team collectively during sprint/iteration planning and then during the iteration help mentor individual team members. [Coaching Agile Teams. Lyssa Adkins.] [Knowledge and Skills: Level 1]

25. B - Having a motivated team is essential for any project, regardless of whether it is agile or not. Motivated teams work together better, have strong productivity, and exceed expectations. Some simple steps to increase motivation are 1) spending quality time together; where team members get to know one another on a personal level to build a sense of community, 2) providing feedback, mentoring and coaching; where team members are congratulated and thanked on jobs well done and also mentored or coached to improve in skill and capability, and 3) empowerment; where the team is empowered to make many key decisions which, along the way, builds trust and shows that leadership believes in the capabilities of the team. [The Art of Agile Development. James Shore.] [Knowledge and Skills: Level 1]

26. D - Value-based analysis strives to understand how value, as defined by the customer, relates to various components of the product, like features and tasks. Features are often prioritized with prioritization based on value and risk. Prioritization can be performed using the MoSCoW or Kano method and through the use of risk-to-value and cost-to-value matrices. [Lean-Agile Software Development: Achieving Enterprise Agility. Alan Shalloway, Guy Beaver, James R. Trott.] [Knowledge and Skills: Level 2]

27. D - In the agile framework scrum, sprint planning and sprint review meetings are often timeboxed at four hours. [The Art of Agile Development. James Shore.] [Planning, monitoring, and adapting]

28. C - Coaching and mentoring within teams can be helpful for nascent agile teams and even for more experienced agile teams. Coaching and mentoring is the act of helping a person or team improve performance and achieve realistic goals. Because agile has a value of continuous improvement, coaching and mentoring is not solely for new or immature teams, but experienced ones too where coaching can help achieve higher levels of performance. The amount of coaching and mentoring an agile team needs is variable. Some newer teams will need a coach guiding the team nearly all the time while others may need a coach only for particularly challenging situations. A not uncommon scenario is to have a coach help the team collectively during sprint/iteration planning and then during the iteration help mentor individual team members. [Coaching Agile Teams. Lyssa Adkins.] [Knowledge and Skills: Level 1]

29. D - The Agile Manifesto defines 12 supporting principles. Agile principles include 1) Our highest priority is to satisfy the customer through early and continuous delivery of valuable software. 2) Welcome changing requirements, even late in development. Agile processes harness change for the customer's competitive advantage. 3) Deliver working software frequently, from a couple of weeks to a couple of months, with preference to the shorter timescale. 4) Business people and developers must work together daily throughout the project. 5) Build projects around motivated individuals. Give them the environment and support they need, and trust them to get the job done. 6) The most efficient and effective method of conveying information to and within a development team is face-to-face conversation. 7) Working software is the primary measure of progress. 8) Agile processes promote sustainable development. The sponsors, developers, and users should be able to maintain a constant pace indefinitely. 9) Continuous attention to technical excellence and good design enhances agility. 10) Simplicity--the art of maximizing the amount of work not done--is essential. 11) The best architectures, requirements, and designs emerge from self-organizing teams. 12) At regular intervals, the team reflects on how to become more effective, then tunes and adjusts its behavior accordingly. [Manifesto for Agile Software Development. Agile Alliance.] [Knowledge and Skills: Level 1]

30. D - Two to three minutes is a typical time-boxed value for discussing user stories when playing planning poker. [Agile Estimating and Planning. Mike Cohn.] [Agile estimation]

31. C - The acronym INVEST (independent, negotiable, valuable, estimable, small, and testable) helps the agile practitioner remember the characteristics of a good user story. I – Independent stories can be developed in any order and avoid dependencies which can make development more complex. N – Negotiable user stories mean that both the customer and developer should feel free to analyze and adapt a user story to meet customer needs. V – A valuable user story describes how the product feature will provide value to the customer. E – Estimable user stories are ones that developers can readily estimate the effort or duration required for developing them. S- Small user stories are ones that take about two to five days of work to implement. T - Testable user stories are ones that can be verified according to acceptance criteria to ensure value. [Agile Retrospectives: Making Good Teams Great. Esther Derby, Diana Larsen, Ken Schwaber.] [Planning, monitoring, and adapting]

32. C - Peter used the principle of osmotic communication to understand Paul's dilemma. Osmotic communication includes picking up visual cues, like body language. [Agile Software Development: The Cooperative Game – 2nd Edition. Alistair Cockburn.] [Communications]

33. C - Kanban, Japanese for billboard or signboard, is a scheduling system for just-in-time (JIT) production developed by Toyota in the 1940s and 1950s. It is a way of controlling and reducing inventory by using cards or signs to order (demand signal) requisite parts for a manufacturing process from other dependent systems (supply). Kanban has been adopted by agile to help control workflow. [Lean-Agile Software Development: Achieving Enterprise Agility. Alan Shalloway, Guy Beaver, James R. Trott.] [Planning, monitoring, and adapting]

34. D - Video conferencing and instant messaging are technologies that can provide some level of osmotic communication. [Agile Software Development: The Cooperative Game – 2nd Edition. Alistair Cockburn.] [Communications]

35. A - Building a high-performance team is critical to any project's success. A high performance team has the right team members, is empowered, has built trust, works at a sustainable pace, has consistently high velocity/productivity, takes regular time for reflection to review work, has a team lead that removes any obstacles and provides mentoring and coaching, is self-organized and self-disciplined, and is collocated. Several management techniques can be used to build or foster a high-performance team environment, some techniques include: removing obstacles that slow down a team's performance, having high expectations of team performance, and coaching and mentoring the team to achieve its best performance. [Coaching Agile Teams. Lyssa Adkins.] [Knowledge and Skills: Level 2]

36. C - A lean manufacturing philosophy is to eliminate waste. One defined waste type in the lean philosophy is inventory, which is also referred to as work in process (WIP). WIP is material or parts that have started production but are not yet a finished or "done" product. Inventory is considered wasteful because it costs money to purchase, store, and maintain. One way of reducing inventory is to reduce the WIP at individual machines or servers by only moving as fast as your slowest machine or processor (the system bottleneck). Agile also strives to control its WIP through WIP limits by completing all features to a "done" state before beginning development of new features. One can think of an iteration or sprint as a process that can develop a certain amount of features. In this analogy, the WIP limit is equivalent to the sprint backlog. By maintaining a WIP limit equal to the sprint backlog, no features should be incomplete at the sprint review. [Lean-Agile Software Development: Achieving Enterprise Agility. Alan Shalloway, Guy Beaver, James R. Trott.] [Planning, monitoring, and adapting]

37. B - A lean manufacturing philosophy is to eliminate waste. One defined waste type in the lean philosophy is inventory, which is also referred to as work in process (WIP). WIP is material or parts that have started production but are not yet a finished or "done" product. Inventory is considered wasteful because it costs money to purchase, store, and maintain. One way of reducing inventory is to reduce the WIP at individual machines or servers by only moving as fast as your slowest machine or processor (the system bottleneck). Agile also strives to control its WIP through WIP limits by completing all features to a "done" state before beginning development of new features. One can think of an iteration or sprint as a process that can develop a certain amount of features. In this analogy, the WIP limit is equivalent to the sprint backlog. By maintaining a WIP limit equal to the sprint backlog, no features should be incomplete at the sprint review. [Lean-Agile Software Development: Achieving Enterprise Agility. Alan Shalloway, Guy Beaver, James R. Trott.] [Planning, monitoring, and adapting]

38. A - Velocity is a measure of the number of user story points or stories completed by a team per iteration. An agile team can use its previous velocity recordings as a method of estimating how many user story points it may complete in the next iteration. [Agile Estimating and Planning. Mike Cohn.] [Agile estimation]

39. A - Stakeholder management is a growing topic area within strategic management that brings awareness to the importance of managing stakeholders (i.e., facilitating active participation of stakeholders and fostering a strong collaborative environment) for a project's success. Stakeholder management is typically defined in the context of guiding principles and values. R. E. Freeman's 'Managing for Stakeholders' includes 10 principles: 1) Stakeholder interests need to go together over time. 2) We need a philosophy of volunteerism – to engage stakeholders and manage relationships ourselves rather than leave it to government. 3) We need to find solutions to issues that satisfy multiple stakeholders simultaneously. 4) Everything that we do serves stakeholders. We never trade off the interests of one versus the other continuously over time. 5) We act with purpose that fulfills our commitment to stakeholders. We act with aspiration towards fulfilling our dreams and theirs. 6) We need intensive communication and dialogue with stakeholders – not just those who are friendly. 7)Stakeholders consist of real people with names and faces and children. They are complex. 8)We need to generalize the marketing approach. 9) We engage with both primary and secondary stakeholders. 10) We constantly monitor and redesign processes to make them better serve our stakeholders. Because stakeholder involvement is critical for the success of a project, where projects without active participation from stakeholders are prone to failure, stakeholder management should be a topic that every agile team knows well. [The Art of Agile Development. James Shore.] [Knowledge and Skills: Level 1]

40. C - Acceptance criteria is typically defined in tandem with user story definition during release planning; however, acceptance criteria can also be defined during iteration planning once a story has been picked for the iteration. The one steadfast rule is that acceptance criteria must be defined before development begins. Like agile planning, the definition of acceptance criteria is constantly evolving as the conversation with the product owner matures. [The Art of Agile Development. James Shore.] [Planning, monitoring, and adapting]

Knowledge Area Quiz
Metrics
Practice Questions

Test Name: Knowledge Area Test: Metrics
Total Questions: 15
Correct Answers Needed to Pass:
11 (73.33%)
Time Allowed: 25 Minutes

Test Description

This practice quiz specifically targets your knowledge of the Metrics exam topic area.

Test Questions

1. What is an escaped defect?

- **A.** A defect that is almost impossible to duplicate.
- **B.** A defect that cannot be replicated.
- **C.** A defect that escapes from a previous defect-free build to the most recent build iteration.
- **D.** A defect that is not found by the development or testing team and later found by an end-user.

2. When is value and progress typically measured in an agile effort?

- **A.** After a release planning event
- **B.** After an affinity planning event
- **C.** After the envisioning phase
- **D.** After an iteration.

3. EVM is a frequently used project management abbreviation. What does EVM stand for?

- **A.** Extra value management
- **B.** Earned velocity management
- **C.** Earned value management
- **D.** Earned value maintenance

4. Calculate the SPI of the following project EVM snapshot. BAC is $100,000. AC is $10,000. PV is $5,000. EV is $7,000.

- **A.** 0.50
- **B.** 1.40
- **C.** 71%
- **D.** 0.71

5. If a bar on a product burndown bar chart extends below the horizontal axis, what does it indicate?

- **A.** That the team has overrun on cost.
- **B.** That work has been added to the project.
- **C.** That the schedule is slipping.
- **D.** That work has been removed from the project.

6. If, during a sprint review, the product owner does NOT accept a user story or feature, what should the team do?

A. Mark the story as done because it would not be reviewed if it didn't pass the acceptance criteria written on the back of the card.

B. Mark the user story as incomplete and collaborate with the product owner whether to include the user story in a subsequent iteration.

C. Postpone the sprint review until the user story is accepted.

D. Remove the user story from the product backlog.

7. If the bottom of the bar on a product burndown bar chart is above the horizontal axis, what does it indicate?

A. That the schedule is slipping.

B. That there is a cost variance.

C. That work has been added to the project.

D. That work has been removed from the project and indicating a reduction in scope since initial planning.

8. Why aren't source line of code reports (SLOC) suitable as a reporting metric for project stakeholders?

A. SLOC reports are not a complete source for reporting productivity. Instead, testing line of code reports (TLOC) should be reported.

B. SLOC reports SHOULD be used as a reporting metric to stakeholders.

C. SLOC reports are unsuitable because they can give a false positive indication of the project being near completion.

D. SLOC reports are an imperfect source to be used for productivity reports.

9. During the last iteration, Paul and his agile team completed 2 user stories worth 6 points each, 3 user stories worth 1 point each, and nearly completed one user story point worth 10 points. What was the team's velocity for the previous iteration?

A. 20

B. 19

C. 15

D. 25

10. During the last iteration, Steve and his agile team completed 3 user stories worth 4 points each, 2 user stories worth 3 points each, and nearly completed one user story point worth 20 points. What was the team's velocity for the previous iteration?

A. 18

B. 8

C. 38

D. 28

11. Why might the top of a bar on a product burndown bar chart lower from one iteration to the next?

A. The top of a bar on a product burndown bar chart may lower from one iteration to the next because the team completed work in the previous iteration or the team re-estimated user story effort.

B. The top of a bar on a product burndown bar chart may lower from one iteration to the next because the product owner added work for the project.

C. The top of a bar on a product burndown bar chart may lower from one iteration to the next because the product owner removed work for the project.

D. The top of a bar on a product burndown bar chart may lower from one iteration to the next because the team may have removed work from the project.

12. An executive is reviewing a chart comparing four of his agile teams' velocity for the previous iteration. Is it safe to make assumptions about the most productive team?

A. No, velocity alone is not an apples-to-apples metric with which to compare and contrast team productivity.

B. No, velocity must be included in the context of ideal time to be able to make accurate conclusions about comparing team productivity.

C. Yes, so long as the organization has standardized its baseline user story complexity.

D. Yes, so long as the agile teams were all using story points or all using ideal time.

13. David's agile team just finished building, testing, and releasing 8 user story points in its most recent 3 week iteration. What is the team's velocity?

A. 24

B. 3

C. 8

D. 2.67

14. Calculate the CPI of the following project EVM snapshot. BAC is $100,000. AC is $10,000. PV is $5,000. EV is $7,000.

A. 0.70

B. 0.50

C. 1.43

D. 70%

15. What purpose can EVM serve on an agile project?

A. A technique used to evaluate project performance with respect to quality and value.

B. A technique used to evaluate project performance with respect to velocity and cost.

C. A technique used to evaluate project performance with respect to cost and schedule.

D. A technique used to evaluate project performance with respect to schedule and value.

Knowledge Area Quiz
Metrics
Answer Key and Explanations

1. D - An escaped defect is a software defect that is not found by the development or testing team and later found by an end-user. [Agile Software Development: The Cooperative Game – 2nd Edition. Alistair Cockburn.] [Metrics]

2. D - Because value is delivered incrementally and iteratively through iterations, value and progress is typically measured at the end of each iteration. [The Art of Agile Development. James Shore.] [Metrics]

3. C - EVM or earned value management is a management technique used to evaluate project performance with respect to cost and schedule. [Agile Estimating and Planning. Mike Cohn.] [Metrics]

4. B - EVM or earned value management is a management technique used to evaluate project performance with respect to cost and schedule. EVM relies on other common financial metrics like Budget At Completion (BAC), Actual Cost (AC), Planned Value (PV), Earned Value (EV), Cost Variance (CV), Schedule Variance (SV), Cost Performance Index (CPI), and Schedule Performance Index (SPI). PV is the planned value of work at a given time in a project; you can calculate it by multiplying the BAC by the ratio of current week/scheduled weeks (e.g., 5 weeks into a 15 week $15,000 project = $5,000 PV). EV is value of work actually completed or earned (e.g., you have completed 50% of the project by week 5 of a 15 week $15,000 project = $7,500 EV). SPI = EV / PV. If SPI > 1, the project is ahead of schedule and if SPI < 1, the project is behind schedule. AC is the actual cost the project has incurred to date. [Agile Estimating and Planning. Mike Cohn.] [Metrics]

5. B - If a bar extends below the horizontal axis on a project burndown bar chart, work has been added to the project indicating an increase in scope. [Agile Estimating and Planning. Mike Cohn.] [Metrics]

6. B - If a user story is not accepted by the product owner during a sprint review, the team should not mark the story as complete and collaborate with the product owner to determine if and when the user story should be completed. [Agile Estimating and Planning. Mike Cohn.] [Metrics]

7. D - If the bottom of the bar on a product burndown bar chart is above the horizontal axis, it indicates that work has been removed from the project (scope reduction) since initial planning. [Agile Estimating and Planning. Mike Cohn.] [Metrics]

8. D - SLOC reports are an imperfect source to be used for productivity reports. [The Art of Agile Development. James Shore.] [Metrics]

9. C - The team's velocity is 15. 2 x 6 + 3 x 1 = 15. Story points for partially completed stories are not included in the velocity metric. [Agile Estimating and Planning. Mike Cohn.] [Metrics]

10. A - The team's velocity is 18. 3 x 4 + 2 x 3 = 18. Story points for partially completed stories are not included in the velocity metric. [Agile Estimating and Planning. Mike Cohn.] [Metrics]

11. A - The top of a bar on a product burndown bar chart may lower from one iteration to the next because the team completed work in the previous iteration or the team re-estimated user story development effort. When the team completes planned work during the iteration the top of the bar chart is lowered. Additionally, the top of the bar chart may be lowered if the team re-estimates user stories and finds they are not as challenging as previously believed and therefore represent a smaller story point value. [Agile Estimating and Planning. Mike Cohn.] [Metrics]

12. A - Velocity alone is insufficient for comparing productivity among two or more agile teams. This is because no two teams share the same definition of a story point. [Agile Estimating and Planning. Mike Cohn.] [Metrics]

13. C - Velocity is a measure of the number of user story points completed per iteration. An agile team can use its previous velocity recordings as a method of estimating how many user story points it may complete in the next iteration. David's team's velocity is 8 [Agile Estimating and Planning. Mike Cohn.] [Metrics]

14. A - EVM or earned value management is a management technique used to evaluate project performance with respect to cost and schedule. EVM relies on other common financial metrics like Budget At Completion (BAC), Actual Cost (AC), Planned Value (PV), Earned Value (EV), Cost Variance (CV), Schedule Variance (SV), Cost Performance Index (CPI), and Schedule Performance Index (SPI). EV is value of work actually completed or earned (e.g., you have completed 50% of the project by week 5 of a 15 week $15,000 project = $7,500 EV). CV is the difference between what a project has earned to date and cost to date (i.e., CV = EV - AC). SV is the difference between what a project has earned to date and what it was planned to earn to date (i.e., SV = EV - PV). CPI is a ratio that expresses cost performance. CPI = EV/AC. If CPI > 1, the project is earning more than spending; and if CPI <1, the project is spending more than it is earning. AC is the actual cost the project has incurred to date. [Agile Estimating and Planning. Mike Cohn.] [Metrics]

15. C - EVM or earned value management is a management technique used to evaluate project performance with respect to cost and schedule. EVM relies on other common financial metrics like Budget At Completion (BAC), Actual Cost (AC), Planned Value (PV), Earned Value (EV), Cost Variance (CV), Schedule Variance (SV), Cost Performance Index (CPI), and Schedule Performance Index (SPI). CV and SV can be converted into performance indicators of CPI and SPI, respectively, and tracked and charted to show progress over time. BAC is the total project budget. PV is the planned value of work at a given time in a project; you can calculate it by multiplying the BAC by the ratio of current week/scheduled weeks (e.g., 5 weeks into a 15 week $15,000 project = $5,000 PV). EV is value of work actually completed or earned (e.g., you have completed 50% of the project by week 5 of a 15 week $15,000 project = $7,500 EV). CV is the difference between what a project has earned to date and cost to date (i.e., CV = EV - AC). SV is the difference between what a project has earned to date and what it was planned to earn to date (i.e., SV = EV - PV). CPI is a ratio that expresses cost performance. CPI

= EV/AC. If CPI > 1, the project is earning more than spending; and if CPI 1, the project is ahead of schedule and if SPI < 1, the project is behind schedule. AC is the actual cost the project has incurred to date. [Agile Estimating and Planning. Mike Cohn.] [Metrics]

PMI-ACP Lite Mock Exam 14 Practice Questions

Test Name: PMI-ACP Lite Mock Exam 14
Total Questions: 40
Correct Answers Needed to Pass: 30 (75.00%)
Time Allowed: 60 Minutes

Test Description

This is a cumulative PMI-ACP Mock Exam which can be used as a benchmark for your PMI-ACP aptitude. This practice test includes questions from all exam topic areas, including sections from Agile Tools and Techniques, and all three Agile Knowledge and Skills areas.

Test Questions

1. Should stakeholders be invited to a sprint review?

A. No, the sprint review is reserved only for the product team to make sure the user stories pass the acceptance tests.

B. Yes, the sprint review is exclusively for the stakeholders and product owners, so the product owner should absolutely invite the stakeholders.

C. Absolutely, this is a critical component of the agile framework where the latest increment of product functionality is demonstrated to the stakeholders for inspection, feedback, and adapting.

D. No, review meetings are private to the team so that it may take the necessary time to reflect on its performance and continuously improve.

2. Lisa is new to agile project management, but is eager to learn the methodology. Team members have asked Lisa to post the project burndown chart. Lisa decides to post the burndown chart in the basement where none of the team members regularly visit. What is wrong with Lisa's choice of the information radiator's posting location?

A. Nothing

B. It is still somewhat accessible and should be placed in a secure place where no one but Lisa can access.

C. It is not in a digital format.

D. It is not in highly visible place where all team members can regularly view and update its content.

3. Three daily stand-up participants are holding a disruptive side conversation. How should the team leader approach the issue?

A. Use the daily stand-up stick as a gavel and call out the offending parties to behave properly.

B. Nothing immediately but bring up the issue in the iteration review.

C. Trust that as a self-organizing team, it will notice the issue and correct the problem.

D. Cancel the meeting.

4. How do NPV and IRR differ?

A. NPV is a rate value and IRR is a magnitude value.

B. NPV is a rate value and IRR is a summed value.

C. They do not differ.

D. NPV is a magnitude value and IRR is a rate value.

5. An agile tem has decided to use an information radiator for tracking progress. Where should it post the information radiator?

A. On a website that is firewalled and difficult to access.

B. A conspicuous place where the team and stakeholders can review the information radiator easily.

C. In the company monthly newsletter.

D. In an inconspicuous place where only certain team members can review the information radiator.

6. What is the typical duration of an iteration?

A. Two to four weeks.

B. Three to five weeks.

C. Two months.

D. One week.

7. Steve and his team are using process mapping to understand how inputs in his business are turned into outputs and where bottlenecks form. Process mapping is an example of a

A. Process analysis technique

B. Code refactoring technique

C. Done done technique

D. Defect technique

8. How often are the processes of verification and validation performed on an agile project?

A. Only as requested by the customer

B. Seldom

C. Twice a release

D. Frequently

9. As project leader, Hank is conducting a rolling look ahead plan for a complex project. What type of work should Hank include in the rolling look ahead plan?

A. Only work that is to be completed for the next few iterations

B. Only the iterations involved with other teams excluding his own

C. Only the next iteration

D. All work that is remaining in the project through its completion

10. When value stream mapping it is important to identify areas of waste that exist in the process. The pneumonic device WIDETOM may be used to remember the different forms of muda (or waste). What does the T in WIDETOM stand for with respect to waste?

A. Transportation

B. Torpid

C. Tangible

D. Taciturn

11. Which of the following responses is NOT a community value per the PMI agile community of practice community charter?

A. Inspiring

B. Adaptability

C. Openness

D. Courage

12. When a team shares information unconsciously by the simple fact that it is collocated, what is the communication method known as?

A. Dynamic communication

B. Oral communication

C. Osmotic communication

D. Organic communication

13. According to Cockburn, what is referred to as the "sum of all knowledge from all people on a project team?"

A. Organic knowledge

B. Progressive elaborated knowledge

C. Collective knowledge

D. Tacit knowledge

14. Calculate the return on investment of the following: Gain: $15,000; Cost: $10,000.

A. 67%

B. 60%

C. 50%

D. 40%

15. If a task is expected to take approximately 4 hours to complete, what would be a good timebox value to assign to the task?

A. 12 hours

B. 8 hours

C. 4 hours

D. 2 hours

16. When an agile team performs reflection, what types of topics does it review?

A. Superlative team members

B. Osmotic information radiators

C. Lessons learned from successes and failures

D. Planning for the next iteration

17. In the Crystal framework, what is one benefit of collocation?

A. Osmotic communication

B. Osmotic coding

C. Osmotic integration

D. Osmotic refactoring

18. Drew and his pair programming partner Steve have just finished integrating new code into the production code base. What should happen next according to the XP principle of continuous integration?

A. The production code is postfactored to add redundancy measures.

B. The production code base is tested to identify any integration defects.

C. Other code is integrated before testing the production code at the end of the day.

D. The production code is reviewed in its entirety by pair programmers.

19. What type of team is entrusted to self-organize and make decisions collectively to adapt to change?

A. Bout team

B. Attack team

C. Empowered team

D. Forward team

20. Which of the following responses is a community value per the PMI agile community of practice community charter?

A. Overbearing

B. Fastidious

C. Humble

D. Honesty

21. Which of the following responses is a community value per the PMI agile community of practice community charter?

A. Leading Change

B. Rigid

C. Passionate

D. Melancholy

22. Of the following responses, which is a community value per the PMI agile community of practice community charter?

A. Adaptability

B. Optimistic

C. Contemplative

D. Peaceful

23. Which software development framework stresses a 'sustainable pace' of development, simple design, collective ownership, and an on-site customer?

A. Ultra programming (UP)

B. Peer perfect programming (3P)

C. Paired programming (PP)

D. Extreme programming (XP)

24. EVM is a frequently used project management abbreviation. What does BAC stand for in the EVM technique?

A. Budget at correlation

B. Budget analysis correlation

C. Budget and cost

D. Budget at completion

25. A healthy stand-up meeting has several characteristics. Select the response that lists a majority of these characteristics.

A. Peer pressure, fine-grained coordination, a fine focus, and daily commitment

B. Peer pressure, fine-grained coordination, a broad focus, daily commitment, and obstacle identification

C. Peer pressure, fine-grained coordination, a fine focus, weekly commitment, and obstacle identification

D. Peer pressure, fine-grained coordination, a fine focus, daily commitment, and obstacle identification

26. EVM is a frequently used project management abbreviation. What does PV stand for in the EVM technique?

A. Prioritized value

B. Planned value

C. Proportional value

D. Per value

27. Name the two types of integrity in the lean software development framework.

A. Prescriptive and descriptive

B. Ideal and actual

C. Perceived and actual

D. Perceived and conceptual

28. Steve and his team, in a process mapping workshop, just identified two process steps that are significantly impacting the overall performance of the system. Process mapping is an example of a

A. Business value maximization technique

B. Performance improvement plan technique

C. Process analysis technique

D. Kanban technique

29. Ethan and his team just identified two processes for upcoming Kaizen events in a three day value stream mapping workshop. When an agile team uses value stream mapping like Ethan's team, it is an example of a

A. Performance improvement plan technique

B. Process analysis technique

C. Kanban technique

D. Business value maximization technique

30. As agile team leader, Nathan intends to schedule a brainstorming session to generate ideas that may help solve some of the team's current issues. Which of the following is a good brainstorming technique that Nathan should use?

A. Picking a reserved team member as facilitator.

B. Hosting the meeting in the typical Monday morning conference room that is usually only available to certain team members.

C. Delaying any criticism that may hamper idea generation.

D. Leaving participants in the dark until the day of the meeting to add an element of surprise.

31. Which professional society puts forth a code of conduct that every professional should maintain?

A. Program Management Institute

B. Plan Management Institute

C. Project Management Institute

D. Program Management International

32. Henry has just revealed a card to his agile team that shows a value of 5. He drew the card from a deck of similar shaped cards with other values. What popular agile planning game is Henry most likely playing?

A. Planning stud

B. Planning cards

C. Planning cribbage

D. Planning poker

33. Perry is explaining the MoSCoW technique which is often used in agile to prioritize user stories. What does the S stand for?

A. Should not have

B. Small

C. Specific

D. Should have

34. What agile estimation technique is useful for efficiently estimating the relative work effort of large product backlogs?

A. Planning game

B. MoSCoW

C. Planning poker

D. Affinity estimating

35. Vikki, as project leader, empowers her team to make many important decisions. This helps to build trust and a strong sense of community. What is Vikki doing when she empowers the team?

A. Working the team

B. Criticizing the team

C. Motivating the team

D. Leading the team

36. Stephanie, an agile developer, is at a planning event where the relative development effort of user stories is to be estimated. The planning event is mostly conducted in silence and the team is to assign user stories to a Fibonacci sequence. The planning event is efficient and the user stories are estimated quickly. What type of planning event is Stephanie most likely attending?

A. Infinity estimating

B. Affinity estimating

C. Relative estimating

D. Planning poker

37. Which agile estimation technique involves estimating the relative effort of developing a user story by comparing it against two other user stories?

A. Planning poker

B. Three point estimation

C. Triangulation

D. Comparative analysis

38. Hector, as team leader, wants to design a comfortable, collaborative team space for his agile project. What can he do as a basic guideline?

A. Dedicate wall space for frequently updated information radiators

B. Play loud and motivational background music

C. Have non-opening windows

D. Use cubicle walls to give privacy

39. What is the document authored by PMI that outlines moral behaviors of professionals called?

A. PMI's Code of Ethics and Professional Conduct

B. PMI's Code of Ethics and Professional Morality

C. PMI's Code of Conduct and Professional Morality

D. PMI's Code of Morality

40. Drew and his pair programming partner Steve have just finished building new code. What should happen next according to the XP principle of continuous integration?

A. Extensive testing before integration with the production code base.

B. Complete inspection by the customer or customer representative.

C. Conversion to the target coding language.

D. Postfactoring to add contingency measures.

PMI-ACP Lite Mock Exam 14 Answer Key and Explanations

1. C - Stakeholders are a critical component of the agile framework where the latest increment of product functionality is demonstrated to the stakeholders for inspection, feedback, and adapting. [Agile Estimating and Planning. Mike Cohn.] [Planning, monitoring, and adapting]

2. D - An information radiator should be posted in a highly visible area that is easily accessible by the team and stakeholders. [Agile Software Development: The Cooperative Game – 2nd Edition. Alistair Cockburn.] [Communications]

3. C - A high-performance, self-organizing team should realize and correct the disruptive behavior. [Coaching Agile Teams. Lyssa Adkins.] [Communications]

4. D - The internal rate of return (IRR) is a financial metric used to measure and compare the profitability of investments. The IRR is the "rate" that makes the net present value of all cash flows from a particular investment equal to zero. Unlike NPV which is a dollar amount (i.e., a magnitude) value, the IRR is a rate (i.e.,, a percentage). Often times, the IRR is compared against a threshold rate value to determine if the investment is a suitable risk worth implementing. For example, you might calculate an IRR to be 13% for an investment while a comparative market rate is 2%. The IRR being larger than the comparative market rate, would indicate the investment is worth pursuing. [Agile Estimating and Planning. Mike Cohn.] [Value based prioritization]

5. B - An information radiator should be posted in a highly visible area that is easily accessible by the team and stakeholders. [Agile Software Development: The Cooperative Game – 2nd Edition. Alistair Cockburn.] [Communications]

6. A - A cornerstone of Agile development is 'incremental delivery.' Incremental delivery is the frequent delivery of working products, which are successively improved, to a customer for immediate feedback and acceptance. Typically, a product is delivered at the end of each sprint or iteration for demonstration and feedback. In this feedback technique, a customer can review the product and provide updated requirements. Changed/updated/refined requirements are welcomed in the agile process to ensure the customer receives a valuable and quality product. A sprint or iteration typically lasts from two to four weeks and at the end a new and improved product is delivered, incrementally. [The Art of Agile Development. James Shore.] [Knowledge and Skills: Level 1]

7. A - Value stream mapping is a collaborative process analysis technique where a diverse team depicts/maps a process to identify where waste occurs and where improvements can be made. It is an example of a process analysis technique. Like value stream mapping, process mapping is also used to map a process to identify bottlenecks (places where processing slows and inventory can build). [Lean-Agile Software Development: Achieving Enterprise Agility. Alan Shalloway, Guy Beaver, James R. Trott.] [Knowledge and Skills: Level 2]

8. D - Because each iteration typically produces a working product that is built

and integrated and iterations are typically two to four weeks in length, there is frequent verification and validation to ensure product quality. Verification is the confirmation that a product performs as specified by a customer (e.g. as indicated by a user story) and validation is the confirmation that a product behaves as desired (i.e., meets the customer's need). Sometimes a product may be built and integrated to specification - that is, it can be verified - but it does not meet the intent of the customer - that is, it cannot be validated. [Agile Software Development: The Cooperative Game – 2nd Edition. Alistair Cockburn.] [Product quality]

9. A - When using a rolling wave or rolling look ahead plan for complex projects, only work that is about to be completed for the next few iterations - where requirement details are better understood - are planned. The plan includes all interdependent agile project teams to ensure successful integration of tasks. [Agile Estimating and Planning. Mike Cohn.] [Planning, monitoring, and adapting]

10. A - Value stream mapping is a lean manufacturing analysis technique adopted by agile. A value stream map may be used to analyze the flow of information or materials from origin to destination to identify areas of waste. The identified areas of waste are opportunities for process improvement. Waste can take many forms and can be remembered using the pneumonic device WIDETOM. W - waiting; I - inventory; D - defects; E - extra processing; T - transportation; O - over-production ; M - Motion. A value stream map is typically mapped or charted collaboratively with a team so it may define and view the entire process together, pinpointing areas of waste within the process. Processes that add value (processing of a part or feature) are generally referred to as "value-added" and processes that do not (e.g., waiting for a part to arrive) are generally referred to as "non value-added." Generally speaking, one wants to reduce, to the largest extent possible, the non value-added time (i.e., areas of waste). [Lean-Agile Software Development: Achieving Enterprise Agility. Alan Shalloway, Guy Beaver, James R. Trott.] [Value stream analysis]

11. A - The following are community values of the PMI agile community of practice community charter: Vision, Servant Leadership, Trust, Collaboration, Honesty, Learning, Courage, Openness, Adaptability, Leading Change, Transparency [PMI Agile Community of Practice Community Charter. Project Management Institute.] [Knowledge and Skills: Level 1]

12. C - Osmotic communication is a concept of communication where information is shared between collocated team members unconsciously. By sharing the same work environment, team members are exposed to the same environmental sounds and other environmental input and unconsciously share a common framework that improves communication. [Agile Software Development: The Cooperative Game – 2nd Edition. Alistair Cockburn.] [Communications]

13. D - Tacit knowledge is the "sum of all knowledge from all people on a project team." [Agile Software Development: The Cooperative Game – 2nd Edition. Alistair Cockburn.] [Knowledge and Skills: Level 2]

14. C - Return on Investment (ROI): A metric used to evaluate the efficiency of an investment or to compare efficiency among a number of investments. To calculate ROI, the return of an investment (i.e., the gain minus the cost) is divided by the cost of the investment. The result is usually expressed as a percentage and sometimes a ratio. The product owner is often said to be responsible for the ROI. [Agile Estimating and Planning. Mike Cohn.] [Value based prioritization]

15. C - Timeboxing is a realistic estimate or expectation of how long an action, task, or event will take to perform. Some tasks cannot be performed in the initial timeboxed estimate and are good candidates for reevaluation and possibly further decomposition into more tasks. [The Art of Agile Development. James Shore.] [Planning, monitoring, and adapting]

16. C - During reflection an agile team takes a break after completing an iteration to pause and contemplate about its performance. Topics include: lessons learned from successes and failures, such as programming methods that were highly efficient or inefficient; how to reinforce successful practices, such as new testing standard practices; how to discourage negative practices, like straying from team approved coding standards in order to make an iteration deadline. [Agile Software Development: The Cooperative Game – 2nd Edition. Alistair Cockburn.] [Planning, monitoring, and adapting]

17. A - A high-performance agile team is one that is ideally collocated for osmotic communication and face-to-face interaction. However, collocation isn't always feasible in today's multinational environment. For distributed teams, several practices are available to provide the best form of effective communication in the absence of being collocated: team intranet sites, virtual team rooms, and video conferencing over e-mail when possible. Geographic separation, especially on a world-wide scale, causes the team to consider language and cultural differences, and time zone differences. [The Art of Agile Development. James Shore.] [Knowledge and Skills: Level 2]

18. B - The extreme programming (XP) principle of continuous integration is that code is integrated into the full code base as soon as it is built, tested, and completed. Once integrated, the code base and therefore the entire system is built and tested. Continuous integration is just one principle of XP that promotes rapid delivery of software and the early detection of integration defects. [The Art of Agile Development. James Shore.] [Product quality]

19. C - Empowered teams - ones that are self-organizing and know how to solve problems with minimal management involvement - are a cornerstone of the agile methodology. This is the antithesis to the classic viewpoint of the traditional project manager who is seen as someone that controls all decisions and delegates tasks to a team with little feedback. An agile team must include all members and stakeholders to make decisions, and make decisions expediently. Because it is essential that the user/customer be involved with development, it is encouraged that the user/customer is closely integrated with the agile team with collocation/on-site support being ideal. An agile team feels empowered when it collectively assumes responsibility for the delivery of the product (i.e., taking ownership). [Coaching Agile Teams. Lyssa Adkins.] [Knowledge and Skills: Level 1]

20. D - The following are community values of the PMI agile community of practice community charter: Vision, Servant Leadership, Trust, Collaboration, Honesty, Learning, Courage, Openness, Adaptability, Leading Change, Transparency [PMI Agile Community of Practice Community Charter. Project Management Institute.] [Knowledge and Skills: Level 1]

21. A - The following are community values of the PMI agile community of practice community charter: Vision, Servant Leadership, Trust, Collaboration, Honesty, Learning, Courage, Openness, Adaptability, Leading Change, Transparency [PMI Agile Community of Practice Community Charter. Project Management Institute.] [Knowledge and Skills: Level 1]

22. A - The following are community values of the PMI agile community of practice community charter: Vision, Servant Leadership, Trust, Collaboration, Honesty, Learning, Courage, Openness, Adaptability, Leading Change, Transparency [PMI Agile Community of Practice Community Charter. Project Management Institute.] [Knowledge and Skills: Level 1]

23. D - Extreme programming (XP) is a programmer-centric agile framework that focuses on small, ongoing releases. XP highlights several principles: pair programming, sustainable pace, ongoing automated testing, effective communication, simplicity, feedback, courage, collective ownership, continuous integration, energized work, shared workspaces, on-site customer representation, and the use of metaphor to describe concepts. [Agile Software Development: The Cooperative Game – 2nd Edition. Alistair Cockburn.] [Knowledge and Skills: Level 2]

24. D - EVM or earned value management is a management technique used to evaluate project performance with respect to cost and schedule. EVM relies on other common financial metrics like Budget At Completion (BAC), Actual Cost (AC), Planned Value (PV), Earned Value (EV), Cost Variance (CV), Schedule Variance (SV), Cost Performance Index (CPI), and Schedule Performance Index (SPI). [Agile Estimating and Planning. Mike Cohn.] [Metrics]

25. D - The key characteristics of a healthy stand-up meeting include: peer pressure - the team is dependent upon each other so expectations of peers drives progress; fine-grained coordination - the team should understand the necessity for focus and working dependently; fine focus - the team should understand the need for brevity in the stand-up meeting so the team can be productive; daily commitment - the team should understand the value of daily commitments to each other and uphold those commitments; identification of obstacles - the team collectively should be aware of each other's obstacles so that the team collectively can try to resolve them. [The Art of Agile Development. James Shore.] [Communications]

26. B - EVM or earned value management is a management technique used to evaluate project performance with respect to cost and schedule. EVM relies on other common financial metrics like Budget At Completion (BAC), Actual Cost (AC), Planned Value (PV), Earned Value (EV),

Cost Variance (CV), Schedule Variance (SV), Cost Performance Index (CPI), and Schedule Performance Index (SPI). [Agile Estimating and Planning. Mike Cohn.] [Metrics]

27. D - In lean software development, there are two forms of integrity: conceptual and perceived. Conceptual integrity is determined by the developers and is generally high if the product integrates well and functions as specified. Perceived integrity is judged by the customer and is high if the customer is happy with the product, first and foremost, and secondly if the product meets requirements. [Lean-Agile Software Development: Achieving Enterprise Agility. Alan Shalloway, Guy Beaver, James R. Trott.] [Knowledge and Skills: Level 2]

28. C - Value stream mapping is a collaborative process analysis technique where a diverse team depicts/maps a process to identify where waste occurs and where improvements can be made. It is an example of a process analysis technique. Like value stream mapping, process mapping is also used to map a process to identify bottlenecks (places where processing slows and inventory can build). [Lean-Agile Software Development: Achieving Enterprise Agility. Alan Shalloway, Guy Beaver, James R. Trott.] [Knowledge and Skills: Level 2]

29. B - Value stream mapping is a collaborative process analysis technique where a diverse team depicts/maps a process to identify where waste occurs and where improvements can be made. It is an example of a process analysis technique. Like value stream mapping, process mapping is also used to map a process to identify bottlenecks (places where processing slows and inventory can build). [Lean-Agile Software Development: Achieving Enterprise Agility. Alan Shalloway, Guy Beaver, James R. Trott.] [Knowledge and Skills: Level 2]

30. C - A successful brainstorming event should strive to consider the following points - Host the meeting in a neutral and comfortable environment - Have an engaging and experienced facilitator lead the event - Send participants an overview, with goals, schedule, and what ground rules, beforehand - Have a multi-disciplinary/diverse team to get a broader perspective - Delay any criticism that may stifle idea generation. [Agile Retrospectives: Making Good Teams Great. Esther Derby, Diana Larsen, Ken Schwaber.] [Knowledge and Skills: Level 1]

31. C - The Project Management Institute (PMI) outlines a professional code of conduct in the PMI Code of Ethics and Professional Conduct document. [PMI Code of Ethics and Professional Conduct. Project Management Institute.] [Knowledge and Skills: Level 2]

32. D - Planning poker is a popular agile game used to estimate the relative work effort of developing a user story. Each team member has a deck of cards with various numbered values which he or she can draw from to "play (showing one card)" to indicate an estimated point value of developing a user story. [Coaching Agile Teams. Lyssa Adkins.] [Knowledge and Skills: Level 3]

33. D - The MoSCoW technique is commonly used in agile to prioritize user stories and create a story map. The MoSCoW technique prioritizes user stories into the following groups in descending order of priority: M - Must have; S - Should have; C - Could have; W - Would have. Must have items are those product features which are absolutely essential to develop. Should have items are product features that are not essential but have significant business value. Could have items are product features that would add some business value. Would have items are product features that have marginal business value. [User Stories Applied: For Agile Software Development. Mike Cohn.] [Agile analysis and design]

34. D - Affinity estimating is a method to predict the work effort, typically in story points, of developing a user story. It is particularly useful for large product backlogs. Although several methods exist, the basic affinity estimating model involves sizing user stories on a scale from small to large. The scale can be a Fibonacci sequence or t-shirt sizes and is typically taped to a wall in a large conference room. Participants then attach their user stories to the wall as estimates. It is often done in silence and has several iterations until the user stories have been estimated. [The Art of Agile Development. James Shore.] [Agile estimation]

35. C - Having a motivated team is essential for any project, regardless of whether it is agile or not. Motivated teams work together better, have strong productivity, and exceed expectations. Some simple steps to increase motivation are 1) spending quality time together; where team members get to know one another on a personal level to build a sense of community, 2) providing feedback, mentoring and coaching; where team members are congratulated and thanked on jobs well done and also mentored or coached to improve in skill and capability, and 3) empowerment; where the team is empowered to make many key decisions which, along the way, builds trust and shows that leadership believes in the capabilities of the team. [The Art of Agile Development. James Shore.] [Knowledge and Skills: Level 1]

36. B - Affinity estimating is a method to predict the work effort, typically in story points, of developing a user story. It is particularly useful for large product backlogs. Although several methods exist, the basic affinity estimating model involves sizing user stories on a scale from small to large. The scale can be a Fibonacci sequence or t-shirt sizes and is typically taped to a wall in a large conference room. Participants then attach their user stories to the wall as estimates. It is often done in silence and has several iterations until the user stories have been estimated. [The Art of Agile Development. James Shore.] [Agile estimation]

37. C - Triangulation involves estimating the relative effort of developing a user story by comparing it against two other user stories. [Agile Estimating and Planning. Mike Cohn.] [Agile estimation]

38. A - A warm, welcoming environment that promotes effective communication, innovation, and motivated team members is an important aspect to consider when designing team space. Guidelines for a better agile team space include: collocation of team members; reduction of non-essential noise/distractions; dedicated whiteboard and wall space for information radiators; space for the daily stand-up meeting and other meetings; pairing workstations; and other pleasantries like plants and comfortable furniture. [Agile

Retrospectives: Making Good Teams Great. Esther Derby, Diana Larsen, Ken Schwaber.] [Communications]

39. A - The Project Management Institute (PMI) outlines a professional code of conduct in the PMI Code of Ethics and Professional Conduct document. [PMI Code of Ethics and Professional Conduct. Project Management Institute.] [Knowledge and Skills: Level 2]

40. A - The extreme programming (XP) principle of continuous integration is that code is integrated into the full code base as soon as it is built, tested, and completed. Once integrated, the code base and therefore the entire system is built and tested. Continuous integration is just one principle of XP that promotes rapid delivery of software and the early detection of integration defects. [The Art of Agile Development. James Shore.] [Product quality]

Knowledge Area Quiz
Value Stream Analysis
Practice Questions

Test Name: Knowledge Area Test: Value Stream Analysis
Total Questions: 15
Correct Answers Needed to Pass:
11 (73.33%)
Time Allowed: 25 Minutes

Test Description

This practice quiz specifically targets your knowledge of the Value Stream Analysis exam topic area.

Test Questions

1. Which of the following best defines value stream mapping?

A. A lean manufacturing technique used to analyze the flow of material and information that form a product to the consumer.

B. A six sigma manufacturing technique used to analyze the occurrence of defects.

C. A lean manufacturing technique used to control the flow of inventory (WIP) in a manufacturing plant.

D. A six sigma manufacturing technique used to control the visual management board.

2. What manufacturing technique is generally credited with the creation of value stream mapping?

A. Intrepid

B. Lean / Toyota production system

C. Agile

D. Six sigma

3. What is one purpose of value stream mapping?

A. Identify areas of Kaizen in a process.

B. Identify areas of Yokoten in a process.

C. Identify areas of Kanban in a process.

D. Identify areas of waste in a process.

4. What is a purpose of value stream mapping?

A. Identify areas of waste throughout a process.

B. Identify areas of Yokoten in a process.

C. Identify areas of value in a process.

D. Identify areas of WIP in a process.

5. What is total lead time considered as in a value stream map?

A. Waste

B. Value-forma

C. Value-pro

D. Value-added

6. Karen is reviewing a value stream map that she and her agile team just created. The team is debating whether it should reduce a lead time by 90% or increase a process time by 20%. Which of the previous two actions would you suggest her team take?

A. Increase process time by 20%

B. Reduce lead time by 90%

C. Both.

D. Neither. Both represent adding more waste into the value stream.

7. Karen is reviewing a value stream map that she and her agile team just created. The team is debating whether it should increase a lead time by 60% or decrease a process time by 30%. Which of the previous two actions would you suggest her team take?

A. Neither. Both represent adding more waste into the value stream.

B. Both.

C. Reduce process time by 30%

D. Increase lead time by 60%

8. If you were shown a diagram of a proposed design to improve an existing system and the diagram had process steps, information flow, lead times, and process times, what type of diagram would you believe it to be?

A. Future-state value stream map

B. Waste stream map

C. Value stream analysis

D. Current-state value stream map

9. If you were shown a diagram of an existing system and the diagram had process steps, information flow, lead times, and process times, what type of diagram would you believe it to be?

A. Current-state value stream map

B. Value stream analysis

C. Future-state value stream map

D. Waste stream map

10. What is one purpose of value stream mapping?

A. To understand how sigmas are delivered to a customer.

B. To understand how quality is delivered to a customer.

C. To understand how agility is delivered to a customer.

D. To understand how value is delivered to a customer.

11. Harry's agile team has just finished creating a value stream map for one of its products. On the value stream map, Harry's team has

identified two types of data. Which of the following are these two types of data most likely to be?

A. Defect-stream and Value-stream

B. Information-flow and information-owner

C. Value-added and non value-added

D. Sigma-ranked and Theta-prioritized

12. If a business is interested in streamlining its processes to remove and reduce waste and increase the efficiency with which value is delivered to its customers, what technique, adopted from lean manufacturing, might it consider?

A. Operations research

B. Management science

C. Value stream mapping

D. Systems engineering

13. Jill and Stephanie are reviewing a large chart that visually depicts the flow of information from origin to customer. On the chart are times indicating the duration of value-added processes and non value-added processes. What are Jill and Stephanie reviewing?

A. A muda stream map

B. A kaizen stream map

C. A lean stream map

D. A value stream map

14. What is it called when a team collaboratively charts the flow of information or material of a process from origin to destination along with all its instances of waste?

A. Procedure charting

B. Multiple regression

C. Value stream mapping

D. Process shortening mapping

15. When value stream mapping it is important to identify areas of waste that exist in the process. The pneumonic device WIDETOM may be used to remember the different forms of muda (or waste). What does the D in WIDETOM stand for with respect to waste?

A. Deterrent

B. Deleterious

C. Defect

D. Detriment

Knowledge Area Quiz
Value Stream Analysis
Answer Key and Explanations

1. A - Value stream mapping is a lean manufacturing technique used to analyze the flow of material and information (i.e., value) that form a product or service to a consumer. There is roughly five steps in the implementation of value stream mapping: 1) Identification of the product, customer, and scope (i.e., the beginning and end of the process). 2) Map as a team or individual the current value stream, identifying process steps, delays, information requirements. Estimate process step durations and lead time durations. A lead time is how long a process or event must wait before happening. 3) Analyze the map to determine where waste exists (e.g., lead times) an where processes can be improved (process times are generally seen as value-added time, but on the whole process times should try to be reduced to reduce the overall time it takes the stream to deliver value to the customer). 4) From the analysis, draw a future state value stream map that represents a vision or goal the value stream should strive to become. 5) Work towards the goal through process improvement events (i.e., Kaizen) or other methods. [Lean-Agile Software Development: Achieving Enterprise Agility. Alan Shalloway, Guy Beaver, James R. Trott.] [Value stream analysis]

2. B - Value stream mapping is a lean manufacturing technique used to analyze the flow of material and information (i.e., value) that form a product or service to a consumer. There is roughly five steps in the implementation of value stream mapping: 1) Identification of the product, customer, and scope (i.e., the beginning and end of the process). 2) Map as a team or individual the current value stream, identifying process steps, delays, information requirements. Estimate process step durations and lead time durations. A lead time is how long a process or event must wait before happening. 3) Analyze the map to determine where waste exists (e.g., lead times) an where processes can be improved (process times are generally seen as value-added time, but on the whole process times should try to be reduced to reduce the overall time it takes the stream to deliver value to the customer). 4) From the analysis, draw a future state value stream map that represents a vision or goal the value stream should strive to become. 5) Work towards the goal through process improvement events (i.e., Kaizen) or other methods. [Lean-Agile Software Development: Achieving Enterprise Agility. Alan Shalloway, Guy Beaver, James R. Trott.] [Value stream analysis]

3. D - Value stream mapping is a lean manufacturing technique used to analyze the flow of material and information (i.e., value) that form a product or service to a consumer. There is roughly five steps in the implementation of value stream mapping: 1) Identification of the product, customer, and scope (i.e., the beginning and end of the process). 2) Map as a team or individual the current value stream, identifying process steps, delays, information requirements. Estimate process step durations and lead time durations. A lead time is how long a process or event must wait before happening. 3) Analyze the map to determine where waste exists (e.g., lead times) an where processes can be improved (process times are generally seen as value-added time, but on the whole process times

should try to be reduced to reduce the overall time it takes the stream to deliver value to the customer). 4) From the analysis, draw a future state value stream map that represents a vision or goal the value stream should strive to become. 5) Work towards the goal through process improvement events (i.e., Kaizen) or other methods. [Lean-Agile Software Development: Achieving Enterprise Agility. Alan Shalloway, Guy Beaver, James R. Trott.] [Value stream analysis]

4. A - Value stream mapping is a lean manufacturing technique used to analyze the flow of material and information (i.e., value) that form a product or service to a consumer. There is roughly five steps in the implementation of value stream mapping: 1) Identification of the product, customer, and scope (i.e., the beginning and end of the process). 2) Map as a team or individual the current value stream, identifying process steps, delays, information requirements. Estimate process step durations and lead time durations. A lead time is how long a process or event must wait before happening. 3) Analyze the map to determine where waste exists (e.g., lead times) an where processes can be improved (process times are generally seen as value-added time, but on the whole process times should try to be reduced to reduce the overall time it takes the stream to deliver value to the customer). 4) From the analysis, draw a future state value stream map that represents a vision or goal the value stream should strive to become. 5) Work towards the goal through process improvement events (i.e., Kaizen) or other methods. [Lean-Agile Software Development: Achieving Enterprise Agility. Alan Shalloway, Guy Beaver, James R. Trott.] [Value stream analysis]

5. A - Value stream mapping is a lean manufacturing technique used to analyze the flow of material and information (i.e., value) that form a product or service to a consumer. There is roughly five steps in the implementation of value stream mapping: 1) Identification of the product, customer, and scope (i.e., the beginning and end of the process). 2) Map as a team or individual the current value stream, identifying process steps, delays, information requirements. Estimate process step durations and lead time durations. A lead time is how long a process or event must wait before happening. 3) Analyze the map to determine where waste exists (e.g., lead times) an where processes can be improved (process times are generally seen as value-added time, but on the whole process times should try to be reduced to reduce the overall time it takes the stream to deliver value to the customer). 4) From the analysis, draw a future state value stream map that represents a vision or goal the value stream should strive to become. 5) Work towards the goal through process improvement events (i.e., Kaizen) or other methods. [Lean-Agile Software Development: Achieving Enterprise Agility. Alan Shalloway, Guy Beaver, James R. Trott.] [Value stream analysis]

6. B - Value stream mapping is a lean manufacturing technique used to analyze the flow of material and information (i.e., value) that form a product or service to a consumer. There is roughly five steps in the implementation of value stream mapping: 1) Identification of the product, customer, and scope (i.e., the beginning and end of the process). 2) Map as a team or individual the current value stream, identifying process steps, delays, information requirements.

Estimate process step durations and lead time durations. A lead time is how long a process or event must wait before happening. 3) Analyze the map to determine where waste exists (e.g., lead times) an where processes can be improved (process times are generally seen as value-added time, but on the whole process times should try to be reduced to reduce the overall time it takes the stream to deliver value to the customer). 4) From the analysis, draw a future state value stream map that represents a vision or goal the value stream should strive to become. 5) Work towards the goal through process improvement events (i.e., Kaizen) or other methods. [Lean-Agile Software Development: Achieving Enterprise Agility. Alan Shalloway, Guy Beaver, James R. Trott.] [Value stream analysis]

7. C - Value stream mapping is a lean manufacturing technique used to analyze the flow of material and information (i.e., value) that form a product or service to a consumer. There is roughly five steps in the implementation of value stream mapping: 1) Identification of the product, customer, and scope (i.e., the beginning and end of the process). 2) Map as a team or individual the current value stream, identifying process steps, delays, information requirements. Estimate process step durations and lead time durations. A lead time is how long a process or event must wait before happening. 3) Analyze the map to determine where waste exists (e.g., lead times) an where processes can be improved (process times are generally seen as value-added time, but on the whole process times should try to be reduced to reduce the overall time it takes the stream to deliver value to the customer). 4) From the analysis, draw a future state value stream map that represents a vision or goal the value stream should strive to become. 5) Work towards the goal through process improvement events (i.e., Kaizen) or other methods. [Lean-Agile Software Development: Achieving Enterprise Agility. Alan Shalloway, Guy Beaver, James R. Trott.] [Value stream analysis]

8. A - Value stream mapping is a lean manufacturing technique used to analyze the flow of material and information (i.e., value) that form a product or service to a consumer. There is roughly five steps in the implementation of value stream mapping: 1) Identification of the product, customer, and scope (i.e., the beginning and end of the process). 2) Map as a team or individual the current value stream, identifying process steps, delays, information requirements. Estimate process step durations and lead time durations. A lead time is how long a process or event must wait before happening. 3) Analyze the map to determine where waste exists (e.g., lead times) an where processes can be improved (process times are generally seen as value-added time, but on the whole process times should try to be reduced to reduce the overall time it takes the stream to deliver value to the customer). 4) From the analysis, draw a future state value stream map that represents a vision or goal the value stream should strive to become. 5) Work towards the goal through process improvement events (i.e., Kaizen) or other methods. [Lean-Agile Software Development: Achieving Enterprise Agility. Alan Shalloway, Guy Beaver, James R. Trott.] [Value stream analysis]

9. A - Value stream mapping is a lean manufacturing technique used to analyze the flow of material and information (i.e., value) that form a product or service to a consumer. There is roughly five steps in the implementation of value stream mapping: 1) Identification of the product, customer, and scope (i.e., the beginning and end of the process). 2) Map as a team or individual the current value stream, identifying process steps, delays, information requirements. Estimate process step durations and lead time durations. A lead time is how long a process or event must wait before happening. 3) Analyze the map to determine where waste exists (e.g., lead times) an where processes can be improved (process times are generally seen as value-added time, but on the whole process times should try to be reduced to reduce the overall time it takes the stream to deliver value to the customer). 4) From the analysis, draw a future state value stream map that represents a vision or goal the value stream should strive to become. 5) Work towards the goal through process improvement events (i.e., Kaizen) or other methods. [Lean-Agile Software Development: Achieving Enterprise Agility. Alan Shalloway, Guy Beaver, James R. Trott.] [Value stream analysis]

10. D - Value stream mapping is a lean manufacturing technique used to analyze the flow of material and information (i.e., value) that form a product or service to a consumer. There is roughly five steps in the implementation of value stream mapping: 1) Identification of the product, customer, and scope (i.e., the beginning and end of the process). 2) Map as a team or individual the current value stream, identifying process steps, delays, information requirements. Estimate process step durations and lead time durations. A lead time is how long a process or event must wait before happening. 3) Analyze the map to determine where waste exists (e.g., lead times) an where processes can be improved (process times are generally seen as value-added time, but on the whole process times should try to be reduced to reduce the overall time it takes the stream to deliver value to the customer). 4) From the analysis, draw a future state value stream map that represents a vision or goal the value stream should strive to become. 5) Work towards the goal through process improvement events (i.e., Kaizen) or other methods. [Lean-Agile Software Development: Achieving Enterprise Agility. Alan Shalloway, Guy Beaver, James R. Trott.] [Value stream analysis]

11. C - Value stream mapping is a lean manufacturing analysis technique adopted by agile. A value stream map may be used to analyze the flow of information or materials from origin to destination to identify areas of waste. The identified areas of waste are opportunities for process improvement. Waste can take many forms and can be remembered using the pneumonic device WIDETOM. W - waiting; I - inventory; D - defects; E - extra processing; T - transportation; O - over-production ; M - Motion. A value stream map is typically mapped or charted collaboratively with a team so it may define and view the entire process together, pinpointing areas of waste within the process. Processes that add value (processing of a part or feature) are generally referred to as "value-added" and processes that do not (e.g., waiting for a part to arrive) are generally referred to as "non value-added." Generally speaking, one wants to reduce, to the largest extent possible, the non value-added time (i.e., areas of waste). [Lean-Agile Software Development: Achieving Enterprise Agility.

Alan Shalloway, Guy Beaver, James R. Trott.] [Value stream analysis]

12. C - Value stream mapping is a lean manufacturing analysis technique adopted by agile. A value stream map may be used to analyze the flow of information or materials from origin to destination to identify areas of waste. The identified areas of waste are opportunities for process improvement. Waste can take many forms and can be remembered using the pneumonic device WIDETOM. W - waiting; I - inventory; D - defects; E - extra processing; T - transportation; O - over-production ; M - Motion. A value stream map is typically mapped or charted collaboratively with a team so it may define and view the entire process together, pinpointing areas of waste within the process. Processes that add value (processing of a part or feature) are generally referred to as "value-added" and processes that do not (e.g., waiting for a part to arrive) are generally referred to as "non value-added." Generally speaking, one wants to reduce, to the largest extent possible, the non value-added time (i.e., areas of waste). [Lean-Agile Software Development: Achieving Enterprise Agility. Alan Shalloway, Guy Beaver, James R. Trott.] [Value stream analysis]

13. D - Value stream mapping is a lean manufacturing analysis technique adopted by agile. A value stream map may be used to analyze the flow of information or materials from origin to destination to identify areas of waste. The identified areas of waste are opportunities for process improvement. Waste can take many forms and can be remembered using the pneumonic device WIDETOM. W - waiting; I - inventory; D - defects; E - extra processing; T - transportation; O - over-production ; M - Motion. A value stream map is typically mapped or charted collaboratively with a team so it may define and view the entire process together, pinpointing areas of waste within the process. Processes that add value (processing of a part or feature) are generally referred to as "value-added" and processes that do not (e.g., waiting for a part to arrive) are generally referred to as "non value-added." Generally speaking, one wants to reduce, to the largest extent possible, the non value-added time (i.e., areas of waste). [Lean-Agile Software Development: Achieving Enterprise Agility. Alan Shalloway, Guy Beaver, James R. Trott.] [Value stream analysis]

14. C - Value stream mapping is a lean manufacturing analysis technique adopted by agile. A value stream map may be used to analyze the flow of information or materials from origin to destination to identify areas of waste. The identified areas of waste are opportunities for process improvement. Waste can take many forms and can be remembered using the pneumonic device WIDETOM. W - waiting; I - inventory; D - defects; E - extra processing; T - transportation; O - over-production ; M - Motion. A value stream map is typically mapped or charted collaboratively with a team so it may define and view the entire process together, pinpointing areas of waste within the process. Processes that add value (processing of a part or feature) are generally referred to as "value-added" and processes that do not (e.g., waiting for a part to arrive) are generally referred to as "non value-added." Generally speaking, one wants to reduce, to the largest extent possible, the non value-added time (i.e., areas of waste). [Lean-Agile Software Development: Achieving Enterprise Agility. Alan Shalloway, Guy Beaver, James R. Trott.] [Value stream analysis]

15. C - Value stream mapping is a lean manufacturing analysis technique adopted by agile. A value stream map may be used to analyze the flow of information or materials from origin to destination to identify areas of waste. The identified areas of waste are opportunities for process improvement. Waste can take many forms and can be remembered using the pneumonic device WIDETOM. W - waiting; I - inventory; D - defects; E - extra processing; T - transportation; O - over-production ; M - Motion. A value stream map is typically mapped or charted collaboratively with a team so it may define and view the entire process together, pinpointing areas of waste within the process. Processes that add value (processing of a part or feature) are generally referred to as "value-added" and processes that do not (e.g., waiting for a part to arrive) are generally referred to as "non value-added." Generally speaking, one wants to reduce, to the largest extent possible, the non value-added time (i.e., areas of waste). [Lean-Agile Software Development: Achieving Enterprise Agility. Alan Shalloway, Guy Beaver, James R. Trott.] [Value stream analysis]

PMI-ACP Lite Mock Exam 15 Practice Questions

Test Name: PMI-ACP Lite Mock Exam 15
Total Questions: 40
Correct Answers Needed to Pass:
30 (75.00%)
Time Allowed: 60 Minutes

Test Description

This is a cumulative PMI-ACP Mock Exam which can be used as a benchmark for your PMI-ACP aptitude. This practice test includes questions from all exam topic areas, including sections from Agile Tools and Techniques, and all three Agile Knowledge and Skills areas.

Test Questions

1. According to Highsmith and his definition of adaptive leadership, what is one item a project leader can do for "doing agile?"

A. Coach and mentor

B. Practice and preach

C. Remove and deliver

D. Engage and inspire

2. Identify the goal in the following example user story: "As a preferred customer, I need to be able to quickly choose among any available car so that I will remain loyal to the brand."

A. Car

B. Preferred customer

C. Quickly choose among any available car

D. Will remain loyal to the brand

3. Identify the achieved business value in the following example user story: "As a preferred customer, I need to be able to quickly choose among any available car so that I will remain loyal to the brand."

A. Preferred customer

B. Car

C. Will remain loyal to the brand

D. Quickly choose among any available car

4. What is an essential knowledge and skill area of the agile team?

A. Problem-mitigation strategies

B. Problem-first strategies

C. Problem-solving strategies

D. Problem-prioritization strategies

5. In agile and other project management styles, team motivation is a critical factor for success. What is one method to improve team motivation?

A. Providing minimal leadership.

B. Providing a forum for anonymous criticism.

C. Providing constructive feedback.

D. Providing minimal supervision.

6. Jim Highsmith's agile project management model divides project management into five phases. Which response includes items from those five phases?

A. Unit testing, quality control, and content management

B. Reflection and parsing

C. Requirements definition, scoping, and scheduling

D. Envisioning, exploring, and closing

7. What is the relationship between scrum and XP?

A. Scrum is used for software development, whereas XP can be applied to software and hardware

B. Scrum is modeled after XP

C. Scrum and XP share no similarities

D. XP is modeled after scrum

8. According to Highsmith and his definition of adaptive leadership, what is one item a project leader can focus on for "doing agile?"

A. Speed-to-risk

B. Speed-to-value

C. Speed-to-quality

D. Speed-to-refinement

9. If the NPV of an investment is zero, what does that indicate to the potential buyer?

A. That it would neither add to nor subtract value from the buyer's portfolio.

B. That it would add value to the buyer's portfolio.

C. That it would subtract value from the buyer's portfolio.

D. None of the above.

10. In scrum, what serves as the common bridge or connection between the product owner and team?

A. The product datasheet

B. The release plan

C. The retrospective

D. The product backlog

11. A customer demo has just completed on Vanessa's agile team, what activity can Vanessa's team perform to focus on continuous improvement?

A. Through immediately planning for the next iteration.

B. Through writing a solid business case.

C. Through reserving time for reflection.

D. Through updating the project vision.

12. What can an agile team do to promote a warm, welcoming environment to foster effective communication?

A. Use pairing or sharing workstations

B. Use fluorescent lighting

C. Use headphones so developers can drown out background noise

D. Update information radiators infrequently

13. Peter knows that effective communication is highly important for an agile team. What is the knowledge and skill area that deals with communication?

A. Communications management

B. Process flow mapping

C. Value stream mapping

D. Task-network modeling

14. Hector's agile team just finished building, testing, and releasing 10 user story points in its most recent 4 week iteration. What is the team's velocity?

A. 10

B. 4

C. 5

D. 40

15. Hank's agile team is currently initiating a new project and determining which agile practices, standards, techniques it will use through the course of the project. What is Hank's agile team doing?

A. Process kindling

B. Process tailoring

C. Process adapting

D. Process initiating

16. Lisa is describing the four Agile Manifesto values to her co-workers. Which response lists one of its primary values?

A. Following a plan

B. Customer collaboration

C. Processes and tools

D. Contract negotiation

17. Select the response that holds the two backlogs that are used in an agile project.

A. Product backlog and sprint backlog

B. Product backlog and project backlog

C. Sprint backlog and scrum backlog

D. Sprint backlog and iteration backlog

18. What does performing frequent verification and validation help ensure?

A. Product schedule

B. Product quality

C. Product cost

D. Product value

19. Select the response that holds one layer of Highsmith's agile enterprise framework.

A. Portfolio governance layer

B. Risk management layer

C. Methodology management layer

D. Product layer

20. Which of the following holds one layer of Highsmith's agile enterprise framework.

A. Risk management layer

B. Project management layer

C. Product layer

D. Methodology management layer

21. Select the response that holds one layer of Highsmith's agile enterprise framework.

A. Product layer

B. Methodology management layer

C. Risk management layer

D. Iteration management layer

22. Of the following select the response that holds one layer of Highsmith's agile enterprise framework.

A. Technical practices layer

B. Risk management layer

C. Methodology management layer

D. Product layer

23. What are the four layers of Highsmith's agile enterprise framework?

A. Portfolio governance layer, Methodology management layer, iteration management layer, and the technical practices layer

B. Product layer, project management layer, iteration management layer, and the technical practices layer

C. Portfolio governance layer, project management layer, iteration management layer, and the technical practices layer

D. Portfolio governance layer, project management layer, risk management layer, and the technical practices layer

24. What person in the agile framework "serves as a coach, mentor, and counselor?"

A. Project leader

B. Product owner

C. Business analyst

D. Business executive

25. What is NOT a key agile project management characteristic?

A. Delegation of all tasks to team members by the project manager

B. Working with trusted, cross-functional team

C. Increasing product functionality with each iteration

D. Conveying information to the customer about iteration progress

26. When estimating the relative work effort required to develop a user story, the time allotted to each user story is typically Timeboxed. What is the typical Timeboxed value per user story?

A. Two to three minutes

B. 10 to 15 minutes

C. 5 to 15 minutes

D. 15 minutes

27. Of the following, which type of team is entrusted to take ownership of a product and make timely decisions?

A. Counter-alienation team

B. Empowered team

C. Engagement team

D. Engineering team

28. Identify the role in the following example user story: "As an online customer, I need to be able to search by product name and description so that I may add products to my shopping cart."

A. Description

B. Online customer

C. Shopping cart

D. Product name

29. Becky, as project leader, intends on building a high-performance team. What is a practice or technique she can use to build a high performance team?

A. Building in pressure

B. Working at a sustainable pace

C. Preventing the customer for interfering

D. Empowering the customer

30. The Crystal development process has four primary steps when building the project charter. What are the steps?

A. Choosing the product owner; Performing an Exploratory 360; Picking team conventions and practices; Building the initial project plan

B. Building the team; Performing an Exploratory 360; Fine tuning the methodology; Building the initial project plan

C. Building the team; Performing an Exploratory 360; Picking story points or ideal days; Building the initial project plan

D. Building the team; Performing an Exploratory 180; Picking team conventions and practices; Building the initial project plan

31. Thomas, his agile team, and the customer are building the product roadmap. When is it first created?

A. After the first iteration.

B. After the first release.

C. At the beginning of the project.

D. At the end of the project.

32. What agile artifact outlines the project's required investment cost?

A. Business case

B. Risk burndown chart

C. Kanban board

D. Product roadmap

33. High product quality is a cornerstone of the agile project management methodology, what process, performed frequently, helps ensure this standard?

A. Speculation

B. Release planning

C. Product roadmapping

D. Verification and validation

34. What are three essential elements of a user story?

A. Product, goal, process

B. Role, product, process

C. Role, goal, achieved business value

D. Role, goal, process

35. Select the response that holds the most secondary values per the Agile Manifesto.

A. Frequent 'customer-agile team' collaboration and short iteration durations

B. Products work as intended because of frequent delivery iterations

C. Documentation supports working software and appropriate processes and tools aid the development process

D. Customers must collaborate with the agile team to provide feedback and stakeholders must interact effectively to create business value

36. Select the response that holds a secondary value per the Agile Manifesto.

A. Contracts need to be negotiated and plans followed

B. Products work as intended because of frequent delivery iterations

C. Stakeholders must interact effectively to create business value

D. Customers must collaborate with the agile team to provide feedback

37. Gina's agile team is beginning a large, complex project estimated to last for three years. Her team has decided to only plan in detail for the next few iterations and keep iterations further removed at only a high-level of detail. What type of planning technique is Gina's team using?

A. Progressive wave planning

B. Release planning

C. Progressive elaboration

D. Rolling wave planning

38. Affinity planning, where agile team members and product owners assemble to order and categorize user stories, is an example of:

A. An assessment decision model

B. A participatory decision model

C. A preemptive decision model

D. A risk-based decision model

39. An agile task board usually tracks the progress of what key piece of information?

A. Tasks based on user stories

B. Defects

C. Test modules

D. Project backlog lists

40. In which step of the project chartering activity of the Crystal development methodology is project soundness evaluated?

A. Exploratory 360

B. Team convention and standards assignment

C. Team formation

D. Project plan definition

PMI-ACP Lite Mock Exam 15 Answer Key and Explanations

1. D - Highsmith defines adaptive leadership as two dimensional: Being agile and doing agile. Being agile includes focusing on cornerstones of agile project management, like incremental delivery, continuous integration, and adapting to changing requirements. Doing agile includes several activities that an agile leader must do: do less; speed-to-value, quality, and engage and inspire. [Agile Project Management: Creating Innovative Products – 2nd Edition. Jim Highsmith.] [Soft skills negotiation]

2. C - A user story is written with three essential elements: a role, a goal, and an achieved business value. It typically takes the form of: "As a , I need to , so that I can ." A simple example is, "As an online customer, I need to be able to search by product name and description so that I may add products to my shopping cart." [User Stories Applied: For Agile Software Development. Mike Cohn.] [Agile analysis and design]

3. C - A user story is written with three essential elements: a role, a goal, and an achieved business value. It typically takes the form of: "As a , I need to , so that I can ." A simple example is, "As an online customer, I need to be able to search by product name and description so that I may add products to my shopping cart." [User Stories Applied: For Agile Software Development. Mike Cohn.] [Agile analysis and design]

4. C - Literally thousands of decisions are made in the course of a project. Many of these decisions are made in response to problems that inevitably arise and confront the agile team. Therefore it is essential that an agile team is properly versed in problem-solving strategies, tools, and techniques. Some common problem-solving techniques include: ask it loud; revisit the problem; 5Y; sunk cost fallacy; devil's advocate; be kind, rewind; asking probing questions; and reflective/active listening. [Agile Retrospectives: Making Good Teams Great. Esther Derby, Diana Larsen, Ken Schwaber.] [Knowledge and Skills: Level 1]

5. C - Having a motivated team is essential for any project, regardless of whether it is agile or not. Motivated teams work together better, have strong productivity, and exceed expectations. Some simple steps to increase motivation are 1) spending quality time together; where team members get to know one another on a personal level to build a sense of community, 2) providing feedback, mentoring and coaching; where team members are congratulated and thanked on jobs well done and also mentored or coached to improve in skill and capability, and 3) empowerment; where the team is empowered to make many key decisions which, along the way, builds trust and shows that leadership believes in the capabilities of the team. [The Art of Agile Development. James Shore.] [Knowledge and Skills: Level 1]

6. D - Jim Highsmith's agile project management model consists of the following five phases: Envisioning, speculating, exploring, adapting, and closing. [Agile Project Management: Creating Innovative Products – 2nd Edition. Jim Highsmith.] [Knowledge and Skills: Level 1]

7. B - Scrum is generally considered to be modeled after XP and shares many similar concepts and techniques. [User Stories Applied: For Agile Software Development. Mike Cohn.] [Knowledge and Skills: Level 2]

8. B - Highsmith defines adaptive leadership as two dimensional: Being agile and doing agile. Being agile includes focusing on cornerstones of agile project management, like incremental delivery, continuous integration, and adapting to changing requirements. Doing agile includes several activities that an agile leader must do: do less; speed-to-value, quality, and engage and inspire. [Agile Project Management: Creating Innovative Products – 2nd Edition. Jim Highsmith.] [Soft skills negotiation]

9. A - Net Present Value: A metric used to analyze the profitability of an investment or project. NPV is the difference between the present value of cash inflows and the present value of cash outflows. NPV considers the likelihood of future cash inflows that an investment or project will yield. NPV is the sum of each cash inflow/outflow for the expected duration of the investment. Each cash inflow/outflow is discounted back to its present value (PV) (i.e.,, what the money is worth in terms of today's value). NPV is the sum of all terms: NPV = Sum of [Rt/(1 + i)^t] where t = the time of the cash flow, i = the discount rate (the rate of return that could be earned on in the financial markets) , and Rt = the net cash inflow or outflow. For example, consider the following two year period. The discount rate is 5% and the initial investment cost is $500. At the end of the first year, a $200 inflow is expected. At the end of the second year, a $1,000 is expected. NPV = -500 + 200/(1.05)^1 + 1000/(1.05)^2 = ~$597. If NPV is positive, it indicates that the investment will add value to the buyer's portfolio. If NPV is negative, it will subtract value. If NPV is zero, it will neither add or subtract value. [Agile Estimating and Planning. Mike Cohn.] [Value based prioritization]

10. D - The product backlog serves as the common bridge or connection between the product owner and team. [Lean-Agile Software Development: Achieving Enterprise Agility. Alan Shalloway, Guy Beaver, James R. Trott.] [Knowledge and Skills: Level 2]

11. C - Agile project management places strong emphasis on 'continuous improvement.' Continuous improvement processes are built into the agile methodology, from customers providing feedback after each iteration to the team reserving time to reflect on its performance through retrospectives after each iteration. Ongoing unit and integration testing and keeping up with technological/industry developments also play a part in the continuous improvement process. Continuous improvement is also a key principle in the lean methodology, where a focus of removing waste from the value stream is held. [The Art of Agile Development. James Shore.] [Knowledge and Skills: Level 2]

12. A - A warm, welcoming environment that promotes effective communication, innovation, and motivated team members is an important aspect to consider when designing team space. Guidelines for a better agile team space include: collocation of team members; reduction of non-essential noise/distractions; dedicated

whiteboard and wall space for information radiators; space for the daily stand-up meeting and other meetings; pairing workstations; and other pleasantries like plants and comfortable furniture. [Agile Retrospectives: Making Good Teams Great. Esther Derby, Diana Larsen, Ken Schwaber.] [Communications]

13. A - Effective communication is a cornerstone of agile. Communication is the act of transferring information among various parties. Communications management is a knowledge and skill area of agile that highlights this importance. PMI has several definitions regarding communications management and agile builds on top of these to add its own perspective: 1) Communications Planning: Determining the information and communication needs of the projects stakeholders 2) Information Distribution: Making needed information available to project stakeholders in a timely manner, 3) Performance Reporting: Collecting and distributing performance information. This includes status reporting, progress measurement, and forecasting, and 4) Managing Stakeholders: Managing communications to satisfy the requirements and resolve issues with project stakeholders. From an agile perspective: communication among the team is built into the process and facilitated through collocation, information radiators, daily stand-up meetings, retrospectives etc.; Although it is hoped that the product owner, customer, and user can be heavily involved with the project and also use these communication techniques, a plan for conveying information to stakeholders may be needed if this is not the case. [Agile Software Development: The Cooperative Game – 2nd Edition. Alistair Cockburn.] [Knowledge and Skills: Level 1]

14. A - Velocity is a measure of the number of user story points completed per iteration. An agile team can use its previous velocity recordings as a method of estimating how many user story points it may complete in the next iteration. David's team's velocity is 10. [Agile Estimating and Planning. Mike Cohn.] [Metrics]

15. B - When initiating a new agile development effort the project team should determine its agile approach. This is also known as process tailoring, where the agile team determines which agile practices or standards it will follow for the project, like whether it will hold a daily stand-up meeting and what its duration will be, whether it will use any information radiators, how it will estimate and plan for product features, etc. [Agile Software Development: The Cooperative Game – 2nd Edition. Alistair Cockburn.] [Planning, monitoring, and adapting]

16. B - The Agile Manifesto defines four values. The four values list primary values and secondary values, with primary values superseding secondary values. The values are 1) individuals and interactions over processes and tools, 2) working software over comprehensive documentation, 3) customer collaboration over contract negotiation, and 4) responding to change over following a plan. [Manifesto for Agile Software Development. Agile Alliance.] [Knowledge and Skills: Level 1]

17. A - The two backlogs found on agile projects are the product backlog and the sprint/iteration backlog [Lean-Agile Software Development: Achieving

Enterprise Agility. Alan Shalloway, Guy Beaver, James R. Trott.] [Agile analysis and design]

18. B - Because each iteration typically produces a working product that is built and integrated and iterations are typically two to four weeks in length, there is frequent verification and validation to ensure product quality. Verification is the confirmation that a product performs as specified by a customer (e.g. as indicated by a user story) and validation is the confirmation that a product behaves as desired (i.e., meets the customer's need). Sometimes a product may be built and integrated to specification - that is, it can be verified - but it does not meet the intent of the customer - that is, it cannot be validated. [Agile Software Development: The Cooperative Game – 2nd Edition. Alistair Cockburn.] [Product quality]

19. A - The four layers of Highsmith's agile enterprise framework include the: portfolio governance layer, project management layer, iteration management layer, and the technical practices layer. [Agile Project Management: Creating Innovative Products – 2nd Edition. Jim Highsmith.] [Knowledge and Skills: Level 3]

20. B - The four layers of Highsmith's agile enterprise framework include the: portfolio governance layer, project management layer, iteration management layer, and the technical practices layer. [Agile Project Management: Creating Innovative Products – 2nd Edition. Jim Highsmith.] [Knowledge and Skills: Level 3]

21. D - The four layers of Highsmith's agile enterprise framework include the: portfolio governance layer, project management layer, iteration management layer, and the technical practices layer. [Agile Project Management: Creating Innovative Products – 2nd Edition. Jim Highsmith.] [Knowledge and Skills: Level 3]

22. A - The four layers of Highsmith's agile enterprise framework include the: portfolio governance layer, project management layer, iteration management layer, and the technical practices layer. [Agile Project Management: Creating Innovative Products – 2nd Edition. Jim Highsmith.] [Knowledge and Skills: Level 3]

23. C - The four layers of Highsmith's agile enterprise framework include the: portfolio governance layer, project management layer, iteration management layer, and the technical practices layer. [Agile Project Management: Creating Innovative Products – 2nd Edition. Jim Highsmith.] [Knowledge and Skills: Level 3]

24. A - A common misconception in agile is that an agile team does not need a leader. In fact, all agile teams need a leader, but the way in which the leader leads is fundamentally different than the typical traditional project manager/project leader method. Some have theorized that this misconception stems from the desired 'self-organizing' quality of the agile team. And although the 'self-organizing' agile team is empowered to take ownership and responsibility of the product and make some decisions itself, it nevertheless requires a leader to help provide guidance, mentoring, coaching, problem solving, and decision making. Some key aspects required of an agile leader include: empowering team members to decide what standard agile practices and methods it will use; allowing the team to be self-organized and self-disciplined; empowering the team members to make decisions collaboratively with the customer; inspire the team to be innovative and explore new ideas and technology capabilities; be a champion of and articulate the product vision to team members so it will be motivated to accomplish the overall objective; remove any obstacles and solve any problems the team may face in its effort; communicate and endorse the values and principles of agile project management to stakeholders that may be unfamiliar with agile; ensure that all stakeholders, including business managers and developers, are collaborating effectively; and, be able to adapt the leadership style to the working environment to ensure that the agile values and principles are effectively upheld. [The Art of Agile Development. James Shore.] [Knowledge and Skills: Level 1]

25. A - Agile teams should be self-organizing and not have tasks delegated upon. The Agile Manifesto defines four values and 12 supporting principles. The values are 1) individuals and interactions over processes and tools, 2) working software over comprehensive documentation, 3) customer collaboration over contract negotiation, and 4) responding to change over following a plan. Agile principles include 1) focusing on satisfying the customer, 2) welcoming change, 3) delivering working software frequently, 4) ensuring that business people and developers work together, 5) motivating the individuals involved in development, 6) using face-to-face communication whenever possible, 7) using working software as the primary measure of progress, 8) maintaining a constant pace of development, 9) paying continuous attention to technical excellence and good design, 10) aiming for simplicity, 11) using self-organizing teams, and 12) regularly reflecting on how to become more effective. [Manifesto for Agile Software Development. Agile Alliance.] [Knowledge and Skills: Level 1]

26. A - Two to three minutes is a typical time-boxed value for discussing user stories when playing planning poker. [Agile Estimating and Planning. Mike Cohn.] [Agile estimation]

27. B - Empowered teams - ones that are self-organizing and know how to solve problems with minimal management involvement - are a cornerstone of the agile methodology. This is the antithesis to the classic viewpoint of the traditional project manager who is seen as someone that controls all decisions and delegates tasks to a team with little feedback. An agile team must include all members and stakeholders to make decisions, and make decisions expediently. Because it is essential that the user/customer be involved with development, it is encouraged that the user/customer is closely integrated with the agile team with collocation/on-site support being ideal. An agile team feels empowered when it collectively assumes responsibility for the delivery of the product (i.e., taking ownership). [Coaching Agile Teams. Lyssa Adkins.] [Knowledge and Skills: Level 1]

28. B - A user story is written with three essential elements: a role, a goal, and an achieved business value. It typically takes the form of: "As a , I need to , so that I can ." A simple example is, "As an online customer, I need to be able to search by product name and description so that I may add products to my shopping cart." [User Stories Applied: For Agile Software

Development. Mike Cohn.] [Agile analysis and design]

29. B - Building a high-performance team is critical to any project's success. A high performance team has the right team members, is empowered, has built trust, works at a sustainable pace, has consistently high velocity/productivity, takes regular time for reflection to review work, has a team lead that removes any obstacles and provides mentoring and coaching, is self-organized and self-disciplined, and is collocated. Several management techniques can be used to build or foster a high-performance team environment, some techniques include: removing obstacles that slow down a team's performance, having high expectations of team performance, and coaching and mentoring the team to achieve its best performance. [Coaching Agile Teams. Lyssa Adkins.] [Knowledge and Skills: Level 2]

30. B - The Crystal development process is cyclical/iterative. Its primary components are chartering, delivery cycles, and project wrap-up. Chartering involves creating a project charter, which can last from a few days to a few weeks. Chartering consists of four activities: 1) Building the core project team, 2) performing an Exploratory 360° assessment, 3) fine tuning the methodology, and 3) building the initial project plan. [Agile Software Development: The Cooperative Game – 2nd Edition. Alistair Cockburn.] [Agile analysis and design]

31. C - The product roadmap - owned by the product owner - serves as a high level overview of the product requirements. It is used as a tool for prioritizing features , organizing features into categories, and assigning rough time frames. Creating a product roadmap has four basic steps: 1) Identify requirements (these will become part of the product backlog), 2) Organize requirements into categories or themes, 3) Estimate relative work effort (e.g., planning poker or affinity estimation) and prioritize (value), and 4) Estimate rough time frames (estimate velocity, sprint duration, and rough release dates). [The Art of Agile Development. James Shore.] [Agile analysis and design]

32. A - Business case development is an important initial step in agile project management. The business case is a concise document that outlines the project's vision, goals, strategies for achieving goals, milestones, required investment and expected return/payback. A business case articulates the why and how a project will deliver value to a customer. [Lean-Agile Software Development: Achieving Enterprise Agility. Alan Shalloway, Guy Beaver, James R. Trott.] [Knowledge and Skills: Level 2]

33. D - Because each iteration typically produces a working product that is built and integrated and iterations are typically two to four weeks in length, there is frequent verification and validation to ensure product quality. Verification is the confirmation that a product performs as specified by a customer (e.g. as indicated by a user story) and validation is the confirmation that a product behaves as desired (i.e., meets the customer's need). Sometimes a product may be built and integrated to specification - that is, it can be verified - but it does not meet the intent of the customer - that is, it cannot be validated. [Agile Software Development: The

Cooperative Game – 2nd Edition. Alistair Cockburn.] [Product quality]

34. C - A user story is written with three essential elements: a role, a goal, and an achieved business value. It typically takes the form of: "As a , I need to , so that I can ." A simple example is, "As an online customer, I need to be able to search by product name and description so that I may add products to my shopping cart." [User Stories Applied: For Agile Software Development. Mike Cohn.] [Agile analysis and design]

35. C - The agile secondary values include: documentation of software, processes and tools, contract negotiation, and following project plans. [Manifesto for Agile Software Development. Agile Alliance.] [Knowledge and Skills: Level 1]

36. A - The agile secondary values include: documentation of software, processes and tools, contract negotiation, and following project plans. [Manifesto for Agile Software Development. Agile Alliance.] [Knowledge and Skills: Level 1]

37. D - Rolling wave planning (or rolling look ahead planning) involves planning in waves or phases and is especially useful for large, complex projects. Only the next few iterations are planned in detail and iterations more distant are planned only at a high-level. Progressive elaboration is continuous planning that assumes that details and requirements will be better refined later and will be incorporated into the planning process at the appropriate time. [Agile Estimating and Planning. Mike Cohn.] [Agile analysis and design]

38. B - To build trust among the team, agile believes heavily in participatory decision models where team members collaborate to make decisions. Although a team leader or scrum master will need to make some decisions individually, many decisions can be made by the team collectively. These agile principles are also known as collective ownership, self-organization, and self-discipline. In collective ownership, the team members are equally responsible for project results and are empowered to participate in decision making and problem solving processes. [Agile Retrospectives: Making Good Teams Great. Esther Derby, Diana Larsen, Ken Schwaber.] [Knowledge and Skills: Level 2]

39. A - Typical agile task boards track and monitor tasks that have been chosen for the active iteration. One column holds all the tasks selected for development during the iteration. Each task has an associated card which is placed in one of several other columns on the task board – such as 'To do,' 'In progress,' 'Ready for testing,' and 'Done' – according to current task status. Different teams may use variations of these columns, depending on project needs and their preferences. [Lean-Agile Software Development: Achieving Enterprise Agility. Alan Shalloway, Guy Beaver, James R. Trott.] [Planning, monitoring, and adapting]

40. A - The Crystal development process is cyclical/iterative. Its primary components are chartering, delivery cycles, and project wrap-up. Chartering involves creating a project charter, which can last from a few days to a few weeks. Chartering consists of four activities: 1) Building the core project team, 2) performing an Exploratory 360° assessment, 3) fine tuning the methodology, and 3) building the initial project plan. [Agile Software Development: The Cooperative Game – 2nd Edition. Alistair Cockburn.] [Agile analysis and design]

Knowledge Area Quiz Knowledge and Skills: Level 1 Practice Questions

Test Name: Knowledge Area Test: Knowledge and Skills: Level 1
Total Questions: 15
Correct Answers Needed to Pass: 11 (73.33%)
Time Allowed: 25 Minutes

Test Description

This practice quiz specifically targets your knowledge of the Knowledge and Skills: Level 1 exam topic area.

Test Questions

1. Lisa is describing the four Agile Manifesto values to her co-workers. Of the following, which response lists two of the four values?

A. 1) Customer collaboration over contract negotiation, and 2) Responding to change over following a plan.

B. 1) Customer collaboration over contract negotiation, and 2) Following a plan over responding to change.

C. 1) Contract negotiation over customer collaboration, and 2) Responding to change over following a plan.

D. 1) Teams and interactions over processes and tools, 2) Working software over comprehensive documentation

2. Lisa is describing the four Agile Manifesto values to her co-workers. Which response lists two of the four values?

A. 1) Team member collaboration over contract negotiation, and 2) Responding to change over following a plan.

B. 1) Individuals and interactions over processes and tools, 2) Working software over comprehensive documentation

C. 1) Teams and interactions over processes and tools, 2) Working software over comprehensive documentation

D. 1) Customer collaboration over contract negotiation, and 2) Following a plan over responding to change.

3. Which of the following is the best definition of brainstorming?

A. A collaborative activity held for the purpose of reviewing user stories.

B. An individual exercise performed for the purpose of generating ideas.

C. A collaborative activity held for the purpose of generating ideas.

D. A formal meeting led by a project leader to introduce previously defined ideas.

4. Select a technique that promotes agile 'knowledge sharing.'

A. A high specialized team

B. A team composed of generalized specialists

C. A uni-functional team

D. A monolithic team

5. Which of the following lists a key agile project management characteristic?

A. Incremental development of products and services

B. A singular-dimensioned team consisting of highly specialized experts all of the same skill

C. Short iterations and the use of baselines for strict schedule and budget control

D. Detailed change management processes

6. Juan is listening to an agile project management brief at the annual agile capstone conference. The speaker's topic is empowered teams. What does an empowered team mean?

A. A team that is self-organizing, cross-functional and can manage itself with little external influence.

B. A team that is profit-oriented and focused solely on meeting cost and schedule constraints.

C. A team that relies on external management to give it direction.

D. A team that is capable of exceeding sustainable development velocities in "power" iterations to meet backlog goals.

7. Which of the following is the best definition of 'feedback technique?'

A. A technique used in extreme programming to provide criticism of coding syntax.

B. A technique that facilitates constructive criticism to improve product quality and value.

C. A technique used in paired programming to provide criticism of coding syntax.

D. A technique that facilitates ever increasing amounts of spectral magnitude.

8. Of the following responses, which is NOT a community value per the PMI agile community of practice community charter?

A. Adaptability

B. Leading Change

C. Openness

D. Commandeering

9. What phase do both Highsmith's agile project management and traditional project management share?

A. Speculating

B. Closing

C. Adapting

D. Executing

10. Select the first phase of Jim Highsmith's agile project management model.

A. Envisioning

B. Closing

C. Adapting

D. Exploring

11. Jerry has just entered Highsmith's agile project management closing phase. What are he and his team focusing on?

A. Completing all outstanding project work, like recording lessons learned and performing other tasks with the product release

B. Making adjustments to the feature breakdown structure specification

C. Adapting product features to customer feedback

D. Adapting project plans for the next iteration

12. As project leader of an agile effort, in Highsmith's agile project management adapting phase you are expected to make adjustments. What are some of the types of adjustments that a project leader may perform in the adapting phase?

A. Adjustments to the cost sheet

B. Adjustments to any team dynamics, like handling problems raised by team members

C. Adjustments to the feature breakdown structure specification

D. Adjustments to software licenses

13. While Gerald is discussing to Lisa his take on the most prominent risks the project is facing, Lisa uses encouraging body language. What type of listening technique is Lisa using?

A. Excited

B. Alert

C. Tuned

D. Active

14. Ryan as project leader, has been discussing the importance of 'stakeholder management' with his team. Why is stakeholder management so important?

A. An agile project relies on the monitoring and controlling of stakeholders.

B. An agile project relies on active participation from its stakeholders.

C. An agile project relies on the absence of participation of stakeholders.

D. An agile project relies on the intermittent participation of stakeholders.

15. Which of the following is the best definition of 'feedback?'

A. A maturing process where future innovation is taken into consideration.

B. A dynamic process where past information influences the future behavior of the same process.

C. An evolving process where past information is disregarded.

D. A static process where future information stagnates the previous behavior of the same process.

Knowledge Area Quiz
Knowledge and Skills: Level 1
Answer Key and Explanations

1. A - The Agile Manifesto defines four values. The four values list primary values and secondary values, with primary values superseding secondary values. The values are 1) individuals and interactions over processes and tools, 2) working software over comprehensive documentation, 3) customer collaboration over contract negotiation, and 4) responding to change over following a plan. [Manifesto for Agile Software Development. Agile Alliance.] [Knowledge and Skills: Level 1]

2. B - The Agile Manifesto defines four values. The four values list primary values and secondary values, with primary values superseding secondary values. The values are 1) individuals and interactions over processes and tools, 2) working software over comprehensive documentation, 3) customer collaboration over contract negotiation, and 4) responding to change over following a plan. [Manifesto for Agile Software Development. Agile Alliance.] [Knowledge and Skills: Level 1]

3. C - Brainstorming is a group activity held for the purpose of generating new ideas. The idea is that through collaboration, a team can generate more potentially valuable ideas than an individual, while at the same time forming a positive bonding experience for the team. [Agile Retrospectives: Making Good Teams Great. Esther Derby, Diana Larsen, Ken Schwaber.] [Knowledge and Skills: Level 1]

4. B - In agile, effective 'knowledge sharing' is a critical factor for success. It involves the near real time communication of key information among all team members and stakeholders. To promote knowledge sharing, agile uses standard practices built into its process, such as using generalized specialists/cross functional teams, self-organizing and self-disciplined teams, collocation, daily stand-up meetings, iteration/sprint planning, release planning, pair programming and pair rotation, project retrospectives/reflection, and on-site customer support. And, of course, the sixth principle of Agile is " The most efficient and effective method of conveying information to and within a development team is face-to-face conversation." In this sense, Agile prefers and encourages collocation for all stakeholders and team members for the simple fact that face-to-face conversation is the best method of communication and, in turn, effective knowledge sharing. [Becoming Agile: ...in an imperfect world. Greg Smith, Ahmed Sidky.] [Knowledge and Skills: Level 1]

5. A - Key characteristics of agile project management include: continuous improvement, cross-functional teams, short iterations, an incremental approach, and business priorities and customer value. [The Art of Agile Development. James Shore.] [Knowledge and Skills: Level 1]

6. A - Empowered teams - ones that are self-organizing and know how to solve problems with minimal management involvement - are a cornerstone of the agile methodology. An agile team feels empowered when it collectively assumes responsibility for the delivery of the product (i.e., taking ownership). [Coaching Agile Teams. Lyssa Adkins.] [Knowledge and Skills: Level 1]

7. B - There are several feedback techniques - techniques that facilitate constructive criticism to improve product value and quality - built into the agile process. In the classic definition, feedback is a dynamic process where past information influences the behavior of the same process in the future. Agile feedback techniques include prototyping, simulation, demonstration, evaluations, pair programming, unit testing, continuous integration, daily stand-up meetings, sprint planning. Because agile prides itself on a transparent and collaborative environment, feedback is essentially ubiquitous. [Agile Retrospectives: Making Good Teams Great. Esther Derby, Diana Larsen, Ken Schwaber.] [Knowledge and Skills: Level 1]

8. D - The following are community values of the PMI agile community of practice community charter: Vision, Servant Leadership, Trust, Collaboration, Honesty, Learning, Courage, Openness, Adaptability, Leading Change, Transparency [PMI Agile Community of Practice Community Charter. Project Management Institute.] [Knowledge and Skills: Level 1]

9. B - The agile and traditional project management methods share closing as a phase name. Closing occurs as the last phase in both methods. [Agile Project Management: Creating Innovative Products – 2nd Edition. Jim Highsmith.] [Knowledge and Skills: Level 1]

10. A - Jim Highsmith's agile project management model consists of the following sequential five phases: Envisioning, speculating, exploring, adapting, and closing. [Agile Project Management: Creating Innovative Products – 2nd Edition. Jim Highsmith.] [Knowledge and Skills: Level 1]

11. A - In the closing phase, the agile team completes all remaining project work. In a software project, remaining work can be such tasks as user training documentation and installation manuals. [Agile Project Management: Creating Innovative Products – 2nd Edition. Jim Highsmith.] [Knowledge and Skills: Level 1]

12. B - In the adapting phase, the agile team leader may make adjustments to the team makeup, like problems raised by team members, if any team dynamic problems arise. [Agile Project Management: Creating Innovative Products – 2nd Edition. Jim Highsmith.] [Knowledge and Skills: Level 1]

13. D - One communication technique to reduce misunderstanding and miscommunication is active listening. A well run agile project necessitates both good listeners and communicators, active listening helps work towards both of these necessities. The basics of active listening include: 1) Being present and focusing your attention on the speaker. 2) Taking notes instead of interrupting. 3) Paraphrasing to confirm and review what you have heard. 4) Summarizing the conversation once it has concluded for posterity. Using open ended questions, good body language, and silence can help improve listening skills. [Coaching Agile Teams. Lyssa Adkins.] [Knowledge and Skills: Level 1]

14. B - Stakeholder management is a growing topic area within strategic management that brings awareness to the importance of managing stakeholders (i.e., facilitating active participation of stakeholders and fostering a strong collaborative

environment) for a project's success. Stakeholder management is typically defined in the context of guiding principles and values. R. E. Freeman's 'Managing for Stakeholders' includes 10 principles: 1) Stakeholder interests need to go together over time. 2) We need a philosophy of volunteerism – to engage stakeholders and manage relationships ourselves rather than leave it to government. 3) We need to find solutions to issues that satisfy multiple stakeholders simultaneously. 4) Everything that we do serves stakeholders. We never trade off the interests of one versus the other continuously over time. 5) We act with purpose that fulfills our commitment to stakeholders. We act with aspiration towards fulfilling our dreams and theirs. 6) We need intensive communication and dialogue with stakeholders – not just those who are friendly. 7)Stakeholders consist of real people with names and faces and children. They are complex. 8)We need to generalize the marketing approach. 9) We engage with both primary and secondary stakeholders. 10) We constantly monitor and redesign processes to make them better serve our stakeholders. Because stakeholder involvement is critical for the success of a project, where projects without active participation from stakeholders are prone to failure, stakeholder management should be a topic that every agile team knows well. [The Art of Agile Development. James Shore.] [Knowledge and Skills: Level 1]

15. B - There are several feedback techniques - techniques that facilitate constructive criticism to improve product value and quality - built into the agile process. In the classic definition, feedback is a dynamic process where past information influences the behavior of the same process in the future. Agile feedback techniques include prototyping, simulation, demonstration, evaluations, pair programming, unit testing, continuous integration, daily stand-up meetings, sprint planning. Because agile prides itself on a transparent and collaborative environment, feedback is essentially ubiquitous. [Agile Retrospectives: Making Good Teams Great. Esther Derby, Diana Larsen, Ken Schwaber.] [Knowledge and Skills: Level 1]

PMI-ACP Lite Mock Exam 16 Practice Questions

Test Name: PMI-ACP Lite Mock Exam 16
Total Questions: 40
Correct Answers Needed to Pass:
30 (75.00%)
Time Allowed: 60 Minutes

Test Description

This is a cumulative PMI-ACP Mock Exam which can be used as a benchmark for your PMI-ACP aptitude. This practice test includes questions from all exam topic areas, including sections from Agile Tools and Techniques, and all three Agile Knowledge and Skills areas.

Test Questions

1. According to Highsmith, in governing agile projects, executives are most interested in which of the following project details?

A. Project retrograde

B. Project vision and scope

C. Investment performance and risk

D. Follow-on business

2. In Highsmith's agile project management speculation phase you develop which of the following?

A. Project schedule

B. Feature breakdown structure

C. Estimated iteration and release plans

D. Project vision

3. Tom is currently executing the speculation phase of Highsmith's agile project management model. In addition to estimating iteration and release plans, what else will Tom be developing?

A. Project requirements

B. Feature breakdown and a rough project plan

C. Project schedule and constraints

D. Project vision and scope

4. In agile and other project management styles, team motivation is a critical factor for success. What is one method to improve team motivation?

A. Providing minimal structure.

B. Providing minimal leadership.

C. Providing mentoring.

D. Providing a platform to focus on personal deficiencies.

5. What is an essential knowledge and skill area of the agile team?

A. Problem-mitigation techniques

B. Problem-prioritization techniques

C. Problem-first techniques

D. Problem-solving techniques

6. Which of the following duties is expected of a servant leader?

A. Providing product insight.

B. Providing support.

C. User story authoring.

D. Burndown charting.

7. What type of delivery style ensures that a customer or product owner has the chance to review a working product that is improved in intervals and ready for feedback frequently?

A. Push delivery

B. Incremental delivery

C. Pull delivery

D. Lead time delivery

8. Henrietta is managing an agile effort and her team, although on the company campus, is separated over several offices. What might Henrietta strive to do to improve communication?

A. Push for a remote working environment

B. Push for more overtime

C. Push for moving the daily scrum to a weekly scrum

D. Push for collocating the team

9. The traditional iron triangle includes which of the following parameters?

A. Constraints

B. Schedule

C. Value

D. Quality

10. According to Highsmith, agility is the ability to balance

A. quality and value

B. change and planning

C. flexibility and stability

D. constraints and value

11. Gerald is working on a multi-national agile project. What is one thing Gerald should be sensitive of in a multi-national effort?

A. Cultural norms and social customs

B. Quality differences

C. Risk-based spike tasks

D. Product burndown charts

12. Select a common agile framework/methodology.

A. Feature driven development (FDD)

B. Quality driven development (QDD)

C. Product driven development (PDD)

D. Data driven development (DDD)

13. Andy always makes sure he invites a diverse audience when he holds Kaizen events. Having a diverse audience is generally considered a

A. Facilitation method

B. Waste reduction method

C. Yokoten method

D. Quality stream method

14. When an agile team decomposes user stories into tasks and prioritizes them based on value what is the process called?

A. Agile-based decomposition and prioritization.

B. Risk-based decomposition and prioritization

C. Quality-based decomposition and prioritization.

D. Value-based decomposition and prioritization.

15. When an agile team decomposes user stories into tasks and prioritizes them based on risk what is the process called?

A. Risk-based decomposition and prioritization

B. Quality-based decomposition and prioritization.

C. Agile-based decomposition and prioritization.

D. Risk-based decomposition and prioritization.

16. Quinn is estimating the amount of days it will take him to develop a user story. In his estimate he is considering holidays, non-working days, possibilities of delays, and the possibility that other developers on the team may help with the user story. If Quinn is using ideal days to estimate the relative work effort of the user story, what is he doing incorrectly?

A. Quinn is considering multiple-developer involvement when he should be considering single-developer involvement only.

B. Quinn is forgetting to also consider coding obstacles in his estimate.

C. Quinn is forgetting to consider the positive impact that reflection will have on the team's productivity.

D. Quinn is considering non-working days, delays, and multiple-developer involvement, which should be excluded when estimating work effort using ideal days.

17. In agile modeling, what is a poor example of a name given to a persona?

A. Ralph West

B. End user

C. Oscar Gill

D. Veronica Poolie

18. Select a key element of a project charter?

A. Success criteria

B. Risk-to-value matrix

C. Planned value

D. Rate of return

19. Select the response that defines an information radiator.

A. A visual representation of project-related data to illustrate project status.

B. A schema for organizing information into related datum.

C. A highly detailed section of the agile project management waterfall plan.

D. Raw data organized into information to show data access and modification dates.

20. Christy is confused about the purpose of a product roadmap. She asks Thomas, her project manager, to identify a benefit of a product roadmap to help her understand a product roadmaps purpose. Select the benefit of a product roadmap.

A. Helps facilitate iteration development.

B. Helps facilitate daily stand-up meetings.

C. Helps facilitate the assignment of rough time frames

D. Helps facilitate reflection meetings.

21. Which communication technique values silence just as much as speaking to reduce miscommunication and misunderstanding?

A. Mime

B. Gesture

C. Active

D. Reactive

22. Bob is reviewing the upcoming user stories for the next iteration. He notices that there will be a few tasks with high risk. What is a risk management technique Bob and his agile team can use to reduce risk?

A. Risk-based spike tasks.

B. Risk-based set tasks.

C. Risk-based bump tasks.

D. Risk-based slam tasks.

23. What is an iteration backlog?

A. A list of all product features to be developed in a release.

B. A list of the product features to be developed in an iteration.

C. A list of possible product features to be developed in an iteration.

D. A list of product features.

24. Jules is describing the SMART acronym used for task analysis in an agile seminar. What does the R stand for?

A. Realistic

B. Ready

C. Rule-based

D. Relevant

25. If a product owner must expedite the release of a product, what two options are available to him or her to advance the release date?

A. Reducing the number of features released and increasing the depth, or complexity, of features.

B. Reducing the number of features released and reducing the depth, or complexity, of features.

C. Increasing the number of features released and increasing the depth, or complexity, of features.

D. Reducing the number of features released and increasing the depth, or complexity, of features.

26. What type of testing is encouraged throughout an agile project on completed software to test system design and potentially identify new features that may add value to the product?

A. Refactor testing

B. Exploratory testing

C. Interface testing

D. Unit testing

27. TDD has four basic steps. What is the second step in TDD?

A. Write product code and apply the test

B. Refactor the product code

C. Verify and validate that the test fails

D. Write test code that will fail

28. TDD has four basic steps. What is the third step in TDD?

A. Write test code that will fail

B. Verify and validate that the test fails

C. Refactor the product code

D. Write product code and apply the test

29. Jill, as project lead, has been using coaching to help mentor her team to improve its performance. What is Jill doing when she provides coaching?

A. Motivating the team

B. Mobilizing the team

C. Guiding the team

D. Refactoring the team

30. Neve and her agile team are dividing user stories into smaller, manageable tasks. What is this process called?

A. Task assessment

B. Reflection

C. Decomposition

D. Incremental design

31. One of the twelve agile principles is termed 'reflection.' What does 'reflection' mean?

A. Reflection refers to the process of improving code to make it more efficient.

B. Reflection refers to making a regular habit of reviewing team performance and processes to identify opportunities for improvement.

C. Reflection refers to accessing attributes of a program's metadata.

D. Reflection refers to reflecting product requirements back at the customer through the delivery of working software.

32. From the following, select a technique that promotes agile 'knowledge sharing.'

A. sprint roadmap

B. Project roadmap

C. Reflection roadmap

D. Product roadmap

33. Andy, as project leader, has been building a sense of community among his team by focusing, in part, on making sure each team member receives some quality time attention. What is Andy doing when he makes sure quality time is being spent?

A. Motivating the team

B. Leading the team

C. Guiding the team

D. Reforming the team

34. What is the process called when a person performs a self-assessment to understand how he or she may improve performance?

A. Returning

B. Reimaging

C. Refactoring

D. Reflection

35. Nathan, a new agile practitioner, is at a planning event where the relative development effort of user stories of a large product backlog is to be estimated. The planning event is mostly conducted in silence and the team is to assign user stories to various t-shirt sizes (small, medium, large, extra-large). The planning event is efficient and the user stories are estimated quickly. What type of planning event is Nathan most likely attending?

A. T-shirt estimating

B. Infinity estimating

C. Affinity estimating

D. Relative estimating

36. When information is shared between collocated team members unconsciously, it is known as?

A. Osmotic communication

B. Active listening

C. Chaordic communication

D. Entropic communication

37. Ryan and his agile team are subdividing user stories into manageable tasks to help plan the upcoming sprint. What is this process called?

A. Meta-tasking

B. Decomposition

C. Front end analysis

D. Refactoring

38. When value stream mapping it is important to identify areas of waste that exist in the process. The pneumonic device WIDETOM may be used to remember the different forms of muda (or waste). What does the W in WIDETOM stand for with respect to waste?

A. Wanting

B. Watching

C. Waiting

D. Working

39. Hector knows that a delivery concept of agile is defined as "the frequent delivery of a working product for immediate customer feedback." Which term is this delivery concept?

A. WIP delivery

B. Incremental delivery

C. Release delivery

D. Iterative delivery

40. Select from the following types of contracts, the one most suited for the agile framework.

A. Specific service contract for the initial phase with separate fixed-price contracts for each user story.

B. Specific service contract for the initial phase with separate fixed-schedule contracts for each user story.

C. General service contract for the initial phase with separate fixed-price contracts for each user story.

D. General service contract for the initial phase with separate fixed-schedule contracts for each user story.

PMI-ACP Lite Mock Exam 16 Answer Key and Explanations

1. C - When governing agile projects, executives are most interested in investment performance and risk. [Agile Project Management: Creating Innovative Products – 2nd Edition. Jim Highsmith.] [Knowledge and Skills: Level 2]

2. C - The focus in the envisioning phase is on project vision, scope (and requirements), project schedule, and assembling a project team. [Agile Project Management: Creating Innovative Products – 2nd Edition. Jim Highsmith.] [Knowledge and Skills: Level 1]

3. B - The focus in the speculation phase is on estimating iteration and release plans, defining feature breakdown, developing a rough project plan, considering project risk and risk mitigation strategies, and estimating project costs. [Agile Project Management: Creating Innovative Products – 2nd Edition. Jim Highsmith.] [Knowledge and Skills: Level 1]

4. C - Having a motivated team is essential for any project, regardless of whether it is agile or not. Motivated teams work together better, have strong productivity, and exceed expectations. Some simple steps to increase motivation are 1) spending quality time together; where team members get to know one another on a personal level to build a sense of community, 2) providing feedback, mentoring and coaching; where team members are congratulated and thanked on jobs well done and also mentored or coached to improve in skill and capability, and 3) empowerment; where the team is empowered to make many key decisions which, along the way, builds trust and shows that leadership believes in the capabilities of the team. [The Art of Agile Development. James Shore.] [Knowledge and Skills: Level 1]

5. D - Literally thousands of decisions are made in the course of a project. Many of these decisions are made in response to problems that inevitably arise and confront the agile team. Therefore it is essential that an agile team is properly versed in problem-solving strategies, tools, and techniques. Some common problem-solving techniques include: ask it loud; revisit the problem; 5Y; sunk cost fallacy; devil's advocate; be kind, rewind; asking probing questions; and reflective/active listening. [Agile Retrospectives: Making Good Teams Great. Esther Derby, Diana Larsen, Ken Schwaber.] [Knowledge and Skills: Level 1]

6. B - Servant leadership has its roots with an essay written in 1970 by Robert K Greenleaf. Greenleaf defined servant leaders as humble stewards devoted to their company and work to serve their peers, teams, and customers. In a self-organizing team, a servant leader, as Greenleaf defined it, is ideal as the team leader is an enabler, listening to the agile team's needs, removing obstacles, and providing tools or other support to promote high productivity. [Coaching Agile Teams. Lyssa Adkins.] [Soft skills negotiation]

7. B - A cornerstone of Agile development is 'incremental delivery.' Incremental delivery is the frequent delivery of working products, which are successively improved, to a customer for immediate feedback and acceptance. Typically, a product is delivered at the end of each sprint or iteration for demonstration and feedback. In this feedback technique, a customer can review the product and provide updated requirements. Changed/updated/refined requirements are welcomed in the agile process to ensure the customer receives a valuable and quality product. A sprint or iteration typically lasts from two to four weeks and at the end a new and improved product is delivered, incrementally. [The Art of Agile Development. James Shore.] [Knowledge and Skills: Level 1]

8. D - A high-performance agile team is one that is ideally collocated for osmotic communication and face-to-face interaction. However, collocation isn't always feasible in today's multinational environment. For distributed teams, several practices are available to provide the best form of effective communication in the absence of being collocated: team intranet sites, virtual team rooms, and video conferencing over e-mail when possible. Geographic separation, especially on a world-wide scale, causes the team to consider language and cultural differences, and time zone differences. [The Art of Agile Development. James Shore.] [Knowledge and Skills: Level 2]

9. B - The traditional iron triangle includes scope, schedule, and cost as its parameters Value, quality, and constraints are parameters of the agile triangle. [Agile Project Management: Creating Innovative Products – 2nd Edition. Jim Highsmith.] [Knowledge and Skills: Level 1]

10. C - Agility is the ability to balance flexibility and stability. [Agile Project Management: Creating Innovative Products – 2nd Edition. Jim Highsmith.] [Knowledge and Skills: Level 2]

11. A - A high-performance agile team is one that is ideally collocated for osmotic communication and face-to-face interaction. However, collocation isn't always feasible in today's multinational environment. For distributed teams, several practices are available to provide the best form of effective communication in the absence of being collocated: team intranet sites, virtual team rooms, and video conferencing over e-mail when possible. Geographic separation, especially on a world-wide scale, causes the team to consider language and cultural differences, and time zone differences. [The Art of Agile Development. James Shore.] [Knowledge and Skills: Level 2]

12. A - Common frameworks or methodologies used within agile include: scrum, extreme programming (XP), lean software development, crystal, feature driven development (FDD), dynamic systems development method (DSDM), agile unified process (AUP). [Agile Software Development: The Cooperative Game – 2nd Edition. Alistair Cockburn.] [Knowledge and Skills: Level 2]

13. A - As a project leader or scrum master, effective facilitation methods are critical for building a high-performance and motivated team. Facilitation of meetings, discussions, demonstrations, etc., is a constant on an agile project. Some general facilitation methods include: using a small number of people for brainstorming events; hosting events in a non-threatening/comfortable environment; having an agenda that is shared with the group ahead of time; using open-ended questions instead of closed-ended questions; including a diverse representation to gain a broader perspective of the topic. [Agile Retrospectives: Making

Good Teams Great. Esther Derby, Diana Larsen, Ken Schwaber.] [Knowledge and Skills: Level 2]

14. D - In iteration planning, an agile team, collaboratively with the customer, chooses user stories to include for development. Although the user stories are prioritized in the product backlog initially during release planning, an agile team and customer should review prioritization based on progressive elaboration (i.e., gained knowledge and perspective). Prioritization is often based on value and risk and can be performed using the MoSCoW or Kano method and through the use of risk-to-value and cost-to-value matrices. An agile team performs decomposition to sub-divide user stories into more manageable tasks so that it may estimate task time. Tasks for an iteration may also be prioritized based on value, similar to how user stories are prioritized. [Lean-Agile Software Development: Achieving Enterprise Agility. Alan Shalloway, Guy Beaver, James R. Trott.] [Knowledge and Skills: Level 1]

15. D - In iteration planning, an agile team, collaboratively with the customer, chooses user stories to include for development. Although the user stories are prioritized in the product backlog initially during release planning, an agile team and customer should review prioritization based on progressive elaboration (i.e., gained knowledge and perspective). Prioritization is often based on value and risk and can be performed using the MoSCoW or Kano method and through the use of risk-to-value and cost-to-value matrices. An agile team performs decomposition to sub-divide user stories into more manageable tasks so that it may estimate task time. Tasks for an iteration may also be prioritized based on value, similar to how user stories are prioritized. [Lean-Agile Software Development: Achieving Enterprise Agility. Alan Shalloway, Guy Beaver, James R. Trott.] [Knowledge and Skills: Level 1]

16. D - Instead of using story points, agile teams may estimate the relative sizes of user stories using ideal days. Ideal days represents the amount of days - uninterrupted by meetings, personal life, non-working days, or any other delays, obstacles or distractions - that it would take a single person to build, test, and release the user story, relative to other user stories in the backlog. [Agile Estimating and Planning. Mike Cohn.] [Agile estimation]

17. B - A persona is a notional user of the system under development. Being much more detailed than actors in use case modeling where generic user names are assigned (e.g., end user), personas try to elaborate on users with detailed descriptions to provide context to the developers. Some personas have such notional details as name, address, age, income, likes and dislikes, and other specific details. [User Stories Applied: For Agile Software Development. Mike Cohn.] [Agile analysis and design]

18. A - The project charter is an important governing document that requires all stakeholder participation. Although experts recommend it not be longer than a page in length, creating a project charter can be challenging, as all stakeholders must participate and come to a consensus. Three key elements should be included in a project charter: vision, mission, and success criteria. Vision is the 'why' or rationale of a project. Mission is the 'what' of the project and describes what the team will accomplish to reach the vision. Success criteria are management metrics that define 'how' the project will be deemed successful. [Lean-Agile Software Development: Achieving Enterprise Agility. Alan Shalloway, Guy Beaver, James R. Trott.] [Knowledge and Skills: Level 2]

19. A - An information radiator is a visual representation of project status data. [Agile Software Development: The Cooperative Game – 2nd Edition. Alistair Cockburn.] [Communications]

20. C - The product roadmap - owned by the product owner - serves as a high level overview of the product requirements. It is used as a tool for prioritizing features , organizing features into categories, and assigning rough time frames. Creating a product roadmap has four basic steps: 1) Identify requirements (these will become part of the product backlog), 2) Organize requirements into categories or themes, 3) Estimate relative work effort (e.g., planning poker or affinity estimation) and prioritize (value), and 4) Estimate rough time frames (estimate velocity, sprint duration, and rough release dates). [The Art of Agile Development. James Shore.] [Agile analysis and design]

21. C - One communication technique to reduce misunderstanding and miscommunication is active listening. A well run agile project necessitates both good listeners and communicators, active listening helps work towards both of these necessities. The basics of active listening include: 1) Being present and focusing your attention on the speaker. 2) Taking notes instead of interrupting. 3) Paraphrasing to confirm and review what you have heard. 4) Summarizing the conversation once it has concluded for posterity. Using open ended questions, good body language, and silence can help improve listening skills. [Coaching Agile Teams. Lyssa Adkins.] [Knowledge and Skills: Level 1]

22. A - Risked-based spike is a risk management technique and is often thought of as a task. A risked-based spike is a task used to gain knowledge in an area of uncertainty to reduce risk. For example, a development team may need to understand how migrating from Windows 7 to Windows 8 may impact the look and feel of the interface. Risked-based spikes typically are included in iteration planning directly before a the task that holds the uncertainty. [The Art of Agile Development. James Shore.] [Risk management]

23. B - The iteration backlog is a list of product features or work items to be completed in an iteration. It is typically fixed for the iteration unless it is overcome by important customer requirements. [Lean-Agile Software Development: Achieving Enterprise Agility. Alan Shalloway, Guy Beaver, James R. Trott.] [Agile analysis and design]

24. D - The acronym SMART (specific, measurable, achievable, relevant, and time-boxed) helps the agile practitioner remember the characteristics of a well-defined task. S – Specific tasks are ones that clearly contribute to the development of a user story. It should not be vague. M – Measurable tasks are ones that the team and customer can verify. A - Achievable tasks are ones that developers may realistically implement and understand. R - Relevant tasks are ones that unequivocally add value to the user story. T - Timeboxed tasks are ones that can have an estimate assigned of the amount of effort or time needed for development. [Agile Retrospectives: Making Good Teams Great. Esther Derby, Diana Larsen, Ken Schwaber.] [Planning, monitoring, and adapting]

25. B - When a product owner is trying to advance a release date, he or she may reduce the number of features released and reduce the depth or scope of the features to be released. [Agile Estimating and Planning. Mike Cohn.] [Planning, monitoring, and adapting]

26. B - Regular exploratory testing is encouraged to improve product quality. Typically, exploratory testing is performed on completed product software to test the system design for any bugs and to identify any new features that may add value to the customer. Exploratory testing should cover what a developer is unable to anticipate through the course of normal unit testing. A project charter is often used as a general overview of the product that exploratory testers use for testing guidance. [The Art of Agile Development. James Shore.] [Product quality]

27. C - The TDD process has four basic steps: 1) Write a test, 2) Verify and validate the test, 3) Write product code and apply the test, 4) Refactor the product code. An example may be that a user has to enter an age value. A good test is to make sure the user data entry is a positive number and not a different type of input, like a letter (i.e., write the test). The programmer would verify that entering a letter instead of a number would cause the program to cause an exception (i.e., v&v the test). The programmer would then write product code that takes user entry for the age value (i.e., write the product code). The programmer would then run the product code and enter correct age values and incorrect age values (i.e., apply the test). If the product code is successful, the programmer would refactor the product code to improve its design. Using these four steps iteratively ensures that programmers think about how a software program might fail first and to build product code that is holistically being tested. This helps produce high quality code. [The Art of Agile Development. James Shore.] [Product quality]

28. D - The TDD process has four basic steps: 1) Write a test, 2) Verify and validate the test, 3) Write product code and apply the test, 4) Refactor the product code. An example may be that a user has to enter an age value. A good test is to make sure the user data entry is a positive number and not a different type of input, like a letter (i.e., write the test). The programmer would verify that entering a letter instead of a number would cause the program to cause an exception (i.e., v&v the test). The programmer would then write product code that takes user entry for the age value (i.e., write the product code). The programmer would then run the product code and enter correct age values and incorrect age values (i.e., apply the test). If the product code is successful, the programmer would refactor the product code to improve its design. Using these four steps iteratively ensures that programmers think about how a software program might fail first and to build product code that is holistically being tested. This helps produce high quality code. [The

Art of Agile Development. James Shore.] [Product quality]

29. A - Having a motivated team is essential for any project, regardless of whether it is agile or not. Motivated teams work together better, have strong productivity, and exceed expectations. Some simple steps to increase motivation are 1) spending quality time together; where team members get to know one another on a personal level to build a sense of community, 2) providing feedback, mentoring and coaching; where team members are congratulated and thanked on jobs well done and also mentored or coached to improve in skill and capability, and 3) empowerment; where the team is empowered to make many key decisions which, along the way, builds trust and shows that leadership believes in the capabilities of the team. [The Art of Agile Development. James Shore.] [Knowledge and Skills: Level 1]

30. C - In iteration planning, an agile team, collaboratively with the customer, chooses user stories to include for development. Although the user stories are prioritized in the product backlog initially during release planning, an agile team and customer should review prioritization based on progressive elaboration (i.e., gained knowledge and perspective). Prioritization is often based on value and risk and can be performed using the MoSCoW or Kano method and through the use of risk-to-value and cost-to-value matrices. An agile team performs decomposition to sub-divide user stories into more manageable tasks so that it may estimate task time. Tasks for an iteration may also be prioritized based on value, similar to how user stories are prioritized. [Lean-Agile Software Development: Achieving Enterprise Agility. Alan Shalloway, Guy Beaver, James R. Trott.] [Knowledge and Skills: Level 1]

31. B - Reflection refers to the agile principle of reviewing work and performance at regular intervals. By doing so an agile team can identify areas of weakness and identify opportunities for improvements. Devoting time to reflection ensures high performance standards. [Agile Software Development: The Cooperative Game – 2nd Edition. Alistair Cockburn.] [Planning, monitoring, and adapting]

32. D - In agile, effective 'knowledge sharing' is a critical factor for success. It involves the near real time communication of key information among all team members and stakeholders. To promote knowledge sharing, agile uses standard practices built into its process, such as using generalized specialists/cross functional teams, self-organizing and self-disciplined teams, collocation, daily stand-up meetings, iteration/sprint planning, release planning, pair programming and pair rotation, project retrospectives/reflection, and on-site customer support. And, of course, the sixth principle of Agile is " The most efficient and effective method of conveying information to and within a development team is face-to-face conversation." In this sense, Agile prefers and encourages collocation for all stakeholders and team members for the simple fact that face-to-face conversation is the best method of communication and, in turn, effective knowledge sharing. [Becoming Agile: ...in an imperfect world. Greg Smith, Ahmed Sidky.] [Knowledge and Skills: Level 1]

33. A - Having a motivated team is essential for any project, regardless of whether it is agile or not. Motivated teams work together better, have strong productivity, and exceed expectations. Some simple steps to increase motivation are 1) spending quality time together; where team members get to know one another on a personal level to build a sense of community, 2) providing feedback, mentoring and coaching; where team members are congratulated and thanked on jobs well done and also mentored or coached to improve in skill and capability, and 3) empowerment; where the team is empowered to make many key decisions which, along the way, builds trust and shows that leadership believes in the capabilities of the team. [The Art of Agile Development. James Shore.] [Knowledge and Skills: Level 1]

34. D - During reflection or retrospectives, an agile team reserves time to reflect on the work it has completed with the objective of continuous improvement. In these self-assessment/team-assessment events, topics can include: lessons learned from successes and failures; team standards that worked, failed, or were not properly followed; and other areas of improvement. [Agile Retrospectives: Making Good Teams Great. Esther Derby, Diana Larsen, Ken Schwaber.] [Knowledge and Skills: Level 2]

35. C - Affinity estimating is a method to predict the work effort, typically in story points, of developing a user story. It is particularly useful for large product backlogs. Although several methods exist, the basic affinity estimating model involves sizing user stories on a scale from small to large. The scale can be a Fibonacci sequence or t-shirt sizes and is typically taped to a wall in a large conference room. Participants then attach their user stories to the wall as estimates. It is often done in silence and has several iterations until the user stories have been estimated. [The Art of Agile Development. James Shore.] [Agile estimation]

36. A - Osmotic communication is a concept of communication where information is shared between collocated team members unconsciously. [Agile Software Development: The Cooperative Game – 2nd Edition. Alistair Cockburn.] [Communications]

37. B - In iteration planning, an agile team, collaboratively with the customer, chooses user stories to include for development. Although the user stories are prioritized in the product backlog initially during release planning, an agile team and customer should review prioritization based on progressive elaboration (i.e., gained knowledge and perspective). Prioritization is often based on value and risk and can be performed using the MoSCoW or Kano method and through the use of risk-to-value and cost-to-value matrices. An agile team performs decomposition to sub-divide user stories into more manageable tasks so that it may estimate task time. Tasks for an iteration may also be prioritized based on value, similar to how user stories are prioritized. [Lean-Agile Software Development: Achieving Enterprise Agility. Alan Shalloway, Guy Beaver, James R. Trott.] [Knowledge and Skills: Level 1]

38. C - Value stream mapping is a lean manufacturing analysis technique adopted by agile. A value stream map may be used to analyze the flow of information or materials from origin to destination to identify areas of waste. The identified areas of waste are opportunities for process improvement. Waste can take many forms and can be remembered using the pneumonic device WIDETOM. W - waiting; I - inventory; D - defects; E - extra processing; T - transportation; O - over-production ; M - Motion. A value stream map is typically mapped or charted collaboratively with a team so it may define and view the entire process together, pinpointing areas of waste within the process. Processes that add value (processing of a part or feature) are generally referred to as "value-added" and processes that do not (e.g., waiting for a part to arrive) are generally referred to as "non value-added." Generally speaking, one wants to reduce, to the largest extent possible, the non value-added time (i.e., areas of waste). [Lean-Agile Software Development: Achieving Enterprise Agility. Alan Shalloway, Guy Beaver, James R. Trott.] [Value stream analysis]

39. B - A cornerstone of Agile development is 'incremental delivery.' Incremental delivery is the frequent delivery of working products, which are successively improved, to a customer for immediate feedback and acceptance. Typically, a product is delivered at the end of each sprint or iteration for demonstration and feedback. In this feedback technique, a customer can review the product and provide updated requirements. Changed/updated/refined requirements are welcomed in the agile process to ensure the customer receives a valuable and quality product. A sprint or iteration typically lasts from two to four weeks and at the end a new and improved product is delivered, incrementally. [The Art of Agile Development. James Shore.] [Knowledge and Skills: Level 1]

40. C - Time, budget, and cost estimation is an important knowledge and skill area of agile. According to Highsmith, the nature of the agile method, whereby it welcomes changing scope, means that it lends itself well to fixed budgets and a fixed schedule because changing scope makes it difficult to estimate a total cost. Generally speaking, the budget and schedule constraints are known but before a project will commence there needs to be an agreed upon set of base product functionality defined in an initiation phase; fixing scope reduces an agile team's innovative tendency to provide improved value. For companies that are familiar with fixed-price contracts, where requirements are agreed upon before contract closing, adopting agile can be a weary initial venture. Instead, other contract vehicle types are recommended for agile efforts. These include: a general service contract for the initiation phase and separate fixed-price contracts for iterations or user stories; time-and-material contracts; not-to-exceed with fixed-fee contracts; and, incentive contracts (e.g., fixed price with incentive; cost-reimbursable with award fee). [Agile Project Management: Creating Innovative Products – 2nd Edition. Jim Highsmith.] [Knowledge and Skills: Level 1]

Knowledge Area Quiz
Knowledge and Skills: Level 2
Practice Questions

Test Name: Knowledge Area Test: Knowledge and Skills: Level 2
Total Questions: 15
Correct Answers Needed to Pass: 11 (73.33%)
Time Allowed: 25 Minutes

Test Description

This practice quiz specifically targets your knowledge of the Knowledge and Skills: Level 2 exam topic area.

Test Questions

1. What is the ideal team member location in the agile framework?

A. Distributed

B. Isolation

C. Collocation

D. Separation

2. How is continuous improvement built into the agile framework?

A. Through strict adherence to the agile project standards defined at the beginning of a project.

B. Through the use of overtime to meet deadlines earlier than planned.

C. Through demonstrating a working product only at the end of a release.

D. Through listening and responding to customer feedback after each iteration.

3. Which framework is adapted from the unified process (UP) for use in agile?

A. Agile unified process (AUP)

B. Extreme unified process (EUP)

C. Simple unified process (SUP)

D. Adapted unified process (AdUP)

4. Sarah is a scrum master for an agile project. She practices using open-ended questions with her team to promote idea generation. The use of open ended questions is a…

A. Facilitation method

B. Crystal method

C. Passive listening method

D. Dynamic product development method (DPDM)

5. What is the difference between aspirational and mandatory standards, as referred to in the PMI Code?

A. Aspirational standards are not mandatory but good practice and encouraged.

B. Aspirational standards are backed by federal law and mandatory backed by state and local law.

C. Aspirational standards are enforced by state law and mandatory standards are backed by federal law.

D. Both are compulsory standards and backed by law.

6. Becky, as project leader, intends on building a high-performance team. What is a practice she should follow to build a high-performance team?

A. Using overtime to incentivize the team to delivery early

B. Building in pressure

C. Empowering the customer

D. Having the right team members (i.e., a cross-functional team)

7. What agile artifact outlines the project's vision?

A. Kanban board

B. Business case

C. Product backlog

D. Scope document

8. What is Cohn's definition of product knowledge?

A. Intrinsic knowledge of the product domain and industry

B. Knowledge about what the threshold features are about a product.

C. Extrinsic knowledge of the product domain and industry

D. Knowledge about what features will or will not be developed in a project

9. Select a common agile framework/methodology.

A. Sprint

B. Scrum

C. LP

D. PMI

10. Which of the following best describes the crystal framework?

A. A technical approach that can be used in the agile framework that is a family of methodologies for flexible and lightweight software development.

B. A technical approach that can be used in the agile framework that focuses on simple design and constant testing.

C. A technical approach that can be used in the agile framework that focuses on the elimination of waste and amplification of learning.

D. A technical approach that can be used in the agile framework that focuses on paired programming and integrated testing.

11. What is the process called when a team constructively criticizes its performance for the purpose of improving performance going forward?

A. Reflection

B. Refactoring

C. Returning

D. Reimaging

12. Which agile framework emphasizes a heavy focus on proving the 'fitness' or marketability of a product (i.e., has a strong business emphasis)?

A. Static systems development method (SSDM)

B. Extreme systems development method (XSDM)

C. Dynamic systems development method (DSDM)

D. Dynamic product development method (DPDM)

13. Which software development framework stresses the use of 'metaphor' to describe concepts?

A. Ultra programming (UP)

B. Paired programming (PP)

C. Peer perfect programming (3P)

D. Extreme programming (XP)

14. Which software development framework used in agile uses a prescriptive model where the development process is planned, managed, and tracked by feature?

A. Acceptance test driven development (ATDD)

B. Test driven development (TDD)

C. Feature driven development (FDD)

D. Defect driven development (3D)

15. How do high-performance teams approach conflict?

A. Know that conflict is inevitable and approach conflict with an open mind knowing that it can manage conflict itself.

B. Take an anonymous vote among team members to identify which team members should leave the project.

C. Avoid talking about or dealing with conflict, knowing that that all problems will eventually pass.

D. Know that all conflict is completely self-imposed and the best course of action is to ignore conflict until it goes away.

Knowledge Area Quiz
Knowledge and Skills: Level 2
Answer Key and Explanations

1. C - A high-performance agile team is one that is ideally collocated for osmotic communication and face-to-face interaction. However, collocation isn't always feasible in today's multinational environment. For distributed teams, several practices are available to provide the best form of effective communication in the absence of being collocated: team intranet sites, virtual team rooms, and video conferencing over e-mail when possible. Geographic separation, especially on a world-wide scale, causes the team to consider language and cultural differences, and time zone differences. [The Art of Agile Development. James Shore.] [Knowledge and Skills: Level 2]

2. D - Agile project management places strong emphasis on 'continuous improvement.' Continuous improvement processes are built into the agile methodology, from customers providing feedback after each iteration to the team reserving time to reflect on its performance through retrospectives after each iteration. Ongoing unit and integration testing and keeping up with technological/industry developments also play a part in the continuous improvement process. Continuous improvement is also a key principle in the lean methodology, where a focus of removing waste from the value stream is held. [The Art of Agile Development. James Shore.] [Knowledge and Skills: Level 2]

3. A - Agile Unified Process (AUP) is a simplified version of the Unified Process, or UP (UP itself is a more detailed framework for iterative and incremental software development). AUP simplifies UP for the agile framework. AUP projects use four phases: 1) inception, 2) elaboration, 3) construction, and 4) transition. At the end of each short iteration, the team delivers a working product. [Agile Software Development: The Cooperative Game – 2nd Edition. Alistair Cockburn.] [Knowledge and Skills: Level 2]

4. A - As a project leader or scrum master, effective facilitation methods are critical for building a high-performance and motivated team. Facilitation of meetings, discussions, demonstrations, etc., is a constant on an agile project. Some general facilitation methods include: using a small number of people for brainstorming events; hosting events in a non-threatening/comfortable environment; having an agenda that is shared with the group ahead of time; using open-ended questions instead of closed-ended questions; including a diverse representation to gain a broader perspective of the topic. [Agile Retrospectives: Making Good Teams Great. Esther Derby, Diana Larsen, Ken Schwaber.] [Knowledge and Skills: Level 2]

5. A - Aspirational standards are standards that every professional should strive to uphold, but are not compulsory. Mandatory standards are required and often backed by law. [PMI Code of Ethics and Professional Conduct. Project Management Institute.] [Knowledge and Skills: Level 2]

6. D - Building a high-performance team is critical to any project's success. A high performance team has the right team members, is empowered, has built trust, works at a sustainable pace, has consistently high velocity/productivity, takes regular time for reflection to review work, has a team lead that removes any obstacles and provides mentoring and coaching, is self-organized and self-disciplined, and is collocated. Several management techniques can be used to build or foster a high-performance team environment, some techniques include: removing obstacles that slow down a team's performance, having high expectations of team performance, and coaching and mentoring the team to achieve its best performance. [Coaching Agile Teams. Lyssa Adkins.] [Knowledge and Skills: Level 2]

7. B - Business case development is an important initial step in agile project management. The business case is a concise document that outlines the project's vision, goals, strategies for achieving goals, milestones, required investment and expected return/payback. A business case articulates the why and how a project will deliver value to a customer. [Lean-Agile Software Development: Achieving Enterprise Agility. Alan Shalloway, Guy Beaver, James R. Trott.] [Knowledge and Skills: Level 2]

8. D - Cohn's definition of product knowledge is knowledge about what features will or will not be developed in a project. [User Stories Applied: For Agile Software Development. Mike Cohn.] [Knowledge and Skills: Level 2]

9. B - Common frameworks or methodologies used within agile include: scrum, extreme programming (XP), lean software development, crystal, feature driven development (FDD), dynamic systems development method (DSDM), agile unified process (AUP). [Agile Software Development: The Cooperative Game – 2nd Edition. Alistair Cockburn.] [Knowledge and Skills: Level 2]

10. A - Crystal is a family of methodologies for a flexible and lightweight approach to software development. The family of methodologies is color coded to differentiate its members (e.g., clear, yellow, orange, red.) The color chosen depends on the level of effort required. On one end of the spectrum is crystal clear, which is for smaller efforts, while crystal red is for larger efforts. Regardless of color, the crystal framework is cyclical and has three fundamental processes: chartering, delivery cycles, and wrap-up. Crystal chartering includes building the team, doing an Exploratory 360, defining standards of practice for the team, and building the project plan. In the delivery cycle, the crystal team iteratively develops, integrates, tests, and releases the product in iterations that last from one week to two months. Like other agile frameworks, crystal includes collaborative events, like stand-up meetings and reflective improvement workshops. In wrap-up the team concludes the project and holds a completion ritual where the team reflects on the entire project. [Agile Software Development: The Cooperative Game – 2nd Edition. Alistair Cockburn.] [Knowledge and Skills: Level 2]

11. A - During reflection or retrospectives, an agile team reserves time to reflect on the work it has completed with the objective of continuous improvement. In these self-assessment/team-assessment events, topics can include: lessons learned from successes and failures; team standards that worked, failed, or were not properly followed; and other areas of improvement. [Agile Retrospectives: Making Good Teams Great.

Esther Derby, Diana Larsen, Ken Schwaber.] [Knowledge and Skills: Level 2]

12. C - Dynamic Systems Development Method (DSDM) is a structured framework that emphasizes a business perspective with a heavy focus on proving the 'fitness' or marketability. Similar to scrum, DSDM has three major phases: initiating project activities, project life cycle activities, and closing project activities (i.e., similar to scrum's pre-game, game, post-game). The project life cycle has five stages: feasibility study, business study, functional model iteration, design and build iteration, and implementation. [Agile Software Development: The Cooperative Game – 2nd Edition. Alistair Cockburn.] [Knowledge and Skills: Level 2]

13. D - Extreme programming (XP) is a programmer-centric agile framework that focuses on small, ongoing releases. XP highlights several principles: pair programming, sustainable pace, ongoing automated testing, effective communication, simplicity, feedback, courage, collective ownership, continuous integration, energized work, shared workspaces, on-site customer representation, and the use of metaphor to describe concepts. [Agile Software Development: The Cooperative Game – 2nd Edition. Alistair Cockburn.] [Knowledge and Skills: Level 2]

14. C - Feature driven development (FDD) uses a prescriptive model where the software development process is planned, managed, and tracked from the perspective of individual software features. FDD uses short iterations of two weeks or less to develop a set amount of features. The five step FDD process is: 1. Develop overall model; 2. Create the features list; 3. Plan by feature; 4. Design by feature; 5 Build by feature. [Agile Software Development: The Cooperative Game – 2nd Edition. Alistair Cockburn.] [Knowledge and Skills: Level 2]

15. A - High-performance teams differ from low-performance teams with how they deal with conflict. Conflict is inevitable even for the most experienced agile team. The difference is that high-performance teams approach conflict with an open mind and as self-organizing often navigate and resolve conflict organically. [Coaching Agile Teams. Lyssa Adkins.] [Knowledge and Skills: Level 2]

PMI-ACP Lite Mock Exam 17 Practice Questions

Test Name: PMI-ACP Lite Mock Exam 17
Total Questions: 40
Correct Answers Needed to Pass:
30 (75.00%)
Time Allowed: 60 Minutes

Test Description

This is a cumulative PMI-ACP Mock Exam which can be used as a benchmark for your PMI-ACP aptitude. This practice test includes questions from all exam topic areas, including sections from Agile Tools and Techniques, and all three Agile Knowledge and Skills areas.

Test Questions

1. What person in the agile framework "adapts the leadership style to the working environment?"

   A. Release planner

   B. Project leader

   C. Project scheduler

   D. Product owner

2. Select the response that lists the three main levels of agile planning.

   A. Release planning, daily planning, daily stand-up planning

   B. Release planning, rolling waveform planning, daily planning

   C. Release planning, iteration planning, daily planning

   D. Sprint planning, iteration planning, iteration planning

3. Reggie realizes that the timeboxed value for the current user story he is developing is too short a duration. What should Reggie do?

   A. Aggregate the task with other tasks that are equally as difficult

   B. Take a corrective measure as soon as possible and notify the team about the realization

   C. Remove the user story from the current iteration and place it in the product backlog

   D. Simply update the timebox to what he thinks is appropriate and continue to work without notifying the team

4. Which of the following is an agile principle per the Agile Manifesto?

   A. Defect reduction

   B. Test-driven development

   C. Paying continuous attention to technical excellence and good design.

   D. Removing waste

5. Which of the following is a key soft skill negotiation quality?

A. Conflict resolution

B. Requirement resolution

C. Negotiation resolution

D. Specification resolution

6. What is an essential knowledge and skill area of the agile team?

A. Problem-prioritization tools

B. Problem-solving tools

C. Problem-mitigation tools

D. Problem-first tools

7. Lisa is describing the four Agile Manifesto values to her co-workers. Which response lists a secondary value?

A. Responding to change

B. Customer collaboration

C. Following a plan

D. Individuals and interactions

8. Two of the Agile Manifesto's four core values cover communication values. Select these values from the list.

A. Individuals and interactions over processes and tools, and customer collaboration over contract negotiation

B. Working software over comprehensive documentation, and individuals and interactions over processes and tools

C. Individuals and interactions over processes and tools, and responding to change over following a plan

D. Responding to change over following a plan, and individuals and interactions over processes and tools

9. How is iterative customer evaluation of a product incorporated into iteration planning?

A. Results from the customer evaluation help the team prioritize which user stories should be tested and integrated during the next iteration.

B. Customer evaluation is used during release planning which holds the work breakdown structure of the iteration plan

C. Customer evaluation is not incorporated into iteration planning. The agile team plans for the iteration independently of customer evaluation.

D. Customer feedback helps the agile team plan for the next iteration.

10. Which of the following responses is a community value per the PMI agile community of practice community charter?

A. Openness

B. Introspective

C. Weary

D. Reticent

11. Select a common agile problem-solving technique.

A. Reflection listening

B. Retrospective listening

C. Passive listening

D. Active listening

12. Select a common agile problem-solving technique.

A. Reflective listening

B. Passive listening

C. Reflection listening

D. Retrospective listening

13. Select the agile knowledge and skill area that concerns itself with effective communication.

A. Brainstorm facilitation management

B. Feedback management

C. Retrospective management

D. Communications management

14. Select a key element of a project charter?

A. Impact statement

B. Return on investment

C. Investment cost

D. Vision

15. Select a key element of a project charter?

A. Stakeholder analysis

B. Risk analysis

C. Cost-to-value matrix

D. Mission

16. Gerald is working on a multi-national agile project. What is one thing Gerald should be sensitive of in a multi-national effort?

A. Risk-based spike tasks

B. Time zones

C. Risk burndown chart

D. Quality differences

17. What agile artifact outlines the project's goals?

A. Product roadmap

B. Business case

C. Risk burndown chart

D. Iteration backlog

18. What agile estimation technique originates from the wideband Delphi estimation technique?

A. Planning games

B. Affinity poker

C. Risk games

D. Planning poker

19. What is typically plotted in a risk burndown graph?

A. Risk impact

B. Risk severity

C. Risk mitigation factors

D. Risk likelihood

20. Which of the following agile knowledge and skill areas involves the management of effective communication?

A. Risk management

B. Communications management

C. Operations research

D. Timeboxing management

21. John and his agile team are planning an iteration with several tasks having high risk. To manage the risk, what type of task can John and his team build into the iteration plan?

A. Risk-based spike tasks.

B. Risk-mitigation reflection tasks.

C. Risk-seeking tasks.

D. Risk-averse tasks.

22. Calculate the return on investment of the following: Gain: $10,000; Cost: $1,000.

A. 1000%

B. 700%

C. 900%

D. 800%

23. Gerald is working on a multi-national agile project. What is one thing Gerald should be sensitive of in a multi-national effort?

A. Language

B. Quality differences

C. Kanban board

D. Risk-based spike tasks

24. Select a method that is commonly used to help prioritize user stories.

A. Risk-to-cost matrix

B. Risk-to-mitigate matrix

C. Risk-to-reward matrix

D. Risk-to-value matrix

25. What is one reason to perform a risk-based spike task?

A. To learn more about release planning.

B. To learn more about certain tasks.

C. To learn more about uncertain tasks.

D. To learn more about iteration delays.

26. Jill has been tasked with exploring a release of the software product for any bugs or flaws in the system design. What type of testing is Jill performing?

A. User testing

B. Role testing

C. Ad hoc testing

D. Exploratory testing

27. Select a common agile problem-solving technique.

A. Sunk cost fallacy

B. Root reflection

C. 2Y

D. Inspection

28. Select a common agile problem-solving technique.

A. Ask it loud

B. Root reflection

C. Root inspection

D. Probe it loud

29. Select a common agile problem-solving technique.

A. Root inspection

B. Root reflection

C. Revisit the problem

D. Probe it loud

30. Select a common agile problem-solving technique.

A. 5Y

B. Root reflection

C. Root inspection

D. Probe it loud

31. Of the following, which type of team is expected and trusted to make decisions to adapt to changing needs and requirements?

A. Rehearsed team

B. Revolving team

C. Rotating team

D. Empowered team

32. What topic area within strategic management deals with promoting a work environment where the agile team and stakeholders collaborate?

A. Schedule management

B. Cooperative management

C. Social management

D. Stakeholder management

33. What agile estimation technique is conducted using a deck of cards with non-sequential numbers for quickly estimating the relative work effort of developing user stories in a product backlog?

A. Planning poker

B. Affinity estimation

C. Planning game

D. SMART

34. In the SMART acronym, which is used to guide the creation of well-defined tasks, what does the T stand for?

A. Tangible

B. Testable

C. Torrent

D. Timeboxed

35. Which of the following is the best definition of 'knowledge sharing?'

A. The heavily controlled conveyance of information to only key team members.

B. The tightly controlled flow of information among team members to maintain clear organizational hierarchies.

C. The conveyance of data between refactored code modules.

D. The conveyance of important information among all stakeholders and team members.

36. EVM is a frequently used project management abbreviation. What does SPI stand for in the EVM technique?

A. Schedule performance indicator

B. Schedule performance index

C. Specification performance indicator

D. Schedule parametric index

37. EVM is a frequently used project management abbreviation. What does SV stand for in the EVM technique?

A. Schedule value

B. Specification value

C. Specification variance

D. Schedule variance

38. Patrick is reviewing an information radiator that shows the current progress of items in the product backlog. Unlike a traditional burnup chart, the information radiator that Patrick is reviewing shows the items' total scope, including completion details of 'not started,' 'started,' and 'completed.' What type of information radiator is Patrick most likely reviewing?

A. Total scope diagram

B. Cumulative flow diagram

C. Done done diagram

D. Schematic diagram

39. Gina's agile team is beginning a large, complex project estimated to last for three years. Her team has decided to only plan in detail for the next few iterations and keep iterations further removed at only a high-level of detail. Gina's team assumes that customer requirements and other details will change and become more detailed in the future. What project management technique is the basis of this assumption?

A. Scope creep

B. Progressive elaboration

C. Rolling wave elaboration

D. Scope bloat

40. Which of the following helps an agile team promote simple and effective communication?

A. Through focusing on quality

B. Through focusing on constraints

C. Through focusing on value

D. Through retrospectives

PMI-ACP Lite Mock Exam 17 Answer Key and Explanations

1. B - A common misconception in agile is that an agile team does not need a leader. In fact, all agile teams need a leader, but the way in which the leader leads is fundamentally different than the typical traditional project manager/project leader method. Some have theorized that this misconception stems from the desired 'self-organizing' quality of the agile team. And although the 'self-organizing' agile team is empowered to take ownership and responsibility of the product and make some decisions itself, it nevertheless requires a leader to help provide guidance, mentoring, coaching, problem solving, and decision making. Some key aspects required of an agile leader include: empowering team members to decide what standard agile practices and methods it will use; allowing the team to be self-organized and self-disciplined; empowering the team members to make decisions collaboratively with the customer; inspire the team to be innovative and explore new ideas and technology capabilities; be a champion of and articulate the product vision to team members so it will be motivated to accomplish the overall objective; remove any obstacles and solve any problems the team may face in its effort; communicate and endorse the values and principles of agile project management to stakeholders that may be unfamiliar with agile; ensure that all stakeholders, including business managers and developers, are collaborating effectively; and, be able to adapt the leadership style to the working environment to ensure that the agile values and principles are effectively upheld. [The Art of Agile Development. James Shore.] [Knowledge and Skills: Level 1]

2. C - The three main levels of agile planning are release planning, iteration planning, and daily planning. [The Art of Agile Development. James Shore.] [Planning, monitoring, and adapting]

3. B - When a developer notices that a user story/task is taking longer than the timebox indicates, he or she should notify the team and take a corrective measure. Corrective measures include splitting the task into smaller user stories or changing team members. [The Art of Agile Development. James Shore.] [Planning, monitoring, and adapting]

4. C - The Agile Manifesto defines 12 supporting principles. Agile principles include 1) Our highest priority is to satisfy the customer through early and continuous delivery of valuable software. 2) Welcome changing requirements, even late in development. Agile processes harness change for the customer's competitive advantage. 3) Deliver working software frequently, from a couple of weeks to a couple of months, with preference to the shorter timescale. 4) Business people and developers must work together daily throughout the project. 5) Build projects around motivated individuals. Give them the environment and support they need, and trust them to get the job done. 6) The most efficient and effective method of conveying information to and within a development team is face-to-face conversation. 7) Working software is the primary measure of progress. 8) Agile processes promote sustainable development. The sponsors, developers, and users should be able to maintain a constant pace indefinitely. 9) Continuous attention to technical excellence and good design enhances agility. 10) Simplicity--the

art of maximizing the amount of work not done--is essential. 11) The best architectures, requirements, and designs emerge from self-organizing teams. 12) At regular intervals, the team reflects on how to become more effective, then tunes and adjusts its behavior accordingly. [Manifesto for Agile Software Development. Agile Alliance.] [Knowledge and Skills: Level 1]

5. A - Key soft skills negotiation qualities for the effective implementation and practice of agile are: emotional intelligence, collaboration, adaptive leadership, negotiation, conflict resolution, servant leadership. [Coaching Agile Teams. Lyssa Adkins.] [Soft skills negotiation]

6. B - Literally thousands of decisions are made in the course of a project. Many of these decisions are made in response to problems that inevitably arise and confront the agile team. Therefore it is essential that an agile team is properly versed in problem-solving strategies, tools, and techniques. Some common problem-solving techniques include: ask it loud; revisit the problem; 5Y; sunk cost fallacy; devil's advocate; be kind, rewind; asking probing questions; and reflective/active listening. [Agile Retrospectives: Making Good Teams Great. Esther Derby, Diana Larsen, Ken Schwaber.] [Knowledge and Skills: Level 1]

7. C - The Agile Manifesto defines four values. The four values list primary values and secondary values, with primary values superseding secondary values. The values are 1) individuals and interactions over processes and tools, 2) working software over comprehensive documentation, 3) customer collaboration over contract negotiation, and 4) responding to change over following a plan. [Manifesto for Agile Software Development. Agile Alliance.] [Knowledge and Skills: Level 1]

8. A - The Agile Manifesto developed by the Agile Alliance covers 4 values and 12 principles. The four values are: 1) individuals and interactions over processes and tools, 2) working software over comprehensive documentation, 3) customer collaboration over contract negotiation, and 4) responding to change over following a plan. The 12 principles are: 1) focusing on satisfying the customer, 2) welcoming change, 3) delivering working software frequently, 4) ensuring that business people and developers work together, 5) motivating the individuals involved in development, 6) using face-to-face communication whenever possible, 7) working software as the primary measure of progress, 8) maintaining a constant pace of development, 9) paying continuous attention to technical excellence and good design, 10) aiming for simplicity, 11) using self-organizing teams, and 12) regularly reflecting on how to become more effective. [Manifesto for Agile Software Development. Agile Alliance.] [Communications]

9. D - Once completing an iteration, the team and customer evaluate the most recently developed product features. The customer's evaluation provides the agile team with key insights and objectives for the next iteration. Iteration planning is highly dependent on customer evaluation to ensure quality is built into the product. [The Art of Agile Development. James Shore.] [Planning, monitoring, and adapting]

10. A - The following are community values of the PMI agile community of practice community charter: Vision, Servant

Leadership, Trust, Collaboration, Honesty, Learning, Courage, Openness, Adaptability, Leading Change, Transparency [PMI Agile Community of Practice Community Charter. Project Management Institute.] [Knowledge and Skills: Level 1]

11. D - Literally thousands of decisions are made in the course of a project. Many of these decisions are made in response to problems that inevitably arise and confront the agile team. Therefore it is essential that an agile team is properly versed in problem-solving strategies, tools, and techniques. Some common problem-solving techniques include: ask it loud; revisit the problem; 5Y; sunk cost fallacy; devil's advocate; be kind, rewind; asking probing questions; and reflective/active listening. [Agile Retrospectives: Making Good Teams Great. Esther Derby, Diana Larsen, Ken Schwaber.] [Knowledge and Skills: Level 1]

12. A - Literally thousands of decisions are made in the course of a project. Many of these decisions are made in response to problems that inevitably arise and confront the agile team. Therefore it is essential that an agile team is properly versed in problem-solving strategies, tools, and techniques. Some common problem-solving techniques include: ask it loud; revisit the problem; 5Y; sunk cost fallacy; devil's advocate; be kind, rewind; asking probing questions; and reflective/active listening. [Agile Retrospectives: Making Good Teams Great. Esther Derby, Diana Larsen, Ken Schwaber.] [Knowledge and Skills: Level 1]

13. D - Effective communication is a cornerstone of agile. Communication is the act of transferring information among various parties. Communications management is a knowledge and skill area of agile that highlights this importance. PMI has several definitions regarding communications management and agile builds on top of these to add its own perspective: 1) Communications Planning: Determining the information and communication needs of the projects stakeholders 2) Information Distribution: Making needed information available to project stakeholders in a timely manner, 3) Performance Reporting: Collecting and distributing performance information. This includes status reporting, progress measurement, and forecasting, and 4) Managing Stakeholders: Managing communications to satisfy the requirements and resolve issues with project stakeholders. From an agile perspective: communication among the team is built into the process and facilitated through collocation, information radiators, daily stand-up meetings, retrospectives etc.; Although it is hoped that the product owner, customer, and user can be heavily involved with the project and also use these communication techniques, a plan for conveying information to stakeholders may be needed if this is not the case. [Agile Software Development: The Cooperative Game – 2nd Edition. Alistair Cockburn.] [Knowledge and Skills: Level 1]

14. D - The project charter is an important governing document that requires all stakeholder participation. Although experts recommend it not be longer than a page in length, creating a project charter can be challenging, as all stakeholders must participate and come to a consensus. Three key elements should be included in a project charter: vision, mission, and success criteria. Vision is the 'why' or rationale of a project. Mission is the 'what' of the project and describes what the team will accomplish to reach the vision. Success criteria are management metrics that define 'how' the project will be deemed successful. [Lean-Agile Software Development: Achieving Enterprise Agility. Alan Shalloway, Guy Beaver, James R. Trott.] [Knowledge and Skills: Level 2]

15. D - The project charter is an important governing document that requires all stakeholder participation. Although experts recommend it not be longer than a page in length, creating a project charter can be challenging, as all stakeholders must participate and come to a consensus. Three key elements should be included in a project charter: vision, mission, and success criteria. Vision is the 'why' or rationale of a project. Mission is the 'what' of the project and describes what the team will accomplish to reach the vision. Success criteria are management metrics that define 'how' the project will be deemed successful. [Lean-Agile Software Development: Achieving Enterprise Agility. Alan Shalloway, Guy Beaver, James R. Trott.] [Knowledge and Skills: Level 2]

16. B - A high-performance agile team is one that is ideally collocated for osmotic communication and face-to-face interaction. However, collocation isn't always feasible in today's multinational environment. For distributed teams, several practices are available to provide the best form of effective communication in the absence of being collocated: team intranet sites, virtual team rooms, and video conferencing over e-mail when possible. Geographic separation, especially on a world-wide scale, causes the team to consider language and cultural differences, and time zone differences. [The Art of Agile Development. James Shore.] [Knowledge and Skills: Level 2]

17. B - Business case development is an important initial step in agile project management. The business case is a concise document that outlines the project's vision, goals, strategies for achieving goals, milestones, required investment and expected return/payback. A business case articulates the why and how a project will deliver value to a customer. [Lean-Agile Software Development: Achieving Enterprise Agility. Alan Shalloway, Guy Beaver, James R. Trott.] [Knowledge and Skills: Level 2]

18. D - Planning poker is based upon the wideband Delphi estimation technique. It is a consensus-based technique for estimating effort. Sometimes called scrum poker, it is a technique for a relative estimation of effort, typically in story points, to develop a user story. At a planning poker meeting, each estimator is given an identical deck of planning poker cards with a wide range of values. The Fibonacci sequence is often used for values for planning poker (i.e., 0, 1, 1, 2, 3, 5,8,etc.); another common sequence is (question mark, 0, 1/2, 1, 2, 3, 5, 8, 13, 20, 40, and 100). A planning poker meeting works as follows: 1) a moderator, not estimating, facilitates the meeting. 2) the product owner/manager provides a short overview of the user story and answers clarifying questions posed by the developers. Typically the product owner does not vote. 3) Each estimator selects an estimate of work effort by selecting a card, 4) Once everyone has selected a card, everyone overturns their card concurrently, 5) Estimators with high and low estimates are given a chance to defend positions. 6) The process repeats until there is consensus.

The developer who owns the user story is typically given higher credence. [Agile Estimating and Planning. Mike Cohn.] [Agile estimation]

19. B - A risk burndown chart is a risk management technique used to track project risk over time. It allows stakeholders to quickly review project risk management performance (e.g., increasing, decreasing, and by how much) over time. Severity (a product of impact and probability) is charted along the vertical axis with time on the horizontal axis. Impact typically takes a value from 0 to 5 in increasing order of risk and probability/likelihood typically takes a value from 0 to 5 in increasing order of probability. In this example, the worst severity a risk could have is 25 (5 x 5 = 25) and the least harmful severity a risk could have is 0. The agile team and customer/product owner identifies its risks and assigns severity values in a risk register and tracks those values over time. Ideally, risk severity will decrease over time. [The Art of Agile Development. James Shore.] [Risk management]

20. B - Effective communication is a cornerstone of agile. Communication is the act of transferring information among various parties. Communications management is a knowledge and skill area of agile that highlights this importance. PMI has several definitions regarding communications management and agile builds on top of these to add its own perspective: 1) Communications Planning: Determining the information and communication needs of the projects stakeholders 2) Information Distribution: Making needed information available to project stakeholders in a timely manner, 3) Performance Reporting: Collecting and distributing performance information. This includes status reporting, progress measurement, and forecasting, and 4) Managing Stakeholders: Managing communications to satisfy the requirements and resolve issues with project stakeholders. From an agile perspective: communication among the team is built into the process and facilitated through collocation, information radiators, daily stand-up meetings, retrospectives etc.; Although it is hoped that the product owner, customer, and user can be heavily involved with the project and also use these communication techniques, a plan for conveying information to stakeholders may be needed if this is not the case. [Agile Software Development: The Cooperative Game – 2nd Edition. Alistair Cockburn.] [Knowledge and Skills: Level 1]

21. A - Risked-based spike is a risk management technique and is often thought of as a task. A risked-based spike is a task used to gain knowledge in an area of uncertainty to reduce risk. For example, a development team may need to understand how migrating from Windows 7 to Windows 8 may impact the look and feel of the interface. Risked-based spikes typically are included in iteration planning directly before a the task that holds the uncertainty. [The Art of Agile Development. James Shore.] [Risk management]

22. C - Return on Investment (ROI): A metric used to evaluate the efficiency of an investment or to compare efficiency among a number of investments. To calculate ROI, the return of an investment (i.e., the gain minus the cost) is divided by the cost of the investment. The result is usually expressed as a percentage and sometimes a ratio. The product owner is often said to be responsible for the ROI. [Agile Estimating and Planning. Mike Cohn.] [Value based prioritization]

23. A - A high-performance agile team is one that is ideally collocated for osmotic communication and face-to-face interaction. However, collocation isn't always feasible in today's multinational environment. For distributed teams, several practices are available to provide the best form of effective communication in the absence of being collocated: team intranet sites, virtual team rooms, and video conferencing over e-mail when possible. Geographic separation, especially on a world-wide scale, causes the team to consider language and cultural differences, and time zone differences. [The Art of Agile Development. James Shore.] [Knowledge and Skills: Level 2]

24. D - An agile team must always face the prioritization of product features in its product backlog. From release planning to iteration planning, an agile team must prioritize the user stories/ features of its product to ensure that high-quality and high-value features are developed first to help facilitate an optimized and early return on investment (ROI). An agile team typically prioritizes requirements or user stories/features in terms of relative value and risk; value is defined by the customer (i.e., customer-value prioritization). Two common methods to prioritize product features are: MoSCoW and Kano. The MoSCoW method categorizes features into 'Must have,' 'Should have,' 'Could have,' and 'Would have' features. The Kano method categorizes features into 'Must haves (threshold),' 'Dissatisfiers,' 'Satisfiers,' and 'Delighters.' Must haves are features that are requisite. Dissatisfiers are features that adversely impact perceived value and should be eliminated. 'Satisfiers' are features that increase perceived value linearly, where the more you add the more the customer is pleased, but are not required, and 'Delighters' are features that increase perceived value exponentially to please the customer. To prioritize features based on risk, a risk-to-value matrix can be used. A risk-to-value matrix has four quadrants, with the horizontal axis having low and high value, and the vertical axis having low and high risk. User stories are assigned to one of the four categories/quadrants: low-value, low-risk; low-value, high-risk; high-value, low-risk; high-value, high-risk. A cost-to-value matrix can also be made in this manner. All prioritization in agile is 'relative,' meaning that the priority of one user story is relative to other user stories and not prioritized on a fixed scale. [Lean-Agile Software Development: Achieving Enterprise Agility. Alan Shalloway, Guy Beaver, James R. Trott.] [Knowledge and Skills: Level 1]

25. C - Risked-based spike is a risk management technique and is often thought of as a task. A risked-based spike is a task used to gain knowledge in an area of uncertainty to reduce risk. For example, a development team may need to understand how migrating from Windows 7 to Windows 8 may impact the look and feel of the interface. Risked-based spikes typically are included in iteration planning directly before a the task that holds the uncertainty. [The Art of Agile Development. James Shore.] [Risk management]

26. D - Regular exploratory testing is encouraged to improve product quality. Typically, exploratory testing is performed on completed product software to test the system design for any bugs and to identify any new features that may add value to the customer. Exploratory testing should cover what a developer is unable to anticipate through the course of normal unit testing. A project charter is often used as a general overview of the product that exploratory testers use for testing guidance. [The Art of Agile Development. James Shore.] [Product quality]

27. A - Literally thousands of decisions are made in the course of a project. Many of these decisions are made in response to problems that inevitably arise and confront the agile team. Therefore it is essential that an agile team is properly versed in problem-solving strategies, tools, and techniques. Some common problem-solving techniques include: ask it loud; revisit the problem; 5Y; sunk cost fallacy; devil's advocate; be kind, rewind; asking probing questions; and reflective/active listening. [Agile Retrospectives: Making Good Teams Great. Esther Derby, Diana Larsen, Ken Schwaber.] [Knowledge and Skills: Level 1]

28. A - Literally thousands of decisions are made in the course of a project. Many of these decisions are made in response to problems that inevitably arise and confront the agile team. Therefore it is essential that an agile team is properly versed in problem-solving strategies, tools, and techniques. Some common problem-solving techniques include: ask it loud; revisit the problem; 5Y; sunk cost fallacy; devil's advocate; be kind, rewind; asking probing questions; and reflective/active listening. [Agile Retrospectives: Making Good Teams Great. Esther Derby, Diana Larsen, Ken Schwaber.] [Knowledge and Skills: Level 1]

29. C - Literally thousands of decisions are made in the course of a project. Many of these decisions are made in response to problems that inevitably arise and confront the agile team. Therefore it is essential that an agile team is properly versed in problem-solving strategies, tools, and techniques. Some common problem-solving techniques include: ask it loud; revisit the problem; 5Y; sunk cost fallacy; devil's advocate; be kind, rewind; asking probing questions; and reflective/active listening. [Agile Retrospectives: Making Good Teams Great. Esther Derby, Diana Larsen, Ken Schwaber.] [Knowledge and Skills: Level 1]

30. A - Literally thousands of decisions are made in the course of a project. Many of these decisions are made in response to problems that inevitably arise and confront the agile team. Therefore it is essential that an agile team is properly versed in problem-solving strategies, tools, and techniques. Some common problem-solving techniques include: ask it loud; revisit the problem; 5Y; sunk cost fallacy; devil's advocate; be kind, rewind; asking probing questions; and reflective/active listening. [Agile Retrospectives: Making Good Teams Great. Esther Derby, Diana Larsen, Ken Schwaber.] [Knowledge and Skills: Level 1]

31. D - Empowered teams - ones that are self-organizing and know how to solve problems with minimal management involvement - are a cornerstone of the agile methodology. An agile team feels empowered when it collectively assumes responsibility for the delivery of the product (i.e., taking ownership). [Coaching Agile Teams. Lyssa Adkins.] [Knowledge and Skills: Level 1]

32. D - Stakeholder management is a growing topic area within strategic management that brings awareness to the importance of managing stakeholders (i.e., facilitating active participation of stakeholders and fostering a strong collaborative environment) for a project's success. Stakeholder management is typically defined in the context of guiding principles and values. R. E. Freeman's 'Managing for Stakeholders' includes 10 principles: 1) Stakeholder interests need to go together over time. 2) We need a philosophy of volunteerism – to engage stakeholders and manage relationships ourselves rather than leave it to government. 3) We need to find solutions to issues that satisfy multiple stakeholders simultaneously. 4) Everything that we do serves stakeholders. We never trade off the interests of one versus the other continuously over time. 5) We act with purpose that fulfills our commitment to stakeholders. We act with aspiration towards fulfilling our dreams and theirs. 6) We need intensive communication and dialogue with stakeholders – not just those who are friendly. 7)Stakeholders consist of real people with names and faces and children. They are complex. 8)We need to generalize the marketing approach. 9) We engage with both primary and secondary stakeholders. 10) We constantly monitor and redesign processes to make them better serve our stakeholders. Because stakeholder involvement is critical for the success of a project, where projects without active participation from stakeholders are prone to failure, stakeholder management should be a topic that every agile team knows well. [The Art of Agile Development. James Shore.] [Knowledge and Skills: Level 1]

33. A - Planning poker is based upon the wideband Delphi estimation technique. It is a consensus-based technique for estimating effort. Sometimes called scrum poker, it is a technique for a relative estimation of effort, typically in story points, to develop a user story. At a planning poker meeting, each estimator is given an identical deck of planning poker cards with a wide range of values. The Fibonacci sequence is often used for values for planning poker (i.e., 0, 1, 1, 2, 3, 5,8,etc.); another common sequence is (question mark, 0, 1/2, 1, 2, 3, 5, 8, 13, 20, 40, and 100). A planning poker meeting works as follows: 1) a moderator, not estimating, facilitates the meeting. 2) the product owner/manager provides a short overview of the user story and answers clarifying questions posed by the developers. Typically the product owner does not vote. 3) Each estimator selects an estimate of work effort by selecting a card, 4) Once everyone has selected a card, everyone overturns their card concurrently, 5) Estimators with high and low estimates are given a chance to defend positions. 6) The process repeats until there is consensus. The developer who owns the user story is typically given higher credence. [Agile Estimating and Planning. Mike Cohn.] [Agile estimation]

34. D - In the SMART acronym, the T stands for 'Timeboxed' meaning that a well-defined task can be performed in a specific duration. [Agile Retrospectives: Making Good Teams Great. Esther Derby, Diana Larsen, Ken Schwaber.] [Planning, monitoring, and adapting]

35. D - In agile, effective 'knowledge sharing' is a critical factor for success. It involves the near real time communication of key information among all team members and stakeholders. To promote knowledge sharing, agile uses standard practices built into its process, such as using generalized specialists/cross functional teams, self-organizing and self-disciplined teams, collocation, daily stand-up meetings, iteration/sprint planning, release planning, pair programming and pair rotation, project retrospectives/reflection, and on-site customer support. And, of course, the sixth principle of Agile is " The most efficient and effective method of conveying information to and within a development team is face-to-face conversation." In this sense, Agile prefers and encourages collocation for all stakeholders and team members for the simple fact that face-to-face conversation is the best method of communication and, in turn, effective knowledge sharing. [Becoming Agile: ...in an imperfect world. Greg Smith, Ahmed Sidky.] [Knowledge and Skills: Level 1]

36. B - EVM or earned value management is a management technique used to evaluate project performance with respect to cost and schedule. EVM relies on other common financial metrics like Budget At Completion (BAC), Actual Cost (AC), Planned Value (PV), Earned Value (EV), Cost Variance (CV), Schedule Variance (SV), Cost Performance Index (CPI), and Schedule Performance Index (SPI). [Agile Estimating and Planning. Mike Cohn.] [Metrics]

37. D - EVM or earned value management is a management technique used to evaluate project performance with respect to cost and schedule. EVM relies on other common financial metrics like Budget At Completion (BAC), Actual Cost (AC), Planned Value (PV), Earned Value (EV), Cost Variance (CV), Schedule Variance (SV), Cost Performance Index (CPI), and Schedule Performance Index (SPI). [Agile Estimating and Planning. Mike Cohn.] [Metrics]

38. B - Like burnup charts, cumulative flow diagrams are information radiators that can track progress for agile projects. CFDs differ from traditional burnup charts because they convey total scope (not started, started, completed) of the entire backlog. Tracked items can be features, stories, tasks, or use cases. By tracking total scope, CFDs communicate absolute progress and give a proportional sense of project progress (e.g., On Day 14: 15% of features have been completed; 15% have been started; and, 70% have not been started). [Lean-Agile Software Development: Achieving Enterprise Agility. Alan Shalloway, Guy Beaver, James R. Trott.] [Planning, monitoring, and adapting]

39. B - Rolling wave planning (or rolling look ahead planning) involves planning in waves or phases and is especially useful for large, complex projects. Only the next few iterations are planned in detail and iterations more distant are planned only at a high-level. Progressive elaboration is continuous planning that assumes that details and requirements will be better refined later and will be incorporated into the planning process at the appropriate time. [Agile Estimating and Planning. Mike Cohn.] [Agile analysis and design]

40. D - Effective communication is a cornerstone of agile. Communication is the act of transferring information among various parties. Communications management is a knowledge and skill area of agile that highlights this importance. PMI has several definitions regarding communications management and agile builds on top of these to add its own perspective: 1) Communications Planning:

Determining the information and communication needs of the projects stakeholders 2) Information Distribution: Making needed information available to project stakeholders in a timely manner, 3) Performance Reporting: Collecting and distributing performance information. This includes status reporting, progress measurement, and forecasting, and 4) Managing Stakeholders: Managing communications to satisfy the requirements and resolve issues with project stakeholders. From an agile perspective: communication among the team is built into the process and facilitated through collocation, information radiators, daily stand-up meetings, retrospectives etc.; Although it is hoped that the product owner, customer, and user can be heavily involved with the project and also use these communication techniques, a plan for conveying information to stakeholders may be needed if this is not the case. [Agile Software Development: The Cooperative Game – 2nd Edition. Alistair Cockburn.] [Knowledge and Skills: Level 1]

Knowledge Area Quiz
Knowledge and Skills: Level 3
Practice Questions

Test Name: Knowledge Area Test: Knowledge and Skills: Level 3
Total Questions: 15
Correct Answers Needed to Pass:
11 (73.33%)
Time Allowed: 25 Minutes

Test Description

This practice quiz specifically targets your knowledge of the Knowledge and Skills: Level 3 exam topic area.

Test Questions

1. What term is often used to describe complex adaptive systems (CAS)?

   A. Chaordic

   B. Entropic

   C. Facile

   D. Static

2. Mark's agile team is geographically dispersed throughout the world. What is one factor the team should consider when conducting its business?

   A. Whether or not to demonstrate the product at the end of each iteration.

   B. Whether or not to have daily stand-up meetings.

   C. Whether or not to consider time zone differences when scheduling meetings.

   D. Whether or not to perform continuous testing and integration.

3. When an agile team authors documents to conform with local or federal regulations it is known as?

   A. Risk-aversion compliance

   B. Mandatory compliance

   C. Documentation compliance

   D. Regulatory compliance

4. When a non-agile company migrates to an agile framework what is often the most challenging task?

   A. Changing company culture

   B. Changing communication styles from top-down to face-to-face

   C. Changing the mindset from following rigid plans to adapting to change

   D. Changing project status meetings to daily stand-ups

5. Describe the type of organizational compliance an agile team upholds itself to when hired by an independent organization.

   A. The agile team ignores the organization's code of ethics and conduct.

B. The agile team complies with the organization's code of ethics and conduct.

C. The agile team follows its own code of ethics and conduct.

D. The agile team chooses what to comply with of the organization's code of ethics and conduct.

6. Ron is setting up control limits using a Shewhart control chart for his agile project. What control limit is typically used on a Shewhart control chart?

A. Six-sigma

B. One-sigma

C. Three-sigma

D. Five-sigma

7. Which agile framework uses an Exploratory 360 in its formal chartering process?

A. AUP

B. DSDM

C. Crystal

D. XP

8. What does the earned value management (EVM) accounting variable 'CPI' measure?

A. The cost performance index is a ratio of earned value over actual cost.

B. The cost performance indicator is a ratio of expected value over actual cost.

C. The cost performance index is a ratio of actual cost over earned value.

D. The cost performance indicator is a ratio of actualized cost over expected value.

9. Which agile framework emphasizes the practice of using a 40-hour work week?

A. XP

B. Scrum

C. Agile unified process (AUP)

D. DSDM

10. Which software development framework has a development process that is planned, managed, and tracked by feature?

A. Acceptance test driven development (ATDD)

B. Defect driven development (3D)

C. Test driven development (TDD)

D. Feature driven development (FDD)

11. Which type of contract is the least suitable for the agile development method?

A. Time and materials

B. Fixed-price

C. Cost-reimbursable

D. Not-to-exceed with fixed-fee

12. What popular agile game is used to estimate the relative effort of developing user stories?

A. Planning poker

B. Story point poker

C. Point poker

D. Poker

13. What does the earned value management (EVM) accounting variable 'SPI' measure?

A. The schedule performance index is a ratio of expected value over planned value.

B. The schedule performance index is a ratio of earned value over planned value.

C. The schedule performance index is a ratio of planned value over earned value.

D. The schedule performance index is a ratio of planned value over expected value.

14. Which agile framework emphasizes the always having a product that you could potentially ship/release?

A. XP

B. FDD

C. Crystal

D. Scrum

15. In which agile framework is the customer referred to as the "product owner?"

A. Extreme programming (XP)

B. Agile unified process (AUP)

C. Scrum

D. Lean software development

Knowledge Area Quiz
Knowledge and Skills: Level 3
Answer Key and Explanations

1. A - A complex adaptive system, or CAS, is a system composed of interacting, adaptive agents or components. The term is used in agile to remind practitioners that the development of a product is adaptive in that previous interactions, events, decisions influence future behavior. The term chaordic (a made up word blending chaotic and order) is sometimes used when describing CASs. Literature points to three key characteristics of chaordic projects: alignment and cooperation, emergence and self-organization, and learning and adaptation. [Agile Project Management: Creating Innovative Products – 2nd Edition. Jim Highsmith.] [Knowledge and Skills: Level 3]

2. C - A high-performance agile team is one that is ideally collocated for osmotic communication and face-to-face interaction. However, collocation isn't always feasible in today's multinational environment. For distributed teams, several practices are available to provide the best form of effective communication in the absence of being collocated: team intranet sites, virtual team rooms, and video conferencing over e-mail when possible. Geographic separation, especially on a world-wide scale, causes the team to consider language and cultural differences, and time zone differences. [Agile Software Development: The Cooperative Game – 2nd Edition. Alistair Cockburn.] [Knowledge and Skills: Level 3]

3. D - Although in agile project management, it is generally practiced to generate minimal documentation to support the project, some specific documents, like those required by regulatory bodies need to be created to comply with local and federal law. [Agile Project Management: Creating Innovative Products – 2nd Edition. Jim Highsmith.] [Knowledge and Skills: Level 3]

4. A - Changing company culture is typically the most difficult when migrating to an agile framework. [The Art of Agile Development. James Shore.] [Knowledge and Skills: Level 3]

5. B - Compliance with a company's code of ethics and professional conduct is standard practice in agile. [PMI Agile Community of Practice Community Charter. Project Management Institute.] [Knowledge and Skills: Level 3]

6. C - Control limits - those which set an objective range to indicate whether a process is controlled or stabilized or defect free (e.g., within three sigmas of the mean) - may be used in an agile project. Generally, a control limit of three-sigma (s) is used on a Shewhart control chart. A sigma refers to one standard deviation. So three sigmas indicates a limit three standard deviations away from the mean in both the positive and negative direction. This applies to normal data, where a normal distribution curve has been obtained. [Lean-Agile Software Development: Achieving Enterprise Agility. Alan Shalloway, Guy Beaver, James R. Trott.] [Knowledge and Skills: Level 3]

7. C - Crystal is a family of methodologies for a flexible and lightweight approach to software development. The family of methodologies is color coded to differentiate its members (e.g., clear, yellow,

orange, red.) The color chosen depends on the level of effort required. On one end of the spectrum is crystal clear, which is for smaller efforts, while crystal red is for larger efforts. Regardless of color, the crystal framework is cyclical and has three fundamental processes: chartering, delivery cycles, and wrap-up. Crystal chartering includes building the team, doing an Exploratory 360, defining standards of practice for the team, and building the project plan. In the delivery cycle, the crystal team iteratively develops, integrates, tests, and releases the product in iterations that last from one week to two months. Like other agile frameworks, crystal includes collaborative events, like stand-up meetings and reflective improvement workshops. In wrap-up the team concludes the project and holds a completion ritual where the team reflects on the entire project. [Agile Software Development: The Cooperative Game – 2nd Edition. Alistair Cockburn.] [Knowledge and Skills: Level 3]

8. A - EVM or earned value management is a management technique used to evaluate project performance with respect to cost and schedule. EVM relies on other common financial metrics like Budget At Completion (BAC), Actual Cost (AC), Planned Value (PV), Earned Value (EV), Cost Variance (CV), Schedule Variance (SV), Cost Performance Index (CPI), and Schedule Performance Index (SPI). CV and SV can be converted into performance indicators of CPI and SPI, respectively, and tracked and charted to show progress over time. BAC is the total project budget. AC is the actual cost incurred to date. PV is the planned value of work at a given time in a project; you can calculate it by multiplying the BAC by the ratio of current week/scheduled weeks (e.g., 5 weeks into a 15 week $15,000 project = $5,000 PV). EV is value of work actually completed or earned (e.g., you have completed 50% of the project by week 5 of a 15 week $15,000 project = $7,500 EV). CV is the difference between what a project has earned to date and cost to date (i.e., CV = EV - AC). SV is the difference between what a project has earned to date and what it was planned to earn to date (i.e., SV = EV - PV). CPI is a ratio that expresses cost performance. CPI = EV/AC. If CPI > 1, the project is earning more than spending; and if CPI 1, the project is ahead of schedule and if SPI < 1, the project is behind schedule. [Agile Estimating and Planning. Mike Cohn.] [Knowledge and Skills: Level 3]

9. A - Extreme Programming (XP) uses the following practices: pair programming, collective ownership, continuous integration, 40-hour week, on-site customer, coding standards, open workspace, and team rules [Agile Software Development: The Cooperative Game – 2nd Edition. Alistair Cockburn.] [Knowledge and Skills: Level 3]

10. D - Feature driven development (FDD) uses a prescriptive model where the software development process is planned, managed, and tracked from the perspective of individual software features. FDD uses short iterations of two weeks or less to develop a set amount of features. The five step FDD process is: 1. Develop overall model; 2. Create the features list; 3. Plan by feature; 4. Design by feature; 5 Build by feature. [Agile Software Development: The Cooperative Game – 2nd Edition. Alistair Cockburn.] [Knowledge and Skills: Level 3]

11. B - Fixed-price contracts, although typical of traditional projects where scope is

defined ahead of time, are not well suited for agile. When scope is fixed it can deter a team from exploring out-of-scope solutions that may add value to the product. Contracts suited for agile include: general service for the initial phase with fixed-price contracts for successive phases; cost-reimbursable/time and materials; not-to-exceed with fixed-fee; and a combination with incentives. [Agile Software Development: The Cooperative Game – 2nd Edition. Alistair Cockburn.] [Knowledge and Skills: Level 3]

12. A - Planning poker is a popular agile 'game' used to estimate the relative work effort (story points) of developing user stories. [Coaching Agile Teams. Lyssa Adkins.] [Knowledge and Skills: Level 3]

13. B - Schedule Performance Index (SPI). SPI is a ratio that expresses schedule performance. SPI = EV / PV. If SPI > 1, the project is ahead of schedule and if SPI < 1, the project is behind schedule. AC is the actual cost the project has incurred to date. [Agile Estimating and Planning. Mike Cohn.] [Knowledge and Skills: Level 3]

14. D - Scrum emphasizes, in part, the following principles: always have a product you can theoretically ship, speak a common language, and continuously test the product as you build it. [Agile Project Management with Scrum. Ken Schwaber.] [Knowledge and Skills: Level 3]

15. C - The core roles in scrum are the product owner, scrum master and development team. [Agile Project Management with Scrum. Ken Schwaber.] [Knowledge and Skills: Level 3]

PMI-ACP Lite Mock Exam 18 Practice Questions

Test Name: PMI-ACP Lite Mock Exam 18
Total Questions: 40
Correct Answers Needed to Pass: 30 (75.00%)
Time Allowed: 60 Minutes

Test Description

This is a cumulative PMI-ACP Mock Exam which can be used as a benchmark for your PMI-ACP aptitude. This practice test includes questions from all exam topic areas, including sections from Agile Tools and Techniques, and all three Agile Knowledge and Skills areas.

Test Questions

1. If a team believes during sprint planning that a task is expected to take approximately 8 hours to complete, what would be a good timebox value to assign to the task?

A. 16 hours

B. 8 hours

C. 4 hours

D. 24 hours

2. What topic area within strategic management deals with fostering a work environment to engage stakeholders?

A. Stakeholder management

B. Value management

C. Scope management

D. Executive management

3. During the last iteration, Paula and her agile team completed 10 user stories worth 1 point each, 2 user stories worth 5 points each, and nearly completed one user story point worth 5 points. What was the team's velocity for the previous iteration?

A. 30

B. 20

C. 5

D. 10

4. Which of the following is a process analysis technique.

A. Process mapping

B. Reflection agenda

C. Scrum

D. Product roadmap

5. Which software development framework stresses the use of pair-programming and shared workspaces?

A. Extreme programming (XP)

B. Lean software development

C. Agile unified process (AUP)

D. Scrum

6. What is a typical scrum timebox value for a sprint planning meeting?

A. 16 hours

B. 24 hours

C. 4 hours

D. 8 hours

7. What is the typical duration of a sprint?

A. Three to five weeks.

B. Two months.

C. One week.

D. Two to four weeks.

8. The scrum framework what stakeholders compose the three "managers?"

A. Scrum master, executive sponsor, and product owner

B. Scrum master, executive sponsor, and business analyst

C. Product owner, scrum master, and team

D. Scrum master, product team, and development team

9. Of the following, which is a key soft skill negotiation quality?

A. Strong leadership

B. Seismic leadership

C. Servant leadership

D. Safety leadership

10. Having a high emotional intelligence is important to promote effective communication in an agile team. What is one of the seven components of emotional intelligence as defined by Higgs & Dulewicz?

A. Emotional resilience

B. Reticence

C. Confidence

D. Self-aggrandizement

11. Having a high emotional intelligence is important to promote effective communication in an agile team. Which of the following\ is one of the seven components of emotional intelligence as defined by Higgs & Dulewicz?

A. Conscientiousness

B. Reticence

C. Confidence

D. Self-aggrandizement

12. Jessica is using active listening to help her agile team member work through a design

challenge she is facing. In this context, what agile knowledge and skill area does active listening fall under?

A. Problem-mitigation strategies, tools, and techniques

B. Problem-solving strategies, tools, and techniques

C. Problem-reversing strategies, tools, and techniques

D. Problem-saturation strategies, tools, and techniques

13. Why is the quality of servant leadership desirable for agile team leaders?

A. Self-organizing teams need a key enabler to remove obstacles and provide effective coaching.

B. Self-organizing teams need an authoritative figure that assigns tasks and makes sure the project is on schedule and budget.

C. Self-organizing teams do not need servant leadership.

D. Self-organizing teams need an ambassador between it and the product owner to reduce interruptions.

14. Stacey intends to schedule a brainstorming session to generate ideas that may help solve some of the team's current issues. Which of the following is NOT a good brainstorming technique that Stacey should use?

A. Leaving participants in the dark until the day of the meeting to add an element of surprise.

B. Having a multi-disciplinary/diverse group so that many different perspectives are available.

C. Sending participants preparatory material, so they know what to expect and what is expected of them.

D. Having an engaging and experienced facilitator lead the brainstorming session.

15. When are user stories initially defined?

A. During iteration planning

B. During release planning

C. During project vision planning

D. During sprint planning

16. Paula, as team leader, wants to design a comfortable, collaborative team space for her agile project. What can she do as a basic guideline?

A. Separate of team members by function

B. Collocate team members

C. Rotate team member roles

D. Isolate team members

17. Stephanie, as team leader, wants to design a comfortable, collaborative team space for her agile project. What can she do as a basic guideline?

A. Reserve a space for daily stand-up meetings

B. Arrange seating to group by team function

C. Rotate team member roles

D. Separate team members by function

18. In agile modeling, what is a good example of a name given to a persona?

A. ATM user

B. ATM maintainer

C. Ronald Herbert

D. ATM machine

19. Christy is confused about the purpose of a product roadmap. She asks Thomas, her project manager, to identify a benefit of a product roadmap to help her understand a product roadmaps purpose. Select the benefit of a product roadmap.

A. Helps facilitate daily stand-up meetings.

B. Helps facilitate the organization of features into categories or themes.

C. Helps facilitate reflection meetings.

D. Helps facilitate iteration development.

20. In the lean manufacturing, just-in-time concept of kanban, is inventory control based on pull or push?

A. Push

B. Both pull and push

C. Neither pull or push

D. Pull

21. Jane and her team are demonstrating to the business stakeholder recently developed product code. At the demonstration, the team reviews what the expected behavior of the code is based on previous collaborative discussions with the stakeholders and also brings up any risks the team found during the development process (e.g., other ways the code may fail that were not thought of in previous discussions). What step is Jane on in the ATDD four step process?

A. 2nd

B. 4th

C. 1st

D. 3rd

22. Of the following responses, which is NOT a community value per the PMI agile community of practice community charter?

A. Peaceful

B. Vision

C. Trust

D. Servant Leadership

23. Which of the following is a key soft skill negotiation quality?

A. Serial leadership

B. Service leadership

C. Servile leadership

D. Servant leadership

24. Jan is looking at an important agile document that includes the project mission and success criteria. What document is Jan most likely reviewing?

A. Statement of work

B. Team virtual page

C. Project charter

D. Mission statement

25. What is one method that can be used to improve communication for a team that cannot be collocated?

A. Setting up a team intranet site

B. Setting up an RSS feed

C. Setting up a listserv

D. Setting up a message board

26. According to Highsmith, what type of contract does agile lend itself well to?

A. Firm fixed-price

B. Fixed-budget and fixed-schedule

C. Fixed-schedule and fixed-price

D. Fixed-budget and fixed-price

27. How is risk severity, as used in a risk burndown chart, typically calculated?

A. Severity = impact * planned cost

B. Severity = impact * planned value

C. Severity = impact * actual cost

D. Severity = impact * probability/likelihood

28. Which of the following is NOT a characteristic of agile project management?

A. Short iterations

B. Top-down decision making

C. Cross-functional teams

D. Continuous improvement

29. According to the PMI Code, unethical or illegal conduct

A. Should be reported to the offending parties for resolution.

B. Should be reported to appropriate parties.

C. Should be reported to upper management.

D. Should be reported to the human resources office.

30. Stacey knows that feedback techniques are ubiquitous in agile projects. Which of the following lists an agile 'feedback technique for product?'

A. Spike task

B. Slam task

C. Risk reduction task

D. Sprint planning

31. What is the agile technique of affinity estimation notably useful for?

A. Eliminating the need for task duration estimation

B. Slowing down the estimation process

C. Large product backlogs

D. Small product backlogs

32. What acronym helps the agile practitioner remember the characteristics of a well-defined task?

A. SPORT

B. SMART

C. STRONG

D. SMALL

33. What topic area within strategic management deals with promoting a work environment where stakeholders are constantly engaged?

A. Schedule management

B. Stakeholder management

C. Risk management

D. Interaction management

34. Of the following, select a method used in agile for the purpose of prioritization.

A. SMART

B. INVEST

C. Kano

D. WIDETOM

35. Becky and her agile team have just performed decomposition on several user stories and wants to prioritize them. What common technique might she and her team use to prioritize the user stories?

A. SMART

B. INVEST

C. WoSCoM

D. MoSCoW

36. What is the fourth step of the ATDD four step process?

A. Demo

B. Develop

C. Distill

D. Discuss

37. How might an agile team continuously improve its product?

A. By performing work breakdown structure reviews.

B. By performing ongoing integration testing.

C. By using comprehensive documentation to define team values.

D. By performing integration testing near the end of a release.

38. Ginny has recently started an agile project where she is to be the project leader. What should Ginny aspire to be as agile leader?

A. Someone who builds team trust and removes any obstacles a team may face during its effort.

B. Someone that drives the team to maximum and unsustainable performance levels to exceed customer expectations.

C. Someone who constantly criticizes team members so that they are aware of their defects and can improve their performance.

D. Someone who builds an authoritative air so that team members know who is in charge.

39. Victoria has recently started an agile project where she is to be the project leader. What should Victoria aspire to be as agile leader?

A. Someone who constantly criticizes team members so that they are aware of their defects and can improve their performance.

B. Someone that drives the team to maximum and unsustainable performance levels to exceed customer expectations.

C. Someone who communicates and endorses the values and principles of agile project management to stakeholders that may be unfamiliar with agile.

D. Someone who espouses agile project management as the best and therefore only management method that can succeed in today's volatile marketplace.

40. Kyle knows that a delivery concept of agile is defined as "frequent delivery of working products, which are successively improved, to a customer for immediate feedback and acceptance." Which term is this delivery concept?

A. Release delivery

B. Incremental delivery

C. Value stream delivery

D. Sprint delivery

PMI-ACP Lite Mock Exam 18 Answer Key and Explanations

1. B - Timeboxing is a realistic estimate or expectation of how long an action, task, or event will take to perform. Some tasks cannot be performed in the initial timeboxed estimate and are good candidates for reevaluation and possibly further decomposition into more tasks. [The Art of Agile Development. James Shore.] [Planning, monitoring, and adapting]

2. A - Stakeholder management is a growing topic area within strategic management that brings awareness to the importance of managing stakeholders (i.e., facilitating active participation of stakeholders and fostering a strong collaborative environment) for a project's success. Stakeholder management is typically defined in the context of guiding principles and values. R. E. Freeman's 'Managing for Stakeholders' includes 10 principles: 1) Stakeholder interests need to go together over time. 2) We need a philosophy of volunteerism – to engage stakeholders and manage relationships ourselves rather than leave it to government. 3) We need to find solutions to issues that satisfy multiple stakeholders simultaneously. 4) Everything that we do serves stakeholders. We never trade off the interests of one versus the other continuously over time. 5) We act with purpose that fulfills our commitment to stakeholders. We act with aspiration towards fulfilling our dreams and theirs. 6) We need intensive communication and dialogue with stakeholders – not just those who are friendly. 7)Stakeholders consist of real people with names and faces and children. They are complex. 8)We need to generalize the marketing approach. 9) We engage with both primary and secondary stakeholders. 10) We constantly monitor and redesign processes to make them better serve our stakeholders. Because stakeholder involvement is critical for the success of a project, where projects without active participation from stakeholders are prone to failure, stakeholder management should be a topic that every agile team knows well. [The Art of Agile Development. James Shore.] [Knowledge and Skills: Level 1]

3. B - The team's velocity is 20. 10 x 1 + 2 x 5 = 20. Story points for partially completed stories are not included in the velocity metric. [Agile Estimating and Planning. Mike Cohn.] [Metrics]

4. A - Value stream mapping is a collaborative process analysis technique where a diverse team depicts/maps a process to identify where waste occurs and where improvements can be made. It is an example of a process analysis technique. Like value stream mapping, process mapping is also used to map a process to identify bottlenecks (places where processing slows and inventory can build). [Lean-Agile Software Development: Achieving Enterprise Agility. Alan Shalloway, Guy Beaver, James R. Trott.] [Knowledge and Skills: Level 2]

5. A - Extreme programming (XP) is a programmer-centric agile framework that focuses on small, ongoing releases. XP highlights several principles: pair programming, sustainable pace, ongoing automated testing, effective communication, simplicity, feedback, courage, collective ownership, continuous integration, energized work, shared workspaces, on-site customer representation, and the use of metaphor to describe concepts. [Agile

Software Development: The Cooperative Game – 2nd Edition. Alistair Cockburn.] [Knowledge and Skills: Level 2]

6. C - In the agile framework scrum, sprint planning and sprint review meetings are often timeboxed at four hours. [The Art of Agile Development. James Shore.] [Planning, monitoring, and adapting]

7. D - A cornerstone of Agile development is 'incremental delivery.' Incremental delivery is the frequent delivery of working products, which are successively improved, to a customer for immediate feedback and acceptance. Typically, a product is delivered at the end of each sprint or iteration for demonstration and feedback. In this feedback technique, a customer can review the product and provide updated requirements. Changed/updated/refined requirements are welcomed in the agile process to ensure the customer receives a valuable and quality product. A sprint or iteration typically lasts from two to four weeks and at the end a new and improved product is delivered, incrementally. [The Art of Agile Development. James Shore.] [Knowledge and Skills: Level 1]

8. C - The three "managers" of the scrum framework include the product owner, scrum master, and team. [Agile Project Management with Scrum. Ken Schwaber.] [Knowledge and Skills: Level 2]

9. C - Key soft skills negotiation qualities for the effective implementation and practice of agile are: emotional intelligence, collaboration, adaptive leadership, negotiation, conflict resolution, servant leadership. [Coaching Agile Teams. Lyssa Adkins.] [Soft skills negotiation]

10. A - Higgs & Dulewicz (1999) defines emotional intelligence using seven components: 1) Self-awareness, 2) Emotional resilience, 3) Motivation, 4) Interpersonal sensitivity, 5) Influence, 6) Intuitiveness, and 7) Conscientiousness. [Coaching Agile Teams. Lyssa Adkins.] [Soft skills negotiation]

11. A - Higgs & Dulewicz (1999) defines emotional intelligence using seven components: 1) Self-awareness, 2) Emotional resilience, 3) Motivation, 4) Interpersonal sensitivity, 5) Influence, 6) Intuitiveness, and 7) Conscientiousness. [Coaching Agile Teams. Lyssa Adkins.] [Soft skills negotiation]

12. B - Literally thousands of decisions are made in the course of a project. Many of these decisions are made in response to problems that inevitably arise and confront the agile team. Therefore it is essential that an agile team is properly versed in problem-solving strategies, tools, and techniques. Some common problem-solving techniques include: ask it loud; revisit the problem; 5Y; sunk cost fallacy; devil's advocate; be kind, rewind; asking probing questions; and reflective/active listening. [Agile Retrospectives: Making Good Teams Great. Esther Derby, Diana Larsen, Ken Schwaber.] [Knowledge and Skills: Level 1]

13. A - Servant leadership has its roots with an essay written in 1970 by Robert K Greenleaf. Greenleaf defined servant leaders as humble stewards devoted to their company and work to serve their peers, teams, and customers. In a self-organizing team, a servant leader, as Greenleaf defined it, is ideal as the team leader is an enabler, listening to the agile team's needs, removing obstacles, and providing tools or other

support to promote high productivity. [Coaching Agile Teams. Lyssa Adkins.] [Soft skills negotiation]

14. A - A successful brainstorming event should strive to consider the following points - Host the meeting in a neutral and comfortable environment - Have an engaging and experienced facilitator lead the event - Send participants an overview, with goals, schedule, and what ground rules, beforehand - Have a multi-disciplinary/diverse team to get a broader perspective - Delay any criticism that may stifle idea generation. [Agile Retrospectives: Making Good Teams Great. Esther Derby, Diana Larsen, Ken Schwaber.] [Knowledge and Skills: Level 1]

15. B - Release planning is important because the customer and development team collaborate to create a high-level plan for product release. User stories are initially defined during release planning. The release plan typically includes a schedule that includes several iterations and an estimate for when the product will be released. The development team discusses each user story in detail to, along with the customer, assign them to the project's iterations. [The Art of Agile Development. James Shore.] [Planning, monitoring, and adapting]

16. B - A warm, welcoming environment that promotes effective communication, innovation, and motivated team members is an important aspect to consider when designing team space. Guidelines for a better agile team space include: collocation of team members; reduction of non-essential noise/distractions; dedicated whiteboard and wall space for information radiators; space for the daily stand-up meeting and other meetings; pairing workstations; and other pleasantries like plants and comfortable furniture. [Agile Retrospectives: Making Good Teams Great. Esther Derby, Diana Larsen, Ken Schwaber.] [Communications]

17. A - A warm, welcoming environment that promotes effective communication, innovation, and motivated team members is an important aspect to consider when designing team space. Guidelines for a better agile team space include: collocation of team members; reduction of non-essential noise/distractions; dedicated whiteboard and wall space for information radiators; space for the daily stand-up meeting and other meetings; pairing workstations; and other pleasantries like plants and comfortable furniture. [Agile Retrospectives: Making Good Teams Great. Esther Derby, Diana Larsen, Ken Schwaber.] [Communications]

18. C - A persona is a notional user of the system under development. Being much more detailed than actors in use case modeling where generic user names are assigned (e.g., end user), personas try to elaborate on users with detailed descriptions to provide context to the developers. Some personas have such notional details as name, address, age, income, likes and dislikes, and other specific details. [User Stories Applied: For Agile Software Development. Mike Cohn.] [Agile analysis and design]

19. B - The product roadmap - owned by the product owner - serves as a high level overview of the product requirements. It is used as a tool for prioritizing features , organizing features into categories, and assigning rough time frames. Creating a product roadmap has four basic steps: 1)

Identify requirements (these will become part of the product backlog), 2) Organize requirements into categories or themes, 3) Estimate relative work effort (e.g., planning poker or affinity estimation) and prioritize (value), and 4) Estimate rough time frames (estimate velocity, sprint duration, and rough release dates). [The Art of Agile Development. James Shore.] [Agile analysis and design]

20. D - Kanban, Japanese for billboard or signboard, is a scheduling system for just-in-time (JIT) production developed by Toyota in the 1940s and 1950s. It is a way of controlling and reducing inventory by using cards or signs to order (demand signal) requisite parts for a manufacturing process from other dependent systems (supply). Kanban has been adopted by agile to help control workflow. Kanban is based on the concept of 'pull.' Where the demand signal for production originates from the end customer requesting a product. When the customer orders a product (e.g., car) it sends a cascading "pull" signal that triggers through the manufacturing process. [Lean-Agile Software Development: Achieving Enterprise Agility. Alan Shalloway, Guy Beaver, James R. Trott.] [Planning, monitoring, and adapting]

21. B - Acceptance Test Driven Development (ATDD) is similar to Test-driven development (TDD) in that it requires programmers to create tests first before any product code. The tests in ATDD are aimed at confirming features/behaviors that the intended software will have. The iterative cycle of ATDD with its four steps can be remembered as the four Ds: 1) Discuss, 2) Distill, 3) Develop, and 4) Demo. 1) Discuss: The agile team and customer or business stakeholder discuss a user story in detail. Talking about the expected behaviors the user story should have and what it should not. 2) The development team takes those items learned from the discussion and distills them into tests that will verify and validate those behaviors. The distillation process is where the entire team should have a good understanding of what "done" (or completed) means for a user story. That is, what the acceptance criteria are. 3) After distillation, the team develops the test code and product code to implement the product features. 4) Once the product features have been developed, the team demonstrates them to the customer or business stakeholders for feedback. [Lean-Agile Software Development: Achieving Enterprise Agility. Alan Shalloway, Guy Beaver, James R. Trott.] [Product quality]

22. A - The following are community values of the PMI agile community of practice community charter: Vision, Servant Leadership, Trust, Collaboration, Honesty, Learning, Courage, Openness, Adaptability, Leading Change, Transparency [PMI Agile Community of Practice Community Charter. Project Management Institute.] [Knowledge and Skills: Level 1]

23. D - Key soft skills negotiation qualities for the effective implementation and practice of agile are: emotional intelligence, collaboration, adaptive leadership, negotiation, conflict resolution, servant leadership. [Coaching Agile Teams. Lyssa Adkins.] [Soft skills negotiation]

24. C - The project charter is an important governing document that requires all stakeholder participation. Although experts recommend it not be longer than a page in length, creating a project charter can be challenging, as all stakeholders must participate and come to a consensus. Three key elements should be included in a project charter: vision, mission, and success criteria. Vision is the 'why' or rationale of a project. Mission is the 'what' of the project and describes what the team will accomplish to reach the vision. Success criteria are management metrics that define 'how' the project will be deemed successful. [Lean-Agile Software Development: Achieving Enterprise Agility. Alan Shalloway, Guy Beaver, James R. Trott.] [Knowledge and Skills: Level 2]

25. A - A high-performance agile team is one that is ideally collocated for osmotic communication and face-to-face interaction. However, collocation isn't always feasible in today's multinational environment. For distributed teams, several practices are available to provide the best form of effective communication in the absence of being collocated: team intranet sites, virtual team rooms, and video conferencing over e-mail when possible. Geographic separation, especially on a world-wide scale, causes the team to consider language and cultural differences, and time zone differences. [The Art of Agile Development. James Shore.] [Knowledge and Skills: Level 2]

26. B - Time, budget, and cost estimation is an important knowledge and skill area of agile. According to Highsmith, the nature of the agile method, whereby it welcomes changing scope, means that it lends itself well to fixed budgets and a fixed schedule because changing scope makes it difficult to estimate a total cost. Generally speaking, the budget and schedule constraints are known but before a project will commence there needs to be an agreed upon set of base product functionality defined in an initiation phase; fixing scope reduces an agile team's innovative tendency to provide improved value. For companies that are familiar with fixed-price contracts, where requirements are agreed upon before contract closing, adopting agile can be a weary initial venture. Instead, other contract vehicle types are recommended for agile efforts. These include: a general service contract for the initiation phase and separate fixed-price contracts for iterations or user stories; time-and-material contracts; not-to-exceed with fixed-fee contracts; and, incentive contracts (e.g., fixed price with incentive; cost-reimbursable with award fee). [Agile Project Management: Creating Innovative Products – 2nd Edition. Jim Highsmith.] [Knowledge and Skills: Level 1]

27. D - A risk burndown chart is a risk management technique used to track project risk over time. It allows stakeholders to quickly review project risk management performance (e.g., increasing, decreasing, and by how much) over time. Severity (a product of impact and probability) is charted along the vertical axis with time on the horizontal axis. Impact typically takes a value from 0 to 5 in increasing order of risk and probability/likelihood typically takes a value from 0 to 5 in increasing order of probability. In this example, the worst severity a risk could have is 25 (5 x 5 = 25) and the least harmful severity a risk could have is 0. The agile team and customer/product owner identifies its risks and assigns severity values in a risk register and tracks those values over time. Ideally, risk severity will decrease over time. [The Art of Agile Development. James Shore.] [Risk management]

28. B - Key characteristics of agile project management include: continuous improvement, cross-functional teams, short iterations, an incremental approach, and business priorities and customer value. [The Art of Agile Development. James Shore.] [Knowledge and Skills: Level 1]

29. B - The PMI Code of Ethics and Professional Conduct states that it is mandatory for a project manager to: inform yourself about and uphold the policies, rules, regulations, and laws that govern your work, including professional and volunteer activities; report unethical or illegal conduct to appropriate parties and, if necessary, to those affected by the misconduct; ensure that any allegations of misconduct or illegal activity are substantiated and file only complaints that are supported by facts; never take part or help someone else take part in illegal activities. [PMI Code of Ethics and Professional Conduct. Project Management Institute.] [Knowledge and Skills: Level 2]

30. D - There are several feedback techniques - techniques that facilitate constructive criticism to improve product value and quality - built into the agile process. In the classic definition, feedback is a dynamic process where past information influences the behavior of the same process in the future. Agile feedback techniques include prototyping, simulation, demonstration, evaluations, pair programming, unit testing, continuous integration, daily stand-up meetings, sprint planning. Because agile prides itself on a transparent and collaborative environment, feedback is essentially ubiquitous. [Agile Retrospectives: Making Good Teams Great. Esther Derby, Diana Larsen, Ken Schwaber.] [Knowledge and Skills: Level 1]

31. C - Affinity estimating is a method to predict the work effort, typically in story points, of developing a user story. It is particularly useful for large product backlogs. Although several methods exist, the basic affinity estimating model involves sizing user stories on a scale from small to large. The scale can be a Fibonacci sequence or t-shirt sizes and is typically taped to a wall in a large conference room. Participants then attach their user stories to the wall as estimates. It is often done in silence and has several iterations until the user stories have been estimated. [The Art of Agile Development. James Shore.] [Agile estimation]

32. B - The acronym SMART (specific, measurable, achievable, relevant, and time-boxed) helps the agile practitioner remember the characteristics of a well-defined task. S – Specific tasks are ones that clearly contribute to the development of a user story. It should not be vague. M – Measurable tasks are ones that the team and customer can verify. A - Achievable tasks are ones that developers may realistically implement and understand. R - Relevant tasks are ones that unequivocally add value to the user story. T - Timeboxed tasks are ones that can have an estimate assigned of the amount of effort or time needed for development. [Agile Retrospectives: Making Good Teams Great. Esther Derby, Diana Larsen, Ken Schwaber.] [Planning, monitoring, and adapting]

33. B - Stakeholder management is a growing topic area within strategic management that brings awareness to the importance of managing stakeholders (i.e., facilitating active participation of stakeholders and fostering a strong collaborative environment) for a project's success. Stakeholder management is typically defined in the context of guiding principles and values. R. E. Freeman's 'Managing for Stakeholders' includes 10 principles: 1) Stakeholder interests need to go together over time. 2) We need a philosophy of volunteerism – to engage stakeholders and manage relationships ourselves rather than leave it to government. 3) We need to find solutions to issues that satisfy multiple stakeholders simultaneously. 4) Everything that we do serves stakeholders. We never trade off the interests of one versus the other continuously over time. 5) We act with purpose that fulfills our commitment to stakeholders. We act with aspiration towards fulfilling our dreams and theirs. 6) We need intensive communication and dialogue with stakeholders – not just those who are friendly. 7)Stakeholders consist of real people with names and faces and children. They are complex. 8)We need to generalize the marketing approach. 9) We engage with both primary and secondary stakeholders. 10) We constantly monitor and redesign processes to make them better serve our stakeholders. Because stakeholder involvement is critical for the success of a project, where projects without active participation from stakeholders are prone to failure, stakeholder management should be a topic that every agile team knows well. [The Art of Agile Development. James Shore.] [Knowledge and Skills: Level 1]

34. C - An agile team must always face the prioritization of product features in its product backlog. From release planning to iteration planning, an agile team must prioritize the user stories/ features of its product to ensure that high-quality and high-value features are developed first to help facilitate an optimized and early return on investment (ROI). An agile team typically prioritizes requirements or user stories/features in terms of relative value and risk; value is defined by the customer (i.e., customer-value prioritization). Two common methods to prioritize product features are: MoSCoW and Kano. The MoSCoW method categorizes features into 'Must have,' 'Should have,' 'Could have,' and 'Would have' features. The Kano method categorizes features into 'Must haves (threshold),' 'Dissatisfiers,' 'Satisfiers,' and 'Delighters.' Must haves are features that are requisite. Dissatisfiers are features that adversely impact perceived value and should be eliminated. 'Satisfiers' are features that increase perceived value linearly, where the more you add the more the customer is pleased, but are not required, and 'Delighters' are features that increase perceived value exponentially to please the customer. To prioritize features based on risk, a risk-to-value matrix can be used. A risk-to-value matrix has four quadrants, with the horizontal axis having low and high value, and the vertical axis having low and high risk. User stories are assigned to one of the four categories/quadrants: low-value, low-risk; low-value, high-risk; high-value, low-risk; high-value, high-risk. A cost-to-value matrix can also be made in this manner. All prioritization in agile is 'relative,' meaning that the priority of one user story is relative to other user stories and not prioritized on a fixed scale. [Lean-Agile Software Development: Achieving Enterprise Agility. Alan Shalloway, Guy Beaver, James R. Trott.] [Knowledge and Skills: Level 1]

35. D - In iteration planning, an agile team, collaboratively with the customer, chooses user stories to include for development.

Although the user stories are prioritized in the product backlog initially during release planning, an agile team and customer should review prioritization based on progressive elaboration (i.e., gained knowledge and perspective). Prioritization is often based on value and risk and can be performed using the MoSCoW or Kano method and through the use of risk-to-value and cost-to-value matrices. An agile team performs decomposition to sub-divide user stories into more manageable tasks so that it may estimate task time. Tasks for an iteration may also be prioritized based on value, similar to how user stories are prioritized. [Lean-Agile Software Development: Achieving Enterprise Agility. Alan Shalloway, Guy Beaver, James R. Trott.] [Knowledge and Skills: Level 1]

36. A - Acceptance Test Driven Development (ATDD) is similar to Test-driven development (TDD) in that it requires programmers to create tests first before any product code. The tests in ATDD are aimed at confirming features/behaviors that the intended software will have. The iterative cycle of ATDD with its four steps can be remembered as the four Ds: 1) Discuss, 2) Distill, 3) Develop, and 4) Demo. 1) Discuss: The agile team and customer or business stakeholder discuss a user story in detail. Talking about the expected behaviors the user story should have and what it should not. 2) The development team takes those items learned from the discussion and distills them into tests that will verify and validate those behaviors. The distillation process is where the entire team should have a good understanding of what "done" (or completed) means for a user story. That is, what the acceptance criteria are. 3) After distillation, the team develops the test code and product code to implement the product features. 4) Once the product features have been developed, the team demonstrates them to the customer or business stakeholders for feedback. [Lean-Agile Software Development: Achieving Enterprise Agility. Alan Shalloway, Guy Beaver, James R. Trott.] [Product quality]

37. B - Agile project management places strong emphasis on 'continuous improvement.' Continuous improvement processes are built into the agile methodology, from customers providing feedback after each iteration to the team reserving time to reflect on its performance through retrospectives after each iteration. Ongoing unit and integration testing and keeping up with technological/industry developments also play a part in the continuous improvement process. Continuous improvement is also a key principle in the lean methodology, where a focus of removing waste from the value stream is held. [The Art of Agile Development. James Shore.] [Knowledge and Skills: Level 2]

38. A - A common misconception in agile is that an agile team does not need a leader. In fact, all agile teams need a leader, but the way in which the leader leads is fundamentally different than the typical traditional project manager/project leader method. Some have theorized that this misconception stems from the desired 'self-organizing' quality of the agile team. And although the 'self-organizing' agile team is empowered to take ownership and responsibility of the product and make some decisions itself, it nevertheless requires a leader to help provide guidance, mentoring, coaching, problem solving, and decision making. Some key aspects required of an agile leader include: empowering team members to decide what standard agile practices and methods it will use; allowing the team to be self-organized and self-disciplined; empowering the team members to make decisions collaboratively with the customer; inspire the team to be innovative and explore new ideas and technology capabilities; be a champion of and articulate the product vision to team members so it will be motivated to accomplish the overall objective; remove any obstacles and solve any problems the team may face in its effort; communicate and endorse the values and principles of agile project management to stakeholders that may be unfamiliar with agile; ensure that all stakeholders, including business managers and developers, are collaborating effectively; and, be able to adapt the leadership style to the working environment to ensure that the agile values and principles are effectively upheld. [The Art of Agile Development. James Shore.] [Knowledge and Skills: Level 1]

39. C - A common misconception in agile is that an agile team does not need a leader. In fact, all agile teams need a leader, but the way in which the leader leads is fundamentally different than the typical traditional project manager/project leader method. Some have theorized that this misconception stems from the desired 'self-organizing' quality of the agile team. And although the 'self-organizing' agile team is empowered to take ownership and responsibility of the product and make some decisions itself, it nevertheless requires a leader to help provide guidance, mentoring, coaching, problem solving, and decision making. Some key aspects required of an agile leader include: empowering team members to decide what standard agile practices and methods it will use; allowing the team to be self-organized and self-disciplined; empowering the team members to make decisions collaboratively with the customer; inspire the team to be innovative and explore new ideas and technology capabilities; be a champion of and articulate the product vision to team members so it will be motivated to accomplish the overall objective; remove any obstacles and solve any problems the team may face in its effort; communicate and endorse the values and principles of agile project management to stakeholders that may be unfamiliar with agile; ensure that all stakeholders, including business managers and developers, are collaborating effectively; and, be able to adapt the leadership style to the working environment to ensure that the agile values and principles are effectively upheld. [The Art of Agile Development. James Shore.] [Knowledge and Skills: Level 1]

40. B - A cornerstone of Agile development is 'incremental delivery.' Incremental delivery is the frequent delivery of working products, which are successively improved, to a customer for immediate feedback and acceptance. Typically, a product is delivered at the end of each sprint or iteration for demonstration and feedback. In this feedback technique, a customer can review the product and provide updated requirements. Changed/updated/refined requirements are welcomed in the agile process to ensure the customer receives a valuable and quality product. A sprint or iteration typically lasts from two to four weeks and at the end a new and improved product is delivered, incrementally. [The Art of Agile Development. James Shore.] [Knowledge and Skills: Level 1]

PMI-ACP Lite Mock Exam 19 Practice Questions

Test Name: PMI-ACP Lite Mock Exam 19
Total Questions: 40
Correct Answers Needed to Pass:
30 (75.00%)
Time Allowed: 60 Minutes

Test Description

This is a cumulative PMI-ACP Mock Exam which can be used as a benchmark for your PMI-ACP aptitude. This practice test includes questions from all exam topic areas, including sections from Agile Tools and Techniques, and all three Agile Knowledge and Skills areas.

Test Questions

1. Which of the following is the best definition of an agile leader?

A. Someone that provides guidance, mentoring, coaching, and makes decisions when needed, but empowers the team to make its own decisions collaboratively a predominant amount of the time.

B. Someone that makes all decisions in the face of team adversity to quell unfavorable team dynamics.

C. Someone who is minimally available but present enough to make all decisions.

D. Someone that provides minimal guidance, mentoring, coaching, but makes all decisions without informing the team until required.

2. Edward has recently started an agile project where she is to be the project leader. What should Edward aspire to be as agile leader?

A. Someone who empowers the team to be self-organized and self-disciplined.

B. Someone who empowers the team to be self-sufficient and independent of any leadership.

C. Someone who empowers the team to be self-scrumming and self-introspective.

D. Someone who empowers the team to make all decisions by itself.

3. Xavier has just verified and validated that the test code he just wrote fails as part of the four step process of TDD. What step is Xavier performing?

A. 4th

B. 1st

C. 2nd

D. 3rd

4. In a self-assessment or reflection event, what is a likely topic a team will focus on?

A. Team standards that failed

B. The tester who caught the fewest bugs

C. Customer inconsistencies in requirements

D. Product owner values

5. Calculate the Net Present Value of the following investment candidate. The initial investment cost is $2,000. The discount rate is 5%. At the end of year 1, $2000 is expected. At the end of year 2, $2000 is expected. At the end of year 3, $2000 is expected.

A. $3,447

B. $3,337

C. $3,227

D. $3,667

6. Which is NOT a phase of Highsmith's agile project management?

A. Envisioning

B. Adapting

C. Speculating

D. Executing

7. Stephanie's agile team is always looking to improve its performance. Her team has decided to use an experienced agile practitioner and facilitator to come in and provide guidance to the team on how it may improve. What knowledge and skill area is this practitioner providing to the team?

A. Speculating and closing

B. Envisioning and elaborating

C. Knowledge building and mentoring

D. Coaching and mentoring

8. Jessica is using 'ask it loud' to help her understand the nature of an issue she is facing on the project. What agile knowledge and skill area does 'ask it loud' fall under?

A. Problem-saturation strategies, tools, and techniques

B. Problem-reversing strategies, tools, and techniques

C. Problem-mitigation strategies, tools, and techniques

D. Problem-solving strategies, tools, and techniques

9. EVM is a frequently used project management abbreviation. How is SPI calculated?

A. SPI = EV / PV

B. SPI = BAC / EV

C. SPI = PV / EV

D. SPI = BAC / PV

10. What person in the agile framework "empowers team members to decide what standard agile practices and methods it will use?"

A. Business executive

B. Project leader

C. Business analyst

D. sprint planner

11. What is the typical unit of work effort used for sizing user stories in planning poker and affinity estimation?

A. Story days

B. Sprint points

C. Story points

D. Agile points

12. David's agile team just finished building, testing, and releasing 12 user story points in its most recent 3 week iteration. What is the team's velocity?

A. 0.8

B. 4

C. 36

D. 12

13. Of the following, which event is typically the one where acceptance criteria is first defined?

A. Release planning

B. sprint retrospective

C. Product roadmapping

D. Envisioning

14. What type of team uses collaboration to solve problems and decides on the path forward?

A. Sprint team

B. Empowered team

C. Parry team

D. Iteration team

15. Which of the following is NOT a primary agile value per the Agile Manifesto?

A. Products work as intended because of frequent delivery iterations

B. Customers must collaborate with the agile team to provide feedback

C. Stakeholders must interact effectively to create business value

D. Comprehensive software specification and precise contract terms and conditions

16. Jan is looking at an important agile document that includes the project vision and mission. What document is Jan most likely reviewing?

A. Statement of work

B. Request for proposal

C. Project home page

D. Project charter

17. Stacey is concerned with the recent stagnant performance of her agile team. She believes it just needs some outside, independent guidance to improve What agile knowledge and skill technique might Stacey consider?

A. Crowdsourcing and mentoring

B. Symptom and solution

C. Coaching and mechanizing

D. Coaching and mentoring

18. Ursula's agile team is in need of outside guidance and leadership to help it reach new levels of performance. Her team has decided to use an experienced agile practitioner and facilitator. What knowledge and skill area is this practitioner providing to the team?

A. Envisioning and elaborating

B. Coaching and mechanizing

C. Coaching and mentoring

D. Symptom and solution

19. Of the following responses, which is a community value per the PMI agile community of practice community charter?

A. Inspiring

B. Persistent

C. Collaboration

D. Streamlined

20. Select a technique used for value-based analysis?

A. AGILE

B. Risk-to-value matrix

C. Strength

D. IDEF

21. Oswald and his agile team are subdividing user stories into manageable tasks so that it may plan the upcoming iteration with more accuracy. What is this process called?

A. Sub-tasking

B. Decomposition

C. Function task analysis

D. Sub-functioning

22. Coaching and mentoring can be a powerful knowledge and skill technique to improve the performance of an agile team. What is the perfect amount of coaching and mentoring for an agile team?

A. Coaching and mentoring is not a knowledge and skill technique within agile.

B. Minimal to reduce distracting the development team.

C. Non-stop.

D. It varies depending on the needs of the team.

23. Of the following, which is NOT a part of active listening?

A. Being present and focusing your attention on the speaker.

B. Thinking about what to say next to move the conversation flow.

C. Summarizing.

D. Paraphrasing.

24. Of the following, which is NOT a part of active listening?

A. Interrupting the speaker.

B. Being present and focusing your attention on the speaker.

C. Taking notes.

D. Summarizing.

25. Which of the following responses is NOT a part of active listening?

A. Taking notes.

B. Summarizing.

C. Paraphrasing.

D. Allowing yourself to get distracted.

26. Ralph is describing the INVEST acronym used for user story development in an agile practitioner seminar. What does the S in INVEST stand for?

A. Smart

B. Small

C. Superlative

D. Specific

27. Jules is describing the SMART acronym used for task analysis in an agile seminar. What does the S stand for?

A. Small

B. Stable

C. Specific

D. Superlative

28. What earned value management (EVM) variable captures schedule variance?

A. SV = AC - PV

B. SV = PV - EV

C. SV = PV - AC

D. SV = EV - PV

29. Which of the following is an agile 'feedback technique for product?'

A. Developing

B. Refactoring

C. Simulation

D. Coding

30. Hanson has shared an agenda for an upcoming product demonstration with key stakeholders. Sharing an agenda is generally considered a

A. Iteration method

B. Facilitation method

C. Business case method

D. Synchronization method

31. Of the following responses, which is a community value per the PMI agile community of practice community charter?

A. Confident

B. Courage

C. Deliberate

D. Taciturn

32. What should the persons with the highest and lowest estimated story point value do when playing a game of planning poker?

A. Remove their estimate values from the game.

B. Carry their values forward to the next user story.

C. Take the average of the their scores and then see if it is within 10% of the average of the other scores.

D. Defend their positions to the group so it may help to arrive at a consensus.

33. Which of the following responses is NOT a part of active listening?

A. Paraphrasing.

B. Focusing your full attention on a speaker.

C. Taking notes.

D. Focusing your full attention on environmental surroundings.

34. What topic area within strategic management deals with promoting a work environment of active participation of stakeholders?

A. Schedule management

B. Team member management

C. Agile management

D. Stakeholder management

35. Oscar and his agile team are subdividing user stories into manageable tasks. What is this process called?

A. Sub-functioning

B. Subdividing

C. Task analysis

D. Decomposition

36. Esther is looking at a document that holds a list of all the product features to be developed in the upcoming sprint/iteration. What document is Ester reviewing?

A. Product backlog

B. Task backlog

C. Scrum backlog

D. Sprint backlog

37. What agile artifact outlines the project's strategies for achieving goals?

A. Burndown chart

B. Business case

C. Task board

D. Value stream map

38. Select a technique that promotes agile 'knowledge sharing.'

A. Assimilation planning

B. Doctrine planning

C. Release planning

D. Manifesto planning

39. Process mapping is an example of a

A. Process analysis technique

B. Error proofing technique

C. Sprint planning technique

D. Team reflection technique

40. A core agile philosophy is effective information sharing among team members. Which communication method ensures this and is an Agile Manifesto principle?

A. WebEx

B. E-mail

C. Telephone

D. Face-to-face communication

PMI-ACP Lite Mock Exam 19 Answer Key and Explanations

1. A - A common misconception in agile is that an agile team does not need a leader. In fact, all agile teams need a leader, but the way in which the leader leads is fundamentally different than the typical traditional project manager/project leader method. Some have theorized that this misconception stems from the desired 'self-organizing' quality of the agile team. And although the 'self-organizing' agile team is empowered to take ownership and responsibility of the product and make some decisions itself, it nevertheless requires a leader to help provide guidance, mentoring, coaching, problem solving, and decision making. Some key aspects required of an agile leader include: empowering team members to decide what standard agile practices and methods it will use; allowing the team to be self-organized and self-disciplined; empowering the team members to make decisions collaboratively with the customer; inspire the team to be innovative and explore new ideas and technology capabilities; be a champion of and articulate the product vision to team members so it will be motivated to accomplish the overall objective; remove any obstacles and solve any problems the team may face in its effort; communicate and endorse the values and principles of agile project management to stakeholders that may be unfamiliar with agile; ensure that all stakeholders, including business managers and developers, are collaborating effectively; and, be able to adapt the leadership style to the working environment to ensure that the agile values and principles are effectively upheld. [The Art of Agile Development. James Shore.] [Knowledge and Skills: Level 1]

2. A - A common misconception in agile is that an agile team does not need a leader. In fact, all agile teams need a leader, but the way in which the leader leads is fundamentally different than the typical traditional project manager/project leader method. Some have theorized that this misconception stems from the desired 'self-organizing' quality of the agile team. And although the 'self-organizing' agile team is empowered to take ownership and responsibility of the product and make some decisions itself, it nevertheless requires a leader to help provide guidance, mentoring, coaching, problem solving, and decision making. Some key aspects required of an agile leader include: empowering team members to decide what standard agile practices and methods it will use; allowing the team to be self-organized and self-disciplined; empowering the team members to make decisions collaboratively with the customer; inspire the team to be innovative and explore new ideas and technology capabilities; be a champion of and articulate the product vision to team members so it will be motivated to accomplish the overall objective; remove any obstacles and solve any problems the team may face in its effort; communicate and endorse the values and principles of agile project management to stakeholders that may be unfamiliar with agile; ensure that all stakeholders, including business managers and developers, are collaborating effectively; and, be able to adapt the leadership style to the working environment to ensure that the agile values and principles are effectively upheld. [The Art of Agile Development. James Shore.] [Knowledge and Skills: Level 1]

3. C - The TDD process has four basic steps: 1) Write a test, 2) Verify and validate the test, 3) Write product code and apply the

test, 4) Refactor the product code. An example may be that a user has to enter an age value. A good test is to make sure the user data entry is a positive number and not a different type of input, like a letter (i.e., write the test). The programmer would verify that entering a letter instead of a number would cause the program to cause an exception (i.e., v&v the test). The programmer would then write product code that takes user entry for the age value (i.e., write the product code). The programmer would then run the product code and enter correct age values and incorrect age values (i.e., apply the test). If the product code is successful, the programmer would refactor the product code to improve its design. Using these four steps iteratively ensures that programmers think about how a software program might fail first and to build product code that is holistically being tested. This helps produce high quality code. [The Art of Agile Development. James Shore.] [Product quality]

4. A - During reflection or retrospectives, an agile team reserves time to reflect on the work it has completed with the objective of continuous improvement. In these self-assessment/team-assessment events, topics can include: lessons learned from successes and failures; team standards that worked, failed, or were not properly followed; and other areas of improvement. [Agile Retrospectives: Making Good Teams Great. Esther Derby, Diana Larsen, Ken Schwaber.] [Knowledge and Skills: Level 2]

5. A - Net Present Value: A metric used to analyze the profitability of an investment or project. NPV is the difference between the present value of cash inflows and the present value of cash outflows. NPV considers the likelihood of future cash inflows that an investment or project will yield. NPV is the sum of each cash inflow/outflow for the expected duration of the investment. Each cash inflow/outflow is discounted back to its present value (PV) (i.e.,, what the money is worth in terms of today's value). NPV is the sum of all terms: NPV = Sum of [Rt/(1 + i)^t] where t = the time of the cash flow, i = the discount rate (the rate of return that could be earned on in the financial markets) , and Rt = the net cash inflow or outflow. For example, consider the following two year period. The discount rate is 5% and the initial investment cost is $500. At the end of the first year, a $200 inflow is expected. At the end of the second year, a $1,000 is expected. NPV = -500 + 200/(1.05)^1 + 1000/(1.05)^2 = ~$597. If NPV is positive, it indicates that the investment will add value to the buyer's portfolio. If NPV is negative, it will subtract value. If NPV is zero, it will neither add or subtract value. [Agile Estimating and Planning. Mike Cohn.] [Value based prioritization]

6. D - The agile project management phases, in sequence, are: Envisioning, speculating, exploring, adapting, closing. [Manifesto for Agile Software Development. Agile Alliance.] [Knowledge and Skills: Level 1]

7. D - Coaching and mentoring within teams can be helpful for nascent agile teams and even for more experienced agile teams. Coaching and mentoring is the act of helping a person or team improve performance and achieve realistic goals. Because agile has a value of continuous improvement, coaching and mentoring is not solely for new or immature teams, but experienced ones too where coaching can

help achieve higher levels of performance. The amount of coaching and mentoring an agile team needs is variable. Some newer teams will need a coach guiding the team nearly all the time while others may need a coach only for particularly challenging situations. A not uncommon scenario is to have a coach help the team collectively during sprint/iteration planning and then during the iteration help mentor individual team members. [Coaching Agile Teams. Lyssa Adkins.] [Knowledge and Skills: Level 1]

8. D - Literally thousands of decisions are made in the course of a project. Many of these decisions are made in response to problems that inevitably arise and confront the agile team. Therefore it is essential that an agile team is properly versed in problem-solving strategies, tools, and techniques. Some common problem-solving techniques include: ask it loud; revisit the problem; 5Y; sunk cost fallacy; devil's advocate; be kind, rewind; asking probing questions; and reflective/active listening. [Agile Retrospectives: Making Good Teams Great. Esther Derby, Diana Larsen, Ken Schwaber.] [Knowledge and Skills: Level 1]

9. A - EVM or earned value management is a management technique used to evaluate project performance with respect to cost and schedule. EVM relies on other common financial metrics like Budget At Completion (BAC), Actual Cost (AC), Planned Value (PV), Earned Value (EV), Cost Variance (CV), Schedule Variance (SV), Cost Performance Index (CPI), and Schedule Performance Index (SPI). CV and SV can be converted into performance indicators of CPI and SPI, respectively, and tracked and charted to show progress over time. SPI = EV / PV. If SPI > 1, the project is ahead of schedule and if SPI < 1, the project is behind schedule. [Agile Estimating and Planning. Mike Cohn.] [Metrics]

10. B - A common misconception in agile is that an agile team does not need a leader. In fact, all agile teams need a leader, but the way in which the leader leads is fundamentally different than the typical traditional project manager/project leader method. Some have theorized that this misconception stems from the desired 'self-organizing' quality of the agile team. And although the 'self-organizing' agile team is empowered to take ownership and responsibility of the product and make some decisions itself, it nevertheless requires a leader to help provide guidance, mentoring, coaching, problem solving, and decision making. Some key aspects required of an agile leader include: empowering team members to decide what standard agile practices and methods it will use; allowing the team to be self-organized and self-disciplined; empowering the team members to make decisions collaboratively with the customer; inspire the team to be innovative and explore new ideas and technology capabilities; be a champion of and articulate the product vision to team members so it will be motivated to accomplish the overall objective; remove any obstacles and solve any problems the team may face in its effort; communicate and endorse the values and principles of agile project management to stakeholders that may be unfamiliar with agile; ensure that all stakeholders, including business managers and developers, are collaborating effectively; and, be able to adapt the leadership style to the working environment to ensure that the agile values and principles are effectively upheld. [The

Art of Agile Development. James Shore.] [Knowledge and Skills: Level 1]

11. C - Story points is the typical unit used for estimating the relative work effort involved with developing a user story. [Agile Estimating and Planning. Mike Cohn.] [Agile estimation]

12. D - Velocity is a measure of the number of user story points completed per iteration. An agile team can use its previous velocity recordings as a method of estimating how many user story points it may complete in the next iteration. David's team's velocity is 12. [Agile Estimating and Planning. Mike Cohn.] [Agile estimation]

13. A - Acceptance criteria is typically defined in tandem with user story definition during release planning; however, acceptance criteria can also be defined during iteration planning once a story has been picked for the iteration. The one steadfast rule is that acceptance criteria must be defined before development begins. Like agile planning, the definition of acceptance criteria is constantly evolving as the conversation with the product owner matures. [The Art of Agile Development. James Shore.] [Planning, monitoring, and adapting]

14. B - Empowered teams - ones that are self-organizing and know how to solve problems with minimal management involvement - are a cornerstone of the agile methodology. This is the antithesis to the classic viewpoint of the traditional project manager who is seen as someone that controls all decisions and delegates tasks to a team with little feedback. An agile team must include all members and stakeholders to make decisions, and make decisions expediently. Because it is essential that the user/customer be involved with development, it is encouraged that the user/customer is closely integrated with the agile team with collocation/on-site support being ideal. An agile team feels empowered when it collectively assumes responsibility for the delivery of the product (i.e., taking ownership). [Coaching Agile Teams. Lyssa Adkins.] [Knowledge and Skills: Level 1]

15. D - The agile primary values include: individuals and interactions, working software, customer collaboration, and responding to change. [Manifesto for Agile Software Development. Agile Alliance.] [Knowledge and Skills: Level 1]

16. D - The project charter is an important governing document that requires all stakeholder participation. Although experts recommend it not be longer than a page in length, creating a project charter can be challenging, as all stakeholders must participate and come to a consensus. Three key elements should be included in a project charter: vision, mission, and success criteria. Vision is the 'why' or rationale of a project. Mission is the 'what' of the project and describes what the team will accomplish to reach the vision. Success criteria are management metrics that define 'how' the project will be deemed successful. [Lean-Agile Software Development: Achieving Enterprise Agility. Alan Shalloway, Guy Beaver, James R. Trott.] [Knowledge and Skills: Level 2]

17. D - Coaching and mentoring within teams can be helpful for nascent agile teams and even for more experienced agile teams. Coaching and mentoring is the act of helping a person or team improve performance and achieve realistic goals. Because agile has a value of continuous improvement, coaching and mentoring is not solely for new or immature teams, but experienced ones too where coaching can help achieve higher levels of performance. The amount of coaching and mentoring an agile team needs is variable. Some newer teams will need a coach guiding the team nearly all the time while others may need a coach only for particularly challenging situations. A not uncommon scenario is to have a coach help the team collectively during sprint/iteration planning and then during the iteration help mentor individual team members. [Coaching Agile Teams. Lyssa Adkins.] [Knowledge and Skills: Level 1]

18. C - Coaching and mentoring within teams can be helpful for nascent agile teams and even for more experienced agile teams. Coaching and mentoring is the act of helping a person or team improve performance and achieve realistic goals. Because agile has a value of continuous improvement, coaching and mentoring is not solely for new or immature teams, but experienced ones too where coaching can help achieve higher levels of performance. The amount of coaching and mentoring an agile team needs is variable. Some newer teams will need a coach guiding the team nearly all the time while others may need a coach only for particularly challenging situations. A not uncommon scenario is to have a coach help the team collectively during sprint/iteration planning and then during the iteration help mentor individual team members. [Coaching Agile Teams. Lyssa Adkins.] [Knowledge and Skills: Level 1]

19. C - The following are community values of the PMI agile community of practice community charter: Vision, Servant Leadership, Trust, Collaboration, Honesty, Learning, Courage, Openness, Adaptability, Leading Change, Transparency [PMI Agile Community of Practice Community Charter. Project Management Institute.] [Knowledge and Skills: Level 1]

20. B - Value-based analysis strives to understand how value, as defined by the customer, relates to various components of the product, like features and tasks. Features are often prioritized with prioritization based on value and risk. Prioritization can be performed using the MoSCoW or Kano method and through the use of risk-to-value and cost-to-value matrices. [Lean-Agile Software Development: Achieving Enterprise Agility. Alan Shalloway, Guy Beaver, James R. Trott.] [Knowledge and Skills: Level 2]

21. B - In iteration planning, an agile team, collaboratively with the customer, chooses user stories to include for development. Although the user stories are prioritized in the product backlog initially during release planning, an agile team and customer should review prioritization based on progressive elaboration (i.e., gained knowledge and perspective). Prioritization is often based on value and risk and can be performed using the MoSCoW or Kano method and through the use of risk-to-value and cost-to-value matrices. An agile team performs decomposition to sub-divide user stories into more manageable tasks so that it may estimate task time. Tasks for an iteration may also be prioritized based on value, similar to how user stories are prioritized. [Lean-Agile Software Development: Achieving Enterprise Agility. Alan Shalloway, Guy Beaver, James R. Trott.] [Knowledge and Skills: Level 1]

22. D - Coaching and mentoring within teams can be helpful for nascent agile teams and even for more experienced agile teams. Coaching and mentoring is the act of helping a person or team improve performance and achieve realistic goals. Because agile has a value of continuous improvement, coaching and mentoring is not solely for new or immature teams, but experienced ones too where coaching can help achieve higher levels of performance. The amount of coaching and mentoring an agile team needs is variable. Some newer teams will need a coach guiding the team nearly all the time while others may need a coach only for particularly challenging situations. A not uncommon scenario is to have a coach help the team collectively during sprint/iteration planning and then during the iteration help mentor individual team members. [Coaching Agile Teams. Lyssa Adkins.] [Knowledge and Skills: Level 1]

23. B - One communication technique to reduce misunderstanding and miscommunication is active listening. A well run agile project necessitates both good listeners and communicators, active listening helps work towards both of these necessities. The basics of active listening include: 1) Being present and focusing your attention on the speaker. 2) Taking notes instead of interrupting. 3) Paraphrasing to confirm and review what you have heard. 4) Summarizing the conversation once it has concluded for posterity. Using open ended questions, good body language, and silence can help improve listening skills. [Coaching Agile Teams. Lyssa Adkins.] [Knowledge and Skills: Level 1]

24. A - One communication technique to reduce misunderstanding and miscommunication is active listening. A well run agile project necessitates both good listeners and communicators, active listening helps work towards both of these necessities. The basics of active listening include: 1) Being present and focusing your attention on the speaker. 2) Taking notes instead of interrupting. 3) Paraphrasing to confirm and review what you have heard. 4) Summarizing the conversation once it has concluded for posterity. Using open ended questions, good body language, and silence can help improve listening skills. [Coaching Agile Teams. Lyssa Adkins.] [Knowledge and Skills: Level 1]

25. D - One communication technique to reduce misunderstanding and miscommunication is active listening. A well run agile project necessitates both good listeners and communicators, active listening helps work towards both of these necessities. The basics of active listening include: 1) Being present and focusing your attention on the speaker. 2) Taking notes instead of interrupting. 3) Paraphrasing to confirm and review what you have heard. 4) Summarizing the conversation once it has concluded for posterity. Using open ended questions, good body language, and silence can help improve listening skills. [Coaching Agile Teams. Lyssa Adkins.] [Knowledge and Skills: Level 1]

26. B - The acronym INVEST (independent, negotiable, valuable, estimable, small, and testable) helps the agile practitioner remember the characteristics of a good user story. I – Independent stories can be developed in any order and avoid dependencies which can make development more complex. N – Negotiable user stories mean that both the customer and developer should feel free to analyze and adapt a user story to meet customer needs. V – A valuable user story describes how the product feature will provide value to the customer. E – Estimable user stories are ones that developers can readily estimate the effort or duration required for developing them. S- Small user stories are ones that take about two to five days of work to implement. T - Testable user stories are ones that can be verified according to acceptance criteria to ensure value. [Agile Retrospectives: Making Good Teams Great. Esther Derby, Diana Larsen, Ken Schwaber.] [Planning, monitoring, and adapting]

27. C - The acronym SMART (specific, measurable, achievable, relevant, and time-boxed) helps the agile practitioner remember the characteristics of a well-defined task. S – Specific tasks are ones that clearly contribute to the development of a user story. It should not be vague. M – Measurable tasks are ones that the team and customer can verify. A - Achievable tasks are ones that developers may realistically implement and understand. R - Relevant tasks are ones that unequivocally add value to the user story. T - Timeboxed tasks are ones that can have an estimate assigned of the amount of effort or time needed for development. [Agile Retrospectives: Making Good Teams Great. Esther Derby, Diana Larsen, Ken Schwaber.] [Planning, monitoring, and adapting]

28. D - Unlike traditional project management methods that evaluate risk and variance and trends in formal meetings, agile incorporates risk analysis and variance and trend analysis into iteration review meetings. Risk and variance and trend analysis may be performed in agile using information radiators, like a risk burndown chart, and the use of traditional earned value management (EVM) to measure cost and schedule variance (CV and SV, respectively). [Agile Estimating and Planning. Mike Cohn.] [Knowledge and Skills: Level 3]

29. C - There are several feedback techniques - techniques that facilitate constructive criticism to improve product value and quality - built into the agile process. In the classic definition, feedback is a dynamic process where past information influences the behavior of the same process in the future. Agile feedback techniques include prototyping, simulation, demonstration, evaluations, pair programming, unit testing, continuous integration, daily stand-up meetings, sprint planning. Because agile prides itself on a transparent and collaborative environment, feedback is essentially ubiquitous. [Agile Retrospectives: Making Good Teams Great. Esther Derby, Diana Larsen, Ken Schwaber.] [Knowledge and Skills: Level 1]

30. B - As a project leader or scrum master, effective facilitation methods are critical for building a high-performance and motivated team. Facilitation of meetings, discussions, demonstrations, etc., is a constant on an agile project. Some general facilitation methods include: using a small number of people for brainstorming events; hosting events in a non-threatening/comfortable environment; having an agenda that is shared with the group ahead of time; using open-ended questions instead of closed-ended questions; including a diverse representation to gain a broader perspective of the topic. [Agile Retrospectives: Making Good Teams Great. Esther Derby, Diana

Larsen, Ken Schwaber.] [Knowledge and Skills: Level 2]

31. B - The following are community values of the PMI agile community of practice community charter: Vision, Servant Leadership, Trust, Collaboration, Honesty, Learning, Courage, Openness, Adaptability, Leading Change, Transparency [PMI Agile Community of Practice Community Charter. Project Management Institute.] [Knowledge and Skills: Level 1]

32. D - Planning poker is based upon the wideband Delphi estimation technique. It is a consensus-based technique for estimating effort. Sometimes called scrum poker, it is a technique for a relative estimation of effort, typically in story points, to develop a user story. At a planning poker meeting, each estimator is given an identical deck of planning poker cards with a wide range of values. The Fibonacci sequence is often used for values for planning poker (i.e., 0, 1, 1, 2, 3, 5,8,etc.); another common sequence is (question mark, 0, 1/2, 1, 2, 3, 5, 8, 13, 20, 40, and 100). A planning poker meeting works as follows: 1) a moderator, not estimating, facilitates the meeting. 2) the product owner/manager provides a short overview of the user story and answers clarifying questions posed by the developers. Typically the product owner does not vote. 3) Each estimator selects an estimate of work effort by selecting a card, 4) Once everyone has selected a card, everyone overturns their card concurrently, 5) Estimators with high and low estimates are given a chance to defend positions. 6) The process repeats until there is consensus. The developer who owns the user story is typically given higher credence. [Agile Estimating and Planning. Mike Cohn.] [Agile estimation]

33. D - One communication technique to reduce misunderstanding and miscommunication is active listening. A well run agile project necessitates both good listeners and communicators, active listening helps work towards both of these necessities. The basics of active listening include: 1) Being present and focusing your attention on the speaker. 2) Taking notes instead of interrupting. 3) Paraphrasing to confirm and review what you have heard. 4) Summarizing the conversation once it has concluded for posterity. Using open ended questions, good body language, and silence can help improve listening skills. [Coaching Agile Teams. Lyssa Adkins.] [Knowledge and Skills: Level 1]

34. D - Stakeholder management is a growing topic area within strategic management that brings awareness to the importance of managing stakeholders (i.e., facilitating active participation of stakeholders and fostering a strong collaborative environment) for a project's success. Stakeholder management is typically defined in the context of guiding principles and values. R. E. Freeman's 'Managing for Stakeholders' includes 10 principles: 1) Stakeholder interests need to go together over time. 2) We need a philosophy of volunteerism – to engage stakeholders and manage relationships ourselves rather than leave it to government. 3) We need to find solutions to issues that satisfy multiple stakeholders simultaneously. 4) Everything that we do serves stakeholders. We never trade off the interests of one versus the other continuously over time. 5) We act with purpose that fulfills our commitment to stakeholders. We act with aspiration towards fulfilling our dreams and theirs. 6) We need intensive communication and dialogue with stakeholders – not just those who are friendly. 7)Stakeholders consist of real people with names and faces and children. They are complex. 8)We need to generalize the marketing approach. 9) We engage with both primary and secondary stakeholders. 10) We constantly monitor and redesign processes to make them better serve our stakeholders. Because stakeholder involvement is critical for the success of a project, where projects without active participation from stakeholders are prone to failure, stakeholder management should be a topic that every agile team knows well. [The Art of Agile Development. James Shore.] [Knowledge and Skills: Level 1]

35. D - In iteration planning, an agile team, collaboratively with the customer, chooses user stories to include for development. Although the user stories are prioritized in the product backlog initially during release planning, an agile team and customer should review prioritization based on progressive elaboration (i.e., gained knowledge and perspective). Prioritization is often based on value and risk and can be performed using the MoSCoW or Kano method and through the use of risk-to-value and cost-to-value matrices. An agile team performs decomposition to sub-divide user stories into more manageable tasks so that it may estimate task time. Tasks for an iteration may also be prioritized based on value, similar to how user stories are prioritized [Lean-Agile Software Development: Achieving Enterprise Agility. Alan Shalloway, Guy Beaver, James R. Trott.] [Knowledge and Skills: Level 1]

36. D - The sprint backlog is a list of product features or work items to be completed in a sprint. It is typically fixed for the sprint unless it is overcome by important customer requirements. [Lean-Agile Software Development: Achieving Enterprise Agility. Alan Shalloway, Guy Beaver, James R. Trott.] [Agile analysis and design]

37. B - Business case development is an important initial step in agile project management. The business case is a concise document that outlines the project's vision, goals, strategies for achieving goals, milestones, required investment and expected return/payback. A business case articulates the why and how a project will deliver value to a customer. [Lean-Agile Software Development: Achieving Enterprise Agility. Alan Shalloway, Guy Beaver, James R. Trott.] [Knowledge and Skills: Level 2]

38. C - In agile, effective 'knowledge sharing' is a critical factor for success. It involves the near real time communication of key information among all team members and stakeholders. To promote knowledge sharing, agile uses standard practices built into its process, such as using generalized specialists/cross functional teams, self-organizing and self-disciplined teams, collocation, daily stand-up meetings, iteration/sprint planning, release planning, pair programming and pair rotation, project retrospectives/reflection, and on-site customer support. And, of course, the sixth principle of Agile is " The most efficient and effective method of conveying information to and within a development team is face-to-face conversation." In this sense, Agile prefers and encourages collocation for all stakeholders and team members for the simple fact that face-to-face conversation is the best method of communication and, in turn, effective knowledge sharing. [Becoming Agile: ...in an imperfect world. Greg Smith, Ahmed Sidky.] [Knowledge and Skills: Level 1]

39. A - Value stream mapping is a collaborative process analysis technique where a diverse team depicts/maps a process to identify where waste occurs and where improvements can be made. It is an example of a process analysis technique. Like value stream mapping, process mapping is also used to map a process to identify bottlenecks (places where processing slows and inventory can build). [Lean-Agile Software Development: Achieving Enterprise Agility. Alan Shalloway, Guy Beaver, James R. Trott.] [Knowledge and Skills: Level 2]

40. D - The Agile Manifesto developed by the Agile Alliance covers 4 values and 12 principles. The four values are: 1) individuals and interactions over processes and tools, 2) working software over comprehensive documentation, 3) customer collaboration over contract negotiation, and 4) responding to change over following a plan. The 12 principles are: 1) focusing on satisfying the customer, 2) welcoming change, 3) delivering working software frequently, 4) ensuring that business people and developers work together, 5) motivating the individuals involved in development, 6) using face-to-face communication whenever possible, 7) working software as the primary measure of progress, 8) maintaining a constant pace of development, 9) paying continuous attention to technical excellence and good design, 10) aiming for simplicity, 11) using self-organizing teams, and 12) regularly reflecting on how to become more effective. [Manifesto for Agile Software Development. Agile Alliance.] [Communications]

PMI-ACP Lite Mock Exam 20 Practice Questions

Test Name: PMI-ACP Lite Mock Exam 20
Total Questions: 40
Correct Answers Needed to Pass:
30 (75.00%)
Time Allowed: 60 Minutes

Test Description

This is a cumulative PMI-ACP Mock Exam which can be used as a benchmark for your PMI-ACP aptitude. This practice test includes questions from all exam topic areas, including sections from Agile Tools and Techniques, and all three Agile Knowledge and Skills areas.

Test Questions

1. Which of the following is a key agile artifact that requires all stakeholders come to a consensus?

A. Terms and conditions

B. Project charter

C. Story point estimation document

D. Statement of work

2. Of the following, which is an agile principle per the Agile Manifesto?

A. Aiming for simplicity.

B. Defect reduction

C. Test-driven development

D. Removing waste

3. Of the following, which is an agile principle per the Agile Manifesto?

A. Removing waste

B. Test-driven development

C. Focus on product value

D. Maintaining a constant pace of development.

4. According to the PMI Code, you should accept assignments

A. that are consistent with your aspirations.

B. that are consistent with your background, experience, skills, and qualifications

C. that are consistent with your interests regardless of whether your background, experience, and skills qualify.

D. that are beyond your capabilities but that will allow you to grow as an organization

5. As an agile practitioner, Barry believes heavily in transparency. What does the principle of transparency mean with respect to communication?

A. That every e-mail and other written communication is shared with every stakeholder immediately

B. That team members should expect no privacy in the work place

C. Open and honest communication about successes and failures to all stakeholders

D. A need-to-know information sharing policy where important information regarding project failures is only shared with key personnel

6. If a task is said to have the characteristic of being specific, what does it indicate?

A. That it has been specified in the product backlog.

B. That is has been specified in the work breakdown structure.

C. That is meets specific customer criteria.

D. That it clearly contributes to the development of a user story and is not vague.

7. If the NPV of an investment is above zero, what does that indicate to the potential buyer?

A. That it would neither add to nor subtract value from the buyer's portfolio.

B. That it would add value to the buyer's portfolio.

C. That it would subtract value from the buyer's portfolio.

D. None of the above.

8. In a rolling look ahead plan how many iterations are planned for at one time?

A. The next few iterations

B. Only the next iteration

C. 8 two-week iterations or 16 one-week iterations depending on the iteration cycle

D. The previous iterations that had leftover user stories

9. What is an information radiator?

A. A website holding project documentation.

B. A visual representation of a project status metric.

C. An organizational chart with pictures of agile team members.

D. The world wide web.

10. Vanessa is reviewing her team's risk burndown chart. She notices that the severity for all identified risks are continuing to grow in value. What does this mean briefly?

A. That project risk is not successfully being mitigated.

B. That project risk is remaining static.

C. That project risk is not an area of concern.

D. That project risk is successfully being mitigated.

11. Jacob's agile team just finished building, testing, and releasing 24 user story points in its most recent 3 week iteration. What is the team's velocity?

A. 3

B. 24

C. 72

D. 8

12. Vanessa is reviewing her team's risk burndown chart. She notices that the severity for all identified risks are continuing to decrease in value. What does this mean briefly?

A. That project risk is successfully being mitigated.

B. That project risk is remaining static.

C. That project risk is not an area of concern.

D. That project risk is not successfully being mitigated.

13. Jack and his agile team want to incorporate test-driven development (TDD) into standard practice. Briefly, what does test-driven development mean?

A. That the product owner tests the customer during the definition of the product vision to ensure the business value is clearly stated.

B. That software developers test the customer during release planning to ensure user stories are properly outlined.

C. That software developers design and develop product software first and use extensive unit testing afterwards to ensure code meets acceptance criteria.

D. That software developers design and develop tests first before developing product software to ensure code meets acceptance criteria.

14. What is a positive indicator that agile may be appropriate to an organization as a new project methodology?

A. That the adopting organization emphasizes the negotiation of contracts over individuals and interactions.

B. That the adopting organization emphasizes the perk of remote working.

C. That the adopting organization values strict, inflexible project management techniques.

D. That the adopting organization emphasizes collocation of project team members.

15. Becky, as project leader, intends on building a high-performance team. What is

a practice or technique she can use to build a high performance team?

A. Assigning more work than can be accomplished in an iteration to set a sense of urgency

B. Empowering the team

C. Never pausing to reflect on performance until the end of the project

D. Making all decisions for the team

16. Of the following, which is the best definition of coaching and mentoring?

A. Helping a person or team prioritize features in the backlog.

B. Helping a person or team come up with new ideas.

C. Helping a person or team achieve new goals by providing guidance and insight.

D. Helping a person or team communicate with one another.

17. If you have a cost variance of negative $2,000 what does it imply?

A. That the earned value exceeds the actual costs of the project.

B. That the planned costs of the project exceed the earned value.

C. That the expected value of the project exceeds the actual costs of the project.

D. That the actual costs incurred by the project exceed the earned value.

18. If a task is said to have the characteristic of being measurable, what does it indicate?

A. That the task is achievable.

B. That the task can be verified by the team and customer.

C. That the task is timeboxed.

D. That the task is specific.

19. Cody is trying to explain Mike Cohn's square root of the sum of squares method that is used to estimate a project buffer to his agile team. He decides to start with the definition of a local safety. What is a local safety?

A. The 100% confidence estimate

B. The difference between the 50% confidence estimate and the 10% confidence estimate

C. The 60% confidence estimate

D. The difference between the 90% confidence estimate and 50% confidence estimate

20. Select the response that is a typical information radiator for an agile project.

A. Local emergency numbers

B. A burndown chart

C. The agile manifesto

D. A project schedule

21. What is one piece of information a stakeholder can review using a risk-based burnup chart?

A. The amount of defects identified to date in a release.

B. The amount of story points remaining to complete in an iteration.

C. The amount of remaining use stories to decompose in a release.

D. The most likely amount of story points that will be completed in a project.

22. What is one piece of information a stakeholder can review using a risk-based burnup chart?

A. The amount of remaining use stories to decompose in a release.

B. The amount of story points remaining to complete in an iteration.

C. The amount of defects identified to date in a release.

D. The amount of story points that will be completed in a project in a best-case scenario.

23. Which of the following is a key soft skill negotiation quality?

A. Emotional equivalence

B. Emotional rigidity

C. Emotional obsolescence

D. Emotional intelligence

24. According to the PMI Code, decisions and actions should be based on

A. the best interests of society after first satisfying the customer.

B. the best interests of the customer.

C. the best interests of the parent company's bottom line.

D. the best interests of society, public safety, and the environment.

25. Select the response that best defines the XP practice of continuous integration.

A. The incremental development of software that is immediately integrated into the full code base.

B. The coding of new software directly within the production code base.

C. The incremental development of software that is extensively tested before integrating into the full code base, followed by testing of the full code to ensure successful integration.

D. The coding of integration software for new product features.

26. Kaitlin is providing an overview of the XP principle of continuous integration. Which response provides the best definition of continuous integration?

A. The integration of built and tested code with the production code base. Once the test code is integrated the entire product code base is tested.

B. The integration of new code with the production code base. One the code is integrated, the product may be released to the customer for feedback.

C. The coding of new software directly within the production code base.

D. The coding of integration software for new product features.

27. On an agile project, who is responsible for updating the content of an information radiator?

A. The customers

B. External stakeholders

C. The project team members

D. Internal stakeholders

28. From the following, select a technique that promotes agile 'knowledge sharing.'

A. The daily sprint meeting

B. The daily iteration meeting

C. The daily sprint meeting

D. The daily stand-up meeting

29. Jane and her team are developing code to implement unit tests and product code for a user story. This is after the team had distilled information into specific tests to confirm expected behavior of the product. What step is Jane on in the ATDD four step process?

A. 1st

B. 2nd

C. 4th

D. 3rd

30. Which of the following is the best definition of value-based decomposition?

A. The decomposition of user stories into tasks that are in turn prioritized by value.

B. The decomposition of iterations into intervals that are in turn prioritized by value.

C. The decomposition of release plans into intervals that are in turn prioritized by value.

D. The decomposition of story points into intervals that are in turn prioritized by value.

31. EVM is a frequently used project management abbreviation. How is CPI calculated?

A. CPI = BAC / EV

B. CPI = EV / AC

C. CPI = BAC / PV

D. CPI = AC / EV

32. What should an agile team consider when estimating story points?

A. The customer prioritized value of developing a user story.

B. The complexity, cost, radiance, and dependency of developing a user story.

C. The complexity, effort, risk, and dependencies of developing a user story.

D. The ease, value, required quality, and cost of developing a user story.

33. What does sharing and discussing the product vision in detail during release planning help ensure?

A. The establishment of the proper requirements, acceptance criteria, and priorities

B. The establishment of iteration team members

C. The establishment of product value risk assessment criteria

D. The establishment of daily stand-up meeting acceptance criteria

34. Joyce, as a certified agile practitioner, believes in the value of 'knowledge sharing.' Which of the following is the best definition of 'knowledge sharing?'

A. The tightly controlled flow of information among top ranking team members.

B. The conveyance of data between refactored code modules.

C. Keeping all team members and stakeholders informed by the equitable sharing of important project information.

D. The heavily controlled conveyance of information to only certain team members.

35. What topic area within strategic management deals with fostering a welcoming environment where stakeholders actively participate?

A. Team member management

B. Agile management

C. Stakeholder management

D. Schedule management

36. Which of the following is the best definition of 'incremental delivery?'

A. The immediate delivery of a working product to a customer for customer unit testing.

B. The semi-annual delivery of a working product to a customer for continuous feedback and acceptance.

C. The frequent delivery of a working product to a customer for continuous feedback and acceptance.

D. The occasional delivery of a working product, which improves steadily, over non-standard periods of time.

37. Select the response that holds the best definition of work in process (WIP).

A. The inventory of material that is awaiting initial processing.

B. Material that is currently in production or development but has not yet been completed.

C. The production work that is required to process material into finished products.

D. The backlog of features held in the product backlog.

38. Where do all user stories typically reside in an agile project?

A. Kanban board

B. The iteration backlog

C. The product backlog

D. The sprint backlog

39. Ken's agile team has set a feature WIP limit of five. How many features may the team be simultaneously building during the iteration?

A. No more than five.

B. No more than two.

C. No more than one.

D. No more than 10.

40. Which of the following is NOT a secondary agile value per the Agile Manifesto?

A. Customers must collaborate with the agile team to provide feedback

B. Contracts need to be negotiated and plans followed

C. Appropriate processes and tools aid the development process

D. Documentation supports working software and appropriate processes and tools aid the development process

PMI-ACP Lite Mock Exam 20 Answer Key and Explanations

1. B - The project charter is an important governing document that requires all stakeholder participation. Although experts recommend it not be longer than a page in length, creating a project charter can be challenging, as all stakeholders must participate and come to a consensus. Three key elements should be included in a project charter: vision, mission, and success criteria. Vision is the 'why' or rationale of a project. Mission is the 'what' of the project and describes what the team will accomplish to reach the vision. Success criteria are management metrics that define 'how' the project will be deemed successful. [Lean-Agile Software Development: Achieving Enterprise Agility. Alan Shalloway, Guy Beaver, James R. Trott.] [Knowledge and Skills: Level 2]

2. A - The Agile Manifesto defines 12 supporting principles. Agile principles include 1) Our highest priority is to satisfy the customer through early and continuous delivery of valuable software. 2) Welcome changing requirements, even late in development. Agile processes harness change for the customer's competitive advantage. 3) Deliver working software frequently, from a couple of weeks to a couple of months, with preference to the shorter timescale. 4) Business people and developers must work together daily throughout the project. 5) Build projects around motivated individuals. Give them the environment and support they need, and trust them to get the job done. 6) The most efficient and effective method of conveying information to and within a development team is face-to-face conversation. 7) Working software is the primary measure of progress. 8) Agile processes promote sustainable development. The sponsors, developers, and users should be able to maintain a constant pace indefinitely. 9) Continuous attention to technical excellence and good design enhances agility. 10) Simplicity--the art of maximizing the amount of work not done--is essential. 11) The best architectures, requirements, and designs emerge from self-organizing teams. 12) At regular intervals, the team reflects on how to become more effective, then tunes and adjusts its behavior accordingly. [Manifesto for Agile Software Development. Agile Alliance.] [Knowledge and Skills: Level 1]

3. D - The Agile Manifesto defines 12 supporting principles. Agile principles include 1) Our highest priority is to satisfy the customer through early and continuous delivery of valuable software. 2) Welcome changing requirements, even late in development. Agile processes harness change for the customer's competitive advantage. 3) Deliver working software frequently, from a couple of weeks to a couple of months, with preference to the shorter timescale. 4) Business people and developers must work together daily throughout the project. 5) Build projects around motivated individuals. Give them the environment and support they need, and trust them to get the job done. 6) The most efficient and effective method of conveying information to and within a development team is face-to-face conversation. 7) Working software is the primary measure of progress. 8) Agile processes promote sustainable development. The sponsors, developers, and users should be able to maintain a constant pace indefinitely. 9) Continuous attention to technical excellence and good design enhances agility. 10) Simplicity--the art of maximizing the amount of work not done--is essential. 11) The best architectures, requirements, and designs emerge from self-organizing teams. 12) At regular intervals, the team reflects on how to become more effective, then tunes and adjusts its behavior accordingly. [Manifesto for Agile Software Development. Agile Alliance.] [Knowledge and Skills: Level 1]

4. B - The PMI Code of Ethics and Professional Conduct outlines the following aspirational standards based on the core value of responsibility: base your decisions and actions on the best interests of society, public safety, and the environment; accept only assignments that are consistent with your background, experience, skills, and qualifications; honestly disclose gaps or weaknesses in your experience, qualifications, or skills; fulfill the commitments that you undertake – do what you say you will do; take ownership of errors or omissions and make corrections promptly; protect proprietary or confidential information that has been entrusted to you; uphold the PMI Code and hold others accountable to it. [PMI Code of Ethics and Professional Conduct. Project Management Institute.] [Knowledge and Skills: Level 2]

5. C - Transparent communication upholds the virtue of being open and honest about the project's successes or failures. By sharing this information, the team members, and internal and external stakeholders can focus on delivering a high quality and high value product. [Agile Software Development: The Cooperative Game – 2nd Edition. Alistair Cockburn.] [Communications]

6. D - The acronym SMART (specific, measurable, achievable, relevant, and time-boxed) helps the agile practitioner remember the characteristics of a well-defined task. S – Specific tasks are ones that clearly contribute to the development of a user story. It should not be vague. M – Measurable tasks are ones that the team and customer can verify. A - Achievable tasks are ones that developers may realistically implement and understand. R - Relevant tasks are ones that unequivocally add value to the user story. T - Timeboxed tasks are ones that can have an estimate assigned of the amount of effort or time needed for development. [Agile Retrospectives: Making Good Teams Great. Esther Derby, Diana Larsen, Ken Schwaber.] [Planning, monitoring, and adapting]

7. B - Net Present Value: A metric used to analyze the profitability of an investment or project. NPV is the difference between the present value of cash inflows and the present value of cash outflows. NPV considers the likelihood of future cash inflows that an investment or project will yield. NPV is the sum of each cash inflow/outflow for the expected duration of the investment. Each cash inflow/outflow is discounted back to its present value (PV) (i.e.,, what the money is worth in terms of today's value). NPV is the sum of all terms: NPV = Sum of [Rt/(1 + i)^t] where t = the time of the cash flow, i = the discount rate (the rate of return that could be earned on in the financial markets) , and Rt = the net cash inflow or outflow. For example, consider the following two year period. The discount rate is 5% and the initial investment cost is $500. At the end of the first year, a $200 inflow is expected. At the end of the second year, a $1,000 is expected. NPV = -500 + 200/(1.05)^1 + 1000/(1.05)^2 = ~$597. If NPV is positive, it indicates that the investment will add value to the buyer's portfolio. If NPV is negative, it will subtract value. If NPV is zero, it will neither add or subtract value. [Agile Estimating and Planning. Mike Cohn.] [Value based prioritization]

8. A - When using a rolling wave or rolling look ahead plan for complex projects, agile teams plan for work in the next few iterations. A rolling wave or look ahead plan focuses on planning only work that is about to be accomplished, not work beyond this threshold with details that remain unclear because it is too far in the future. [Agile Estimating and Planning. Mike Cohn.] [Planning, monitoring, and adapting]

9. B - An information radiator is a visual representation of project status data. [Agile Software Development: The Cooperative Game – 2nd Edition. Alistair Cockburn.] [Communications]

10. A - A risk burndown chart is a risk management technique used to track project risk over time. It allows stakeholders to quickly review project risk management performance (e.g., increasing, decreasing, and by how much) over time. Severity (a product of impact and probability) is charted along the vertical axis with time on the horizontal axis. Impact typically takes a value from 0 to 5 in increasing order of risk and probability/likelihood typically takes a value from 0 to 5 in increasing order of probability. In this example, the worst severity a risk could have is 25 (5 x 5 = 25) and the least harmful severity a risk could have is 0. The agile team and customer/product owner identifies its risks and assigns severity values in a risk register and tracks those values over time. Ideally, risk severity will decrease over time. [The Art of Agile Development. James Shore.] [Risk management]

11. B - Velocity is a measure of the number of user story points or stories completed by a team per iteration. An agile team can use its previous velocity recordings as a method of estimating how many user story points it may complete in the next iteration. [Agile Estimating and Planning. Mike Cohn.] [Agile estimation]

12. A - A risk burndown chart is a risk management technique used to track project risk over time. It allows stakeholders to quickly review project risk management performance (e.g., increasing, decreasing, and by how much) over time. Severity (a product of impact and probability) is charted along the vertical axis with time on the horizontal axis. Impact typically takes a value from 0 to 5 in increasing order of risk and probability/likelihood typically takes a value from 0 to 5 in increasing order of probability. In this example, the worst severity a risk could have is 25 (5 x 5 = 25) and the least harmful severity a risk could have is 0. The agile team and customer/product owner identifies its risks and assigns severity values in a risk register and tracks those values over time. Ideally, risk severity will decrease over time. [The Art of Agile Development. James Shore.] [Risk management]

13. D - Test-driven development, or TDD, is an agile methodology that has software developers develop automated software tests before developing software that implements product features. This helps ensure quality as each bit of feature software is tested individually to remove bugs and improve performance before it is integrated with the final product. [The Art of Agile Development. James Shore.] [Product quality]

14. D - When considering whether to apply new agile practices, several internal and external factors should be considered. Internal factors include whether the project is developing new processes or products; whether the organization is collaborative and emphasizes trust, adaptability, collective ownership, and has minimal or informal project management processes; the size, location, and skills of the project team. External factors include the industry stability and customer engagement or involvement. Generally, agile is best suited to developing new processes or products for an organization that is collaborative and emphasizes trust, adaptability, collective ownership, and has minimal project management processes by an agile/project team that is relatively small in size, is collocated, and is cross-functional in skill. Additionally, agile is known to succeed in industries that are quickly adapting to disruptive technologies as opposed to industries that are stable and perhaps inflexible to adaptive approaches. And, lastly, the component of customer involvement and engagement cannot be stressed enough; the more participation, the better. [The Art of Agile Development. James Shore.] [Knowledge and Skills: Level 3]

15. B - Building a high-performance team is critical to any project's success. A high performance team has the right team members, is empowered, has built trust, works at a sustainable pace, has consistently high velocity/productivity, takes regular time for reflection to review work, has a team lead that removes any obstacles and provides mentoring and coaching, is self-organized and self-disciplined, and is collocated. Several management techniques can be used to build or foster a high-performance team environment, some techniques include: removing obstacles that slow down a team's performance, having high expectations of team performance, and coaching and mentoring the team to achieve its best performance. [Coaching Agile Teams. Lyssa Adkins.] [Knowledge and Skills: Level 2]

16. C - Coaching and mentoring within teams can be helpful for nascent agile teams and even for more experienced agile teams. Coaching and mentoring is the act of helping a person or team improve performance and achieve realistic goals. [Coaching Agile Teams. Lyssa Adkins.] [Knowledge and Skills: Level 1]

17. D - EVM or earned value management is a management technique used to evaluate project performance with respect to cost and schedule. EVM relies on other common financial metrics like Budget At Completion (BAC), Actual Cost (AC), Planned Value (PV), Earned Value (EV), Cost Variance (CV), Schedule Variance (SV), Cost Performance Index (CPI), and Schedule Performance Index (SPI). CV and SV can be converted into performance indicators of CPI and SPI, respectively, and tracked and charted to show progress over time. BAC is the total project budget. AC is the actual cost incurred to date. PV is the planned value of work at a given time in a project; you can calculate it by multiplying the BAC by the ratio of current week/scheduled weeks (e.g., 5 weeks into a 15 week $15,000 project = $5,000 PV). EV is value of work actually completed or earned (e.g., you have completed 50% of the project by week 5 of a 15 week $15,000 project = $7,500 EV). CV is the difference between what a project has earned to date and cost to date (i.e., CV = EV - AC). [Agile Estimating and Planning. Mike Cohn.] [Knowledge and Skills: Level 3]

18. B - The acronym SMART (specific, measurable, achievable, relevant, and time-boxed) helps the agile practitioner remember the characteristics of a well-defined task. S – Specific tasks are ones that clearly contribute to the development of a user story. It should not be vague. M – Measurable tasks are ones that the team and customer can verify. A - Achievable tasks are ones that developers may realistically implement and understand. R - Relevant tasks are ones that unequivocally add value to the user story. T - Timeboxed tasks are ones that can have an estimate assigned of the amount of effort or time needed for development. [Agile Retrospectives: Making Good Teams Great. Esther Derby, Diana Larsen, Ken Schwaber.] [Planning, monitoring, and adapting]

19. D - The local safety is the difference between the 90% confidence estimate of task time and the 50% confidence estimate of task time. Remember that estimates for task time are typically a range of estimates and not a single value; think of estimates existing as a cumulative distribution function. A 50% confidence estimate is essentially an aggressive estimate where the estimator only has a 50% confidence that the task will be completed within the associated time value. A 90% confidence estimate is essentially a conservative estimate where the estimator has a 90% confidence that the task will be completed within the associated time value. [Agile Estimating and Planning. Mike Cohn.] [Agile estimation]

20. B - Typical information radiators on an agile project include: project burndown charts, task boards, burnup charts, and defect charts. [Agile Software Development: The Cooperative Game – 2nd Edition. Alistair Cockburn.] [Communications]

21. D - A risk-based burnup chart tracks targeted and actual product delivery progress and also includes estimates of how likely the team is to achieve targeted value adjusted for risk. Typically, risk is shown as three different levels: best-case; most likely; and worst-case. For example, if you have a 10 iteration project and the team's current velocity is 10 story points, you can portray the chance of completing 100 story points (most likely case), the chance of completing 80 story points (worst-case), and the chance of completing 120 story points (best-case). In this way, the stakeholders get a feel for the range of risk. [The Art of Agile Development. James Shore.] [Risk management]

22. D - A risk-based burnup chart tracks targeted and actual product delivery progress and also includes estimates of how likely the team is to achieve targeted value adjusted for risk. Typically, risk is shown as three different levels: best-case; most likely; and worst-case. For example, if you have a 10 iteration project and the team's current velocity is 10 story points, you can portray the chance of completing 100 story points (most likely case), the chance of completing 80 story points (worst-case), and the chance of completing 120 story points (best-case). In this way, the stakeholders get a feel for the range of risk. [The Art of Agile Development. James Shore.] [Risk management]

23. D - Key soft skills negotiation qualities for the effective implementation and practice of agile are: emotional intelligence, collaboration, adaptive leadership, negotiation, conflict resolution, servant leadership. [Coaching Agile Teams. Lyssa Adkins.] [Soft skills negotiation]

24. D - The PMI Code of Ethics and Professional Conduct outlines the following aspirational standards based on the core value of responsibility: base your decisions and actions on the best interests of society, public safety, and the environment; accept only assignments that are consistent with your background, experience, skills, and qualifications; honestly disclose gaps or weaknesses in your experience, qualifications, or skills; fulfill the commitments that you undertake – do what you say you will do; take ownership of errors or omissions and make corrections promptly; protect proprietary or confidential information that has been entrusted to you; uphold the PMI Code and hold others accountable to it. [PMI Code of Ethics and Professional Conduct. Project Management Institute.] [Knowledge and Skills: Level 2]

25. C - The extreme programming (XP) principle of continuous integration is that code is integrated into the full code base as soon as it is built, tested, and completed. Once integrated, the code base and therefore the entire system is built and tested. Continuous integration is just one principle of XP that promotes rapid delivery of software and the early detection of integration defects. [The Art of Agile Development. James Shore.] [Product quality]

26. A - The extreme programming (XP) principle of continuous integration is that code is integrated into the full code base as soon as it is built, tested, and completed. Once integrated, the code base and therefore the entire system is built and tested. Continuous integration is just one principle of XP that promotes rapid delivery of software and the early detection of integration defects. [The Art of Agile Development. James Shore.] [Product quality]

27. C - The most correct answer is the project team members. The project team members is the best answer because they will use the information radiator most during the course of the project and will typically be the first entities to know when a metric has been modified. [Agile Software Development: The Cooperative Game – 2nd Edition. Alistair Cockburn.] [Communications]

28. D - In agile, effective 'knowledge sharing' is a critical factor for success. It involves the near real time communication of key information among all team members and stakeholders. To promote knowledge sharing, agile uses standard practices built into its process, such as using generalized specialists/cross functional teams, self-organizing and self-disciplined teams, collocation, daily stand-up meetings, iteration/sprint planning, release planning, pair programming and pair rotation, project retrospectives/reflection, and on-site customer support. And, of course, the sixth principle of Agile is " The most efficient and effective method of conveying information to and within a development team is face-to-face conversation." In this sense, Agile prefers and encourages collocation for all stakeholders and team members for the simple fact that face-to-face conversation is the best method of communication and, in turn, effective knowledge sharing. [Becoming Agile: ...in an imperfect world. Greg Smith, Ahmed Sidky.] [Knowledge and Skills: Level 1]

29. D - Acceptance Test Driven Development (ATDD) is similar to Test-driven development (TDD) in that it requires programmers to create tests first before any product code. The tests in ATDD are aimed at confirming features/behaviors that the intended software will have. The iterative cycle of ATDD with its four steps can be remembered as the four Ds: 1) Discuss, 2) Distill, 3) Develop, and 4) Demo. 1) Discuss: The agile team and customer or business stakeholder discuss a user story in detail. Talking about the expected behaviors the user story should have and what it should not. 2) The development team takes those items learned from the discussion and distills them into tests that will verify and validate those behaviors. The distillation process is where the entire team should have a good understanding of what "done" (or completed) means for a user story. That is, what the acceptance criteria are. 3) After distillation, the team develops the test code and product code to implement the product features. 4) Once the product features have been developed, the team demonstrates them to the customer or business stakeholders for feedback. [Lean-Agile Software Development: Achieving Enterprise Agility. Alan Shalloway, Guy Beaver, James R. Trott.] [Product quality]

30. A - In iteration planning, an agile team, collaboratively with the customer, chooses user stories to include for development. Although the user stories are prioritized in the product backlog initially during release planning, an agile team and customer should review prioritization based on progressive elaboration (i.e., gained knowledge and perspective). Prioritization is often based on value and risk and can be performed using the MoSCoW or Kano method and through the use of risk-to-value and cost-to-value matrices. An agile team performs decomposition to sub-divide user stories into more manageable tasks so that it may estimate task time. Tasks for an iteration may also be prioritized based on value, similar to how user stories are prioritized. [Lean-Agile Software Development: Achieving Enterprise Agility. Alan Shalloway, Guy Beaver, James R. Trott.] [Knowledge and Skills: Level 1]

31. B - EVM or earned value management is a management technique used to evaluate project performance with respect to cost and schedule. EVM relies on other common financial metrics like Budget At Completion (BAC), Actual Cost (AC), Planned Value (PV), Earned Value (EV), Cost Variance (CV), Schedule Variance (SV), Cost Performance Index (CPI), and Schedule Performance Index (SPI). CPI is a ratio that expresses cost performance. CPI = EV/AC. If CPI > 1, the project is earning more than spending; and if CPI <1, the project is spending more than it is earning. [Agile Estimating and Planning. Mike Cohn.] [Metrics]

32. C - Story points represent the relative work effort it takes to develop a user story. Each point represents a fixed value of development effort. When estimating the agile team must consider complexity, effort, risk, and inter-dependencies. [Agile Estimating and Planning. Mike Cohn.] [Agile estimation]

33. A - In release planning, the agile project manager discusses the product vision with the development team in detail. This ensures that the proper requirements, acceptance criteria, and priorities are established. [The Art of Agile Development. James Shore.] [Planning, monitoring, and adapting]

34. C - In agile, effective 'knowledge sharing' is a critical factor for success. It involves the near real time communication of key information among all team members and stakeholders. To promote knowledge sharing, agile uses standard practices built into its process, such as using generalized specialists/cross functional teams, self-organizing and self-disciplined teams, collocation, daily stand-up meetings, iteration/sprint planning, release planning, pair programming and pair rotation, project retrospectives/reflection, and on-site customer support. And, of course, the sixth principle of Agile is " The most efficient and effective method of conveying information to and within a development team is face-to-face conversation." In this sense, Agile prefers and encourages collocation for all stakeholders and team members for the simple fact that face-to-face conversation is the best method of communication and, in turn, effective knowledge sharing. [Becoming Agile: ...in an imperfect world. Greg Smith, Ahmed Sidky.] [Knowledge and Skills: Level 1]

35. C - Stakeholder management is a growing topic area within strategic management that brings awareness to the importance of managing stakeholders (i.e., facilitating active participation of stakeholders and fostering a strong collaborative environment) for a project's success. Stakeholder management is typically defined in the context of guiding principles and values. R. E. Freeman's 'Managing for Stakeholders' includes 10 principles: 1) Stakeholder interests need to go together over time. 2) We need a philosophy of volunteerism – to engage stakeholders and manage relationships ourselves rather than leave it to government. 3) We need to find solutions to issues that satisfy multiple stakeholders simultaneously. 4) Everything that we do serves stakeholders. We never trade off the interests of one versus the other continuously over time. 5) We act with purpose that fulfills our commitment to stakeholders. We act with aspiration towards fulfilling our dreams and theirs. 6) We need intensive communication and dialogue with stakeholders – not just those who are friendly. 7)Stakeholders consist of real people with names and faces and children. They are complex. 8)We need to generalize the marketing approach. 9) We engage with both primary and secondary stakeholders. 10) We constantly monitor and redesign processes to make them better serve our stakeholders. Because stakeholder involvement is critical for the success of a project, where projects without active participation from stakeholders are prone to failure, stakeholder management should be a topic that every agile team knows well. [The Art of Agile Development. James Shore.] [Knowledge and Skills: Level 1]

36. C - A cornerstone of Agile development is 'incremental delivery.' Incremental delivery is the frequent delivery of working products, which are successively improved, to a customer for immediate feedback and acceptance. Typically, a product is delivered at the end of each sprint or iteration for demonstration and feedback. In this feedback technique, a customer can review the product and provide updated requirements. Changed/updated/refined requirements are welcomed in the agile process to ensure the customer receives a valuable and quality product. A sprint or iteration typically lasts from two to four weeks and at the end a new and improved product is delivered, incrementally. [The Art of Agile Development. James Shore.] [Knowledge and Skills: Level 1]

37. B - A lean manufacturing philosophy is to eliminate waste. One defined waste type in the lean philosophy is inventory, which is also referred to as work in process (WIP). WIP is material or parts that have started production but are not yet a finished or "done" product. Inventory is considered wasteful because it costs money to purchase, store, and maintain. One way of reducing inventory is to reduce the WIP at individual machines or servers by only moving as fast as your slowest machine or processor (the system bottleneck). Agile also strives to control its WIP through WIP limits by completing all features to a "done" state before beginning development of new features. One can think of an iteration or sprint as a process that can develop a certain amount of features. In this analogy, the WIP limit is equivalent to the sprint backlog. By maintaining a WIP limit equal to the sprint backlog, no features should be incomplete at the sprint review. [Lean-Agile Software Development: Achieving Enterprise Agility. Alan Shalloway, Guy Beaver, James R. Trott.] [Planning, monitoring, and adapting]

38. C - In an agile project, the product backlog typically holds all the user stories to be developed. [User Stories Applied: For Agile Software Development. Mike Cohn.] [Agile analysis and design]

39. A - A lean manufacturing philosophy is to eliminate waste. One defined waste type in the lean philosophy is inventory, which is also referred to as work in process (WIP). WIP is material or parts that have started production but are not yet a finished or "done" product. Inventory is considered wasteful because it costs money to purchase, store, and maintain. One way of reducing inventory is to reduce the WIP at individual machines or servers by only moving as fast as your slowest machine or processor (the system bottleneck). Agile also strives to control its WIP through WIP limits by completing all features to a "done" state before beginning development of new features. One can think of an iteration or sprint as a process that can develop a certain amount of features. In this analogy, the WIP limit is equivalent to the sprint backlog. By maintaining a WIP limit equal to the sprint backlog, no features should be incomplete at the sprint review. [Lean-Agile Software Development: Achieving Enterprise Agility. Alan Shalloway, Guy Beaver, James R. Trott.] [Planning, monitoring, and adapting]

40. A - The agile secondary values include: documentation of software, processes and tools, contract negotiation, and following project plans. [Manifesto for Agile Software Development. Agile Alliance.] [Knowledge and Skills: Level 1]

Additional Resources

Exam Taking Tips

PMI-ACP Exam Facts

- There are 120 total multiple choice questions which make up the PMI-ACP exam
- 20 randomly placed "pretest questions" are included, and do not count towards the pass/fail determination
- Students have 3 hours to complete the exam
- While PMI does not publish a precise passing score, students should expect to score 65% or higher to pass the exam (65 of 100 questions)
- Students may bring blank "scratch" paper with which to draft responses, such as for formula-based exam questions.

Before the Exam

- Visit the exam location before your exam date so that you are familiar with the address and commute time, especially if you are a nervous test taker.
- Be prepared to fully utilize your blank "scratch" paper in the exam. This means that you have committed important formulas, concepts, and key facts to memory; and you are able to apply them to a blank sheet of paper in less than five minutes.
- Alleviate exam stress and anxiety by taking practice exams that attune you to the pace, subject matter, and difficulty of the real exam.
- On the night before the exam, reduce your study time to one hour or less and get extra sleep. The reduced study time and extra rest will allow your brain to better process the information it has absorbed during earlier, more intense, study sessions.

Taking the Exam

- IMPORTANT: Bring your PMI authorization letter, as well as two forms of ID, to the exam center.
- At the beginning of the PMI-ACP exam, use your scratch paper to "download" all of the formulas, concepts, and key facts you have committed to memory. To save time, perform this activity immediately after the initial computer tutorial which allots 15 minutes.
- Approach each question from PMI's perspective, not your own experience, even if the most correct response seems contrary to your "on-the-job" knowledge.
- Plan your breaks during the exam. A recommended break pattern during the PMI-ACP exam is to stand up and stretch after every 50 questions.
- Smile as you take the exam. It has been proven that smiling alleviates stress and boosts confidence during exceptionally difficult tasks. Use deep breathing techniques to further relax.
- If you have exam time remaining, review the questions you "marked for review". Use all the exam time you have until each question has been reviewed twice.

The PMI-ACP exam is a multiple choice test that asks one to recognize correct answers among a set of four options. The extra options that are not the correct answer are called the "distracters"; and their purpose, unsurprisingly, is to distract the test taker from the actual correct answer among the bunch.

Students usually consider multiple choice exams as much easier than other types of exams; this is not necessarily true with the PMI-ACP exam. Among these reasons are:

- Most multiple choice exams ask for simple, factual information; unlike the PMI-ACP exam which often requires the student to apply knowledge and make a best judgment.

- The majority of multiple choice exams involve a large quantity of different questions – so even if you get a few incorrect, it's still okay. The PMI-ACP exam covers a broad set of material, often times in greater depth than other certification exams.

Regardless of whether or not multiple choice testing is more forgiving; in reality, one must study immensely because of the sheer volume of information that is covered.

Although three hours may seem like more than enough time for a multiple choice exam, when faced with 120 questions, time management is one of the most crucial factors in succeeding and doing well. You should always try and answer all of the questions you are confident about first, and then go back about to those items you are not sure about afterwards. Always read *carefully* through the entire test as well, and do your best to not leave any question blank upon submission– even if you do not readily know the answer.

Many people do very well with reading through each question and not looking at the options before trying to answer. This way, they can steer clear (usually) of being fooled by one of the "distracter" options or get into a tug-of-war between two choices that both have a good chance of being the actual answer.

Never assume that "all of the above" or "none of the above" answers are the actual choice. Many times they are, but in recent years they have been used much more frequently as distracter options on standardized tests. Typically this is done in an effort to get people to stop believing the myth that they are always the correct answer.

You should be careful of negative answers as well. These answers contain words such as "none", "not", "neither", and the like. Despite often times being very confusing, if you read these types of questions and answers carefully, then you should be able to piece together which is the correct answer. Just take your time!

If you ever narrow down a question to two possible answers, then try and slow down your thinking and think about how the two different options/answers differ. Look at the question again and try to apply how this difference between the two potential answers relates to the question. If you are convinced there is literally no difference between the two potential answers (you'll more than likely be wrong in assuming this), then take another look at the answers that you've already eliminated. Perhaps one of them is actually the correct one and you'd made a previously unforeseen mistake.

On occasion, over-generalizations are used within response options to mislead test takers. To help guard against this, always be wary of responses/answers that use absolute words like "always", or "never". These are less likely to actually be the answer than phrases like "probably" or "usually" are. Funny or witty responses are also, most of the time, incorrect – so steer clear of those as much as possible.

Although you should always take each question individually, "none of the above" answers are usually less likely to be the correct selection than "all of the above" is. Keep this in mind with the understanding that it is not an absolute rule, and should be analyzed on a case-by-case (or "question-by-question") basis.

Looking for grammatical errors can also be a huge clue. If the stem ends with an indefinite article such as "an" then you'll probably do well to look for an answer that begins with a vowel instead of a consonant. Also, the longest response is also oftentimes the correct one, since whoever wrote the question item may have tended to load the answer with qualifying adjectives or phrases in an effort to make it correct. Again though, always deal with these on a question-by-question basis, because you could very easily be getting a question where this does not apply.

Verbal associations are oftentimes critical because a response may repeat a key word that was in the question. Always be on the alert for this. Playing the old Sesame Street game "Which of these things is not like the other" is also a very solid strategy, if a bit preschool. Sometimes many of a question's distracters will be very similar to try to trick you into thinking that one choice is related to the other. The answer very well could be completely unrelated however, so stay alert.

Just because you have finished a practice test, be aware that you are not done working. After you have graded your test with all of the necessary corrections, review it and try to recognize what happened in the answers that you got wrong. Did you simply not know the qualifying correct information? Perhaps you were led astray by a solid distracter answer? Going back through your corrected test will give you a leg up on your next one by revealing your tendencies as to what you may be vulnerable with, in terms of multiple choice tests.

It may be a lot of extra work, but in the long run, going through your corrected multiple choice tests will work wonders for you in preparation for the real exam. See if you perhaps misread the question or even missed it because you were unprepared. Think of it like instant replays in professional sports. You are going back and looking at what you did on the big stage in the past so you can help fix and remedy any errors that could pose problems for you on the real exam.

15069285R10244

Made in the USA
Middletown, DE
23 October 2014